Apart
& Together

Studies in
Anabaptist and Mennonite History
No. 30

Apart & Together

Hope Kauffman Lind

Studies in Anabaptist and Mennonite History

Edited by Cornelius J. Dyck, Leonard Gross,
Leland Harder, Albert N. Keim, Walter Klaassen, John S. Oyer,
Theron F. Schlabach, and John H. Yoder

Published by Herald Press, Scottdale, Pennsylvania, and Waterloo, Ontario, in cooperation with Mennonite Historical Society, Goshen, Indiana. The Society is primarily responsible for the content of the studies, and Herald Press for their publication.

1. Two Centuries of American Mennonite Literature, 1727-1928
   By Harold S. Bender, 1929
2. The Hutterian Brethren, 1528-1931
   By John Horsch, 1931
3. Centennial History of the Mennonites in Illinois°
   By Harry F. Weber, 1931
4. For Conscience' Sake°
   By Sanford Calvin Yoder, 1940
5. Ohio Mennonite Sunday Schools°
   By John Umble, 1941
6. Conrad Grebel, Founder of the Swiss Brethren°
   By Harold S. Bender, 1950
7. Mennonite Piety Through the Centuries°
   By Robert Friedmann, 1949
8. Bernese Anabaptists and Their American Descendants°
   By Delbert L. Gratz, 1953
9. Anabaptism in Flanders, 1530-1650
   By A. L. E. Verheyden, 1961
10. The Mennonites in Indiana and Michigan°
    By J. C. Wenger, 1961
11. Anabaptist Baptism: A Representative Study
    By Rollin Stelly Armour, 1966
12. Lost Fatherland: The Story of Mennonite Emigration from Soviet Russia, 1921-1927°
    By John B. Toews, 1967
13. Mennonites of the Ohio and Eastern Conference°
    By Grant M. Stoltzfus, 1969

14. The Mennonite Church in India, 1897-1962
    By John A. Lapp, 1972
15. The Theology of Anabaptism: An Interpretation
    By Robert Friedmann, 1973
16. Anabaptism and Asceticism
    By Kenneth R. Davis, 1974
17. South Central Frontiers°
    By Paul Erb, 1974
18. The Great Trek of the Russian Mennonites to Central Asia, 1880-
    1884°
    By Fred R. Belk, 1976
19. Mysticism and the Early South German-Austrian Anabaptist Movement,
    1525-1531
    By Werner O. Packull, 1976
20. Conscience in Crisis: Mennonites and Other Peace Churches in America, 1739-1789
    By Richard K. MacMaster with Samuel L. Horst and Robert F. Ulle,
    1979
21. Gospel Versus Gospel: Mission and the Mennonite Church, 1863-1944
    By Theron F. Schlabach, 1979
22. Strangers Become Neighbors: Mennonites and Indigenous Relations in
    the Paraguayan Chaco
    By Calvin Redekop, 1980
23. The Golden Years of the Hutterites, 1565-1578°
    By Leonard Gross, 1980
24. Mennonites in Illinois
    By Willard H. Smith, 1983
25. Petr Chelčický: A Radical Separatist in Hussite Bohemia
    By Murray L. Wagner, 1983
26. Maintaining the Right Fellowship: A Narrative Account of Life in the
    Oldest Mennonite Community in North America
    By John L. Ruth, 1984
27. The Life and Thought of Michael Sattler
    By C. Arnold Snyder, 1984
28. American Mennonites and Protestant Movements: A Community
    Paradigm
    By Beulah Stauffer Hostetler, 1987
29. Andreas Fischer and the Sabbatarian Anabaptists
    By Daniel Liechty, 1988
30. Apart and Together: Mennonites in Oregon and Neighboring States,
    1876-1976
    By Hope Kauffman Lind, 1990

°Out of print but available in microfilm or photocopies.

Apart & Together

Mennonites in Oregon and Neighboring States ■ 1876-1976

Hope Kauffman Lind

HERALD PRESS
Scottdale, Pennsylvania
Waterloo, Ontario

Library of Congress Cataloging-in-Publication Data
Lind, Hope Kauffman, 1935-
    Apart and together : Mennonites in Oregon and neighboring states,
1876-1976 / Hope Kauffman Lind.
        p.   cm. — (Studies in Anabaptist and Mennonite history ; no. 30)
    Includes bibliographical references.
    ISBN 0-8361-3106-1
    1. Mennonites—Oregon 2. Oregon—Church history.   I. Title.
II. Series.
BX8117.074L55   1990
289.7'795—dc20   90-30840
                                                                        CIP

The paper used in this publication meets the minimum requirements of American
National Standard for Information Sciences—Permanence of Paper for Printed
Library Materials, ANSI Z39.48-1984.

APART AND TOGETHER
Copyright © 1990 by Herald Press, Scottdale, Pa. 15683
    Published simultaneously in Canada by Herald Press,
    Waterloo, Ont. N2L 6H7. All rights reserved.
Library of Congress Catalog Card Number: 90-30840
International Standard Book Number: 0-8361-3106-1
Printed in the United States of America
Cover and book design by Gwen Stamm

1 2 3 4 5 96 95 94 93 92 91 90

In appreciation for
La Vernae Janzen Dick Hohnbaum
—without her this book would not have been written—
and
Cora Irene Garber Kauffman Gascho
and the memory of Alvin Gascho—
their early nurture influenced my commitment
to Mennonite life and thought

Contents

Foreword by Harold Hochstetler 13
Series Editor's Preface 15
Preface 19
Abbreviations 23

Part I Uprooting and Planting 25
   1. Oregon and Its Mennonite and Related Groups 27
   2. Amish Mennonites in Oregon 41
   3. OMs: From Early Division to Fragile Unity
      (1890s to 1930s) 63
   4. OMs: Unity Tested (1940s and 1950s) 86
   5. OMs: Division and Regrouping (1960-1976) 114
   6. Smaller Mennonite and Related Groups in Oregon 135
   7. Related Mennonite Groups in Neighboring States 183

Part II The Larger Vision 204
   8. Oregon Mennonites Nurturing Their Faith 205
   9. Oregon Mennonites in Mission and Service 235
  10. Oregon Mennonites in the Larger World 266
  11. Oregon Mennonites and War 282
  12. Mennonite Institutions in Oregon 306

Part III The Ongoing Community of Faith 325
  13. Oregon Mennonites: Strangers and Friends 327
  14. Following After Faithfulness 337

Notes 345
Appendix: Leaders in Oregon Mennonite Congregations
   Through 1976 379
Bibliographical Note 389
Index 392
The Author 415

Foreword

The story of the Mennonite Church in Oregon is a moving account of the struggles and triumphs experienced among a people seeking to live out the gospel within an environment that has fostered an independent frontier spirit. Hope Lind has adeptly connected the strands of history which give meaning to this experience. Attitudes and relationships, both within and without the Mennonite community, have been forces giving form to the development of the community's faith and mission.

Hope Lind's research provides refreshing insights into patterns and practices shaping the drama of Mennonite church life as it has unfolded during the first hundred years in Oregon. Life in this faith community has indeed been a journey. Inherent in this mobility have been challenges as well as risks. One gains a renewed appreciation of the operative forces at work in the uprooting and planting processes involved in creating an Anabaptist community in the West.

The Oregon Mennonite communities have been formed within a ferment offering potential either for enhancing mutuality or adding to fragmentation. This historical account identifies forces strengthening both togetherness and independence. The narrative gives a realistic description of the emergence of significant communal relationships amidst tension with independent values impinging on the community's life.

This story of the first hundred years of Mennonites in Oregon can help us grapple with both the past and future of the church in the American West. Our history does influence our attitudes, perceptions, and decisions. A living memory can help shape the future church in Oregon and elsewhere. Our history offers us hope. The Lord of the church can use our history to strengthen our vision and vitalize our fellowship.

Mennonites continue to experience the tensions between independence and togetherness. Critical periods of both opportunity and of peril are before us. The choices made and courses followed must be centered in a faithful people set free to move toward each other—and toward the broadening dimensions of our fellowship and witness.

As a participant in the contemporary Oregon Mennonite experience, I am grateful to Hope Lind for her diligent research. I appreciate the insightful challenges she offers the church in Oregon as well as the broader church community. We are being pointed to the future. This history provides some basis for moving into that future.

—Harold Hochstetler
February 1, 1990

Series Editor's Preface

It has been almost a century since a young historian named Frederick Jackson Turner called on fellow scholars to appreciate the importance of westward migration and the frontier in American history. Turner went on to related topics, especially sectionalism and regionalism. Such emphases led him to various conclusions about U.S. democracy and uniqueness—conclusions which won him high fame. Nowadays not many students of U.S. history accept Turner's conclusions whole, yet almost all see the importance of the frontier and of particular sections, regions, and groups. Those who know American history in depth know the particulars.

Hope Lind's story of Mennonites (and Amish) in Oregon and its region is a search into American history in depth. The history of Mennonites in North America comes bound up with national developments. In the U.S. as the frontier moved west, many Mennonites and Amish were close in its wake. As regions developed their particular economies, Mennonites and Amish got involved and contributed. As frontier communities transplanted social organization and institutions, Mennonites also established congregations, district conferences, and eventually various local or regional schools, missions, and benevolent institutions. A Turnerian analysis would emphasize that the process brought a certain fragmentation and a heightened individualism; and indeed a strong theme of Lind's analysis is a tendency toward such fragmentation, such individualism. Yet Lind offers another theme also, a rather opposite one; namely a continued sense of peoplehood, mutuality, and community. Mennonites who moved to the Far West longed keenly for fellowship and support. They worked both for cohesion among themselves and for fellowship and cooperation with their sisters and brothers back in the distant East.

The tension between fragmentation and individualism on the one hand and community and mutual support on the other was a

15

tension that Mennonites shared with many other Americans, perhaps especially the Americans most influenced by the frontier. But that is only part of the story. The other part is that Mennonites' own history—from the sixteenth-century Anabaptists onward—had a central dilemma that reinforced that tension. The history of Anabaptists, Mennonites, and Amish is a history of people who took very seriously the idea of the church. To them church meant being a new people, a people who as individuals had chosen personally and voluntarily to follow God's will as taught and shown in Jesus Christ, a people working corporately to understand God's saving ways and saving will for humans. With that idea of church they emphasized that the teachings of Jesus and of the Bible—especially the New Testament—were to be taken literally for guiding and instructing Christians in their daily walk. To believe meant to apply biblical example and teaching even to the smallest of acts and decisions—everyday ones, minute ones.

The positive side of that history has been a determined effort to be true disciples of Jesus in practical ways—to be truly and constantly faithful in deed, not only in word or in an ethereal realm labeled the "spiritual." The negative side has been an all-too-frequent tendency to quarrel and often divide over seemingly minor details of dress or entertainment or business dealings or other practical matters. For Mennonites throughout their history the interplay of that positive and that negative has been a great dilemma, perhaps their greatest. Actually, it is a dilemma of all Christians whether they realize it or not; but it seems to have caught Mennonites especially hard in its grip. Yet, paradoxically, Mennonites have also worked diligently to achieve intense fellowship and church life.

So Lind's story is a dynamic one, with Mennonites and Amish being pulled hard toward fragmentation and individualism in one direction, and struggling hard to maintain strong fellowship and close community in the other. That dynamic, with its opposite pulls, comes partly from Oregon Mennonites' entanglement in American history. But it also expresses something inherent in Mennonites' own history, outlook, and understanding of Christian obedience.

Time and again Lind has illuminated that basic dynamic. Meanwhile she has summarized well the details of Oregon Mennonites' moving, settling, congregation-planting, and institution-building, and also of changes in theology and practice. All this she has done with great skill as she worked thoroughly, insightfully, and persistently. She also had some help. The Pacific Coast Conference of the Mennonite Church gave extensive support, both financial and moral. La Vernae Janzen Dick (Hohnbaum) helped with some of the research and planned originally to be coauthor. John A. Lapp of Mennonite Central Committee served the SAMH series as editor for this book. Many others gave support and services in one way or another. The book is Lind's own massive personal effort; yet like all good scholarship, it also grew out of cooperation.

We of the *Studies in Anabaptist and Mennonite History* series enthusiastically welcome this book.

—*Theron F. Schlabach*
Goshen College
SAMH Editor-in-Chief

Preface

This book is my gift to Oregon Mennonites, who have accepted me as an immigrant among many. I hope it will help them to understand how their past has influenced their present, to build on its strengths which they endorse, and to avoid past errors which they deplore. Most of all I would have them remember that, like Christians in all ages and places, Oregon Mennonites attempting to accomplish God's work were and are imperfect people. When they are tempted to censure actors on the stage of this history, may they temper their judgment with the humbling reminder that we ourselves are often guilty of that which we judge in others. When they applaud the cast, may they accept the challenge to likewise live faithfully.

This book is also a gift from Oregon Mennonites to people outside of Oregon Mennonite circles. For other interested persons I have attempted to portray some of the significant developments among Mennonites during their first century in Oregon and to indicate influences that directed their individual lives and church communities. As Oregon Mennonites opened their records to inquiry, they gave the priceless gift of trust. I intended not to betray that trust even as I aimed to be forthrightly honest. Although I cannot claim total objectivity, I have tried to understand what people thought and felt about several sides of an issue and to present a fair picture.

Although Oregon's Mennonite membership remains small compared with much larger Mennonite conferences and communities farther east, it is nonetheless significant. The ratio of members in Oregon's Mennonite and related groups to the total Oregon population is almost twice that of all United States Mennonite and related groups to the total United States population. Like their faith relatives farther east, Oregon Mennonites have held up the light of Christ in their own church communities and other communities as they preached salvation and followed Christ in discipleship. Like Mennonites elsewhere, Oregon Mennonites have sprinkled themselves as salt of the earth as they seasoned their larger communities with integrity and promoted Christ's way of love, peace, and justice for the whole world. Oregon Mennonites, like those farther east, did not always exemplify well in their own church communities the love and unity they preached. But empowered by their forgiving God they became building blocks in the economic, social, and religious structures of their neighborhoods and state.[1]

As historian Henry Steele Commager wrote, "Organization always does some violence to the stream of thought or the chaos of conduct that is life." The story of Oregon Mennonites is a jumble of movements, settlements, influences, practices, thoughts, emotions, actions, reactions, good intentions, and probably a little scheming. It tells of related but separate groups of Mennonites with a common spiritual heritage. It is about dreams and commitments, convictions and controversies, sin and forgiveness, and devoted service with doubtless a sprinkling of self-serving decisions. To tell the story is to organize some of its elements into untidy heaps of facts and understandings and to look at them one by one even while connecting the heaps with lines which repeatedly intersect. Imposing such artificial order on the intricate and forever vibrating life of Mennonite groups gives a false simplification of what they are. But their history cannot be recorded without such constraints.[2]

Three parts divide this book into sections. The first briefly places Oregon Mennonites in their geographical and historical context and discusses them chronologically, group by group. The second part focuses on their primary emphases—how they nurtured their faith and practiced it within their congregations and conferences and in the larger world. The last part considers how Oregon Mennonites related to their denominations and other groups and looks at their continuing attempts to live faithfully.

As this book was conceived, La Vernae Janzen Dick (Hohnbaum) and I planned to write a centennial history commemorating the arrival of Oregon's first Mennonite settlers in 1876. We wanted to tell the most important facts of their story and offer our observations and perceptions to help readers understand why Oregon Mennonites believed and acted as they did. When we invited Oregon's Mennonite groups to authorize our research and writing, two did so—the Pacific Coast Conference of the Mennonite Church (MC) and the Pacific District Conference of the General Conference Mennonite Church (GC). With their assistance we received Schowalter Foundation funds to cover the earliest costs. It soon became evident that we would not complete the history in time for the 1976 centennial celebration. Then in 1978 Johnny A. Dick, La Vernae's husband, died and she later changed careers to become a Methodist minister and the wife of Dick Hohnbaum. After she turned over to me her pertinent files and manuscript drafts, I assumed responsibility for the entire project. But without her early research and writing, this history would be greatly impoverished; the extent of its coverage, impossible.

Other changes occurred along the way. When we began, we intended to include a history of each congregation as well as chapters about joint endeavors and general topics related to being Mennonites in Oregon. But space limitations shortened everything. Congregational histories which appear in this book are much briefer than originally conceived, which will disappoint some readers, particularly those who researched many questions and furnished much information. However, all such material is on file and will be deposited in an appropriate Mennonite archive for future reference.

Oregon Mennonites could not have survived without their sister groups in other states. Particularly among those who organized regional conferences, Mennonites in neighboring states influenced and assisted Oregon Mennonites and often shared the same story. This book briefly touches on the stories of MC and GC congregations in neighboring states. It recognizes their interrelatedness with Oregon Mennonites while it acknowledges the support for this history which their two conferences provided.

From the beginning, La Vernae Dick (Hohnbaum) and I solicited and received interest and encouragement from members of the Mennonite Historical Society. J. C. Wenger, Cornelius J. Dyck, Leonard Gross, John S. Oyer, and the coeditors of this book in the Studies in Anabaptist and Mennonite History book series, Theron Schlabach and John A. Lapp, have all personally helped. Most of them have read part or all of the manuscript in one or more drafts; their questions and suggestions helped me evaluate my observations and critique my analyses. I must assume responsibility, however, for errors which may slip past their scrutiny.

Many other persons assisted, and I can name only a few.

Rufus Franz, David Peterson, Marion Schrock, Margaret Shetler, and Jeanne Zook served on my Oregon Advisory Committee and read the entire manuscript in an early draft. They penned in questions and comments and sat with me for hours discussing content and format and offering suggestions. Others who read and responded to part or all of the manuscript include Harold Hochstetler, Marcus Lind, Wilbert Shenk, and David J. R. Smucker. Hazel Hassan of the Illinois Mennonite Historical and Genealogical Society provided a copy of Harry F. Weber's *Centennial History of the Mennonites of Illinois* as a resource. Several Oregon congregations loaned *Gospel Herald* files from their libraries. John Fretz photocopied a number of articles of incorporation in the Oregon state archives.

To cover a publication subsidy and closing costs, the Pacific Coast Conference (MC) made a major contribution. Other contributors included: Pacific District Conference (GC), Ken and Lilly Berkey, Gerald Brenneman, Marcia Byers, Howard D. Claassen, Amos B. Conrad, a memorial to Ernest and Barbara Garber, Eugene Garber, Cora Irene Gascho, Ted Grimsrud, John Jantzi, Roland Jantzi, Ray Kauffman, Lyle King, Viola King, Charity Kropf, Lester and Viola Kropf, Lloyd Kropf, Merle Kropf, Velda C. Kropf, Carl Lind, Cliff Lind, Janet Lind and Calvin Esh, Julia Lind, Marcus Lind, Myron Lind, Harry D. Miller, Alvin and Wilma Nisly, Alfred and Marjorie Nofziger, David Peterson, Plainview Mennonite Church unidentified members, A. M. Rempel, Mabel A. Roth, Berniece Schmucker, Mr. and Mrs. Enos Schrock, Ralph Shank, Ralph and Margaret Shetler, Anne Smucker, Muriel Ethel Snyder, Lester and Sherry Steckly, Oscar and Louise Wideman, Dan Widmer, and Ray Zehr.

I acknowledge with appreciation my husband, Clifford R. Lind, who encouraged me to undertake this project. As chief family earner, he freed me to follow the story of Oregon Mennonites. I am grateful for his generous support in many ways.

—*Hope Kauffman Lind*
Eugene, Oregon

Abbreviations

Mennonite and Related Groups

ACC Apostolic Christian Church
AM Amish Mennonite
BIC Brethren in Christ
BMF Bible Mennonite Fellowship
CC Central Conference of Mennonites
CGC Church of God in Christ, Mennonite (Holdeman)
EMB Evangelical Mennonite Brethren
GC General Conference Mennonite
KNC Kansas-Nebraska Conference
MB Mennonite Brethren
MC Mennonite Church (OM)
OM (Old) Mennonite (MC)
OMGC (Old) Mennonite General Conference (MC)
OOA Old Order Amish
PCC Pacific Coast Conference (MC)
PDC Pacific District Conference (GC) or (MB)
SWC Southwest Conference (MC)
UM Unaffiliated Mennonite
WDAMC Western District Amish Mennonite Conference

Periodicals and Books

CE *Christian Exponent*
CH *Church History of the Pacific Coast Mennonite Conference District,* by S. G. Shetler
CL *Christian Living*
CM *Christian Monitor*
ChrLead *Christian Leader*
DBH *Descendants of Barbara Hochstedler and Christian Stutzman*
DJH *Descendants of Jacob Hochstetler*
EV *Evangelical Visitor*
FA *Family Almanac*
FL *Family Life*
GH *Gospel Herald*
GVG *Gospel Versus Gospel,* by Theron F. Schlabach
GW *Gospel Witness*
HH *The Hertzler-Hartzler Family History*

HT *Herald of Truth*
HW *Herold der Wahrheit*
J&G *Empire of the Columbia,* by Johansen and Gates
KCC *Kingdom, Cross, Community,* ed. by J. R. Burkholder
    and Calvin Redekop
KN *Kansas-Nebraska Conference Record*
MCD *Mennonite Cyclopedic Dictionary*
MCISWW *The Mennonite Church in the Second World War,*
    by Guy F. Hershberger
ME *Mennonite Encyclopedia*
MHB *Mennonite Historical Bulletin*
MFH *Mennonite Family History*
ML *Mennonite Life*
MPP *My Personal Pentecost,* ed. by Roy and Martha Koch
MQR *Mennonite Quarterly Review*
MWR *Mennonite Weekly Review*
MY *Mennonite Yearbook (MC)*
MY (GC) *Mennonite Yearbook (GC)*
MY&D *Mennonite Yearbook and Directory*
PDM *Pacific District Messenger*
PMH *Pennsylvania Mennonite Heritage*
Record *Western District Amish Mennonite Conference Record*
SFP *Service for Peace,* by Melvin Gingerich
S&T *The Sword and Trumpet*
TM *The Mennonite*
WE *Workers Exchange*
WPN *War, Peace and Nonresistance,* by Guy F. Hershberger
WWM *Who's Who Among the Mennonites,* by A. Warkentin and
    Melvin Gingerich

Other

ca circa (about)
CMBS Center for Mennonite Brethren Studies (Fresno)
DCC Drift Creek Camp
HL Hope Lind
info information
LD La Vernae Janzen Dick (Hohnbaum), Salem, Oregon
MCA Mennonite Church Archives (Goshen)
MHL Mennonite Historical Library (Goshen)
MPH Mennonite Publishing House
ms manuscript

PART I
Uprooting and Planting

Some persons like the straight facts of history—names, dates, places, actions, and interactions, spun together into threads that outline a chronological narrative. In such a manner Part I discusses Oregon Mennonite and related groups one by one, from their early appearance in Oregon through 1976, in most cases. It also briefly surveys some of their related congregations in neighboring states.

Other persons prefer to think about reasons and results of history—influences, issues, topics, and themes, woven among facts to make a tapestry. Parts II and III consider such elements of Oregon Mennonite history. Together the parts give a better perspective for understanding Oregon Mennonites than does any part alone.

Uprooting often hurts, and planting, even while invigorating, can dirty the hands. Part I of the story of Oregon Mennonites is neither painless nor free of mud. Problems developed as individuals from diverse backgrounds settled together in a community and as other influences entered. All groups accepted the Bible as the authoritative Word of God, the guide for their faith. All wanted to make their faith practical, especially in the details of their everyday lives. But they often differed on how to do so. Almost from their first years in Oregon, dismal disagreements shadowed their congregations and conferences and at times sharp contentions divided them. This was particularly true of groups with Amish and (old) Mennonite heritage, which emphasized the church as a community of faith in which individuals subjected themselves to that community's standards. Groups which permitted greater individuality and less church restraint often suffered less contention.

But to understand some of the forces at work among Oregon's Mennonite groups is to back off from harsh judgment. Practices and restrictions which may seem trivial to many were really conscientious attempts to follow Christ obediently and to shun ungodly ways of the world. Amish and (old) Mennonite teaching had emphasized that humility was a key characteristic of those who would follow Christ. In 1866 John M. Brenneman of Ohio had written an article for the new Mennonite publication, *Herald of Truth*, which article was later published in pamphlet form with many printings. Brenneman, after establishing biblical grounds for humility and against pride, noted that many say that "outward appearance is nothing, if the heart [is] right." He argued, however, that "the humble do not make any show or display in their appearance, therefore cannot decorate their person." Other leaders and writers built on that emphasis. Though humility versus pride faded as a dominant theme in the next decades, the motif permeated doctrinal teachings, especially regarding attire, well into the next century.[3]

However, (old) Mennonites were not alone in experiencing division over doctrine or practice. All Oregon Mennonite groups specified doctrine and standards of behavior. Individuals who digressed from the stipulated ways of their church community sometimes isolated themselves but more often shifted loyalty, whether primary or marginal, to a competing community or movement. Another denomination or theology frequently attracted Mennonites. Often peers lured young people and even adults to transfer their loyalty from the church community. Nationalism, militarism, and materialism enticed Mennonites, often under the guise of religion and faith. The Mennonite community combined all such competing communities, movements, and trends into a single category and called it "the world."

Although Oregon Mennonites agonized over honest (if volatile) disagreements, Part I also demonstrates love and cooperation, growth and harvest. Disturbing uprootings and stressful plantings occurred, but those who committed themselves to obey the Christ they loved matured and produced fruit. Individuals formed Christian communities and offered helping hands within and outside. If Part I pushes readers to frustrated impatience, let them note also that in Oregon, as elsewhere, God used faltering humans, motivated by commitment to Christ, to accomplish divine purposes in spite of their imperfections.

Chapter 1

Oregon and Its Mennonite and Related Groups

The Western frontier lured tens of thousands of settlers to Oregon in the 1870s, and Mennonites joined the surging movement. In 1876 the *Herald of Truth* was a Mennonite periodical published at Elkhart, Indiana, with a German counterpart, *Herold der Wahrheit*. In response to frequent requests from fellow Mennonites, Christian C. Wenger wrote from Oregon to the *Herold*. He claimed that he and his wife (Magdalena) were Oregon's first Mennonite settlers. On April 6, 1876, more than three weeks after leaving their Wayne County, Ohio, home, they had arrived in Salem. Sharing the honor were John Lichty and his wife, Elizabeth, who accompanied the Wengers. Within two years, six families, a widowed mother, and a single man comprised a Mennonite membership of fourteen. Their "greatest desire [was] to have a church organization with a minister."[1]

For the Wengers and their friends, being Mennonites in isolation was not easy or even possible. To be a Mennonite was to be an individual within a community, worshiping and serving within a congregation of God's people, gathering because of a personal decision to follow Christ in love and obedience. Certainly their ethnic heritage, with its Germanic origins and speech, contributed to their identity. Without question their culture influenced their faith. Social relationships, especially their close ties with extended families and church friends, offered individuals both approval and security in their religious life. To be a Mennonite brought everything together and related their ethnic, cultural, social, and religious heritage into one unified way of life.

Mennonites defined community as a people following Christ in light of New Testament teachings. The community adopted a strict biblicism, outlining its practices according to its interpretations and understandings of the Bible, to which it gave full authority as God's Word. More than many denominations, Mennonites

27

emphasized the community and its claims on the individual, even while they grounded church authority and discipline within the community of lay and ordained individuals. In practice, however, ordained leaders usually exercised the greater authority.

Mennonites' biblicism gave them such distinctive doctrines as nonresistance, nonconformity, and separation of church and state. Before Mennonite groups began to settle in Oregon, the Amish and (old) Mennonites had resisted revivalism and nationalism and held out humility as a plumb line to separate them from the proud world. They aimed to live their faith Sunday through Saturday. Attention to details for making faith practical opened them to charges of legalism and brought severe stress to their communities, but it also revealed their serious intent to obey God faithfully. Such dynamics, instead of keeping the community strong, too often turned Mennonites to other religious communities. Theologies and ideologies such as Fundamentalism and nationalism were other forces that competed with and within Mennonite communities. Such influences affected Mennonites in their first century in Oregon. But even amid change, following Christ included commitment and accountability to the spiritual community.[2]

The American West added another element, a spirited individualism. It proclaimed that individual interests and rights might supersede social controls. In spite of their aloofness from the larger world, elements of individualism attracted Mennonites. Their own religious heritage in Reformation times had emphasized that individuals should be able to choose faith instead of the state mandating it. Later, revivalism, with its varied strains, promoted a religious individualism that many Mennonites adopted. They knew that individuals were responsible for their everyday beliefs and actions. At the same time, Oregon Mennonites gave much attention to how individuals should fulfill their commitment to Christ and his body, the church community, made up of the congregations and conferences that emerged. How should they balance individual responsibility with faithful church membership? How were they to maintain the right tension between individualism and community? These questions called for answers.

Living in Oregon, far away from the denominational centers of life and thought, sharpened the question. It deprived the settlers of regular personal contact with strong Mennonite leaders in well-established communities, and it fostered an individualism which jeopardized church unity. Mennonites in Oregon lived in both promise and peril.[3]

Compared to the eastern states, the Oregon to which Mennonites came in 1876 was a new country for Caucasians. A century earlier when Paul Revere made his legendary midnight ride on the other side of the continent in 1775, inflaming the American Revolution, only native Americans lived in Oregon. By that time white settlers had tamed the Atlantic seaboard. Mennonites had been living in Pennsylvania for more than ninety years and were agonizing over the conflicting claims of their nonresistant consciences and the colonial revolutionaries. A few weeks later, Bruno Haceta became the first known white man to touch land in the Pacific Northwest.[4]

Who would replace the native Americans and claim Oregon was not clear at first. Spain, then England, and finally the new United States of America, claimed the Pacific Northwest. The United States established the more persistent claim with its land link to the area. Lewis and Clark explored the vast Louisiana Territory and in December 1805 built Fort Clatsop for their winter headquarters, a few miles southeast of the mouth of the Columbia. More than forty years later, in 1846, the permanent British-American boundary settlement gave the United States the portion of the Oregon country south of the 49th parallel. This recognized after-the-fact that it was Americans, not British, who were settling there. After the fickle wind of fashion and a change from beaver to silk hats doomed the fur trade in the 1830s, a few American trappers and traders became Oregon farmers. Also in the 1830s Jason Lee's Methodist mission party and other Protestant and Catholic missionaries came to Oregon to work with Indians. They did not convert many. The Indians resisted being shaped into the white man's molds, and the white man's diseases almost destroyed some tribes. As more white settlers arrived in the 1850s and 1860s, the remaining Oregon Indians were segregated on reservations.[5]

Protestants were more successful as colonizers than as missionaries. Glowing reports of opportunity in Oregon attracted streams of new settlers. The missionaries hoped they would be sober, industrious, and loyal both to the United States and to Protestantism. In 1843, after two thousand miles and almost six months on the emerging Oregon Trail, the first major wagon train reached Oregon. In the next years the trail ruts deepened and more log houses claimed space in Oregon fields and forests. Most of the first settlers were farmers who came from the western fringes of the United States, both north and south. As more people with varied practices and expectations settled in Oregon, missionaries helped the newcomers establish an early temporary government. On February 14, 1859, Oregon became the thirty-third state.[6]

With the Indians subdued, transcontinental railroads—the first in 1869—encouraged increased migrations to Oregon. Those who came by train had to go first to California. So did Oregon's earliest Mennonites. Certainly this was safer and faster than the Oregon Trail, but the trip still took days and nights of travel on hard wooden train seats, without dining cars. From Sacramento the travelers took a river steamboat to San Francisco, where they might wait days for an ocean ship. They traveled more than six hundred miles on the Pacific Ocean and the lower Columbia River before arriving at Portland. From Portland to Salem they could go by river steamboat or railroad. In the years surrounding the arrival of Oregon's first Mennonites, the state population almost doubled between 1870 and 1880: from 90,000 to 175,000. In 1883, the Northern Pacific Railroad completed direct rail connections to the state, bringing the population increase of the three northwestern states in the 1880s to more than three times that of the 1870s. Mennonites became one small part of a popular movement west.[7]

One might wonder how the German-speaking Wengers and Lichtys viewed events and developments in their country. As they traveled west to Oregon in 1876, did they see in passing any results of the great Chicago fire of 1871? As they traveled through southern Wyoming, did they hear about the wonders of the new Yellowstone National Park, established in 1872 to the north? Did they know about the new fencing material called barbed wire for which Joseph Glidden took out a patent in 1874—an invention which changed the Great Plains? Did they pay any attention to the corrupt, disputed 1876 election, which made Rutherford B. Hayes the new president? Did they marvel about the new talking machine which Alexander Graham Bell demonstrated in Philadelphia that same year?[8]

Wenger, first correspondent for Oregon Mennonites, commented about the leading role the press took in Oregon, directing "the attention of the people to general education." He and his Mennonite friends probably noticed articles about the improved Oliver rotary plow, the Deering Company's new twine binder, and the steam threshing machine. (At that time, wheat was a principal agricultural product of Oregon.) Wenger wrote that with "tolerably good cultivation," wheat could yield from twenty to forty-five bushels to the acre. Oats, rye, barley, and buckwheat also flourished. He listed a variety of vegetables that grew "remarkably well" and said it would be hard to find "a better country for fruit than western Oregon." The soil was "very productive, the winters mild, and the heat . . . not so great in the summer." He appreciated the "cool nights" which gave "comfortable rest to the laborer."[9]

The Oregon to which Mennonites came was a large state of 97,000 square miles, larger than the country of England and more than 50 percent larger than Georgia, the largest state east of the Mississippi. Washington and the Columbia River bordered it on the north, Idaho and the Snake River on the east, Nevada and California on the south, and on the west the spectacular Pacific Ocean with its sandy beaches and rocky cliffs. Oregon covered almost four hundred miles east to west, almost three hundred miles north to south. Between the Coast and Cascade ranges of mountains, some fifty miles inland from the Pacific, the fertile Willamette Valley stretched one hundred miles from south to north, thirty miles from east to west. Oregon's first Mennonites settled in the Willamette Valley and learned quickly to pronounce it "wi-la'-mit." Then, as also a century later, it was home to a large majority of the state's people.[10]

By the time Mennonites arrived in Oregon, varied immigrant strains had somewhat diluted the state's original conservatism—the sober industry and patriotic Protestantism which the missionaries had promoted. Portland had a liquor outlet for every forty persons, and the Women's Temperance Prayer League vocally and dramatically combated this evil. But, in general, sobriety, thrift, simplicity, and traditionalism continued. Oregon's first farmers were slow to experiment with crops and methods new to them. However, when a gentleman farmer or someone willing to risk failure demonstrated improved methods or different products more adapted to Oregon climate and soils, others followed suit. Oregon conservatism often held to the old until something new and different proved itself, but it did not reject something just because it was new. One Samuel Bowles wrote in 1869 that the Oregonians had "builded . . . more slowly and more wisely than the Californians." He thought Oregon people had "less to unlearn," that they seemed sure "of organizing . . . a steadily prosperous, healthy, and moral" state, and that they were on the way to becoming "the New England of the Pacific Coast."[11]

Oregon Mennonite Groups

Oregon Mennonites traced their heritage to the Anabaptists of the sixteenth-century Reformation in Europe. Protestant Reformers Luther, Zwingli, and their associates paved the way and influenced Mennonite antecedents. However, a third movement of considerable diversity, rejected by both Catholics and Protestants, arose among individuals and small groups in Switzerland, southern Germany, and the Netherlands. Religious concerns figured largely in the movement, although social, political, and economic influences also pulsed through it. An identifying feature was baptism for adult believers, initiated by a group in Zurich comprised of Conrad Grebel, Felix Manz, and others on January 21, 1525. In later centuries, Mennonites recognized that event as the formal beginning of the movement. Opposing authorities considered such baptism to be rebaptism and dubbed the participants "Anabaptists," meaning rebaptizers—a name widely used, in spite of its disfavor among Anabaptists. They began to emphasize that church and state should be strictly separate, that believers should be able to choose their church rather than the government legislating that they join its approved church. As the diverse movement developed more commonality, nonviolence became another prominent characteristic of most Anabaptists.[12]

Almost immediately, in most areas of Europe where Anabaptists lived, intense persecution began to scatter or eliminate their early leaders and many of the followers. In Switzerland, persecution continued for decades, or even centuries. However, Menno Simons, a Dutch priest who joined the Anabaptists in 1536, escaped with his life and ministered to scattered groups of believers so effectively—personally and in writing—that they acquired the nickname "Mennist." This evolved to "Mennonite," the Americanized form of the word.[13]

Persecution and economic and social disadvantages in Europe prompted Mennonites to emigrate, both to Eastern Europe and to North America. About 150 years after Anabaptism emerged in Switzerland, Mennonites established their first permanent settlement in America. Thirteen families from the Crefeld area of North Germany—all of them formerly Mennonite/Quakers, except for one Mennonite couple—arrived in Philadelphia in 1683. Seven miles to the north they established Germantown, which within three centuries was well within the city of Philadelphia. Other European Mennonites followed in the next decades and centuries. Most nineteenth-century Mennonite immigrants passed by or through Pennsylvania and settled farther west or in Canada.[14]

Before 1800, years before Lewis and Clark opened new vistas in faraway Oregon, long before the last Mennonite immigrants arrived in North America, Mennonites were leaving Pennsylvania for Canada and Virginia. By the early 1800s Mennonites were making new homes and founding congregations in Ohio, and, by 1840, in Indiana, Illinois, and Iowa. Mennonites settled in Missouri in the years surrounding the Civil War. In the early 1870s, Mennonites claimed homes in Kansas, Nebraska, and other prairie states, several years before the first Mennonites settled in Oregon in 1876.[15]

Before Mennonites came to Oregon, a number of distinct groups emerged, both in Europe and North America. All held Anabaptist beliefs in common. What separated them was, in part, their varying understandings of how to apply biblical truth in both religious and secular settings. The time and place from which they immigrated to America and to Oregon also influenced their differences. Earlier immigrants sometimes held convictions different from those of later immigrants, and groups who came from one area of Europe did not always agree with those from another region.[16]

The Amish began in 1693 as a schism from Mennonites in Switzerland, Alsace (now in France), and southern Germany over the issue of the *Meidung,* the shunning of excommunicated members in order to maintain a pure church. They also resisted change more than most Mennonites. In America, during the latter half of the nineteenth century, the Amish divided into more progressive Amish Mennonites (AM) and more conservative Old Order Amish (OOA). About the turn of the century, some AM congregations which were more conservative than most other AM congregations but less so than the OOA became identified as Conservative Amish Mennonite. In the 1920s, the Beachy Amish formed another group, again more progressive than the OOA but less so than AMs. By that time the AMs were completing mergers with the more mainline (old) Mennonites. Differences concerning shunning initiated this division as it had the first one, though for later Beachy Amish congregations it was not an issue.[17]

Two American groups with members in Oregon organized in the nineteenth century. The Church of God in Christ, Mennonite (Holdeman) began in 1859 as a conservative movement, and the General Conference Mennonite Church (GC) organized in 1860 as a progressive one. The Holdemans emphasized church purity and used shunning to enforce discipline. The GC group wished to promote cooperation and fellowship among all Mennonites and emphasized missions, education, and publication several decades ahead of the (old) Mennonites.[18]

Two divisions about thirty years apart originated among Russian Mennonites. The Mennonite Brethren Church began in Russia in 1860 as a call to spiritual renewal and church purity. In 1889 the Evangelical Mennonite Brethren, emphasizing the new birth and firm congregational discipline, organized as the "Bruderthaler" with two congregations among recent immigrants in Nebraska and Minnesota. They separated from Russian Mennonites who had migrated to America in the 1870s and who soon joined the General Conference Mennonites.[19]

The Brethren in Christ originated about 1780 in Pennsylvania. Brethren in Christ based part of their system of beliefs on Anabaptist theology. Several early leaders and considerable numbers of members came from Mennonite congregations or had Mennonite heritage. But twentieth-century Mennonites do not know if the movement originally emerged out of Mennonitism. Brethren in Christ emphasized the new birth as a deeply personal, emotional experience and promoted the need for a second dramatic experience of God's grace more than most Mennonites did.[20]

Members of all these Mennonite and related groups came to Oregon. Before 1900, they had settled mainly in five areas: Salem-Silverton, in Marion County; Hubbard-Needy-Woodburn, along the Marion/Clackamas County line; Dallas, in Polk County; Albany, in Linn County; and Eugene, in Lane County. Scattered Mennonites also settled briefly in other counties and a few located in the Portland area. Before 1900 continuing congregations emerged in four areas. Only Lane County lost its early Mennonite groups. In the 1900s congregations developed in other areas, still mostly in the valley or in the foothills edging it.

Mennonites came to Oregon for reasons similar to those held by other settlers. They wanted reasonably priced land and a healthful climate. A few wanted to start businesses. For some, spiritual concerns also motivated their decision. Recent immigrants from Russia wanted to preserve what new policies there had threatened—their religious/cultural heritage, including their use of the German language and their exemption from military service. Some of the Amish probably moved to Oregon to get away from church troubles. According to John A. Hostetler, the "underlying

Locations of
Oregon
Mennonites
before or in 1976

For Shaded Area,
See Chapter 2

OREGON

PACIFIC OCEAN

Hope Lind

Snake River

River

Columbia
Cascade Locks

•Union
UNION

•Heppner
MORROW

JEFFERSON
Culver•

•Estacada
•Molalla
CLACKAMAS
MARION
•Cascadia
LINN
LANE

•LaPine

MULTNOMAH
Portland•

•Salem
Willamette River
•Eugene

DOUGLAS

Creswell•

•Yoncalla

Sutherlin•
Roseburg•
•Winston

Grants Pass•
JOSEPHINE
•Selma

TILLAMOOK
YAMHILL
POLK
LINCOLN
BENTON

process" of Amish migration was "usually the resolution of a religious problem." Their Mennonite cousins sometimes attempted to solve church problems in the same way. For all who came to Oregon, frontier adventure awaited them.[21]

A need for affordable land attracted many Mennonites to Oregon. Among them was young Peter Neuenschwander, who in 1871, at twenty, had migrated from Switzerland to Wayne County, Ohio. In 1873 he married Emma Biery. By then Ohio was becoming thickly settled and land prices were high. To help young people find land, deacon Jacob J. Moser of Sonnenberg Mennonite Church went to Oregon to assess its opportunities. Perhaps he accompanied Christian C. Wenger, who had traveled and worked in Oregon for several months in 1875 before deciding to move there the following spring. Moser did not move to Oregon himself, but he recommended the Silverton area, where land was selling for seven to thirty dollars per acre. In 1877 the Neuenschwander family and others made the move. Neuenschwander later shortened his name to Neuschwander.[22]

Most settlers regarded Oregon's climate as healthful, and some hoped it would improve their health. Amos P. Troyer of Garden City, Cass County, Missouri, suffered aftereffects of typhoid fever. To find out if the Oregon climate deserved its good reputation, Amos sent his wife, Lyle, as he called her (he did not like her name, Delilah), to spy out the land. Lyle, the mother of seven children, the oldest not yet thirteen, must have welcomed such a purposeful vacation. She liked the Willamette Valley, and Amos was pleased with the potatoes, apples, and gifts of canned fruit that she took back to Missouri. In the fall of 1892 the Troyers sold their Cass County farm and moved by immigrant train to Oregon. It was a wise decision. Amos regained his health and lived to be almost seventy-nine.[23]

Though most of Oregon's early Mennonites were farmers, a few went into business. Isaac S. Miller, an 1880 Amish immigrant from Douglas County, Illinois, bought a sawmill operated by a waterwheel. To use the mill's wood by-products, he soon built a small brick and tile plant across the road and manufactured the first machine-made brick in Oregon. Miller also built a cider mill; did woodworking, tailoring, and blacksmithing; and sold bottles of "medicine," presumably made from recipes later found in the mill books. Some years later the sawmill ceased to operate, but in modern times the Needy Brick and Tile Company prospered on the same site.[24]

Spiritual concerns were among primary reasons Mennonites emigrated from Russia to North America in the 1870s. Those who moved to Oregon, beginning in the 1880s, first stopped in the Midwest or prairie states or provinces. Among them was the Gerhard J. Rempel family, who settled at Mountain Lake, Minnesota. Rempel did not like the cold winters there, so the family moved to Redding, California. The climate there pleased him, but Redding had .no Mennonite community and the Rempel parents feared their children might marry outside the Mennonite church and lose their faith. Already their daughter Anna had met and married Johann George Diehm, a native German, in California. In *Die Mennonitische Rundschau*, which John F. Funk of Indiana published especially for Russian Mennonites, Rempel read that Mennonites lived near Dallas, Oregon. He sent two sons to investigate the area. Based on their favorable report, in 1894 the Rempel family moved to a farm east of Dallas, toward Rickreall. The Diehms also moved in 1894.[25]

Though a degree of frontier adventure awaited all of Oregon's early Mennonites, only a few settled on Oregon's own frontier. Amos Conrad of Wayland, Iowa, was twenty-three when he and his two cousins, John Hostetler and Joe Conrad, walked into the Silverton community of Swiss Mennonites in 1882. Although they were surely looking for a place of promise in which to put down roots, no doubt a sense of adventure contributed to their decision to leave the relative security of the Willamette Valley for the high dry plains of eastern Oregon and a spot near Heppner in Morrow County. They were among the few Mennonites who tried their skills and luck homesteading east of the Cascades.[26]

The state's early Mennonites had disappointments and reversals common in any new region. Although some secured good farmland at affordable prices, others bought cheap land and learned, to their sorrow, that its quality matched the price. *Herald of Truth* readers could have noted C. C. Wenger's comments about the difficulty of making "a commencement" in Oregon. He warned that except for persons "possessed of means," those who had "passed the meridian of life and lost the ability to conform themselves to given circumstances, would risk much" in Oregon. Nor did everyone who came find improved health. Adults and children battled with illness and some lost, to be buried in small country cemeteries. Economic depression contributed to adversity for many, such as Amos Conrad, who kept a store in Tangent after his years of farming in eastern Oregon.[27]

Those who hoped to leave church troubles behind usually found that troubles came along with them. Many young people who came to Oregon with their parents never joined a Mennonite group. Lack of strong leadership and geographical isolation from other Mennonites contributed to such losses. No ministers joined the earliest groups of settlers, and without a minister there could be no church. The hardship of being without a congregation was probably the greatest trial for Oregon's early Mennonites. The frontier which fostered individualism also caused them to yearn for established church communities. Two themes surfaced repeatedly in their correspondence to church periodicals. One was the wide diversity among themselves. The other was their need for ministerial leadership.[28]

After a time even the stronghearted tired of adventure, particularly when rewards did not sustain it. After eight years of unproductive homesteading in eastern Oregon, Amos Conrad and his cousins returned to the Willamette Valley, disappointed and disillusioned. Later they regarded those years of their lives as wasted. Not only did they struggle with marginal farmland; as youths of Mennonite heritage, they also felt alone.[29]

No mission board sent the first Mennonites to Oregon, but their coming was part of the continuous worldwide scattering of Mennonites. Frank Epp, a respected Canadian writer and scholar, described it as "a unique diffusion of salt and light." Eventually, Oregon Mennonites established congregations, began mission work, and provided their own seasoning and light in their communities. In Oregon, as elsewhere, sometimes the salt and light failed, and unfaithfulness troubled the church. Some Mennonites returned to their former communities or moved to another location. Epp concluded that "only a deep sense of calling" could enable new settlers to "survive the disillusionments" they faced "in any new land, however filled with promise." Even when the dream tarnished, many Oregon Mennonites, whether held by such a calling or by other circumstances, stayed and put down lasting roots.[30]

In that era, ordained men provided the primary leadership. Oregon Mennonites needed ministers, but before 1900 few moved to Oregon. Only several who stayed were strong leaders. Most capable ministers in established Mennonite communities to the east lacked the incentive to make a costly move to the distant, unknown west to work with motley, individualistic groups who may have been the discontents of their former communities. For most early Oregon Mennonites, the strongest links with their larger church were visiting ministers. Ministerial visits of several days or even weeks strengthened the members in their faith, gathered in both new and former members, and helped local groups establish congregations. Establishment often included ordaining one or more men from within the new congregation. A few of the new ministers exerted strong leadership that influenced Oregon Mennonites for generations.

■ ■ ■

Most Mennonites who moved to Oregon were either recent European immigrants to North America or were from families of "movers" who had edged their way west with one or more moves in a generation. Only a few came directly from the long-established communities in Pennsylvania. Sometimes the movers were less content with conservative church traditions than those who stayed. Many were less financially secure. Except for those who crossed an ocean, few American Mennonites moved farther from their previous community than did those who settled in Oregon. In contrast to some Mennonites in the East and the Midwest who had settled in territories even before they achieved statehood, Oregon's earliest Mennonites arrived after two or three generations of farmers had taken their pick of land and Oregon had been a state almost twenty years. Some Oregon Mennonites did clear timber and break new sod, but many purchased or rented land which others had already tamed.

Still, they came to a frontier which "was as much psychological as it was geographical," Northwest historians Dorothy O. Johansen and Charles M. Gates judged. Even after generations of movers settled the West, the region retained a frontier mystique as a land of challenge and opportunity. Paradoxically, Oregon's distance from larger centers of Mennonite life fostered both a spirit of independence and a yearning for community. Mennonites in Oregon, far from the revivals and restraints of their former congregations, had to decide how they would live in their new country. Would they continue to be Mennonites? Who would nurture their spirits and smooth their many differences? What would unite them? Even after preachers from east of the Rockies moved to Oregon and congregations chose their own ministers, Mennonites there still felt themselves to be on the edge of the church, far from long-settled Mennonite communities.[31]

Not all the Mennonite groups who settled in Oregon established long-lasting congregations. In the twentieth century, changes brought mergers, divisions, the extinction of some groups and the formation of others. Several congregations had shaky beginnings, but those who continued became a witness to God's unshakable love for and infinite patience with the independent, resourceful, sometimes bickering, and usually warmhearted Mennonites of Oregon. From their early years in Oregon, individualism held their church communities in tension, and other organizations or movements competed with their communities for Mennonite loyalties. In the twentieth century, changing definitions of the church and revivalism's emphasis on religious individualism helped keep the tension tight. In spite of shortcomings and inconsistencies, their faith in Christ and his life-changing power held Mennonites to each other, producing communities like the rough, dull agates some of them collected—communities that sometimes, with God's cutting and tumbling and polishing, shone with bold and breathtaking beauty in unexpected splendor.

Chapter 2
Amish Mennonites in Oregon

The division into Amish Mennonites (AM) and Old Order Amish (OOA) was hardly complete in the Midwest when Amish began to move to Oregon. Amish Mennonites were among the earliest to establish congregations in Oregon. Within half a century most had merged with (old) Mennonites (OM), who soon became Oregon's largest Mennonite group, later designated as Mennonite Church (MC). Amish Mennonites settled first in the Hubbard-Woodburn area, then in counties to the south. Few scattered independently.

Marion/Clackamas County

The first settlers known to be AM when they moved to Oregon were Peter D. and Rachel (Miller) Mishler. However, some earlier settlers usually identified as OOA were without question AM a few years later, and may have made that change even before they arrived. Possibly late in 1880, certainly by 1881, the Mishlers moved to Woodburn from LaGrange County, Indiana, where they had been members of the Forks AM church. Some of Rachel's family were also among the early Oregon Mennonite settlers. Louisa (Miller) and Daniel J. Yoder, of Amish parentage, had moved to Oregon in 1879. The parents, Benedict and Rachel (Mast) Miller, also of Forks, arrived in 1883. Their group included another married daughter, Mattie, with her husband, Jim Troyer, and their two-year-old daughter, Edna, and the Millers' three unmarried children, Abraham, Almira, and Milo. Lovina (Miller) and Frank Burck arrived in 1884 with their eight-month-old son, Harley.[1]

In the 1880s, AM bishop Jonathan P. Smucker of Nappanee, Indiana, visited Oregon several times. In 1883, he accompanied the Miller party to Oregon, organized a church, reinstated several expelled members, and baptized five or six persons. The church

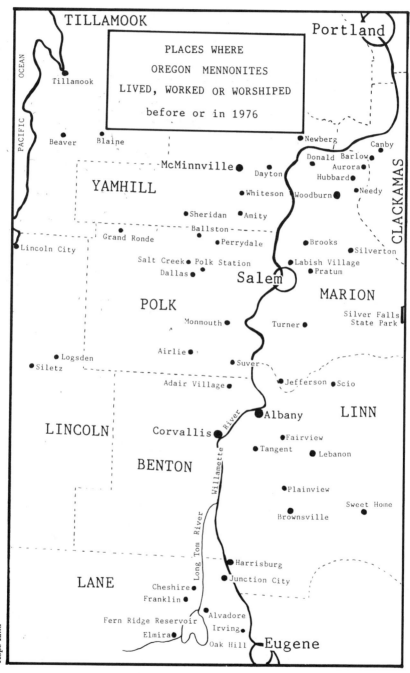

TILLAMOOK

OCEAN

PACIFIC

Portland

PLACES WHERE
OREGON MENNONITES
LIVED, WORKED OR WORSHIPED
before or in 1976

Tillamook

Beaver   Blaine

Newberg   Canby

McMinnville   Donald Barlow
        Dayton   Aurora
YAMHILL   Hubbard
        Whiteson   Woodburn   Needy

Sheridan   Amity

Ballston

Grand Ronde   Perrydale   Brooks
Lincoln City   Silverton

Salt Creek   Polk Station   Labish Village
Dallas   Pratum

CLACKAMAS

Salem

POLK   MARION

Monmouth   Turner   Silver Falls
            State Park

Airlie

Logsden   Suver
Siletz

Adair Village   Jefferson   Scio

LINCOLN   Albany   LINN

Corvallis   Fairview

BENTON   Tangent   Lebanon

Plainview

Sweet Home

Brownsville

Long Tom River

Willamette River

Harrisburg

LANE   Cheshire   Junction City
Franklin

Fern Ridge Reservoir   Alvadore
    Irving
Elmira   Oak Hill   Eugene

Hope Lind

probably consisted of Benedict Miller's extended family and several neighboring Amish families. Perhaps at this time, Peter Christner, who had been ordained an Amish minister in Howard County, Indiana, joined the AMs and became minister of the congregation.[2]

On his 1887 visit, Smucker organized five families into another congregation and ordained Christner as bishop. Most of the families were about to move or were even then living farther south. Joseph Maurer, a native of Alsace-Lorraine, France, and his family had moved from Davis County, Iowa. They arrived in Oregon in 1887 after stopping briefly in Washington. Before settling in Linn County, they stayed several months at Hubbard. The Benedict Miller, Levi J. Yoder, and Peter Christner families had lived near Hubbard several years before they bought land the same spring in Lane County. About that time, Christner ordained Mishler as minister for the AMs remaining in the Woodburn area. Of the five, only the Peter Mishler family remained at Woodburn. Five years later they, too, moved to Lane County.[3]

Smucker's 1888 and 1889 visits to Oregon came when AM families were moving in from other states, multiplying individualism and dividing church community. The John Kropf and Moses Yoder families in 1888 were probably the first from the Sycamore Grove AM congregation in Cass County, Missouri, to move to Oregon. Yoder had been a minister since 1872, but it seems he did not participate with any Oregon Mennonite group. In 1888 P. D. Mishler wrote to *Herald of Truth*: "People are rapidly coming in now and from many different parts; but . . . it seems that each one is inclined to want his church by himself." He prayed that some "able ministers from the East" would come and help "put aside all sectarianism." That year and also the next Smucker visited Oregon, writing after his 1889 visit of "sore trials and afflictions" among the Oregon people. For over a year there had been "trouble" there. But "by the blessing of God, peace was restored." Mishler doubtless welcomed the new settlers, expecting them to meet with his established group. And perhaps most AMs did at first take part in the one congregation of thirty members in Marion County, meeting in a schoolhouse, which the 1890 U.S. Religious Census recorded. But the restored peace proved temporary.[4]

By 1889, George Hostetler from Missouri had arrived at Hubbard with the assigned responsibility of starting a church. Other families from Missouri also arrived about then or within several years. Hostetler, a deacon at Sycamore Grove, had first settled near Rathdrum, Idaho, and Spokane, Washington. His father-in-law, Jacob Easch, formerly of Indiana, offered him forty acres of land if he would start a church there. However, Hostetler's son Simon recalled years later, Emmanuel Kenagy and a few other Missouri people who "had the money" preferred Oregon and repeated the land offer if Hostetler would begin a church in Oregon instead.[5]

The following year, late in 1890, AM ministers Peter Zimmerman of Cass County and Jacob Roth of Thurman, Colorado, visited Oregon. Mishler welcomed them gladly and wrote optimistically, "It seemed that by [their] encouraging words . . . all selfishness and envy had to disappear." The visitors cautioned against going to "a distant country," standing "aloof," and not helping build "up the walls of Zion." They instructed the people "not to find fault" with a congregation not exactly like "the church from which they came," especially when "built upon the same foundation, and seeking to follow Christ in humility, separated from the world and maintaining . . . the non-resistant prinicples of the Gospel."[6]

But such admonitions failed to bring unity. Possibly by 1891, the Indiana and Missouri groups were meeting separately. Families, largely from Missouri, met for Sunday school in Daniel Erb's home, about four miles east of Hubbard. George Hostetler served as superintendent and also preached. About this time, several miles away, another group, probably led by Peter Mishler, had a union Sunday school, and an unidentified correspondent reported that "everything goes peaceably." They also had "meeting" every third Sunday at the schoolhouse, and the United Brethren Church had one every fourth Sunday.

Within a year, in late 1892, Mishler moved to Lane County to serve the AM congregation there, composed of settlers from Indiana and other states, but likely none from Missouri. A few months later, when Zion organized in 1893, none of its charter members were from Indiana AM congregations. The majority were from Missouri, with some from Arkansas, several from the OOA, and the Erb family from Ohio. The Erbs did not remain long at Zion. Later in 1893 they became associated with the fledgling movement, perhaps including Indiana people, that became the neighboring Hopewell Mennonite Church in 1899, though in later years most of the family returned to Zion.[7]

Differences between the Indiana and Missouri people may have related to attire. It is also possible the Missouri people objected to the reputation a recent Indiana settler had for bad financial dealings. But differences among the Missouri people themselves also caused problems. Oral tradition holds that some of them disapproved of changing dress customs and language at Sycamore Grove, their Missouri congregation. The Western District AM Conference, which encompassed AM congregations from Illinois west, had decided in 1884 not to make the wearing of buttons instead of hooks and eyes on men's coats a test of membership, but some who came to Oregon questioned that decision. Another issue was the so-called "sleeping preacher"—John D. Kauffman from Indiana—who preached as if in a trance. He had first visited Sycamore Grove in 1882 and his influence later reached Oregon. And the early leader George Hostetler apparently received criticism.[8]

For reasons unknown to later generations, Hostetler apparently resigned as deacon before Zion organized. Soon thereafter, the Hostetler family moved back to Missouri, perhaps in part because of wife Paulina's poor health, personality conflicts, and disagreements among Zion people. Possibly Hostetler's ideas about healing came under fire. A few years earlier, in a short article in *Herald of Truth*, he had written of Jesus as the great physician not only of the soul but also of the body. After quoting several New Testament Scriptures, he wrote, "These promises stand as firmly to-day as ever, if we only believe." As a personal testimony, he wrote that his wife had been in "delicate health for about four years . . . and confined to her bed part of the time." They had tried "different doctors and patent medicines, but without success. She remained the same," until on February 6, 1884, "through faith in [the] great Physician, she arose and was suddenly endued with new life and strength. The change [was] indescribable." Within five years Paulina lost the use of her limbs. Later her condition again improved. About twenty years after Hostetlers went back to Missouri, they returned to Hubbard. Paulina, in spite of such bodily difficulties, lived to be ninety-three; George, eighty-five.[9]

Joining the Missouri group was John Lais, a Catholic immigrant from Germany. After working in coal mines in Pennsylvania and for an Amish farmer in Indiana, he decided to join the Daniel J. Yoder family when they moved to Oregon in 1879. But he wanted a wife first, and asked to marry Susannah Plank. Susannah's widowed Amish mother approved, so John and Susannah were married. He was 29, she, 19. John wanted to join the Old Order Amish church; Susannah did not. They did not join that church. Some years later, visiting Nebraska bishop Joseph Schlegel baptized John into the AM church. John and Susannah were charter members of Zion and John was in the lot for deacon when Amos P. Troyer was chosen. The AM practice of brotherhood attracted John. For him, the church community superseded individualism, and he resolved to faithfully observe church regulations. After Zion discussed whether men should be allowed to keep buttons on their coats or whether hooks and eyes should be required, Susannah said she would never sew those things on his coat. John reminded her that he had come farther than she had. Whatever the church decided, they would do. Fortunately, the matter was not put to the test. Zion decided not to require hooks and eyes. A short time later, in 1894, John Lais died of pneumonia at age 44, not knowing that many of his descendants would also become part of the church community he had treasured.[10]

The Zion congregation organized in 1893, with visiting bishop Schlegel officiating. For the two-week period covering this event and the preceding meetings, the Hubbard people rented the Rock Creek Methodist Church building, even then an historic little church, just south of Needy. After Schlegel ordained Daniel J. Kropf as minister and Amos P. Troyer as deacon on June 18, 1893, he organized the congregation on June 22 with about forty members. Family names included Erb, Hooley, Hostetler, Johnson, Kauffman, Kenagy, King, Kropf, Lais, Rediger, Roth, Schultz, Troyer, and Yoder.[11]

Zion was a young congregation in a frontier country, and new settlers sometimes missed their well-established "home" congregation. One young mother wrote to a Missouri relative that on Sunday she always thought of the Sycamore Grove church and Sunday school. She saw "quite a difference" between it and Zion and didn't "blame" the "few young folks" from Missouri if they didn't like Oregon. She continued, "I tell you, I am glad I got a man before I [came] to Oregon, for I think surely I should have been an old maid if I had to pick one up here. Ha, Ha!" In another letter she lamented the "wild place [compared to] old Cass," with so many "infidels, unbelievers, hard hearted people, rough," who hunt just as much on Sunday as on any other day of the week. She thought that some who did "profess Christianity [were] most awful slack, never no evangelizing preachers come here [sic]." Sometimes she yearned to "hear a good waking-up sermon." Zion preachers did "preach the Word, of course," as well as they could, she supposed. But she thought Oregon "awful dull."[12]

The congregation met in the home of John Lais or other members or in the Whiskey Hill schoolhouse and later in the small Fir Grove meetinghouse they built in 1894 five miles east of Woodburn. In 1898 they constructed a larger building beside a well-located cemetery three-and-one-half miles east of Hubbard. The story goes that while the men were roofing the building they were singing, "Who will go along with me to Zion?" Emmanuel Kenagy said, "We need a name for our church. Let's call it Zion." And Zion it became. In the 1950s they constructed a new building.[13]

Zion had a minister and a deacon, but only bishops could perform baptisms and lead communion services. Schlegel returned to Oregon late in 1895, planning to ordain a bishop at Zion, and people expected him to use the lot. This method of selection, after a prayer for divine action in the matter, had the nominees choose one of several identical books. The man who chose the book which contained a slip of paper with an appropriate Bible verse became God's chosen leader. On this occasion there was some question about the propriety of allowing a deacon (Troyer) to be in the lot for bishop with a minister (Kropf). So on Thursday, December 12, Schlegel ordained Troyer as minister. On Sunday, December 15, both ministers, Kropf and Troyer, were in the lot. Troyer was chosen.[14]

Both Troyer and Kropf were dedicated leaders. Harold S. Bender, a noted Mennonite historian, considered Troyer Oregon's outstanding AM leader throughout his forty-year career as bishop. But some at Zion would have preferred Kropf, even though God had spoken through the lot and the choice could hardly be disputed. People did not consider Kropf an eloquent speaker, but he was conscientious and concerned about the spiritual welfare of his people. His influence, as a layman, had helped John Lais decide to join Zion.

Troyer and Kropf disagreed on certain matters. Kropf favored requirements for plain clothing and a more decisive discipline, particularly in receiving members who left other congregations. One Oregon historian noted that Kropf was concerned also about the influences on his own family of "seemingly unrestrained youth" who spent time out at the sheds rather than in church services. Troyer tended to be lenient with them, believing that gentle words accomplished more good than a rigid discipline.[15]

In time the differences between Troyer and Kropf deepened, and other influences also contributed to a separation. Their wives, each a strong personality, agreed even less than their husbands. Kropf wished to live in an area where he could farm on a scale larger than at Hubbard. Troyer and Kropf discussed the situation and agreed to part ways because of their differences of conviction and practice. They considered this a peaceful solution to the problem, not a schism. It was not an instance of individualism rejecting community but one of members transferring loyalties from one church community to another.

In March 1911, Kropf, his wife, Anna (Hostetler), and their family, moved south to Harrisburg, in Linn County. Soon eight other Zion families followed, all of them with Hostetler connections. They organized the Harrisburg Conservative Amish Mennonite Church. Most Zion people did not know that Kropf and Troyer had agreed to separate. They thought Kropf simply had left without telling anyone. Later Kropf felt he had done wrong to leave unannounced, and on a Sunday morning in the early 1920s he visited Zion and preached in German, asking for forgiveness. Many in the audience wept.[16]

One additional influence, somewhat discounted by Harrisburg people several generations later, was a phenomenon known as the "sleeping preacher." In the last quarter of the nineteenth century several men in Amish or AM circles began preaching while in a trance. They usually went to sleep in the early evening in a home or meetinghouse, then in some way they indicated that they were ready to be helped to an upright position. Then they prayed and preached with unusual power and clarity, in German or English. One spoke at times in a strange language said to be Italian. Hearers were impressed that such uneducated persons spoke so fluently. Doctors could not explain the condition. Trance preaching, however, has also occurred among other religious groups.[17]

Mennonites and AMs disagreed over how to receive these preachers. Some thought they were spokesmen for God. Others wondered if the evil one might be using them. John D. Kauffman of Elkhart County, Indiana, preached in a trance as early as 1880 or 1881, and his influence continued even after his death in 1913. H. S. Bender described him as "an unordained self-appointed 'preacher.' " Yet, in his era when ordination was ordinarily a requirement for preaching, some people considered Kauffman's words to be as authoritative as those of any ordained man. They believed that a spirit from God was speaking directly through him, that what he said was "Spirit preaching." He promoted conservative practices. Late in life, in 1911, he received ordination as bishop from Peter Zimmerman, without the usual prerequisite of first being a deacon or minister. Zimmerman's ordination as bishop had also been irregular, after he left the Roanoke, Illinois, AM congregation which had ordained him as minister and joined Kauffman's new Mount Herman congregation near Shelbyville, Illinois.[18]

Kauffman had contacts with Oregon people both in Missouri and after they moved to Oregon. In Missouri the community was divided about him. Ministers would not let him preach in the meetinghouse, but on one occasion he preached in a barn owned by David Hostetler, a relative of some of the Oregon Hostetlers. Kauffman visited Hubbard between 1906 and 1911, possibly in 1910, and preached at Zion. Bishop Troyer did not approve of Kauffman but allowed no one to show him disrespect. Levi Hostetler, who was instrumental in getting Kauffman to come to Oregon, was one of those who moved to Harrisburg in 1911.[19]

Several months after the Harrisburg families left, Edward Z. Yoder, a son-in-law of bishop Troyer, was ordained minister at Zion in August 1911. He served Zion over forty years and promoted missions, Christian education, and nonresistance. Alice, his wife, often arranged music for funerals of neighborhood people when Zion preachers officiated. She used her influence in other ways as well. As often happens with strong, talented leaders, she received her share of criticism, but no one could ever say she was apathetic. Several of their children continued the tradition of both lay and ordained leadership in Oregon and elsewhere. Yoder, together with Alice and her father, who died in 1935, probably influenced the character of Zion in its first sixty years more than any other persons.[20]

Soon after the Harrisburg families left, other members transferred to Bethel, which organized to accommodate members who lived in that community. Even so Zion became one of the largest congregations in Oregon. By 1939, membership had increased to a high of 324. In spite of its relatively liberal position on many matters, a large group with even more liberal views withdrew in the mid-1940s to organize a General Conference Mennonite congregation nearby. Zion's membership in 1976 was 267.[21]

Bethel, located in Clackamas County, was the last AM congregation started before Oregon AMs and OMs merged in 1921. By

Kathryn Yoder Miller

Edward Z. (1881-1957) and Alice Pearl (Troyer) (1888-1959)
Yoder, influential Zion leaders, at their marriage in 1909.

the late 1890s some families who had earlier lived in Lane County
or were members of Zion and Hopewell began to settle in an area
where land was cheaper, about eight miles southeast of Canby and
the same distance from Hubbard and Aurora. Because mud or dust
made it difficult to travel five to ten miles to services at Zion and
Hopewell, they organized or participated in Sunday schools in
several schoolhouses in their area. Some started Dryland in 1906.

Others helped in a union school at Bear Creek, which later divided. The Mennonites then began a Sunday school at Eby, three miles away. Hopewell and Zion ministers preached at these and other schools.[22]

Although Bethel existed fifty years as an organized congregation, it functioned a longer time. It began unofficially in 1912, when the Mennonites constructed a meetinghouse on land donated by Christian and Catherine Roth, on the southeast corner of their farm, about five-and-one-half miles east of Zion. In April 1912 the Eby Sunday school moved to the new building, which took the name Bethel Church. Zion and Hopewell ministers continued to fill preaching appointments until Fred J. Gingerich, a minister from Beaver Crossing, Nebraska, moved to Canby in April 1919. When Zion's bishop Troyer organized Bethel in May 1919, he placed Gingerich in charge. Family names of the twenty-eight charter members included Burkholder, Christner, Gingerich, Kauffman, Larson, Nofziger, Schultz, and Yoder. Christian Snyder, a deacon, moved from Creston, Montana, to Bethel in 1920. Both Gingerich and Snyder served Bethel faithfully for several decades, until they died. They also contributed significant vision and leadership to the conference. Bethel membership peaked at eighty-nine in 1942-43, then declined gradually. Some people moved away. Others preferred Zion, which was not so strict in matters of attire—another example of individuals turning from one community to another. In later years better transportation diminished the need for Bethel to exist and contributed to its disbanding in 1969. Membership then was about thirty-five.[23]

Linn County

The Joseph Maurer (pronounced mau-ree) family, which included Barbara (Gerig) Maurer's twice-widowed mother, Barbara Conrad, and several small children, moved to a farm about four miles north of Lebanon in 1887. For seven years they were the only AMs living in Linn County, about halfway between Hubbard and Eugene. Visiting preachers and other AM travelers often stayed with them overnight. The wood-burning train passed near the corner of their farm and would stop upon request. For a time the older Maurer girls attended a nearby Methodist Sunday school and church with neighbors, who could not understand when the parents, fearing the girls might become Methodists, no longer let them attend.[24]

No doubt the Maurers rejoiced when three AM families from Thurman, Colorado, moved to Linn County in the fall of 1894: Jacob and Mary (Eicher) Roth, Daniel and Katherina (Roth) Erb, and Christian R. and Magdalina (Swartzendruber) Kennel. Roth, a minister and soon a bishop, had visited the area twice in the early 1890s. Katherina Erb was a sister of Jacob Roth. Their widowed mother, Catherina Roth, moved to Oregon when her children did. Crop failures in Colorado precipitated the move.[25]

The four families began a Sunday school almost immediately, and probably late in 1894 they organized the Albany AM congregation. The twelve charter members included the four couples, the two grandmothers, and Martin and John Roth, sons of Jacob and Mary. For a short time they worshiped in homes, then in the Dunkard church building located about five miles southeast of Albany. In 1911 they purchased an acre of land nearer Albany and

Oregon Mennonite archival collection, courtesy of Amos Schmucker

The Christian R. Kennel family, one of the first four Fairview families. Back: Eli, Moses; front: John, C. R. (1857-1949), Samuel, Magdalina (Swartzendruber) (1859-1936), Sarah, Emma.

constructed a meetinghouse. C. R. Kennel was the main carpenter. John Heyerly hauled most of the lumber and the benches from Albany with a wagon and team of horses. Since the new building was in the open, with a fine view of nearby farmland and distant mountains, some of them snowcapped, they decided to call their congregation Fairview. In 1951 they constructed a new building and in 1973 a major addition.[26]

Soon after Fairview organized, other families with names including Widmer, Christner, Schlegel, Heyerly, Neuschwander, Eicher, Gerig, Sutter, Ropp, Yutzi, Nofziger, and Schrock moved to the area. Several joined the Albany Mennonite Church when it organized in 1899 and some joined Harrisburg. But most stayed to swell the ranks at Fairview. Later, others moved to Linn County, especially because of prolonged drought in Nebraska and Colorado in the mid-1930s. Fairview became the largest congregation in its conference, with a membership high of 426 in 1965, just before a major withdrawal of members who began the nearby Bethany congregation. Earlier, smaller withdrawals had also occurred, and some members transferred to mission congregations, including East Fairview and Plainview. Membership in 1976 was 350.[27]

Fairview members who withdrew did so for a variety of reasons. Amos Schmucker, Fairview's historian, wrote of an "old Mennonite custom . . . that when some members cannot get along, they start another church." Some of the AMs from Lane County who moved to Linn County in the late 1890's worshiped for a time with the AMs there, but, as George R. Brunk I noted later, they "were not accepted in Bishop Roth's congregation on account of wearing 'buttons' on the outer garments." The question of whether to use the German or English language was another problem. Roth also frowned on telephones. Persons who preferred a less conservative position joined the neighboring Albany Mennonite Church (OM). Those who went to Harrisburg in 1911 or soon after were more conservative regarding the German language and attire. It seems they also disapproved of Sunday school. Some who went to Albany (OM) in the 1920s left because the Fairview bishop disapproved of their participation in a Pentecostal revival campaign in town. Those who withdrew to organize the Tangent congregation in 1950 took a conservative position. Others who left in the 1960s, in some ways more liberal, wanted stronger leadership and faster progress on a building program, but had larger dissatisfactions that soon threatened the Bethany congregation they helped to start.[28]

Oregon Mennonite archival collection, courtesy of Amos Schmucker

Christian R. Gerig (1855-1942), Fairview bishop.

. Few of Fairview's first leaders had long tenure. Most came and went. Exceptions were Daniel Erb and Christian R. Gerig. Erb, ordained deacon in 1897 and minister a year later, served forty years, until he died in 1937 at age eighty-three. Gerig, a brother of Barbara (Gerig) Maurer, was a minister who moved from Iowa to Oregon in 1904. He became perhaps Fairview's strongest early leader. In 1908 he was ordained bishop and served until 1930. Then he resigned—he wanted a younger bishop who could keep up with modern ideas and new thinking. In his later years he said that if he had his life to live over again, he would preach more "Jesus Christ and him crucified," rather than emphasizing so strongly some things that he felt did not amount to much, such as dress and hairstyles. Gerig himself always wore hooks and eyes, a beard and plain-toed shoes, not so much a type of nonconformity as a symbol of nonresistance. He avoided any clothing that suggested military garb such as he remembered from Alsace-Lorraine, France, where he had lived until he was nine. Thus, he did not approve of the plain, regulation coat for ministers which most OMs adopted early in the twentieth century. But he never told his children how they should dress. His first wife wore a cape dress but she matter-of-factly put a necktie on her youngest son when he was four or five years old. Gerig died in 1942 at age eighty-six.[29]

Fairview and Zion were both AM but their corporate personalities soon developed differently. Fairview had more members who had immigrated directly from Europe or come from families of more recent immigrants who had first settled in Ontario, Canada, earlier in the 1800s. More of Zion's members came from immigrant families of the 1700s. Zion aligned itself more closely with the Albany OM congregation, and the two soon became the most liberal in the conference. Fairview developed relationships with the conference but remained more congregational in practice, though Zion, too, was more congregational than some conference leaders wished. But in various matters Fairview held a more conservative and independent position. In 1969 it withdrew from the conference.

The Harrisburg Conservative Amish Mennonite Church in Linn County was a conservative movement away from Zion and Fairview, although the initiators and the largest number came from Zion. Melvin Gingerich, a respected Mennonite historian, clearly attributed the origins of Harrisburg to "sleeping preacher" John D. Kauffman's teachings and influence. Of the nine families from Zion who moved to Harrisburg in 1911 and soon after, all (with the possible exception of one) were closely related to Levi Hostetler of Zion and his brother Christian J. Hostetler of Garden City, Missouri. Both Levi and Christian supported Kauffman and were patriarchs in the so-called "sleeping preacher" congregations of 1911 at Harrisburg and at Pryor, Oklahoma. Most of the Oklahoma Hostetlers soon moved to Shelbyville, Illinois, and became part of the Mount Hermon congregation which Kauffman had established in 1907. For years Mount Hermon and Harrisburg kept in close contact, partly because of family relationships but also because of common religious viewpoints. Ordained men associated with the "sleeping preacher" or from Mount Hermon served Harrisburg at ordinations and in other ways at least through the 1920s. For some years, Harrisburg people spoke of "when the Spirit was with us," meaning Kauffman. Pius Hostetler, an advocate of Kauffman, who in 1916 wrote *Life, Preaching, Labors of John D. Kauffman*, also referred to Kauffman as the "Spirit." It seems, however, that they were not equating Kauffman with the Holy Spirit but rather regarded him as *a* spirit from God.[30]

Some families moved between Fairview and Harrisburg in the early years. The Peter and Emma Neuschwander family of Swiss Mennonites, who had first settled near Salem, transferred to Harrisburg. Neuschwander, a deacon, then withdrew from Harrisburg several years later, partly because he opposed the use of English. Until about 1937 he remained aloof from any church. Then he returned to Harrisburg and retained his membership until he died in 1945. Another, Levi Hostetler, the patriarch, who was approaching eighty when he moved to Harrisburg, moved to Albany in 1914 and was a member at Fairview when he died in 1921 at age eighty-eight. He may have moved partly because of sympathies toward his son Enos, a Harrisburg minister who was silenced in 1913.[31]

In August 1911, within five months after the first families moved to Harrisburg, the congregation organized. Family names of the twenty-eight charter members were Hostetler, Kropf, Miller, Neuschwander, Smucker, Stutzman, and Widmer. Daniel J. Kropf served Harrisburg as minister and, after 1914, as bishop—until 1926, when a voice paralysis incapacitated him. He died a year later. Bishops at Harrisburg included Wilbert D. Kropf, ordained minister in 1955 and bishop in 1957. In the mid-1970s he was still serving, along with other longtime ministers, Levi Kropf and Wilbur D. Kropf, and deacon Herman Kropf. Levi Kropf was a son of Daniel; Wilbur, a son of Levi. The bishop and the deacon were also related to the Daniel J. Kropf family. The congregation never joined a conference.[32]

For four years the Harrisburg group held services in their homes until they built a meetinghouse in 1915. An addition doubled the size in 1936. Fire destroyed it in 1944 during World War II. With special building and materials permits from the United States government, they rebuilt in 1945. The deed to the property originally named this as the Conservative Amish Mennonite Church. However, the community more recently regarded it simply as the Harrisburg Mennonite Church and the congregation, too, adopted that name.[33]

A unique characteristic of Harrisburg for many years was the number of deaf members, as many as fourteen at one time, a total of seven couples and a single male. Levi Hostetler (son of the patriarch and one of the deaf), a layman, was appointed to preach for the deaf in sign language and served in this way about thirty years. Deaf members participated in other ways in worship services through an interpreter. Later, Earl Baker, son of a mute couple, interpreted the spoken word to the deaf. Most of the deaf were children or grandchildren or in-laws of the patriarch Levi Hostetler.[34]

Growth in membership increased gradually to a high of 153 for several years—in the mid-1940s. By 1976 it had dropped to seventy-four. Increases in the earlier years came partly from families moving to the area from Illinois and Indiana, and elsewhere in Oregon, and partly because there were no important defections. In the fall of 1946, when membership was at its peak, one group of families left, as a conservative movement. Within ten years—in the early 1950s—another group of about eight families left because of more liberal leanings. They wanted radios and more relaxed regulations regarding dress and musical instruments. Three of the families moved to Sacramento, California, and began a rescue mission under the conference mission board. When the mission closed about five years later and they returned to Oregon, they transferred their membership from Harrisburg to other congregations. In the early 1970s, a number of families gradually moved from Harrisburg to less conservative congregations, especially to nearby Brownsville. Wilbur D. Kropf noted that some who left also appeared to have "leanings toward Neo-Pentecostalism."[35]

Lane County

The first AMs in Lane County purchased land in the spring of 1887. Levi J. Yoder, Benedict Miller, and Peter Christner bought neighboring properties near Cheshire and Franklin, a few miles northwest of Eugene. That same year, Solomon L. Miller took a homestead in the woods on the Long Tom River west of Eugene, near Elmira. Mattie, Mrs. Miller, was a daughter of Peter and Barbra (Haas) Christner. Times were hard for Sol and Mattie; on March 20, 1889, their house burned down.[36]

Soon other AMs moved to the area. In 1888 young Ben Emmert, eighteen years old, settled near Eugene. By the next year, the J. P. Stutzman family lived near Junction City and Jacob D. Mishler (twin brother of Peter D. Mishler) and family moved to Lane County from Hubbard, where they had lived only a year. Emmert, Stutzmans, and Mishlers had all come from Indiana. In the next years more families and single men moved to Lane County, with names like Berkey, Burck, Burkholder, Eash, Evers, Hamilton, Hershberger, Kilmer, King, Miller, Nofziger, Nusbaum, Schlabach, Schultz, Strubhar, and Yoder. The group was a microcosm of Mennonite diversity. Apparently the Isaac Schlabach family, Amish, from Brewster, Minnesota, were the last to arrive, in September 1897.[37]

The Lane County group worshiped in homes, in an abandoned United Brethren Church building at Oak Hill, which they apparently soon bought, and in a school. Eventually they built their own meetinghouse. Although somewhat scattered, in general the families settled in two neighborhoods, some in the Oak Hill-Fern Ridge area about six miles west of Eugene; others about ten miles farther west, past Elmira. By 1895 there were meetings every other week at Oak Hill and once a month in a schoolhouse near the Long Tom River, in the timber country where the Elmira people lived. About this time Alex Miller, a bachelor, donated land for a meetinghouse about eleven miles west of Eugene along the Siuslaw and Eugene stage road, somewhat centrally located. Short funds and other problems delayed the completion of the building until 1897. Moses Evers donated the hardware for the building and Levi J. Yoder built the church benches.[38]

Early settler Peter Christner, reputed to be the first AM bishop in Oregon, did not lead the new congregation long. In January 1890, soon after J. D. Mishler moved to Lane County, an unidentified correspondent reported that Peter Mishler from Marion County came to Eugene to preach "three very interesting and edifying sermons" to the "little band," at that time six families "without a minister." Mishler continued to travel the ninety miles to Eugene as often as once a month, until he moved there in 1892.

Cliff Lind

Headstone in Oak Hill Cemetery, Eugene, of Peter D. Mishler (1846-1894), one of earliest Amish Mennonite leaders at Woodburn and in Lane County. The verse reads: Farewell my wife and children all/ From you a father Christ [doth call]/ Mourn not for me it is in vain/ To call me to your sight again. (ca. 1967 photo)

Apparently J. D. Mishler and others did not accept Christner's ordained status. But some did; Christner officiated at the marriage of several couples. Why he faded almost into oblivion is unknown, although some considered him "not much of a preacher." His wife died in January 1898 and soon thereafter he moved back to Hubbard. Sometimes he preached for the conservative C. B. Steiner Swiss Mennonite congregation. He died in 1912.[39]

The Mishler brothers led the congregation for most of its short life. Unfortunately, when Peter Mishler moved to Lane County in 1892, he was suffering from cancer. In spite of that, Joseph Schlegel of Nebraska ordained him as bishop in mid-1893. He died in January 1894. In 1893 Schlegel had also ordained Peter's brother Jacob (J. D.) as minister and their brother-in-law, Levi J. Yoder, as deacon. Schlegel returned to Oregon late in 1895 and, accompanied by Amos Troyer and layman A. Yoder of Zion, spent ten days with the Lane County congregation. He ordained J. D. Mishler as bishop and L. J. Yoder as minister. Some Zion people regarded as hypocritical the two men's confessions of their faults, yet J. D. Mishler's influence encompassed countless persons of several generations in a number of congregations. At times it produced separation and division, but some persons considered it an encouragement in their faith. The *Mennonite Cyclopedic Dictionary* noted that he "was active in the service, had many conflicts . . . but was [later] brought into church relationship" with earlier adversaries.[40]

Following the Panic of 1893, Lane County, like the rest of the nation, suffered an economic depression. As an added difficulty, farming there required different methods than the Mennonites had practiced in their former areas. Further, many settled on poor farmland. To supplement meager farm income some of the men worked by the day in Eugene, on the railroad, at carpenter work, at a rock-crushing plant, or elsewhere. Chris Christner lost a hand by falling into a brick machine, and Jacob Berkey lost his right hand to a circular saw in a mill. Most Mennonites in Lane County had trouble making ends meet.[41]

In spite of the hardships, J. D. Mishler wrote consistently glowing reports of the country, the crops, and the climate, picturing Lane County as an ideal place to live and farm. Some of his fellow settlers thought he exaggerated. In 1897, C. I. Kilmer warned *Herald of Truth* readers "not to buy or trade for land in Oregon without seeing it," as the cheap land near the church is "white, wet land or high farm or timber land." Several weeks later, L. J. Yoder wrote about "a brother at Eugene" [Mishler], who described "this part of Oregon . . . as being just as good as Northern Indiana, Ohio, or Pennsylvania for corn, millet, sweet potatoes, peaches, grapes, apricots, etc." Yoder considered him mistaken, because "as a rule, the nights [were] too cool" for such crops "to do well" consistently. And he corrected what was not J. D. Mishler's first or last misstatement, one about a six-year-old Bartlett pear orchard containing 500 trees that had to be propped. Yoder feared that "the reader got the wrong impression, as not all the trees— perhaps only about one in twenty—actually needed props."[42]

Within the congregation itself, problems and tensions at first appeared only normal. It was more progressive than other AM congregations (in the use of the English language). Perhaps it was unreported, underlying disharmony, perhaps apathy, or perhaps inadequate leadership that caused many people, including children of J. D. Mishler, Levi J. Yoder, layman Levi Hershberger, and a Christner who may have been bishop Peter Christner's son, to marry outside the church and leave the Mennonite family. One young man had a drinking problem and his wife left him to move to Illinois with her parents. The congregation had about fifty members at most, except for a time in 1896. Then Mishler included as members the small group at Hubbard, which he had taken under his wing, noting that they brought the Lane County AM membership to nearly seventy.[43]

Visiting ministers tried to keep the congregation on the right path. Preachers J. S. Lehman and J. K. Brubaker, probably from Indiana and Pennsylvania, wrote of visiting the Lane County Mennonites on their long trip west in 1896. They preached in the "Union church" near the Mishler home, in "Bishop Schrock's [elder J. R. Schrag's] congregation" of Russian Mennonites who received them "very cordially," and in the schoolhouse near "Pre. Yoder's" house twelve miles west. They even accepted the Methodist minister's invitation to preach in Elmira. About a service with the AMs in which fourteen accepted Christ, they wrote that they "never did see a more touching sight. . . . Fathers and mothers were weeping for joy; brethren and sisters were rejoicing, and even neighbors that were not Christians seemed to rejoice. . . ." Because they surmised that Russian Mennonite girls were influencing AM girls to wear hats, one of them sent a plain bonnet and bonnet pattern to Oregon.[44]

Coupled with economic difficulties, a dispute over a sawmill surpassed church problems and caused the congregation to disband. One of the members, a Hershberger, borrowed money from two non-Mennonites to purchase a sawmill, and three fellow church members agreed to underwrite his loan. Unfortunately, Hershberger did not meet his financial obligations and filed for bankruptcy. It seems his son also became involved by purchasing the mill back from one of the men loaning money. The other lender sued the cosigners, forcing them to assume financial obligation. It was a great hardship, especially for L. J. Yoder, who lost his farm. Some of the congregation, including J. D. Mishler, sided with Hershberger. Others sided with Yoder. In the midst of hard feelings and financial crisis most families soon moved away—some to Hubbard, some to Albany, and others elsewhere. Some left the Mennonites altogether.

By 1900, only the Moses Evers family remained in Lane County. He often said, "I didn't leave the church. The church left me." He maintained his Mennonite membership throughout his life and most of his children became Mennonites and lived in Mennonite communities in Oregon. Moses Evers stayed on his farm near Elmira, on the road Lane County named Evers Road in his honor. He died in 1955, his wife, Nancy, in 1958. Both were buried in West Lawn Cemetery near Eugene.[45]

Douglas County

The seven families and one unmarried young man who withdrew from Harrisburg in the fall of 1946 felt that Harrisburg had "lost a lot of her conservative viewpoints," according to Ira J. Headings, their leader. Such programs at Harrisburg as Sunday school and summer Bible school influenced the group to leave. In 1947 they moved south to Douglas County and organized the Roseburg Conservative Amish Mennonite congregation at Sutherlin, near Roseburg. At least one spouse in every family, except one, was a descendant of either Levi Hostetler or his brother Christian J. Hostetler, both strong supporters thirty-five years earlier of "sleeping preacher" Kauffman. Melvin Gingerich considered this, too, a "sleeping preacher" church, though about this time Harrisburg was dropping some of Kauffman's more conservative teachings. However, Headings, a Harrisburg deacon since 1942, denied the "sleeping preacher" label. He acknowledged that they "had been stamped by this name by some," but reasoned that they still preached "from the King James Version. Jesus Christ and him crucified." In about two years the group divided. Those who left established the Pleasant Valley Amish Mennonite congregation a few miles distant, near Yoncalla, and started a Sunday school. In 1951 the Roseburg church moved to Allendale, South Carolina, and later to Purdy, Missouri. After a few years the Pleasant Valley group returned to the Linn-Lane County border and about 1963 moved to Muscoda, Wisconsin.[46]

■ ■ ■

Zion, Fairview, and Bethel related to the Western District Amish Mennonite Conference (WDAMC), most of whose congregations were east of the Rockies as far away as Illinois. A few Oregon leaders occasionally attended the annual conferences, but the distance was a distinct handicap. Joseph Schlegel of Nebraska initiated a special WDAMC session in Oregon in 1909, which all of Oregon's ordained AM leaders attended.[47]

By then, AMs and OMs in Oregon and elsewhere were having joint meetings more frequently. Mission meetings, Sunday school conferences, revival meetings and other events helped to emphasize common interests and concerns. They created increasing uniformity in practice and superseded the more pronounced differences of earlier generations. The WDAMC had at first provided only a forum for discussion and sharing of concerns and in 1890 emphasized that its resolutions were not obligatory rules for member congregations. Within thirty years, however, influenced by Mennonite conferences, the WDAMC had reversed its position. Representatives from AM and OM conferences developed merger plans and in 1921 Zion, Fairview and Bethel and OM congregations in the Pacific Northwest organized a joint conference.[48]

Although the new united conference presumed a commitment to unity in belief and practice, it accentuated tensions between individualism and community, between congregationalism and conference regulation. Some individuals had strong notions about how all conference members should practice their faith. Others ascribed less authority to the conference and more to the congregation. The degree to which persons accommodated their individual understandings to the decisions of the conference would determine how they stood in the new circle of Christian community which they called the Pacific Coast Conference.

Chapter 3
OMs: From Early Division to Fragile Unity (1890s to 1930s)

For most of their first century in Oregon, Amish Mennonite (AM) and (old) Mennonite (OM) congregations in Oregon, who merged into one conference in 1921, comprised the state's largest Mennonite group. Many continued to call themselves by the nickname (old) Mennonite even after their denomination adopted the name Mennonite Church (MC) in 1971. Most of Oregon's first OMs had only shortly before been AMs, largely from the Lane County dispersion. But scattered OMs in the northern Willamette Valley joined Hopewell when it organized, and OM leaders east of the Rockies influenced the Oregon congregations strongly, especially in their early years.

Before the first OM congregations organized, hopes flourished briefly for a church in northeastern Oregon near the town of Union, in Union County. Amos and Sabina (Ebersole) Landis and their large family settled in a beautiful valley next to the scenic Wallowa Mountains in 1894. The five members there, who may have included the older Landis children, welcomed other Mennonites to come and join them. Landis liked the climate and reported excellent crops, abundant fruit, reasonably priced farmland, cheap lumber, and good water. In the next years Mennonites from the Midwest occasionally visited northeastern Oregon, but the several families who planned to move there in 1897 apparently changed their minds. Within a few years the Landis family had moved to Goshen, Indiana, after stopping for a time at Palmyra, Missouri.[1]

Amish Mennonites from Lane County who dispersed in the late 1890s settled at Hubbard and Albany. The new groups, in spite of their largely AM heritage, soon became OM congregations, nurtured by visiting OM leaders A. D. Wenger of Lancaster, Pennsylvania; David Garber of Nampa, Idaho; and George R. Brunk I of Canton, Kansas. Brunk was a brother-in-law of Wenger and an enterprising young bishop, although still under thirty when he first visited Oregon. Wenger's presence in Oregon was fleeting, but historian S. G. Shetler has reported that in the summer of 1897, even before the Lane County dispersion, Wenger "partially organized a congregation with six members" at Hubbard, leaving Lane County bishop J. D. Mishler temporarily in charge. Later Mishler, and Lane County families sympathetic with him, joined this group. After his first visit in 1899, Garber visited Oregon various times. He and Brunk played a major role in organizing and reconciling the two groups.[2]

Problems followed the AMs who left Lane County. Hard feelings, broken relationships, and weak leadership demoralized them for several years. About the time of the Lane County dispersion, Mishler withdrew Levi J. Yoder's preaching privileges, leaving the small Linn County group who had gathered around Yoder without a leader. In spite of his congregation's tumultuous early years, Mishler's correspondence to *Herald of Truth* generally portrayed it as prosperous. Yoder, however, wrote about the "sheep" from Lane County being "scattered" and implored readers who cared about members "in the Mennonite fold" to come or send Mennonite bishops and ministers to visit the Oregon people.[3]

In June 1899, about the time Yoder wrote his plea for help, Garber first traveled in Oregon and spent about four weeks visiting various groups, including a brief contact with General Conference Mennonites (GC). Regarding the Lane County dispersion, he wrote of "an act performed, a word spoken," which served as " 'a little fire,' which kindleth a great matter!" He thought that "apparently the *peace* sought for was found." In good faith he temporarily organized congregations at both Albany and Hubbard. By "permission" (of Mishler, perhaps), he "reinstated" Yoder to "the work of the ministry."[4]

In November 1899 Brunk came to Oregon, held a number of meetings at Hubbard and Albany, organized the Hopewell (at Hubbard) and Albany congregations as members of the Kansas-Nebraska Mennonite Conference (KNC), and left, thinking all was well. Garber earlier had left Mishler temporarily in charge of both congregations. Brunk, not knowing that Garber's charge to Mishler was temporary, made it permanent. But Mishler and Yoder, though brothers-in-law, did not get along any better in the next several years than they had in Lane County. Mishler smarted under queries from the East wondering what was "wrong with the churches in Oregon, that they must have help." However, in October 1901 the KNC responded to an "Oregon appeal," perhaps from Yoder, and chose Brunk and Garber to visit the Oregon churches. They would find festering troubles coming to a head.[5]

After Brunk and Garber spent nine days in Oregon in March 1902, Brunk wrote a candid and lengthy report of their visit. He noted that before he had organized Hopewell and Albany in 1899, they "had been much out of order," which caused "friction" and prevented harmonious relationships between the AMs and OMs. Brunk had thought, however, that peace had come between them. What he did not understand was that Hopewell and Albany had not made peace between themselves. His 1902 visit revealed old troubles "still rankling in the hearts with other things that had not come to light before." He discovered "unchristianlike, unfair dealing and even downright dishonesty, which begot hatred and bitterness." Many members "were in this respect entirely free," and not all the guilty shared equally in wrongdoing, and "yet the bishop and minister . . . were not the least among the guilty. All were willing to confess their wrongs and make restitution where possible and forgive one another." Restitution included forgiving loans for those unable to pay, or settling for partial payment. Some "paid in full what was found against them" but some were "so deep in the mire of debt, either of their own or for others for whom they [had] gone security," that Brunk feared they might "shrink from the sacrifice" necessary to do "their duty."[6]

Reconciliation did not come easily and Brunk had reservations about its permanence. A few who said "they were willing to forgive all (?) . . . would first give the accused a sound berating in bitterness and hot displeasure." Then, after venting "their pent up feelings, they would offer to exercise the godly grace of forgiveness." Brunk considered such to be "self-deceived," unable to "truly forgive until their hearts [were] softened through true repentance." Brunk had not known that Mishler had admired GCs after becoming acquainted with them in Lane County. But Mishler denied the charge that he had "used his influence against the church" and "favored a withdrawal" from the conference. He claimed "to have been misunderstood. Upon that ground," Brunk left him in charge of Hopewell. Brunk cautioned "all," however, to "be slow to follow shepherds that call you to leave the fold." He left David Hilty, living temporarily at Albany, in charge there, with "Yoder under him," with the prayer that the work in Oregon would prosper in the future.[7]

Garber's and Brunk's 1902 visit brought reconciliation to the degree that in the next years Mishler occasionally welcomed Yoder to the Hopewell pulpit. But Oregon continued to be a problem to the KNC, which sent Nampa leaders Garber and newly ordained bishop David Hilty to Hopewell for about two weeks in 1904. At this time they ordained Noah Hershberger as minister and Alex Miller as deacon. Strangely, Mishler's report of their visit referred only to the visiting brethren and not to the ordinations. Perhaps he was annoyed that the KNC bypassed him and sent a new bishop to set his congregation in order. Mary Hamilton, who wrote of the "spiritual feast" from Hilty and Garber, expressed thanks that God still remembered them. She noted that those who attain life through Christ would no longer have "room for pride and fashions and the riches of this world."[8]

The Hopewell and Albany congregations were finally living in apparent peace between themselves, and for almost seventy years they were members together of the same conference. But they developed distinct characteristics and varying practices. Mishler soon became a firm proponent of the regulation attire which Brunk was promoting in the (old) Mennonite church about that time, and Hopewell acquired the reputation of being conservative. Albany's early leaders did not promote conservative practices as strongly, and the congregation was considered liberal. Still, leaders and members in both congregations attempted to follow New Testament teachings in their everyday living. Taking their faith seriously accentuated the differences which gradually became more pronounced.

Hopewell's early years were a kaleidoscope of glowing reports and sharp separations, of bright growth and dark reversals. When Brunk organized Hopewell in November 1899, the forty-four charter members included persons named Christner, Emmert, Erb, Hershberger, Johnson, King, Martin, Mishler, Ösch [or Oesch], Schmucker, Unger, Welty, Yoder, and Zook. In the first years internal troubles took their toll. Membership fluctuated greatly, and many persons forfeited their membership because, according to S. G. Shetler, they refused to comply with Garber's and Brunk's "rules and regulations" about behavior and attire. By 1902 membership had dropped to thirty or less. Then by 1908 it increased to seventy-two.[9]

Growth and new vigor followed the early years of turmoil and loss. Bishop Mishler maintained a strict discipline, especially regarding amusements, attire, and the use of tobacco. While some members left because of it, others supported the emphasis. Families from eastern states joined Hopewell. So did a sizable group of Oregon people with non-Mennonite heritage, and several were ordained to the ministry there. For several years after the 1921 AM-OM merger, membership held at an all-time high of 126. Hopewell lost members when some transferred to emerging congregations at Sheridan and Molalla. In 1969 when Bethel disbanded, most Bethel members joined Hopewell. Membership in 1976 was eighty.[10]

In the early period of expectant growth, within six weeks of its organization, Hopewell began to plan for a meetinghouse. The congregation bought an acre of land one-and-one-half miles from the Zion AM meetinghouse and finished a building there in March 1902. Within fifteen years Hopewell outgrew the first building. In 1916, with financial help from Mennonites in the East they completed a new, larger building with a full basement. Until 1964 they used benches from the Lane County meetinghouse (as "temporary seats," Shetler wrote). Even in 1976 a few of the old benches helped to furnish the basement. In 1969 they provided indoor toilet facilities. Otherwise, with only minor remodeling, in 1976 the building retained its original character.[11]

Of Oregon's early Mennonite leaders, bishop J. D. Mishler was probably the most colorful and controversial. He loved to read *Herald of Truth* and *Gospel Herald* and frequently contributed letters. Sometimes he contradicted himself, occasionally he corrected an earlier statement, and now and then other readers corrected him. John F. Funk, *Herald of Truth* editor, did "not doubt" Mishler's "glowing description of Oregon," but he thought the "only thoroughly fair way to describe" any area, Oregon included, was "by being just as particular to mention the unfavorable features" and not to "present the bright side only." Yet Mishler's love for Oregon never waned. At eighty years of age he wrote, "I have been in Oregon nearly 38 years, and have never seen better crops than this year." He also loved the congregations he served. Often he reported growth in membership. Numbers were important to him. He strongly supported having a district conference and helped start the Sunday school conference. Omar Miller, an Oregon minister who was a boy in Mishler's congregation, con-

Sanford G. Shetler

Samuel Grant (S. G.) Shetler and family about 1916, between their years at Hopewell. Back: Luella, Goldie, Rosella; front: Sanford, S. G. (1871-1942), Maggie (Kaufman) (1876-1932), Margaret.

sidered Mishler's prayers a great influence in his life.[12]

Another influential leader at Hopewell was Samuel (S. G.) Shetler, a minister who moved from Johnstown, Pennsylvania, to Oregon at the end of 1913 at Mishler's invitation. When Mishler was nearly seventy and suffering from rheumatism, Hopewell selected Shetler as assisting bishop by majority vote and a few months later, in February 1915, Shetler was ordained as bishop. Mishler hoped that "the dear brother," who had by now learned "some of the Oregon tricks," might "help to get things more on the right way." A churchman of denominational renown, in 1913-1916 and 1920-1921 Shetler left his mark on Oregon Mennonites. In addition to serving Hopewell, he became a teacher and administrator in the Hubbard school district. He worked in the young Pacific Coast Conference (PCC), as moderator, district evangelist, committee member to revise the conference constitution and discipline, and organizer and principal in the new Pacific Coast Bible

School. He also wrote a history of the PCC which appeared in the 1916 *Mennonite Yearbook*. Within the next fifteen years he enlarged and updated it until 1929, when the PCC Church History Committee approved it for 1932 publication. While not documented like modern histories, it has nevertheless been a major resource.[13]

In addition to Mishler, two early ministers served for many years. Noah Hershberger served over fifty years, until his death in 1956. William Bond, of non-Mennonite parentage, a native of Lincolnshire, England, received baptism at Hopewell in his twenty-fifth year and was ordained minister four years later, in 1911. He served thirty years, until his death in 1941.[14]

In its early programming, Hopewell was comparatively progressive. In June 1900 Mishler wrote of their need for a singing teacher, asking for "some good young brother in the East that is willing and that understands music." A year later Hopewell was practicing singing twice a week on the same nights as Bible readings were held, and not a "good young brother" but Sister Lizzie Detweiler of West Liberty, Ohio, was planning to teach vocal music as soon as her books arrived. Sunday evening Bible readings, young people's meetings, midweek prayer meetings, children's meetings, and series of special meetings helped keep young and old active. Isaac L. Kulp was impressed by "a number of young sisters" who were "interested in the work which, if they keep on earnestly, must flourish in the future." Evening revival meetings at first attracted young people from Zion, which did not have such meetings until later. Children's meetings on the front benches at first preceded Sunday evening services, but men and women talking and laughing in the back disrupted them. Floyd Emmert, secretary, decided that children's meetings could not continue thus, and in 1915 they became part of the regular service. Hopewell often hosted intercongregational meetings, including the first Oregon Sunday school conference in 1904; the first (old) Mennonite church conference in Oregon in 1905; the first (old) Mennonite ministers' meeting in Oregon in 1916; and the first half of the first Pacific Coast Bible School in 1920.[15]

Hopewell experienced early tumult, but for even more years the new Albany Mennonite congregation struggled to survive. Except for the C. R. Widmer family, who moved directly to Linn County from Iowa, all of the charter members had earlier lived in Lane County. Though several families worshiped for a time with

Dan Widmer

C. R. Widmer (1864-1945) and Barbara (Roth) (1866-1937) and family, in 1931; back: Gladys (Whitaker), Ezra, Elmer, Joseph, Herbert, Leah (Kenagy); front: Katy (Burck), C. R., Barbara, Dan. Widmers first attended Fairview (AM), were charter members at Albany (MC) in 1899, and some were charter members of Grace Mennonite Church (GC) in 1931.

nearby Fairview, in 1898 or 1899 they organized an interdenominational union Sunday school, with an enrollment of about forty, in the Price schoolhouse east of Albany. About then they also began to hold services in the Methodists' Geisendorfer church, about four miles east of Albany. Here they organized as a congregation in November 1899 with about sixteen members. Family names included Christner, Miller, Mishler, Slabach, Widmer, and Yoder. The Slabachs moved to eastern Oregon the following year. Shetler's 1932 history, which names Ezra Burkholder and wife among eighteen charter members, appears to be in error, though soon after, Burkholders moved to Albany.[16]

For ten years the Albany congregation did not have its own meetinghouse. They used the Geisendorfer church until July 1905.

Gerald Brenneman

*John P. Bontrager (1872-1949) (left) and Moses E. Brenneman
(1881-1957), longtime leaders at Albany Mennonite Church.*

Shortly before they quit, John P. Bontrager arrived to help organize a Mennonite Sunday school so they would not need to
participate longer in a union school. For the next several years,
they used a schoolhouse north of Albany or the nearby Fairmont
Grange Hall. In September 1909 they began using their own building, which they had bought from the Evangelical Church, moved to
their two-acre plot on Twelfth Street in the Albany suburbs, and
remodeled to include basement, gallery, and electric lights.
Hopewell gave fifty dollars toward the purchase as a share of the
sale price of the Lane County building. The congregation then became known as the Twelfth Street Mennonite Church. In June
1952, they moved to a new building under construction about
three miles north of Albany along Highway 99E and took the name
Albany Mennonite Church.[17]

    After a few years of weak or transitory leadership, in 1905
Albany acquired a strong, longtime leader, John P. Bontrager, a
son-in-law of Nampa's David Hilty, who had earlier served for
eighteen months at Albany. Bontrager moved from Ohio to Nampa
in 1900, and served as a lay leader there until Albany called him to
be an exhorter. (Perhaps this was similar to being a licensed minis-

ter half a century later.) In October 1905 he was ordained minister; six years later, bishop. Bontrager was a friendly man, well liked by church and town, and gave his sermons a strong evangelistic emphasis. Often he included an altar call. He loved children and believed in gathering them into the church while "young and tender in years," according to Claud Hostetler, but he did not say at what age. Bontrager participated with vigor in the new PCC which organized soon after he moved to Albany. In 1919 he moved to Los Angeles, but in later years he served for a time as a nonresident bishop of Albany.[18]

The congregation grew little until Bontrager arrived. At least eight young people were baptized in the early years, but other people left, and soon after Bontrager's ordination, Albany had only twenty members. But under his leadership, the Sunday school grew and Sunday evening meetings gained prominence for the congregation and "many of the neighbors" who came, a correspondent noted. Between 1912 and 1915 membership more than doubled. In later years some members withdrew to begin Grace Mennonite Church (GC) in Albany, and others transferred to emerging congregations in Logsden, Salem, Eugene, and Corvallis. In 1968 the membership had reached 267. In 1976 it was 200.[19]

A number of men from Nebraska served in the ministry at Albany, including Moses E. Brenneman, an influential leader for over forty years. He moved to Oregon in 1909, shortly after marrying Orpha Mishler, a daughter of the deceased Lane County bishop, P. D. Mishler, and of Albany charter member Rachel Mishler. Brenneman was ordained deacon in 1911 and minister in 1915. Although ill health at times prevented his preaching, even as an older man he sometimes preached three times a Sunday, in the morning and evening at Albany and in the afternoon at a mission Sunday school. When he died in 1957, he had served Albany longer than any other ordained leader. The congregation also recognized Orpha Brenneman's gifts, as when C. R. Widmer named her to be the first president of the women's sewing circle, sometime before 1921. She was then the only woman who drove a car, and he thought she could provide transportation for the other women.[20]

One other influential leader came to Albany before 1920. Norman A. Lind, a minister from Ohio, moved west for his wife Sarah's health, first to California, then in 1919 to Oregon. In later years Lind felt he erred in coming to Albany without an official invitation, though Bontrager, Brenneman, and some of the members had invited him personally in what was apparently a common procedure of that time. Lind chose Albany because it provided his first opportunity to work with a resident bishop, Bontrager. But it was a short-lived privilege. Bontrager moved to California several months after Lind arrived, and Brenneman became the senior minister, Lind the helping minister. Apparently it was a satisfactory arrangement for both.

When the PCC bishops, Mishler, Bontrager, and Shetler, came to Albany on June 5, 1921, to ordain a bishop, they found that of the three nominees, Brenneman, Lind, and J. E. Whitaker, one had a large majority of the votes. They wished to declare him the new bishop and presented a paper for the three nominees to sign, which stated their willingness to abide by the vote. Both Brenneman and Whitaker were willing, but Lind strongly urged that they use the lot. However, the three bishops did not highly favor the lot. All of them had been ordained without it. So Lind reluctantly signed the paper. The congregation also approved the procedure with no dissenting votes. The bishops then presented Lind as the new bishop. Perhaps persons at Albany later wished the lot had been used. Some felt that Brenneman, as senior minister, should have been the bishop. Friction developed later and Lind left Albany. In 1940 he joined the emerging Sweet Home congregation.[21]

Only for a few years were Oregon's two congregations—Hopewell and Albany—and the Nampa, Idaho, congregation which Brunk also organized in 1899 a part of the distant KNC. While conference leaders came to Oregon several times, only once, in 1901, did Oregon leaders, J. D. Mishler and David Hilty, attend conference across the Rockies. In 1904 the KNC appointed a committee to plan a conference for October 1905, to be held at Hopewell. Guests from Ohio, Illinois, and Tennessee, as well as from member congregations in Kansas, Nebraska and Idaho, attended, as did Oregon's ordained leaders and several Albany laymen. Persons from across the Rockies provided most of the leadership but Westerners did share a few responsibilities. David Garber served on the resolutions committee and M. H. Hostetler and Sarah Kurtz were choristers.

After the visitors discovered how far away Oregon really was, the KNC decided to divide at the Rocky Mountains. Nothing in the records indicates any hesitancy to turn loose those young congregations, barely past adolescence, to be a conference unto themselves. Perhaps the KNC felt somewhat relieved to have them move out as young people establishing their own home. Nor is there any evidence that the Western congregations had any qualms about leaving the parenting group. With the energy, confidence, and enthusiasm of youth, they organized their new conference.[22]

The new Pacific Coast Conference (PCC) first met on November 1 and 2, 1906, at Nampa. Antioch (Nampa) reported 57 members, Hopewell 58, and Albany 20, totaling 135. They adopted the Rules and Discipline of the KNC, with a minor exception, and resolved to "teach the 'all things' commanded in Matt. 28:19, 20." Two ministers discussed the topic "Ministers' Wives—Wings or Weights," and the report noted that wives "should be as wings, lightening the burdens by looking after the affairs at home" when their husbands were absent. The secretaries recorded that "open conference was of much spiritual interest, many testifying for Jesus and expressing their many thanks for this first conference." In the earliest years, women were often choristers, and in 1907 a Kate Blosser was a secretary of conference along with one Harry West.[23]

In the years before the 1921 merger with AM congregations, other congregations organized in the West and joined the PCC, including the Firdale Mennonite Church at Airlie, a small community in Polk County, nearly midway between Monmouth and Corvallis. Suver, a small town to the east, was the address for most of the members. The first settlers there moved to Oregon from California, where they had lived only a few years. The Joseph E. Glick family had left Nampa because of alkaline soil conditions and lived at Corning, California, before moving to Albany in 1910. Others including Weaver, Kilmer, and Shenk families from California settled at Airlie in 1913 and 1914. Some of them and also some of later families were relatives.

The PCC regarded Airlie as a rural mission station at first, and in October 1914 J. P. Bontrager conducted the first service there. When the congregation organized on December 29, 1915, family names of the twenty charter members included Bledsoe, Davis, Glick, Kilmer, Morgan, Pletcher, Sharer, Shenk, and Weaver. During the short lifetime of the congregation, sixty-six persons became members. Additional family names included Berkey, Birky, Boyer, Evers, Fuller, Good, Hamilton, Steckly, Tyson, and Yoder. Gabriel D. Shenk served first as exhorter and then was ordained as minister in December 1916. Five years later he was ordained bishop, and Luke E. Weaver, minister. Though Firdale planned to build a meetinghouse, it never did.[24]

The decline of the congregation was as rapid as its rising. People found the soil unproductive for wheat and many men worked in sawmills to supplement meager farm income. In later years the bishop would tell of a Dr. Wallace coming to the home to deliver a baby. As the doctor left, knowing the family was too poor to pay in cash, he took a loaf of hot homemade bread for his pay. In 1923 some settlers left and the next year the Shenks, Kilmers, and Hamiltons moved to Sheridan. About then most of the remaining families also moved to Sheridan or elsewhere. Firdale's last service was held in September 1924. However, the young minister, Luke Weaver, and his wife, Mary (Glick), kept the Sunday school going until they moved to Terra Bella, California, in 1928. Decades later, the growing of grass seed and commercial fertilizers revolutionized farming in the beautiful rolling countryside between Airlie and Suver. In 1976, Earl Kennel, a prosperous Mennonite, farmed near the land which had disappointed earlier Mennonites.[25]

In 1920 the PCC embraced seven congregations, one each in northwestern Montana and southern California, and two in southern Idaho, in addition to the three in western Oregon. It recorded 451 members, 260 in Oregon. The AM congregations— Zion, Fairview, and Bethel—which merged with the OMs in 1921 totaled 365 members. These congregations held a common faith. But for decades varying beliefs about how to practice it, different concepts of authority, and disagreement about how much their conference, (as a community of faith) should regulate congregations and individuals, threatened conference unity. One understanding, though frequently challenged, was that AM congregations could do their own "housekeeping" and not be subject to conference authority in the way OM congregations were. Years later, in 1950, Omar Miller of Bethel emphasized in his "West Coast Echoes" that "the most important community . . . of the church is the local congregation." He considered it "the primary unit of operation in the administration of the Church of God."[26]

Mennonite publications and increasing interaction which the automobile facilitated helped pave the way for the AM and OM merger in 1921. Both AMs and OMs read and wrote to *Herald of Truth* and its successor, *Gospel Herald*. These periodicals helped systematize doctrine and regulate practice. They also offered news of congregations near and distant. Many a household treasured another Mennonite publication, the annual *Family Almanac*, which not only promoted a distinctly Mennonite religious outlook but also included advice about health, the domestic arts, farm and animal husbandry; advertisements for products ranging from carriages to plain clothes to patent medicine; and the fascinating zodiac calendars which helped many people decide when to plant their potatoes and cabbage.[27]

On June 7-10, 1921, Fairview hosted the first joint AM-OM conference. The church conference followed meetings of its subsidiary organizations, a Sunday school conference, a mission board, and a district sewing circle. In the last session, delegates decided that requirements for being a "communicant member" included "conversion, regeneration, a willingness to learn and obey the commandments of the Bible and regulations of the Church." Membership also required being at peace with God and in "full fellowship with the believers of the all things taught by our Lord." The secretaries, in conclusion, reported that "peace and unity" prevailed.[28]

But the new unity was fragile. One observer of the merger re-

Oregon Mennonite archival collection, courtesy of Amos Schmucker.

Fairview Mennonite Church, site of first joint AM-OM conference in 1921. Men entered one door, women the other. Sheds that sheltered buggies show in the back left. Photo was taken after 1930 annex was built.

membered, half a century later, that it "wasn't as smooth as it sounds." Tensions in the 1920s surrounded the adoption of a constitution, which outlined the organizational structure, and a discipline, which stated requirements, restrictions, and regulations about practices and behavior of members. Apparently persons of AM congregations at first objected to using *Mennonite* in the name, while others objected to omitting it. By 1924 that designation crept into the small print heading and by 1929 the cover page boldly included "Mennonite" in its title.

Even more controversial was what the discipline should include about nonconformity, especially in attire. Hopewell wanted the restrictions to read that ministers be "required" to wear the "regulation coat" (cut straight, without lapel or collar, often called the "plain coat"), with members "encouraged" to do so. But some AM ministers thought the regulation coat resembled military garb and refused to wear it. Specifications for the laity, too, came under attack. Apparently the more conservative leaders wanted to legislate against the necktie. However, the final document required nothing more specific than "plain clothing, nothing that bears the marks of vanity," for both ministers and laymen.[29]

Other concerns also stalled agreement on the controversial document. Finally, in 1924, the delegates at a special "representative meeting" resolved to adopt the conference constitution and discipline with the understanding that "should any congregation not see fit to at once fully subscribe to the wording on some point," they would nevertheless "continue to labor together in brotherly love." As long as what a congregation allowed did not disturb "the peace of the Conference," its standing should not be questioned.[30]

Besides disagreement about the constitution and discipline, other tensions in the 1920s revolved around Fairview's estrangement from the new PCC and procedures for members going from one congregation to another. The aggressive movement to require the regulation coat may have alienated Fairview's ministers. It seems also that they did not understand the new conference structure and objected to the Albany representatives acting "in delegate body" at the 1924 special session. Three years later, in 1927, the executive committee and bishops sent a letter to Fairview, expressing a longing "for a fuller fellowship" than had "prevailed in recent years" and requesting forgiveness. After this, Fairview ministers began to participate again in conference affairs. Members moving from one congregation to another produced tensions when Zion ministers accepted persons Hopewell had excommunicated without first requiring their reinstatement at Hopewell. This was contrary to conference regulations, and the executive committee submitted the case to an arbitration committee.[31]

Amid these tensions of the 1920s, two congregations organized: Sheridan in 1923 and Portland in 1924.

Sheridan Mennonite Church emerged from the request of several Amish or formerly Amish families living in the McMinnville area that Hopewell organize a Sunday school there. Services began in the Durham schoolhouse south of McMinnville on June 11, 1922, and attendance soon increased to forty-five. Hopewell ministers found it costly to travel the forty-five miles one way each Sunday, so Hopewell selected Daniel F. Shenk (their deacon, who in 1915 had been ordained to preach) to move to McMinnville. The Shenk family settled there in October 1922. Six months later the J. M. Mishler family with J. M.'s father, the aged bishop J. D. Mishler, moved to near Sheridan, a smaller town about fourteen miles southwest of McMinnville. In September 1923, the Frank Larrew family of Birch Tree, Missouri, arrived, and in the next two years, Hamiltons and Emmerts from Hubbard; Widemans, Reists, and Brubakers from Alberta, Canada; Shenks, Kilmers and Hamiltons from Airlie; and a Hostetler family from Harrisburg. What began as a Sunday school for progressive Amish soon became a full-blown Mennonite settlement.[32]

In mid-1923 the group began using an historic but unused church building belonging to the Baptists, five miles west of McMinnville. Here Shenk was ordained minister on September 9, 1923, and future bishop Raymond Mishler and Elsie Nice were married that evening. Soon thereafter the congregation moved to an unused church building in Sheridan, and in 1940, they began using a new, larger structure which they were constructing. This building in Sheridan still served them in 1976.[33]

The Sheridan congregation organized on December 23, 1923. Family names of the forty charter members included Beachy, Hamilton, Hostetler, Larrew, Miller, Mishler, Nice, Shenk, Slabaugh, and Yoder. Several weeks later, S. E. Allgyer of Ohio led a series of meetings at Sheridan. "Visible results" included confessions of "new converts, backsliders, and reconsecrations." J. D. Mishler wrote of their rejoicing "in this new field" and trusted the Lord would help them "to keep separated from the world." He lamented

Mildred Schrock

Daniel F. (1886-1962) and Fannie (Schrag) (1884-1969) Shenk, Sheridan minister. Fannie's family were among the earliest Russian Mennonites to settle in Polk and Lane counties.

that the "problem of worldliness, especially the dress question, [had] made its way into some of [their] own beloved churches."[34]

Sheridan became one of the largest congregations in the PCC. A sharp fluctuation in membership at first perhaps reflected the work of the "enemy" who, Mishler confessed, was busy at Sheridan as well as at other places. But by 1926 charter membership had more than doubled, to 102. Membership reached a peak of 360 in 1955, before declining greatly to 125 in 1976. Much of the early growth came from church members' children becoming members and from Mennonite families moving to the community. Some increase came from Sheridan's strong interest in mission outreach. A daughter of a family converted at the Upper Gopher Valley Sunday school (1926-ca. 1932) was still a member at Sheridan in 1976. Declines came as members moved elsewhere and helped establish congregations at Blaine, Ballston, Grants Pass, McMinnville, Grand Ronde (Church in the Wildwood), and Logsden. According to Sheridan historian Mildred Schrock, some loss resulted from backsliding.[35]

Wilma Nisly

Gabriel D. (1878-1961) and Luella (Sharer) (1887-1977) Shenk, Sheridan bishop. Gabe would pile up to 25 children (boys in the trunk, lid up) in his little black 1952 Plymouth to take them to summer Bible school at the Wildwood mission. Luella hosted innumerable house guests, for weeks or even months if people needed a home.

Two of Sheridan's early leaders served for decades. Daniel F. (Dan) Shenk served for most of·forty years, until he died at age seventy-five in 1962. His cousin Gabriel D. (Gabe) Shenk served from 1924 until, in failing health, he resigned in 1956 before he died in 1961 at age eighty-two. In 1933 the congregation appointed Dan Shenk as Local Field Worker, and he spent much time in personal work, visiting shut-ins, hospitals, neighbors, and businessmen. He gave hundreds of Bibles and gospel tracts which he purchased from his own meager income. Through his contacts, at least seventy-five persons came to know Christ.[36]

During the time that Hopewell was beginning Sheridan, Oregon people were also organizing a mission in Portland. It continued as a mission for several decades and the major part of its story belongs with Chapter 9. After Allan and Fannie Good opened the mission in November 1922 they quickly developed a many-sided program which called for a staff of workers. Mennonites who lived and worked in the city also participated. Within a year and a half, on July 27, 1924, the Portland Mennonite Mission Church organized with twenty-three persons accepted by church letter. Family names included Bond, Brubaker, Good, King, Martin, Roth, Snyder, Stauffer, and Yoder. About a month later, on August 31, Paul N. Roth, a charter member formerly of Fairview, was ordained minister, and the congregation received two additional charter members at that time. The mission's needs provided a never-ending challenge and offered people in the PCC many opportunities for service, training and new experiences.[37]

Sheridan and Portland, which joined the newly merged PCC in its first decade, added more voices to conference discussions. Sheridan retained a strict position on attire and, with Hopewell, frequently promoted more restrictive regulations. Allan Good at Portland supported the nonconformity held forth in those days, and the mission workers and converts dressed plainly. But he himself was too busy doing mission work to be a primary spokesman about attire.

Most of the leaders who emerged in other PCC congregations in the 1920s supported conference authority over its congregations and their members. They promoted a uniform standard which they believed not only their members but also all conference congregations should follow. One, E. S. Garber, who was ordained at the Filer, Idaho, congregation in 1927, would exert a strong influence in the PCC for decades. Nonconformity in attire and other matters remained a primary concern in the 1930s.

But a few ministers continued to resist the plain, regulation coat which had not been part of AM practice. On August 26, 1934, Melvin Schrock and Henry Gerig were ordained ministers at Fairview. Schrock was a son of Joseph Schrock, a former minister at Fairview, and Gerig was the youngest son of the aged C. R. Gerig, Fairview's retired bishop. Neither of the AM fathers had worn the plain coat. Of the officiating bishops, N. A. Lind and Fred J. Gingerich thought ministers should wear it but A. P. Troyer, Zion's elderly bishop who died a year later, did not wear it. He did not take part in the private meeting with the nominees in which the other bishops asked if they would let themselves be open to "conviction" about wearing the plain coat. Both Gerig and Schrock said yes. Gerig never did receive the "conviction" to wear it. Schrock did.[38]

Visitors to the PCC from the larger OM church helped make

nonconformity such a dominant concern. Often they referred to it as separation from the world. They emphasized details of attire and also rejected worldly amusements and alliances, tobacco, and other forms of intemperance. Christians were to hold to biblical standards in business, speech, and all practices of life, and speakers often translated generalities into specifics. In the 1930s J. B. Smith, John G. Hochstetler, L. S. Glick, Milton Brackbill, Aaron Mast, J. S. Newhauser, E. W. Kulp, James Bucher, and C. F. Derstine were among conference speakers and evangelists who promoted nonconformity in Oregon congregations.[39]

In that decade PCC Mennonites also dealt with Modernism and the issue of life insurance. Along with much of their larger church they distrusted theology and preferred to speak of doctrines. Theology suggested a rationalistic approach to religion that minimized personal piety and ethics. They regarded as doctrines their carefully outlined beliefs and practices based on their understanding of the Bible. Doctrines called for both a devout spirituality and right living. The system of thought which developed as Modernism seemed more rational than biblical.[40]

Fundamentalism, a conservative movement among Christians of many denominations, refuted Modernism. Fundamentalists emphasized faith in the reliability of the Bible which, they believed, Modernism denied. Mennonites, too, believed the Bible was reliable and attempted to preserve the biblical authority which the new scientific method and liberal views of the Bible seemed to threaten. By 1920 the World Christian Fundamentals Association (WCFA) had adopted a statement which outlined what it considered to be the fundamentals of Christianity. Mennonites adopted these fundamentals in varying degrees and added their own—nonconformity and nonresistance—which, unfortunately, the Fundamentals Association had overlooked. Although many Mennonites embraced premillennialism, one of the WCFA's "fundamentals," many did not, and the church did not require it. Mennonites often defined Modernism as anything they considered to be in opposition to their fundamentals.[41]

The controversy about Modernism surfaced as an issue later in the PCC than among Mennonites farther east, but by 1930 PCC Mennonites were combating it vigorously. Early that year, E. E. Zuercher, a studious minister approaching fifty and one of five ordained men at Nampa, published an article in *Gospel Herald* entitled "The Modern World." Convinced that Mennonites should preach "the simple Word in a simple way," he refuted the "new theology, new thought, newfangled ideas of every kind." A fellow minister at Nampa, Omar G. Miller, a scholarly, conscientious young man with an inquiring mind, was then in his ninth year as secretary of the PCC.

In 1931 Miller, under investigation by PCC bishops because of his expressed "sympathies" toward "decidedly" modernistic writers, asked to be relieved of his duties as minister and was replaced as conference secretary. Miller expressed deep regret for past errors and especially those which had disturbed the peace of the church. He promised not to accept or teach any doctrines or interpretations in conflict with Mennonite faith and standards as long as he remained a member of the (OM) Mennonite Church. The PCC received his confession and several years later he was reinstated as minister at Nampa.[42]

Were Miller's misplaced "sympathies" really as threatening to Nampa and the PCC as they were perceived to be? Certainly his fellow ministers who thought so were doing their best to keep the church pure and faithful. Perhaps denominational unrest within Miller's family (his father had joined the Seventh-Day Adventists) raised caution signals for the bishops. Perhaps, too, Miller was a man ahead of his time, misunderstood and depreciated. Even his wholehearted espousal of plain attire apparently did not restore complete confidence in him. It seems that something held him slightly apart from the center of conference action in subsequent years. Yet he served as a humble and willing worker in several PCC congregations. In 1937, when Miller moved to Oregon, Alvin Rogie reported that Bethel gave him a "hearty welcome."[43]

Early in the 1930s life insurance, more tangible than Modernism, became a divisive issue. Already in the 1920s, church leaders had learned that Dr. George Kenagy, a member at Albany, had life insurance. A crisis ensued. The PCC constitution forbade it in the restrictions against secret orders. Albany bishop Lind and fellow minister Brenneman not only preached against it and issued a strong warning to whoever ignored the restriction; they also refused Kenagy participation in the communion and foot-washing service. Kenagy and some of his extended family soon left the Albany congregation and in June 1931, with people of GC background directed by minister John M. Franz, organized the Grace Mennonite Church (GC).[44]

Amid such questions of theology, doctrine, and practice,

Molalla was Oregon's only PCC congregation to organize in the 1930s. In 1928 Henry C. Lehman of St. Paul moved about twenty miles northwest to Molalla, a little town in Clackamas County about thirty miles south of Portland, to operate a newly purchased truck line. He, with J. B. (Josh) Mishler, also sold used items in what people called a junk store. According to Lehman, "the good Lord put it into [his] heart," and the PCC mission board, too, encouraged him, to build a "mission hall." After four weeks of services in 1929, during which time Nada Strong, an invalid, accepted Christ during evangelistic meetings, the city closed the hall because it did not meet regulations for lighting and ventilation. The building was actually Lehman's truck garage.

In 1930 the mission board asked Joe H. and Ina Yoder to move from Portland to Molalla to revive the work. But it progressed slowly until 1934, when minister D. F. Shenk of Sheridan lived at Molalla for four months to provide regular preaching services. About this time, too, several Emmert families moved to Molalla and pecple who attended a mission Sunday school which Hopewell had started in the nearby Fernwood community agreed to attend services at Molalla, biweekly. On August 19, 1934, forty charter members, most of them from neighboring Hopewell or Bethel, established Molalla Mennonite Church. Some family names were Emmert, Hamilton, Kester, Lehman, Schultz, Strong, and Yoder, and perhaps also Johnson, Mishler, Olsen, and Weber. Joe Yoder was ordained there in February 1935.[45]

The decline of the congregation began even before they constructed a much-needed building in 1940. Membership reached a high of eighty-nine in 1939 and dropped to fifty-seven the next year, after most of the Emmert families, approximately one fourth of the members, had moved to Sweet Home to begin a logging business. The depressed economy contributed to their leaving their feed store and creamery in Molalla and the truck line which they had earlier purchased from Lehman. Problems within the congregation, apparently related to an extension Sunday school and to poor participation in some of the congregation's meetings, contributed to making 1941 a year of low morale from which the congregation never fully recovered. In the next years, others, including pastor Joe H. Yoder, left for health reasons. For a time in the late 1940s, the few remaining members hoped that the Meadowbrook Sunday school, which Zion people had started, might join them. But by 1951 Zion was building a church house for Meadowbrook at Union Mills near Liberal, five miles north of Molalla. The Molalla congregation disbanded in 1951, after only ten years in their new building. Ten of the eleven Molalla members joined Meadowbrook and one returned to Bethel.[46]

As the 1930s ended, the PCC had kept a fragile unity for almost two decades. In spite of recurring tensions, with emphasis on sound doctrine, it had grown in numbers. The annual, sometimes semiannual, revival meetings were common times for young people to accept Christ and prepare to join the church. Conference membership increased steadily during the 1930s, from 1,051 in 1930, to 1,552 in 1938, with a net loss of eleven reported in 1939's total of 1,541. During the Great Depression, in addition to growth from within the congregations, many people, including Mennonites, moved from the drought-plagued prairie states to Oregon. Mission efforts were a third, if the smallest, source of increasing membership.

Although total membership increased, many young people left their Mennonite heritage in the 1930s without ever becoming members, and others withdrew from PCC congregations. For them, the cord of tension between individualism and the church community snapped. They threw their loyalties to other denominations or dropped into the secular, unchurched world. The PCC was not fully united over how to deal with all the issues, but leaders who wished to conserve traditional patterns of life or promote more recent regulations remained dominant. Conference unity remained fragile.[47]

Chapter 4
OMs: Unity Tested (1940s and 1950s)

The fragile unity within the Pacific Coast Conference continued in the 1940s and 1950s—in structure, if not in essence.
Individualism, both personal and congregational, challenged the
authority of the larger church community, the conference. Members left OM congregations to help organize more liberal GC or
more conservative PCC congregations. In the 1950s, the conference discipline, which was supposed to unite members in practice,
drew lines that would eventually divide.

Fortitude and fervor characterized the 1940s. The PCC held
fast to certain positions and practices even while it enthusiastically
developed new programs and institutions. During World War II
many young men performed alternative service in Civilian Public
Service (CPS) camps. Western Mennonite School and the Albany
Home for the Aged opened just after the war. The district mission
board began to operate a children's home and the Lebanon Community Hospital. It also sponsored Jewish mission work, opened a
rescue mission in Portland, and began to publish *Missionary
Evangel.* In addition, for a few years Omar G. Miller independently
published the "District Echoes," also called "West Coast Echoes,"
a small newssheet which had a conservative slant and which could
ask unpopular questions or offer candid opinions that an official
publication did not. Congregations supported the new institutions
and programs and established more mission Sunday schools. Interested persons began mission work in Mexico.

On all of this, the PCC executive committee and the bishop
body attempted to hold a tight rein. Wartime pressures and change
threatened their authority, but through the 1940s they remained
firm. While they welcomed increased mission outreach and new
institutions, they tried to keep their people on the simple, plain
ways of earlier years. Meanwhile, concerned individuals—ordained
and lay—who supported continuing or increased separation from

the world, became dismayed at departures from strict regulations of nonconformity in the PCC, in the larger church, and especially in the colleges. They urged PCC officials and bishops to continue to keep the rein tight and enforce the conference discipline.

Conference records of the 1940s revealed tensions. They referred to problems in the four oldest congregations concerning nonconformity, nonresistance, and authority. Conference speakers frequently referred to doctrines and outlined what they considered the most essential ones. In spite of subtle changes which some congregations were accepting, the PCC officially supported, firmly and fervently, the denominational standards which essentially corresponded with its own discipline statement.[1]

In the late 1930s a difficulty at Albany began over nonconformity. Bishop N. A. Lind held stricter regulations in attire than many members desired, and some felt he became more authoritarian as the years passed. At one communion service he announced from the pulpit that women whose dress sleeves did not reach the elbow could not commune. When he passed out the bread, he did not give it to certain women. Some people objected strongly to this exclusion. Amid resulting tensions, Lind submitted his resignation. Other PCC bishops helped bring understanding and reconciliation between him and the congregation. A few weeks later, early in 1940, the congregation granted the release he requested along with a letter of fellowship.[2]

Zion was dividing over nonresistance, nonconformity, and more. There, Paul N. Roth, an aggressive preacher ordained at Portland almost two decades earlier, challenged the established order. First he brought severe rebuke upon himself when he performed the marriage of a couple, one of whom was not a member of any church. After a confession he was reinstated as a minister. Three years later, during World War II, Roth said that he supported nonresistance and did not encourage young men to join the army. He did believe it was possible for them to do so and still be Christians. He did not support restrictive attire. But Roth's problems were greater than the sum of these issues. Some Zion people regarded him as a young upstart (almost twenty years younger than minister Edward Yoder) who did not recognize the constituted authority of the ministerial body. Others considered him a capable, progressive leader, concerned for the welfare of individuals. His gifts enabled him to teach in winter Bible schools in various congregations. Roth had no family connections with other Zion ministers—a possible handicap—and was originally from Fairview, not Zion. Some felt there was jealousy among the leaders.

When tensions reached a climax, Roth was excommunicated, a measure of discipline Zion seldom used, though it was common in some congregations. It divided Zion, and sixty-six members withdrew in 1944. Most of them, with Roth as pastor, organized the Calvary Mennonite Church (GC) a few miles away near Barlow.[3]

The concerns at Hopewell and Fairview focused more on authority than on nonconformity or nonresistance. An adjustment committee reported that at Hopewell, bishop Henry A. Wolfer was shocked and hurt when someone made a "rash statement" about his wife which two others "sanctioned." Two of the three were among the Hopewell ministry. The committee heard confessions by all involved, effected a reconciliation, and encouraged Wolfer to change location and to continue to work in evangelization among the Jews. At Fairview, an apparent irregularity in the ordination of Verl Nofziger as deacon in July 1948 triggered protest. Quite a number of people voted for a person whom bishop Nick Birky did not include as a candidate for selection by the lot. A committee of ordained men resolved the problem enough to allow Nofziger's ordination to be recognized at the 1950 PCC sessions. However, the issue was one of several that caused a group of people to leave Fairview and begin the Tangent congregation in 1950.[4]

Leaders within the PCC continued to focus on nonconformity. Paul W. Miller of the Indian Cove congregation in Idaho, a brother of Omar G. Miller, prepared a studied presentation titled "The Worldward Drift and Our Attitude Toward It" for the January 1942 ministers' meeting at Sheridan. He noted evidences of drift in business, fashion, political interest, the home, worldly conformity, and in several other trends. He thought that methods and expression of nonconformity might change, but not biblical doctrines. Restrictions were "helps" to shield the church from evil worldly influence, but separation was not "outward forms for every time and place," he asserted. Where Scripture was not clear, "decrees" should be made "after much counsel," but not that of "lay delegates," who he thought should not share in "the solutions and decisions of church problems." He believed that the Holy Spirit did not "prevent differences of opinion" and thought it "not impossible for two people or factions to have the Holy Spirit and His leading at the same time." He proposed that all the ordained men meet for prayer, Bible study, and fellowship, after which the bishops and a problems committee "should take up the points of difference and form a constitution and discipline" that members would be willing to "live out, and practice." However, that same year, 1942, the PCC reprinted the 1924 constitution and discipline without revision.[5]

In the early 1940s visitors from the larger church, too, continued to promote nonconformity, but by the end of the decade the focus was shifting. Abner G. Yoder from Parnell, Iowa, in 1940 stressed the need to keep on the "old paths," such as service, sacrifice, self-denial, humility, regeneration, [traditional] biblical interpretation, and balanced attitudes, noting that "two outstanding old paths are nonconformity and nonresistance." But a few years later representatives from the larger church who visited the PCC gave little attention to standards of attire. Rather, they promoted a new mutual aid plan, a new commission to strengthen Christian education in the congregations, missionary education, and publication interests.[6]

By the end of the 1940s, some Oregon Mennonites had become deeply concerned about relaxed restrictions in sister congregations. Late in 1949, a number of ministers and a layman, with Ernest J. Bontrager as their spokesman, requested a meeting with the PCC executive committee. They pointed out ways in which they thought the PCC and its congregations were drifting away from conference and biblical standards. This meeting was a prelude to the ferment of the 1950s. As variations in practice of nonconformity increased, so did disagreements about the issue. The PCC would not resolve the issue until more years had passed.[7]

In spite of substantial membership losses in several congregations, PCC membership grew steadily in the 1940s, from 1,582 in 1940 to 1,915 in 1948. However, at the 1948 conference, the faraway congregations in California and Arizona requested permission to organize their own conference, which they called the South Pacific Mennonite Conference. Their leaving decreased PCC membership to 1,662 in 1949, only eighty more than when the 1940s began. The PCC had two new Oregon congregations, however: Sweet Home, which organized in 1940, and Western, in 1948.[8]

After a brief Mennonite presence at Sweet Home in 1912 when Elmer McTimmonds taught school at nearby Ames Creek and started a Sunday school, a continuing Mennonite witness began at Sweet Home in 1938 when three Emmert families moved there from Molalla and established a logging company. Large timber

Opal Brubaker

Benjamin Franklin and Anna Emmert, their sons and daughters-in-law, in the early 1940s. Standing: Jess, Eva (Voget) and George, Rolena (Lehman) and Ivan, Mary (Casebeer) and Ralph, Cora (Schlabach) and Albert, Floyd. Seated: Laura (Miller), wife of Jess; Anna (Schrag) (1875-1962); Ben (1870-1942); Grace (Burkholder), wife of Floyd. During their marriage the Emmerts lived near Eugene, Dallas, Hubbard, Sheridan, Molalla, and Sweet Home. Ben helped construct meetinghouses in three communities, including Sweet Home.

companies were opening their vast holdings to harvest, aided by a new railway and an almost completed highway connecting Sweet Home with Lebanon and Albany. Soon more Emmert families from Molalla and Hostetlers and Wolfers from Sheridan joined them. In 1940 the Emmert parents, Ben and Anna, moved from Mollala to Sweet Home. In 1939 the group had called in N. M. Birky and N. A. Lind to help organize a Sunday school, which met in homes. Fairview ministers Melvin Schrock and Henry Gerig frequently drove to Sweet Home for preaching services, in which the people sat on long wooden planks supported by big chunks of wood.[9]

Cliff Lind

Norman A. (1881-1968) Lind, bishop at Albany and Sweet Home, and Sarah (Flohr) (1880-1963) Lind and a great-granddaughter, Janet Lind, in 1960. Even then, Sarah milked her goats, reminiscent of her responsibilities during N. A.'s earlier frequent absences for conference and other church work.

On July 14, 1940, the Mennonites met in a grove of trees at the Ben Emmert home, across the road from the site of the meetinghouse they constructed that fall, to officially organize as a congregation. Forty-three members agreed to the charter. Family names were Emmert (24), Lind (3), Dorsing, Hostetler, McDowell, Roth, Shank, Wolfer (2 each), and Bauman, Brown, Groff, and Johnson (1 each). They requested that N. A. Lind serve as their bishop. Lind, then in his late fifties, had only several months earlier left Albany. Assisted by other ordained men, he served Sweet Home until he retired in 1960. Though a group of members left in the mid-1940s and helped start the Sweet Home Community Chapel (GC), membership reached a high of 145 in 1955. Records name quite a few persons with nontraditional Mennonite names. Later losses came when members transferred to Cascadia, a mission Sunday school, and when persons moved elsewhere for employment or just dropped out of church life. The membership in 1976 was ninety-six. At that time they were discussing whether to remodel their deteriorating old building or to construct a new one on another site.[10]

The impetus for organizing the Western Mennonite congregation came with the beginning of Western Mennonite School (WMS) in 1945. Even before the school moved in the fall of 1946 to its permanent campus on Wallace Road (State Highway 221), about ten miles north of Salem, Mennonite families had begun to settle there. In December 1945 the Reuben Reist family of Portland was the first of the six charter member families to move to the area. In 1946 the Marcus Lind and Willis Byers families moved there from Sheridan, followed, in 1947, by the families of Lloyd Lind from Tangent, Joe Birky from Albany, and Dave Stutzman from Sweet Home. These families wanted a Christian high school education for their children.[11]

After worshiping with other congregations and meeting in homes for some time, the group began using the school facilities in 1947. On March 7, 1948, the congregation organized with twenty-nine charter members plus two newly baptized girls. Minister Marcus Lind, one of the first teachers at the school, became the pastor and served more than twenty-seven years. Many remembered his Sunday evening expository messages on the New Testament books and the Bible stories he told the children. Lind also taught Bible classes at WMS and influenced the PCC and the larger Mennonite church through his teaching, preaching, and writing. On August 31, 1975, he concluded his tenure as pastor but continued to serve as bishop until February 1, 1976. Other ordained men also served at times during Lind's tenure, but he played a decisive role in the congregation for most of its first three decades. Membership grew slowly to a high of ninety-six in 1960. In the next years young people who went away to college or into voluntary service usually did not return. Additional losses came when five families helped begin the new, progressive Salem Mennonite congregation and, later, when four families left to join more conservative congregations. The 1976 membership was sixty-seven.[12]

In the 1940s, as in each decade, changes in the ministerial body influenced both their congregations and the PCC. Whether or not the ordained men were strong conference leaders, all could speak and vote in ministers' meetings. Each death or moving of an ordained man, or the rise of another, tipped the balance of conviction and authority one way or another. A number of influential conference leaders emerged in the older congregations in the 1940s, all of them vigorous participants in mission outreach, some of them committed to conserving detailed nonconformity, others less supportive of specific restrictions. Even while the bishop body held a tight rein in the 1940s, the reins were weakening.

Hilda Reist

Marcus Lind (1908-), pastor of the Western congregation, teacher at Western Mennonite School, and conference leader for several decades.

At Zion, after Paul Roth left in 1944, Chester Kauffman, son of former Zion minister Daniel B. Kauffman and cousin of minister E. Z. Yoder, was chosen by lot and ordained minister in 1945. At this time Zion had several mission Sunday schools and the ministers scattered on Sundays to preach in them. The result of the lot did not please some Zion members. When Kauffman became pastor of the Meadowbrook Sunday school in 1949, they decided they needed another minister. This time they did not use the lot. Instead, members indicated their choice to a committee of ordained men. From a scattered vote the committee chose the new minister, one who had been in the lot with Kauffman four years earlier, and ordained Edward (Kelly) Kenagy, grandson of Zion's first bishop, Amos P. Troyer, and nephew of minister E. Z. Yoder's wife, Alice. Kenagy's wife, Edna, was a daughter of the deacon, John Gingerich. But the Kenagy ordination, too, produced dissatisfaction in some quarters. Within months Kenagy became pastor of the Sunday school in the Silverton Hills, which he had begun that very spring. Zion was again left shorthanded for its home pulpit as well as for various mission efforts.[13]

At Albany, George Kauffman assumed official responsibilities after N. A. Lind left. He served as pastor or assisting minister until 1957, when he moved to Lebanon to serve the new congregation there. One of his strengths in the several congregations he served through the years was his ability to work gracefully and harmoniously with other ordained men. During his pastorate Albany began to provide partial financial support for Kauffman. Beginning in 1949, their next pastor, Paul E. Yoder, served as the first fully supported pastor in any Oregon (MC) congregation. However, the method of support—monthly freewill offerings—did not always produce the necessary income. (By the time David Mann arrived in the 1950s, the congregation provided a specified salary.) Son of Zion's minister, Edward Z. Yoder, Paul was a vigorous, creative leader. Some members felt he was too authoritarian, or too influential in decision-making. Others felt that he provided excellent resources for spiritual growth by opening up the Bible and its meaning and emphasizing the importance of Bible study. During his six years at Albany the congregation began to construct a somewhat controversial new church building. Yoder initiated or encouraged such new things as Mennonite Youth Fellowship, a men's fellowship to serve in times of disaster, a church council, and a constitution. In 1955 he moved to Salem to teach at WMS.[14]

Other emerging leaders in the 1940s who influenced the PCC included Ernest J. Bontrager and his wife, Ida (Boyer), who had moved to Oregon in 1938 to serve in Bethel's rural mission efforts and the next year had begun a mission near Estacada; Max G. Yoder, a son of Sheridan; Ray Mishler, also of Sheridan; and Claud Hostetler at Portland.[15]

Gerald Brenneman

Paul E. Yoder (1912-1987), influential Albany pastor during a period of rapid change. Yoder later served the Western and McMinnville congregations.

Though the PCC maintained a structural unity with fortitude and fervor in the 1940s, increasing diversity among leaders and laity fed a growing ferment in the 1950s that produced increasing pressure on unity. Ten new Oregon congregations joined the PCC in the 1950s, an unprecedented number within one decade. Their pastors and core groups of workers all hoped to gather in the unsaved in their communities as well as among their own youth. Some wanted to conserve or strengthen practices outlined in the conference discipline; others permitted more liberal practices. Ministers who served several of the new congregations had formal education beyond high school, if not seminary training. Albany and Zion, too, added a liberal leavening when they called young out-of-state ministers with seminary training. By the end of the decade, influence and authority were shifting gradually from older to younger leaders, from less- to more-educated men.[16]

When the 1950s began, the group headed by Ernest J. Bontrager had intensified their assertion that conference unity required uniform practice as outlined in the conference discipline. Late in 1949 they had requested that the executive committee "do something" about congregations that did not discipline members who disregarded conference restrictions. The committee and the conference bishops soon appointed five ordained men to "formulate a statement of restrictions on nonconformity, nonresistance, swearing of oaths, secret orders, divorce, and such other points" that they considered "pertinent to [their] present situation." They also charged the new committee to "bring ways and means to carry out the above regulations."[17]

The committee met in March 1950 for two days and prepared a three-page statement which they presented to the ministerial body prior to the June conference. They thought that most details, restrictions, and regulations of the 1942 constitution and discipline were "quite adequate." However, they did remind both ministers and laity of items needing clarification or elaboration, including close communion. The wedding veil was not to be a substitute for the devotional covering, and courting and marrying should be only within (Mennonite) church membership. They emphasized specifics of nonconformity, such as abstinence from intoxicating drinks or tobacco. They included wedding rings, tie clasps, gold watches and neckties—especially "flashy" ones—among additional items of superfluous adornment; added skating rinks to forbidden amusements; enlarged the prohibition regarding musical instruments; and specified television as an innovation to be carefully considered before accepting it "as tolerated." Finally, they emphasized that the PCC had restrictive power over all organizations "under" it.[18]

Within three years the PCC had formed a new constitution and discipline. In the process, delegates approved the document, then congregations acted upon it. Some congregations apparently objected to some parts of the document. At the 1953 conference the executive committee recommended that congregations adopt it "with the understanding that wherein they cannot fully subscribe to the wording on some points . . . they continue to labor together in fellowship with the Spirit and in brotherly love." Whether conservatives wished for more specifics or liberals disapproved increased restrictions, perhaps this exception somewhat modified the document's authority and permitted increasing diversity.

Getting it printed brought additional controversy. Apparently Claud Hostetler, printing committee chairman, did some editing which the executive committee rejected. They felt the printing committee should not have changed one "jot or tittle," whether a "Dutchy" expression (a carryover from more than half a century earlier when many Mennonites still spoke Pennsylvania Dutch, a German dialect) or the numbering or lettering of sections for uniformity. They recalled the documents, which had been printed at a cost of about $235, and noted sternly in 1954 that the committee had "failed to have printed the text . . . adopted . . . in 1953." They made the committee "responsible to reprint a Constitution and Discipline *as passed by Conference*," with "page proof [to] be submitted" to the PCC secretary "before final printing."[19]

Individuals concerned about the drift away from the earlier constitution and discipline hoped that PCC members would acknowledge the authority of the 1953 document. More specific and restrictive than the 1924/1942 constitution and discipline, it spelled out in greater detail what the PCC expected of its members in a rapidly changing world. Bishops, the highest authorities in the church, should be able to hold their members firmly to the stated positions.

Rather than unifying the PCC, the revised document held the yeast of division. Though it was a dedicated effort by the conservative group to produce uniformity, it became the vat which held a fermenting mixture of policies, personalities, and practices.

Later generations may think that many PCC Mennonites had become obsessed with trivia and focused excessively on the practice of nonconformity, particularly attire. But PCC Mennonites were not alone in their emphasis. Sister conferences across the country shared the same focus. Most Mennonites had for centuries stressed simplicity and discouraged pride and costly display in attire. However, American (old) Mennonites sharpened their focus about the turn of the twentieth century when certain influential leaders promoted uniform, prescribed styles of clothing as a visible result of conversion, a demonstration of personal piety, and a safeguard for nonresistance.

In their church, Mennonites experienced security through such visible practices that did not conform to the ways of the world. The church, represented by ordained men who received their authority from God, interpreted the Bible. Being obedient to the Bible meant obeying the leaders, the shepherds of the flock. They largely determined church standards, considered biblical teachings to be clear, and were confident that they understood and interpreted the Bible rightly. Dissenting or questioning voices were to be convicted of their sin or convinced of the rightness of church teachings. Restrictive nonconformity became an essential fruit of their faithfulness to God.[20]

Accepting the Bible as the authority for faith and practice was common ground on which all PCC Mennonites stood. The 1957 conference theme was "We Are Biblicists," and the PCC resolved "with renewal of purpose and loving determination" to "seek more fully to love and obey" Scripture, to uphold its standards in all areas of life, and to "endeavor to be open-minded in . . . attitude toward the teaching of God's Word." A year later a resolution affirmed belief that the Bible is "the inspired Word of God . . . [the] final authority and guide in life . . . and [the] indispensible weapon in resisting the devil" and fulfilling the church's "obligation to the world." It was differing approaches to understanding and interpreting the Bible which produced strong tensions.[21]

Within this milieu of the 1950s, in the midst of these emphases and issues in the PCC, ten congregations organized. Perhaps it was Allen Erb, a mature statesman-bishop, who came from the South Central Conference in 1953 to administer the Lebanon Community Hospital, who largely influenced their organization in that decade. At the 1955 conference, as he discussed "Establishing Churches," he questioned whether the present method of doing mission work was biblical and what was the scriptural method of

Marjorie Nofziger

Allen H. (1888-1975) and Stella (Cooprider) (1888-1959) Erb in 1959. He administered the Lebanon Community Hospital and encouraged mission stations to become congregations.

establishing churches. Apparently he emphasized that mission stations should become congregations, for within the next three years, eight of the ten congregations of the 1950s formally organized. Several had begun as mission stations. Together they added warmth to the already fermenting mixture of policies, personalities, and practices, and brought additional diversity to feed the ferment.[22]

The Tangent Mennonite congregation began as a conservative movement away from nearby Fairview. Minister Melvin Schrock, with his wife and family, left in 1949 because Fairview had no "written or stated standard of faith and practice" and no "guidelines or principles to govern the church." Schrock believed that Fairview was lax in discipline, which permitted "a drifting into unscriptural practices." Later in 1949, seven more families and a single man left Fairview. They shared Schrock's concerns about congregational discipline. Some were interested in a deeper spiritual life. Apparently they were attracted by elements of the holiness movement, which emphasized personal inner peace, piety, at least a degree of perfectionism, and power for service. The movement has attracted many persons who took their Christian faith with utmost seriousness.

The Fairview dissidents began prayer meetings in their homes, meetings open to anyone interested but not officially planned by Fairview leaders and not approved by the bishop. Their withdrawal from Fairview was hardly orthodox and could have brought them censure. But because a conference investigating committee found irregularities in Fairview's administration, they recommended that the Tangent group have the privilege to form a new congregation in good standing in the PCC.[23]

In January 1950, even before the committee's recommendations, the group had begun meeting for regular Sunday services. They soon bought the vacant Bethel Chapel and used it until they moved into a new larger building in 1969. Soon after they began holding services they invited Melvin Schrock to be their minister. Tangent organized on August 9, 1950, with twenty-five charter members. Family names were Hershberger, Kenagy, Reeder, Roth, Schrock, and Stutzman. The membership high of sixty in 1965 came largely from children of member families and transfers in when young people married, though about ten converts were from other-than-Mennonite heritage. One was Ajmer Singh, born a Sikh in India, who married Verna Hershberger of the congregation and later joined the faculty of Oregon College of Education at Monmouth. He left the congregation in the early 1970s. Losses resulted from death, excommunication, and dissatisfaction with the congregation. The 1976 membership was thirty-two.[24]

Some of Tangent's leaders served for several decades, including Melvin Schrock through 1976. Merle Stutzman, another long-term minister, was ordained in January 1952 and served until 1973, when he left because of his position regarding an unfortunate financial transaction between two Tangent members. One of Schrock's sons, Jason, became deacon, then minister in 1976. In the larger Mennonite church, which Tangent viewed with increasing misgivings, another Schrock son, Paul, served for years as a periodical, curriculum, and book editor at Mennonite Publishing House. Tangent leaders hoped that as a congregation affiliated with the PCC, they could help strengthen the enforcement of its discipline. But it soon became clear that the PCC was not regaining but rather increasingly losing the conservative practices dear to the Tangent people. One of the two congregations organized in 1955, Porter, shared their concerns and views.[25]

The impetus for the Porter Mennonite Church began about two decades before it organized. By 1937 Bethel members were concerned about the need for rural mission work in their community and invited Ernest J. and Ida Boyer Bontrager to do house-to-house evangelism. The Bontragers arrived in the spring of 1938 and began a full, organized program of home visits. The work at Porter, a few miles east of Estacada, about thirty miles from Bethel, developed after the Bontragers discovered the community following a huckleberry-picking excursion. People cleaning the Porter schoolhouse favored having a Sunday school there. In fact, one man said that he and his wife had been praying for this. The community of thirty-five homes of mostly poor people along an eight-mile stretch of road had only a few persons claiming salvation. In September 1939 the Bontragers began Sunday morning services there. During the first years Omar G. Miller of Bethel preached on most Sundays. Bontrager was not ordained as a minister until 1943.[26]

Several lay people played significant roles in the work at Porter. Early in 1941 Abraham and Olive Miller and daughter Twila moved from Upland, California, to a farm they had bought in the community. They assisted in services, exemplified a godly home, and provided stability. During most of Bontrager's years at Porter he was frequently away for weeks at a time, serving as evangelist, music teacher, and instructor in Bible schools in Oregon and other states. In 1944 and 1945, Miller was in Civilian Public Service (CPS), the World War II program for conscientious objectors. Except for those two years, the Millers remained the always present, reliable Mennonite family to whom the community people could turn. Another influential person at Porter was Mildred Loucks, who gave much of her time from 1953 to 1959 in visitation work in the community. Some years she also taught a large class of youth. Ida Boyer Bontrager was among the instructors at the first Winter Bible School in 1955.[27]

The work at Porter had its ups and downs. For a time, when both Millers and Bontragers were away from Porter, it appeared the work there might end. But the Millers, returning from CPS, revived it, and Bontragers returned soon after, commuting to Porter while they taught at WMS. The Porter schoolhouse served as their meeting place for several years until 1943, when they dedicated a new meetinghouse. After fire destroyed it in 1967, they constructed a new building with the help of friends across the continent. Sixteen years after the Bontragers began services there, Porter Mennonite Church organized on October 2, 1955, with twenty-six charter members. Family names were Adlon, Bontrager, Hess, Horn, Lanier, Loucks, Miller, Phernetton, Randall, and Schweitzer. Several years later, in 1959, membership dipped to a low of seventeen. A gradual increase in the next decade brought an all-time high of forty-eight in 1969. The 1976 membership was forty-one. Bontrager, who was ordained bishop in 1968, served as pastor from 1943 through 1976.[28]

Winston Mennonite Church, also organized in 1955, was the first Oregon congregation located outside the Willamette and tributary valleys in nearby foothills. It resulted from the vision of I-W men who served under a newly organized program for conscientious objectors at the Veterans' Hospital in Roseburg, one hundred miles south of Albany. They and their wives began having services together on Friday evenings. In 1953 Ivan Headings, an Oklahoma minister who had recently moved to Lebanon, began to pastor the group, visiting them twice a month. Looking for a needy place to hold a summer Bible school in 1953, they chose the small town of Winston, a residential area eight miles south of Roseburg. During Bible school the second summer, several boys accepted Christ and requested baptism. With this beginning, the group started a Sunday school in July 1954. They used the Evergreen Grange Hall until 1954, when they constructed a small building, partly of salvaged materials.[29]

Winston congregation organized on August 7, 1955, with fourteen charter members. Family names were Alliman, Bailey, Baker, Hostetler, Johnstone, Smucker, Yoder, and Zehr. Three were I-W men who stayed to work in the church they helped start. Three were boys who were recent converts. That same day Roy Hostetler, who had returned to Harrisburg after his I-W service, at age twenty-eight the oldest charter member, was chosen by vote and ordained minister. Within several weeks he and his family moved back to Roseburg. He served as pastor fifteen years, until shortly after Winston withdrew from the PCC. During his tenure the membership grew to a peak of forty-eight in 1968. In spite of concentrated emphasis upon outreach into the community and considerable participation of community families or children during those years, the number of community people who remained with the congregation was small. The 1976 membership was thirty.[30]

Two congregations, Logsden and Blaine, organized in 1956. Like Winston, both were outside the Willamette Valley. Both were located across the Coast Range, in small valleys inland a few miles from the Pacific. And for both, Sheridan members provided the initial vision and effort.

Logsden Mennonite Church resulted from the vision of

Dewey Wolfer and David Hostetler of Sheridan. Wolfer and Hostetler noted how people would say a quarterly mission meeting had been the best ever, then go home and seem to forget about the challenges they had heard. They thus agreed to look for open fields for more Bible schools because of high interest in those Sheridan already conducted. One day Hostetler and his wife, Nora, searching for a place to fish along the Siletz River near Logsden, met a girl, Rosalie Kentta, picking blackberries. They talked to her and stopped at the community store. They learned that for fifteen years there had been no Sunday school or church services there and were surprised that about 150 children went by bus to school each day from what appeared to be a small community.[31]

Hostetler, Wolfer, and aging minister Daniel Shenk investigated possibilities at Logsden and recommended beginning a Sunday school there. Because many Sheridan people thought Logsden was too far away for such a work, the committee decided to begin on their own. On Sunday morning, November 26, 1950, Dewey Wolfer and his wife, Florence, got up early to milk their herd of cows, twenty each, then drove to Logsden to begin a Sunday school. The Hostetler and the Melvin Mishler families also went. About thirty community people attended, and the number increased in the next weeks, including both white and Indian children, for a Siletz Indian Tribe reservation was part of the community. When Shenk preached the first sermon, three girls accepted Christ. Once the work was under way, Sheridan accepted it as a mission Sunday school. But it was a long drive for workers every Sunday, seventy-five miles or more each way.

During the first summer Bible school in 1951, the workers camped at Logsden to avoid the daily drive. Realizing that the Sunday school could not survive without a Mennonite presence in the community, Wolfers sold their cows, rented their farm, and in January 1952 moved to Logsden. Considering themselves "just plain farmers" with "no special training," they faced unfamiliar problems, "praying, working, visiting, making mistakes." Attendance fluctuated widely, and some people stayed away because a rumor said that the Mennonites were moving to Logsden to buy up all the land and colonize there.[32]

Several years later, members of Albany Mennonite Church, about half as distant as Sheridan, brought fresh enthusiasm and zeal as they helped in summer Bible school. Sheridan workers were wearing out from the long weekly drive, and Wolfers worked out an agreement in which Sheridan would turn the work over to Albany. Eugene Lemons from Albany became superintendent of the Sunday school and in 1955 several Albany families moved to Logsden to help in the work. The John Jantzi family also moved there about that time for business reasons but soon became long-term workers in the new church.

The Logsden congregation organized on July 29, 1956, with nineteen charter members with the family names of Bilyeu, Carpenter, Grenfell, Hamilton, Hanger, Jantzi, Kennel, Kentta, Lemons, Rariden, and Wolfer. For almost two years Eugene Lemons served as licensed pastor. At first the Mennonites had used the former two-room Logsden schoolhouse. Then in July 1959 they moved into their new building on the first Sunday after the new pastor, Roy D. Roth, arrived from Hesston, Kansas, where he had been president of Hesston College. By 1960 membership was forty-four. Although the reported membership for 1976 was eighty-one, Betty Dickason, Logsden historian, estimated that about forty-five to fifty were then active resident members.[33]

Blaine Mennonite Church organized more than thirty years after the first Mennonites, Frank and May Larrew and their small sons, Loyd and James, homesteaded about six miles above Blaine in 1925. Blaine was located seven miles east of the coastal town of Beaver in Tillamook County, and most people there were dairy farmers or loggers. The Larrews had been charter members at Sheridan, and when they could not drive the fifty-six miles over poor roads across the Coast Range to Sheridan services, they had Sunday school in their home. For years they prayed that God would open the way for church work in Blaine. In 1936 they learned of a union Sunday school in a neighboring district and began attending it. A Presbyterian Sunday school missionary visited it, but infrequently. So in 1937 May asked if ministers from Sheridan might come to preach occasionally. That initiated monthly visits from Sheridan preachers.[34]

By 1946 five other Mennonite families had moved to the Blaine area, and in April the twenty-two Mennonite members petitioned Sheridan that as soon as possible they might organize a church and have a resident minister and a new building. Sheridan granted permission for the three requests and chose minister Daniel F. Shenk by lot to move to Blaine. However, about four months later he moved back to Sheridan because of health problems caused by a noxious weed common in the Blaine area. In

Naomi K. Schrock

Frank (1893-1954) and May (Detwiler) (1893-) Larrew, charter members at Sheridan who homesteaded at Blaine in 1925 and later helped begin the Mennonite congregation there.

January 1947, Jacob Kauffman, a Sheridan member living near Beaver, was ordained to serve as pastor at Blaine, but for about seven years Sheridan ministers still went to Blaine twice a month to help. Kauffman served faithfully for over thirty years. Granting the other two requests took longer, but in 1952 the Blaine people moved into their new building. Though it gave them a stronger Mennonite identity, the small group related more closely with their larger community than many Mennonite congregations did.

On Easter Sunday in 1954, before the third request came to pass, Mennonite pioneer Frank Larrew died at age sixty. Two years later, on August 19, 1956, the Blaine Mennonite Church organized with twenty-eight charter members. Family names were Byers, Hostetler, Kauffman, Larrew, Schrock, and Shenk. The small community offered limited employment opportunities. Few families moved there permanently, and few young people who left to go to college returned. The membership of twenty-eight gradually declined to eleven in 1976.[35]

East Fairview Mennonite Church was one of four PCC congregations organized in 1957, along with Lebanon, Grants Pass, and McMinnville. Only East Fairview began as a mission Sunday school. Jake and Jeanne Roth, Fairview members, moved about 1945 with their young children to the Fairview community, not to be confused with the Fairview congregation at Albany. The Fairview community was named for a store, several sawmills, and an elementary school just off Highway 20, about seven miles southeast of Lebanon and twice that distance from the Fairview Mennonite meetinghouse. The Roths were quietly influential in their community—Jake at the sawmill where he worked, Jeanne in teaching neighborhood children about God.[36]

Some thirty years later one of those children, George Neavoll, by then editor of the editorial pages of the *Wichita* [Kansas] *Eagle and Beacon,* wrote of the Roths' influence. He remembered Jeanne walking the mile or so to the Neavoll home, early in the winter of 1947, to invite the children to Sunday afternoon Sunday school in her home. After missing the first few Sundays because of his father's illness and death, he attended regularly. He considered Jeanne "an authority figure [they] genuinely respected." She did not "attempt to coerce or even gently persuade" the children to join a church or do anything they did not want to do. Yet "as a moral force, Jeanne Roth with her flannelboard lessons . . . was a modern-day equal of St. Augustine or St. Francis." For the first time ever, many of the children faced "the concept of sin, [and] treating others as [they] would like to be treated." They tried to

Alan and Mary Roth

Jake and Jeanne (Robitaille) Roth and family, probably in the early 1950s. Back: Judy, Joyce, and James; Jered between Jeanne and Jake. Roths initiated what later became the East Fairview congregation.

do their best to love their neighbors as themselves, even though sometimes it was "a difficult chore. . . . Parents talked of the change they could see in their children; and the parents themselves were infected by what was happening in the boxlike house that Jake Roth had erected the winter before." The average attendance was about twenty.[37]

In several years the Sunday school moved out of the Roth home and eventually organized as a congregation. Jeanne Roth and Verl Nofziger transported children to the Fairview Church summer Bible school in 1948. In 1949 a committee surveyed people in the Fairview community to learn their interest in a Bible school in their own locale instead. Usually people asked if the committee was from the church that Roths belonged to, commenting that then it must be all right. The Mennonites used the recently vacated one-room schoolhouse for the Bible school and the Sunday school which Fairview soon began. Individuals raised money privately for land and building costs and by the end of 1949 the workers held services in a new church building. A major addition in 1961 provided a sanctuary. Although the community was known as Fairview, by 1952, if not before that time, the mission Sunday school became known as East Fairview to distinguish it from Fairview Mennonite Church. By then Allen Erb was preaching there every other Sunday morning, and the next year Ivan Headings came as pastor. He served for ten years, the last two as helping pastor. East Fairview organized on May 7, 1957, with twenty-nine charter members. Among the family names were Bare, Burk, Cook, Headings, Miller, Reeder, Roth, Stauffer, Stutzman, Wolfer, Wood, and Zimmerman. The membership high may have been fifty-nine, in 1968, when the congregation withdrew from the PCC. Soon after, members such as deacon Ivan Bare and family, who wanted to remain with the PCC, joined other congregations. Others dropped out of church life. The 1976 membership was thirty-two.[38]

Lebanon Mennonite Church began after several Mennonite families moved to the town. Quite a few, along with I-W men, found employment at the new hospital which opened in 1952. Mennonites in the area, including bishop Allen Erb, the first Mennonite administrator of the hospital, thought there should be a church in Lebanon. In October 1955, Erb invited ordained brethren of the Albany, Fairview, Tangent, and Sweet Home congregations, none of them far from Lebanon, to discuss organizing a congregation there. The ordained men approved unanimously. A few weeks later persons considering a congregation at Lebanon met at the East Fairview mission to discuss how its work would be affected if a congregation should organize in Lebanon. The work at both places was encouraged. These were important meetings. During those years most congregations started as mission stations, or because families moved to a new community, or because of conflict and division in a congregation. Lebanon was not a mission station, and other Mennonite congregations surrounded it. But people interested in starting a congregation there wanted the blessing and goodwill of neighboring Mennonites.[39]

With these hurdles cleared, Erb invited anyone interested in starting a congregation in Lebanon to a January 1956 meeting at his home. The sixteen persons present decided to begin by having cottage meetings, the first to be on February 8 at Fannie Schrock's home. Planning and preparation for beginning a congregation progressed with careful and orderly thought. The group agreed upon a "fellowship of purpose" which included reasons for establishing a Mennonite congregation in Lebanon. They made agreements relating to the PCC and soon selected a pastor and a building site. In October 1956 they began regular Sunday morning services in temporary facilities until they moved into their unfinished building in 1958. By 1976 they had enlarged it with two major additions.[40]

On May 8, 1957, three days after East Fairview organized, Lebanon Mennonite Church organized with thirty-two charter members. Family names were Barber, Birky, Burkey, Dillon, Erb, Kanagy, Kauffman, Landis, Miller, Nofziger, Oswald, Schrock,

*Millard Osborne (1932-), early Lebanon pastor and editor of **Missionary Evangel** in the mid-1960s.*

Walker, White, Willems and Wittrig. The charter members came from nine congregations in Oregon, Idaho, Colorado, Nebraska, and Pennsylvania. Allen H. Erb was bishop and George Kauffman interim pastor. Kauffman and Erb served two years until Millard Osborne of Elkhart, Indiana, became half-time pastor in September 1959. Osborne, who had seminary training, also served half-time as chaplain of the Lebanon Community Hospital. During his tenure the congregation tripled its membership, completed its planned building program, and expanded its education and service efforts. In addition, Osborne edited *Missionary Evangel* for a number of years, until he moved to Kansas in 1970. Lebanon became one of the fastest-growing congregations in the PCC, attracting both community people and Mennonites moving to the area. Longtime members believed that prayer, loving acceptance of diverse people, and a focus on their unity in Christ formed the vital spiritual base for their early and continued growth. Membership had increased to 151 in 1976.[41]

Grants Pass Mennonite Church grew out of a vision for extending the borders of Christ's kingdom after a quarterly mission meeting at Sheridan on January 1, 1955. Sheridan members Berle McTimmonds, Howard Nice, and minister Max G. Yoder made several exploratory trips to the Grants Pass area in Oregon's southwestern Josephine County. In March, McTimmonds and Yoder purchased a sawmill at Selma, twenty miles southwest of Grants Pass on the famed Redwood Highway. Soon they moved to the area with their families. Stutzman, Berkey, and Coblentz families and others from Sheridan joined them, as did Elmer and Clysta McTimmonds, parents of Berle. At first the McTimmonds and Yoder families attended Fruitdale Church of the Brethren. However, when the other families arrived, they had Sunday and midweek meetings in their homes. Looking for a suitable location for a church building, they decided on Grants Pass rather than Selma. There was already a Baptist Church in Selma, which was only a small mill community, and they believed another church was not needed there. On the Sunday before Christmas 1957, the Mennonites moved into their unfinished building. In later years they added two annexes.[42]

On August 25, 1957, during the months in which the building was being constructed, the congregation organized at the Chris Coblentz home with thirty-one charter members. Family names were Byers, Coblentz, McTimmonds, Marner, Mitchell, Nice, Stutzman, and Yoder. They accepted Max Yoder as pastor and adopted a

Iris Yoder

Max G. Yoder (1915-), in his early years as pastor at Grants Pass.

constitution. About a year later Yoder was ordained bishop. He served as pastor until 1971, when he moved to Nampa, Idaho.

Grants Pass was far from other Oregon Mennonite congregations, farther even than Winston. The two congregations began semiannual fellowship meetings and meals in the late 1950s which continued into the early 1960s. For both, their isolation from other Mennonite communities made it more difficult to retain a Mennonite identity, and few Mennonite families found the more isolated communities attractive, compared with places such as Lebanon. Both Winston and Grants Pass prospered in their early years with strong leaders. Both experienced later decline. In the late 1960s and early 1970s, some families moved away, and some joined other denominations or dropped out of church completely. But a rapid new increase brought the Grants Pass membership to fifty-three in 1976.[43]

First Mennonite Church of McMinnville started with the five families of Sol Yutzy, John Ratzlaff, Amos Eash, Willard Byers, and Elmer Sharer. They wished for a Mennonite church in McMinnville, where they were employed and where their children attended school. They also thought there should be a Mennonite witness in the town. Ratzlaff, superintendent of the Rock of Ages Home for the Aged, about five miles out in the foothills of the Coast Range, thought a place of worship near the Home would be helpful.

After preliminary planning meetings early in 1957, they met for services at the Home and invited Paul E. Yoder, then a teacher at WMS, as minister. In the next months they located property in

McMinnville and prepared a meetinghouse which they first used on December 1, 1957, the date on which the congregation organized. Yoder was installed as pastor and twenty-nine members from neighboring congregations signed the charter that day. Oscar Wideman, a minister living in the area, then serving at the rescue mission in Portland, also provided leadership for some years. The charter remained open until June 1958 and included forty members. Family names were Beachy, Berkey, Brubaker, Byers, Detweiler, Eash, Eveleth, Hostetler, Kester, Lauber, Phoenix, Ratzlaff, Sharer, Smith, Sommers, Troyer, Wideman, Yoder, and Yutzy. In the 1960s they constructed a new building on their property.[44]

This congregation was organized at a time when undercurrents of ferment were moving within the PCC. Some of Sheridan's ordained men viewed the new congregation with misgivings—with reason. Sheridan was trying to withstand more liberal practices, and many participants at McMinnville preferred a less conservative position. Sheridan leaders feared that this more liberal nearby congregation would make it more difficult to hold Sheridan members to the old ways. Such proved true. A sizable number of early McMinnville members came from Sheridan. When Sheridan withdrew from the PCC about a decade later, some Sheridan members who wished to continue PCC relationships withdrew and joined McMinnville. Many of McMinnville's sixty-eight members in 1976 had family and historic ties with Sheridan, but the McMinnville historian thought that by then the two congregations viewed each other with mutual respect and goodwill.[45]

Plainview Mennonite Church was the last of the ten PCC congregations to organize in the 1950s in Oregon. It, like East Fairview, was a mission outreach of Fairview, and it, too, took its name from a school and community, located about ten miles south of Fairview. However, Plainview was a farming community, whereas East Fairview was a mill community. The Jake Roths had a well-established Sunday school going when Fairview took it over. The first Mennonite effort at Plainview was Fairview's summer Bible school in 1950. Attendance and interest increased in successive Bible schools. When Perry Schrock (that year's Bible school superintendent) and three other Fairview men canvassed the Plainview community, favorable response led them to begin a Sunday school there on June 21, 1953. A few months into the second year of the Sunday school, Gary and Mildred Knuths and Phil Nickel were baptized. Several other community people also became members in the next years. The group constructed a building in 1956 and a decade later built a major addition, which included a sanctuary. During the early years, George Kauffman, then living at Brownsville, six miles to the south, preached frequently at Plainview, before he began to serve at Lebanon. In the fall of 1958, Louis Landis moved from Filer, Idaho, to become pastor of Plainview. He served through January 1966 and again from 1971 through 1976.[46]

Plainview organized on June 28, 1959, with fifty-four charter members. Three were newly baptized and the others were from six congregations: Fairview, Albany, Sheridan, Filer, an Evangelical Mennonite Brethren church, and Grace Mennonite (Albany). Family names were Burkey, Conrad, Ernst, Heyerly, Jantzi, Knuths, Kropf, Landis, Parker, Ruckert, Schrock, Shank, Smucker, Stutzman, and Unrau. Plainview experienced generally steady growth, to 148 in 1974. The 1976 membership was 141. Plainview was well established by 1976, one of the more vigorous congregations in the PCC. Although its people were largely rural (thirteen being farmers), the majority of its members worked in industry, business, and service occupations.[47]

Not only did Oregon's ten new congregations feed the[7] ferment in the PCC in the 1950s; changes in older congregations, particularly in pastoral leadership, also contributed to it. In a decade when bishops still exercised significant power and authority, five congregations acquired new bishops. Most bishops strongly supported conservativism. Allen Erb took a moderately progressive stance. But in several congregations ministers also carried considerable influence. Albany invited David Mann, twenty-five years old and seminary-trained, in 1955. John Lederach, also seminary-trained, was the same age when he arrived at Zion in 1957. With Lebanon's Millard Osborne and Logsden's Roy D. Roth, four new leaders with professional training joined Oregon's leaders in facing issues brought by rapid change in their local and larger church and world. Of the four, three were still in their mid-twenties. In conference matters the new ministers served on influential conference committees along with older bishops and ministers. Before long Mann became assistant conference secretary and Lederach assistant moderator. Osborne and Roth arrived as the 1950s were ending. Their major contributions to the PCC began in the 1960s.[48]

Conference membership grew from 1,752 in 1950 to 2,186 in 1956. One hundred and fifty-one of the 1956 members were under thirteen years of age. Most of the members of new congregations simply took membership letters from their former congregations to their new ones, accounting for little change in actual numbers. By 1959 the membership had dropped slightly to 2,137.[49]

The revised 1953 PCC constitution and discipline did not stop the movement to more liberal practices, and concerned persons began to protest more forcefully. In 1958 Porter sent a letter to the executive committee, objecting strongly to "increasing liberal trends and practices." The PCC secretary wrote for clarification and the Porter minister and trustees cited "the cutting of women's hair in any amount, the wearing of jewelry including the wedding ring, the handling of congregational affairs in a community relationship, the taking part in politics as legal voters . . . television, etc." They believed that if "a sincere and vigorous effort to reestablish and maintain the Scriptural positions" in congregations failed, the conference should use "disciplinary action where necessary." If they observed no evident change by the end of 1959, they believed it necessary to withdraw their membership in the PCC, not wishing to be affiliated with "an organization which condones unscriptural conditions."[50]

To discuss the serious situation, PCC ordained leaders met in August 1959. After the reading of the section in the discipline about adornment, an open discussion focused on violations of the restrictions and what to do about the problem. One emphasized that both liberals and conservatives needed a revival of spiritual life, to observe the Word of God, not just past writings. Some believed that the Bible and the PCC discipline were not necessarily consistent on all points, while others felt that the discipline was biblical, without qualification. But what to do about members who trespassed was admittedly difficult. In response to calls for "disciplinary action," one elderly bishop stated that it was "an awful thing to put someone away from the church."[51]

The meeting produced no solution, and polarization widened. A letter from Tangent expressed sentiments similar to Porter's. Western requested that the PCC urge congregations to pray earnestly for disobedient members and to excommunicate persistent violators. The PCC responded to the appeals with respect and mutual concern and instructed the resolutions committee to draw up a "short resolution of appreciation" to the three congregations, in addition to one relating to the appeals. The latter lengthy resolution acknowledged trends within the brotherhood "contrary to [PCC] interpretation of God's Word" and restated the position of the PCC discipline. Another lengthy 1959 resolution referred to Max G. Yoder's conference sermon, "For in Him We Live and Move and Have Our Being." It emphasized the need for a personal relationship with Christ and an infilling of the Spirit, realizing that "the doctrines of the Word are not our doctrines but His."

But the appeals of concerned congregations and Yoder's emphasis on the centrality of Christ did not contain the ferment of the 1950s. All acknowledged the authority of the Bible, but individual interpretations increasingly differed from the expectations of the traditional conference community. The mixture of new congregations, of new emphases on evangelism and mission, and of younger, educated leaders spilled out of the conference discipline's carefully built structure of restrictions. The discipline was no longer a common wall capable of holding everyone together in uniform mass.[52]

Chapter 5
OMs: Division and Regrouping (1960-1976)

The fragile unity which had held together the Oregon congregations of the PCC since 1921 survived almost four decades before it gave way. It had reflected denominational emphases which emerged about the beginning of the twentieth century, as well as outside influences such as Protestant Fundamentalism. (Old) Mennonite leaders had promoted church authority vested in regional conferences and the denominational general conference, and their discipleship included a biblical literalism that bordered on legalism.

By the 1960s, some Mennonite scholars held different views. Church authority, for them, evolved out of the congregational community of faith, of members together studying the Bible and relying on Holy Spirit guidance to understand its meaning and application for their times. Discipleship meant following Jesus in obedience, love, and ways of peace—in unity of spirit more than uniformity of practice. Clearly, the two approaches permitted their adherents only an uneasy peace with frequent turbulence.

The schisms in the 1960s did not produce a single, unified alternate group. Just before the 1960 conference sessions, after earlier petitions for stronger discipline, Tangent and Porter quietly withdrew from the PCC. They strengthened associations with the Harrisburg congregation and eventually, with like-minded congregations in the Canadian Northwest, formed a loose alliance that acknowledged the authority of each congregation for itself. About the time Tangent and Porter withdrew, two ordained men with similar convictions, Joe Birky from Bethel and Willard L. Stutzman from Sweet Home, transferred to Harrisburg. Near the end of the 1960s, seven congregations (Sheridan, Bethel, Hopewell, East Fairview, Brownsville, Winston, and Fairview) withdrew from the PCC. They shared some concerns of Tangent and Porter, but their reasons were more diverse and they were less united among themselves. Their leaders generally supported the newly organized Bible Mennonite Fellowship, and some of them employed divisive rhetoric to promote their views. Many leaders in the later schisms wanted to conserve practices which the PCC discipline outlined, though they also differed theologically from PCC leaders. As the "Bible fellowship" terminology illustrates, they had come to rely more fully on Protestant Fundamentalism's particular formula for understanding the authority of the Bible. Other factors also contributed to their withdrawal.[1]

The concerns of the withdrawing congregations were not unique to the PCC. By the early 1950s, if not before, in other regional OM conferences in North America, letters, articles in old and new publications, visiting preachers, and informal discussions brought to the foreground issues such as those which concerned Oregon Mennonites. Tangent and Porter, along with other earlier movements away from regional conferences, emphasized personal piety and a conscientious observance of distinctly nonconformed living. They were more separatist, more congregational, less attached to the conference organization. Many leaders who withdrew in the later 1960s, while deeply concerned about "the drift" and lax discipline in the Mennonite church, held more dear their conference relationships, hoping and praying until they withdrew that less restrictive sister congregations might somehow return to earlier practices. Some of them initially hesitated to withdraw because it seemed a violation of conference authority, equal in substance if opposite in form from that of the liberal deviations from the discipline which so concerned them. But eventually leaders and congregations, attempting to live faithfully and grieving because their conferences did not support the practices and discipline they espoused, withdrew from the PCC and a number of other OM conferences.[2]

In Oregon, new congregations in the 1960s affected the balance of power within the PCC and produced greater tensions. But the steady growth in membership of the 1950s continued into the early decade following. Seven Oregon congregations joined the PCC in the 1960s, though by the end of the decade one of the seven had withdrawn. Several mission stations, Meadowbrook, Chapel in the Hills, and Maranatha, developed into independent congregations but did not join the PCC.

Brownsville Mennonite Church resulted from the vision of bishop Henry A. Wolfer. In May 1955 he moved from Sheridan to

Brownsville, about halfway between Lebanon and Harrisburg, to be nearer the Tangent congregation of which he had bishop oversight. In the previous month, Wolfer's strong interest in evangelism and mission, as well as his theological affinity with Fundmentalism's maxims for understanding the Bible, had caused him and other interested persons to organize the Full Gospel Tent Evangelism Association, of which he became chairman. The association purchased a used tent, chairs, songbooks, and other equipment. In June the association had a series of meetings at Lacomb, a small community fifteen miles northeast of Lebanon. They held the second series in July in the Brownsville city park, with Bible school in the daytime directed by Marcus and Leah Lind and staffed by teachers from nearby Mennonite congregations. Within several years Wolfer asked the Ralph Myers, Sr., Earl Baker, Jr., and Lloyd Kropf families from Brownsville and neighboring communities to help begin a congregation in Brownsville. Kropf had earlier been ordained a minister while serving for several years in a rescue mission in Sacramento, California.[3]

The congregation organized on April 10, 1960. The nineteen charter members had family names of Baker, Clay, Kropf, Myers, Paulus, Sills, and Wolfer. Wolfer was the pastor until he died in 1963; Kropf, the assisting minister. Several of the seven families were related. In October 1960 they bought the building they were using and later discussed constructing more adequate facilities, but by the end of 1976 they had not begun a building program. Membership then numbered fifty-six. From Brownsville's beginning, its leaders intended that it would hold to the traditional Mennonite teachings and practices which many were challenging. In the mid-1960s, Kropf became part of a "Concern Group" which later organized as Bible Mennonite Fellowship. Soon he urged Brownsville to withdraw from the PCC. Though Brownsville's bishop, E. S. Garber, shared many of Kropf's concerns, not until a second vote, in December 1968, did he agree to withdraw from the conference in which he had worked for over forty years.[4]

The Church in the Wildwood developed because a nine-year-old boy named Marvin and his foster parents, Alvin and Wilma Nisly, promoted having services in that small, unused meetinghouse located about six miles west of Grand Ronde (Indian) Agency on State Highway 22. Marvin had earlier attended Sunday school there. The Nislys spoke of it to Wilma's father, Sheridan bishop G. D. Shenk. A canvass of the area showed community interest in again having services in the building. In March 1952 the Nislys and other interested Sheridan members opened a Sunday school there. At first bishop Shenk usually preached in the Sunday services. But by 1957 the group wanted a resident minister. Joe and Adah Kropf had earlier served in rescue missions in Portland and Sacramento and attended Wildwood after returning to Oregon. Kropf became pastor in September 1958 and continued to serve in 1976. The church building was in poor repair when the Mennonites began using it, and by the second summer it was too small, as well. In the fall of 1953 they purchased a vacant schoolhouse adjacent to the church building and began using it for services, continuing to use the church and occasionally other nearby buildings for classes. In 1958 they constructed a new building adjoining the schoolhouse and later enlarged their facilities.[5]

On October 29, 1961, the Church in the Wildwood organized with forty-six charter members, with family names including Coblentz, Davies, Fry, Fuller, Krehbiel, Kropf, Moore, Nisly, Shenk, Sims, Smith, and Yoder. Membership reached fifty in 1972, and in 1976 it was forty-four. However, official membership records were "very loosely kept," according to Wilma Nisly, and were perhaps inaccurate. By 1976, although Wildwood had not yet withdrawn from the PCC, it functioned more as a community church, with persons from several denominations participating. It frequently shared in local interdenominational events and took offerings for nondenominational mission organizations.[6]

Salem Mennonite Church was the first PCC congregation to locate in a major Oregon city since services had begun in Portland almost forty years earlier. Salem was Oregon's capital city, third largest in the state, with a 1960 population of approximately 50,000, which almost doubled in the next fifteen years. Salem-area Mennonites had discussed starting a congregation as early as 1955, but nothing developed until January 1960, when eight families met at the Bernard Showalter home to again discuss the possibility. A few weeks later the Merlin Aeschliman, Leo King, Robert Lantz, Bernard Showalter, and Daniel Widmer families began regular weekly prayer meetings. By September 1961, when Wilbert R. Nafziger came from Winton, California, to be pastor, the group included at least ten families.[7]

After beginning a full congregational program in October 1961, they organized officially on November 12. Seven additional persons joined before charter membership closed, making forty-three members named Aeschliman, Becker, Byers, Hochstetler, Holderman, Hostetler, Kauffman, King, Lantz, Martin, Nafziger, Ratzloff, Shenk, Showalter, Widmer and Wolfer. In 1967 John E. Heyerly, seminary-trained, began a five-year term as pastor. In contrast to the professional pastors of other PCC congregations at that time, Heyerly was the only native of Oregon, though, like the others, he did not remain in Oregon. John Willems, his successor in 1973, began a long tenure which would extend well beyond 1976.

Salem soon became a vigorous congregation, moving in 1967 to a new building in the Keizer suburb north of Salem. From its beginning, Salem was a comparatively liberal alternative to the rural Western congregation, from which some of its members came. At times strained relationships occurred, as persons who transferred to Salem left deeply felt vacancies at Western. Although some WMS teachers became members at Salem, others offered their gifts and served in the Western congregation, and by 1976 relationships between the two congregations were open and respectful. Salem's membership was 101 in 1976 and included two farmers.[8]

Cascadia Mennonite Church, like Wildwood, began as a mission station. About thirteen miles east of Sweet Home on Highway 20, in the early 1940s Cascadia was a rapidly growing logging community, without a church. Sweet Home Mennonite Church conducted a summer Bible school there in 1944 and opened a Sunday school soon after. Within several years, Sweet Home ministers began to preach regularly at Cascadia. In 1961 Melvin Paulus, previously a licensed minister in the Brethren in Christ Church, was licensed for the ministry at Cascadia and ordained in 1964. The workers first used the Cascadia schoolhouse for services, then in 1946 they constructed a meetinghouse.[9]

Almost twenty years after the work began, on September 29, 1963, the Cascadia Mennonite Church organized with forty-three charter members. Family names were Cowan, Dimick, Horst, Howes, Hubler, King, Kropf, Paulus, Roth, Schlabach, and Zook. Apparently forty-three was the peak. Membership in 1976 was thirty-eight, including nonresident members. Paulus continued as pastor through 1976. Although he participated in Bible Mennonite Fellowship from its beginning, often as a leader, his congregation remained a member of the PCC. Many community families had moved closer to school and jobs at Sweet Home, and most people who attended services at Cascadia in 1976 lived at Sweet Home or even farther away.[10]

Eugene Mennonite Church developed in Oregon's second largest city, at the upper (southern) end of the Willamette Valley. Early Mennonites in the late 1800s seldom found good farmland nearby and most left before 1900. Later Mennonite families who moved to Eugene joined other denominations In 1960, several university students and their families—Wilbert and Juanita Shenk; Cliff, Hope, and Janet Lind; and Del and Lee Snyder—arrived and with Marlene Roth, another student, met occasionally for informal fellowship. Before the students left Eugene, Jack and Loretta Birky arrived in 1961. They were the first continuing Mennonite family. More Mennonite families moved to the area and in 1963 began to meet periodically for fellowship. In 1964 some of them began regular services. Twelve persons organized as a congregation on June 6, 1965, and several other couples joined Eugene's new MB congregation. Charter membership remained open until January 1967, with family names of Birky, Burkey, Corliss, Hershberger, Lind, Schantz, and Zehr. By then, three had already moved and transferred their membership elsewhere but others had joined. Cleo Mann from Indiana, (father of Albany pastor David) served as interim pastor for two years until June 1968, when Harold Hochstetler from Nampa came as pastor. Hochstetler continued as part-time pastor through 1976, serving also as part-time conference

Cliff Lind

Cleo Mann (1900-1978) and Harold Hochstetler (1922-), in 1968. Hochstetler followed Mann as pastor of Eugene Mennonite Church and later as conference minister.

minister beginning in the early 1970s. The group used the Four Oaks Grange Hall in West Eugene through 1976, with plans to construct a multipurpose facility the following year.[11]

Mobility and diversity of families and an informal membership style brought occasional profound stresses to the Eugene congregation. Many, including university students and their families, invigorated the congregation during their temporary participation but left large vacancies when they moved elsewhere. Often the students brought questions and idealism common to young people and challenged the congregation to cyclic self-examination. Unlike Salem, few Mennonites from other congregations lived close enough to join Eugene without changing occupations or homes. Some who did, for a time, soon left for a more rural Mennonite congregation to the north in place of Eugene's urban diversity. The 1976 membership was thirty-two, with about a third being nonresident or nonparticipating.[12]

Bethany Mennonite Church at Albany began as a division from nearby Fairview. In the early 1960s many Fairview members became dissatisfied with congregational leadership and related issues. Among them were some comparatively progressive members from longtime Fairview families, "natives" whose own leadership gifts were not accepted by Fairview's policy-makers. Others were "immigrants," persons somewhat on the fringes who had moved to Fairview a decade or two earlier from other states and had never become fully integrated into Fairview. What unified the thirty-some families who withdrew in the mid-1960s was a common desire for greater spiritual leadership. Their separation produced considerable tension but the PCC executive committee helped Fairview and the withdrawing group reach an official reconciliation by the end of 1965.

On May 29, 1966, Bethany organized with seventy-four persons. Others soon joined to make a total of eighty-one charter members. Family names were Beckler, Burkey, Eicher, Gerig, Grieser, Haima, Kuhns, Lais, Lehman, Leichty, Miller, Mitchell, Neuschwander, Nice, Nofziger, Ropp, Roth, Schmucker, Smucker, Stutzman, Widmer, and Wisseman. After using the Riverside Grange Hall for about a year, they moved into their new building on Spicer Road in August 1966. Soon after, David Groh of Baden, Ontario, Canada, came as pastor. In the PCC, Groh worked as editor of *Missionary Evangel,* and in other leadership positions until in 1975 he moved to Millersburg, Ohio.[13]

N. M. Birky (1888-1972), Fairview bishop; David Mann (1930-), Albany bishop; David Groh (1930-), who became Bethany pastor on October 1, 1966; and John M. Lederach (1932-), Zion bishop; at the May 29, 1966, chartering service of Bethany Mennonite Church in the Riverside Grange Hall.

Bethany membership increased to ninety-seven by 1968 and the congregation seemed off to a good start. But differences in expectations and understandings soon fractured Bethany's initial unity. In addition, the people had brought with them some unresolved problems. In the fall of 1968, members began drifting away, and by the summer of 1969 about a third had left. Most joined non-Mennonite congregations, with a few returning to Fairview or joining Plainview. At issue, on the surface, at least, was a differing approach among them to the Bible. Those leaving preferred a more fundamentalist, unquestioning approach to that of the pastor's broadly based hermeneutics and resulting social concerns.

Group dynamics also played a part. The natives and the immigrants had not become fully integrrated at Bethany even as they had not at Fairview. Most of the immigrants were related, most from Nebraska. Many who left in the late 1960s were immigrants. Even after this large exodus from Bethany, other problems faced the group. Some who remained favored traditional practices and procedures; others wished for more freedom and innovation. In the next years the people worked at problem-solving among themselves with varying degrees of success. After the membership dipped to a low of fifty-one in 1975, it increased to sixty-four in 1976.[14]

Corvallis Mennonite Church began as an intentional regrouping of members from Albany Mennonite Church. Corvallis, about fifteen miles southwest of Albany along the Willamette River, was the home of Oregon State University. As early as 1964, several Mennonite families living in the Corvallis area met occasionally for fellowship and prayer, but their hopes for a congregation did not mature at that time. Interest revived when in 1968 Albany considered "swarming"—starting a new congregation in a community without a Mennonite witness—as one possible answer to the problem of a crowded church building. A group which included some persons from the local community first met in January 1969 in the attractive but currently unused chapel on the grounds of the Children's Farm Home, several miles northeast of Corvallis on Highway 20.[15]

On September 14, 1969, Corvallis Mennonite Church organized with thirty-eight members. Some family names were Bergey, Bontrager, Buck, Gardner, Holderread, Jones, Kennel, King, Krehbiel, Shenk, Steiner, Stutsman, Whitaker, and Yoder. Three of the families lived in the immediate vicinity of the chapel. The congregation experienced frequent changes of pastors. Paul G. Burkholder, who had served thirteen years in a New York City pastorate and then completed three years of study at Eastern Mennonite College, came as the first one in 1970. Because of unfortunate conflicting expectations concerning the role and qualities of leader, he served only one year before moving to Pennsylvania. The membership, which had reached a high of sixty-five in 1971, dropped quickly after Burkholder left. Some members returned to Albany. Walter Hines, a Methodist minister, then served two and a half years, but his lack of commitment to the peace position produced unease among members and caused some to leave. In 1976, after several additional short-term leaders, George Kauffman agreed to a second short interim assignment. The membership at that time was fifty-three.[16]

The congregations which organized in the 1960s, and their leaders, influenced the PCC, but other congregations and leaders also played significant roles. In the early 1960s, when the position of bishop still carried considerable authority and power, six bishops were ordained. In 1960, Paul Yoder was ordained at McMinnville, David Mann at Albany, Verl Nofziger at Fairview, and John Lederach at Zion. In 1963, Harold Hochstetler was ordained at Nampa and Orie Roth at Sweet Home. Influential ministers new to the PCC included Marcus Smucker at Portland (1963), Paul Brun-

Gerald Brenneman

*George M. Kauffman (1907-   ),
retired from ministering in several
other Oregon congregations, pastored the Corvallis congregation
twice in the 1970s.*

ner at Zion (1966), and Eugene Garber at Sweet Home (1969). All
except Nofziger had some level of advanced professional or biblical
training. None except Nofziger led congregations which later withdrew from the PCC.[17]

In the late 1950s and in the 1960s the balance of power in
the PCC was gradually shifting from the older, native-born leaders
to younger ministers, most of them coming from east of the Rockies with college or seminary training. They were energetic and
articulate, and they soon moved into positions of influence on PCC
committees and boards. At conferences, retreats and camps, they
brought fresh ideas and new but respectful approaches to the
Bible, to the church, to living as Christians. They emphasized commitment to Christ above conformity to a constitution and discipline. They nurtured a greater diversity of convictions and
permitted increasing departures from the PCC discipline. The
younger leaders, like their elder peers, ascribed full authority to
the Bible but they differed on how to determine its authority.

The two groups often used the same words but gave them different meanings. Mutual respect between those who differed
deteriorated rather than improved. To the older, more traditional
leaders, "dedication to faithful living and believing it" meant holding their people firmly to the conference discipline. The PCC thus
became a restless, moving mosaic. Bright spots of caring, coopera-

tion, and respect interspersed dark streaks of anger, resentment, and accusations. Separation loomed closer, and by the time Corvallis had organized, several congregations had already withdrawn from the PCC.

The most controversial issue in the PCC continued to be an increasing deviation from the 1953 discipline. Short hair on the women, the omission of the prayer veiling, and the wearing of jewelry (including the wedding ring) were most consistently mentioned. Ministerial garb also received considerable attention. As before, some leaders hoped that a new discipline might reverse the trends. Others hoped for a document that would reflect contemporary understandings. In 1965 the executive committee appointed a committee of five to begin the process of revising the constitution and discipline. For the first time, the committee included two laypersons, Timothy Strubhar and Ben Kenagy. Instead of simply drafting a new constitution to present to delegates, the committee included congregations in the initial study and discussion about the church, authority, unity, and change.[18]

In the midst of that process PCC leaders who wished to conserve past practices were consolidating their strength. They felt the appeals they made as a "Concern Group" were taken lightly and they began to meet together to plan a future course, turning to men outside the PCC for support and assistance. Sanford Shetler and J. Otis Yoder, Mennonite writers and leaders from Pennsylvania in sympathy with the Concern Group, visited Oregon amid the fears of denominational and conference leaders that they could be facilitating a break with the PCC. For years a few Oregon Mennonites had received and read *The Sword and Trumpet*, a militantly dissenting journal to which both Yoder and Shetler contributed. Probably more were receiving Shetler's newer *Guidelines for Today*, a bit less scholarly and more popular in style. Both periodicals reflected the influence of Protestant Fundamentalism and took a conservative position on theology, doctrine, and practice, in line with the concerns of the Oregon group. Yoder, Shetler, and the two journals helped the Oregonians focus on issues.[19]

Before the June 1966 conference sessions, the Concern Group initiated the process that would eventually divide the PCC. About twenty ministers from ten congregations, with Raymond Mishler as chairman and Melvin Paulus as secretary, prepared an appeal to the PCC. They believed that some PCC and churchwide leaders were promoting ideas and practices contrary to God's

Word. They requested that the PCC withdraw from the larger (old) Mennonite general conference "and adhere to the doctrines stated" in the PCC constitution and discipline. Without corrective steps, they might consider "a peaceable separation."[20]

Before the February 1967 special delegate session to consider the issues, the Concern Group prepared a refined paper. Its six points stated the group's position on the Word of God, on the Confession of Faith, on worldliness, on the prayer veiling, on church and state, and on the ecumenical movement. With language strongly similar to Protestant Fundamentalism, it upheld the "plenary and verbal inspiration of the Bible as the Word of God . . . relevant to every age and culture." The group's paper also endorsed the Dordrecht Confession of Faith and the 1963 Mennonite Confession of Faith and lamented not only the "continual disregard" of the PCC constitution and discipline but also "unwholesome and negative attitudes expressed toward those who attempt to uphold" them. It referred to immodesty and "indecent exposure of the body," jewelry, cut hair for women, and worldly amusements. It noted with concern that many women did not wear the prayer veiling consistently or at all.

There were also overtones of national politics and social upheaval. Separation of church and state, the paper stated, included refusal to "engage in carnal warfare or the use of force," but called Christians to pray for government and obey it when so doing did not conflict with God's Word. However, the statement opposed denominational letters to the government about capital punishment and involvement in the Vietnam War. It opposed engagement in civil rights activism and the Mennonite trend toward involvement in politics. It equated denominational membership in national or world councils of churches and certain other organizations with the unequal yoke because there was not "agreement in faith and practice" on the earlier issues the paper addressed.[21]

The February 25, 1967, special delegate session was the watershed which separated the Concern Group from the PCC. The delegates decided by a two-to-one vote not to withdraw from the larger (old) Mennonite general conference. They did accept by almost as strong a margin the recommendation that conference "take steps to bring an adherence to the doctrines and restrictions" of the discipline. However, they also adopted a motion that this action not affect the work of the conference constitution committee.

This essentially stripped the "adherence" recommendation of meaning and authority. Already talk was circulating about possibly substituting the 1963 Mennonite Confession of Faith for a detailed conference discipline. The Concern Group considered this inadequate, in spite of their statement about the 1963 document being "practical and relevant."[22]

The suggested "separation" in the Concern Group's 1966 appeal to the PCC was no idle threat. Within the year after the February 1967 meeting, Sheridan, Bethel and Hopewell withdrew. East Fairview and Brownsville followed in 1968. By December 1967, five executive officers had established a nonprofit organization, the Bible Mennonite Fellowship (BMF). On or before January 20, 1968, they began periodic meetings welcoming all who were sympathetic to their concerns. The leaders drafted a confession of faith and a constitution and discipline. They provided an application for membership in BMF which either congregations or individuals could submit to the executive committee for approval.[23]

Alongside all of this, the PCC constititon revision committee continued to work in a collaborative rather than an authoritarian process. Much delegate discussion favored the move toward a conference overseer instead of continuing with traditional bishops. And most favored using the 1963 Mennonite Confession of Faith as an adequate statement of doctrine and practice instead of developing a separate discipline. The committee planned to present a third draft of the constitution at the June 1968 conference.[24]

Moving into the time line of the PCC constitution revision, the new BMF scheduled a May 4, 1968, meeting regarding their alternate constitution, which was in essence a restatement of the 1953 PCC constitution and discipline. They had circulated it to all PCC congregations, not just those that had already withdrawn. The conference secretary considered this "a direct affront" not only because they had circulated it without any reference to the constitution revision already in progress but also because the PCC executive committee had already scheduled a May 4 ministers' meeting. Now ministers would have to choose between the two meetings. Apparently PCC leaders spoke to BMF leaders about the conflicting schedule, for BMF rescheduled its meeting to May 11.[25]

When conference delegates in June 1968 began a process that finalized the adoption of a new constitution that December, the break between the conference and the fellowship became complete. At the June 1969 sessions, the PCC implemented the constitution, and boards and committees changed. A resolution noted that now was the time to "take stock" of the present conference position, not to be totally "problem-oriented, but goal-oriented," to move forward optimistically with Christ.

The schisms of the 1960s had not yet ended, however. In the next months, late in 1969, taking stock included receiving notice from Fairview of its withdrawal. Within the next year Winston followed. They shared concerns of the congregations that withdrew earlier, but their decisions came after the denominational general conference met at Turner, Oregon, in 1969. There a few young men known as draft resisters, conscientiously opposed to Selective Service registration for the military draft, presented their position. Their long hair and carefree attire reminded many people of the current "hippie" counterculture movement. Fairview and Winston, attempting to hold their own youth to more established practices, did not approve the respectful official hearing the draft resisters received from general conference and, in protest, withdrew from its affiliated PCC. In spite of these last withdrawals, the 1969 conference theme, "Forward with Christ in Total Commitment," remained a worthy goal.[26]

Conference membership in the 1960s reflected both the withdrawals of some congregations and the emergence and growth of others. In 1960, after Tangent and Porter withdrew, membership was 2,260. An all-time peak of 2,435 in 1965 remained, with only slight losses, for the next two years. Even after additional congregations withdrew, others that remained were growing, and the net loss was smaller than the actual membership of the withdrawing congregations. In 1970 PCC membership was 1,935.[27]

Was there more to the schisms of the 1960s than the issues articulated in the Concern Group's statements? Not all issues that lead to schisms can be clearly defined. Beliefs about what is right do not exist in a vacuum, but within interacting thoughts and emotions of people. Such interaction can influence even what persons regard as unchanging beliefs in ways they do not recognize. How persons interact with each other and how this influences perceptions of issues cannot usually be measured. Often it cannot be documented, except by the observations of thoughtful people. One aged Oregon bishop who had experienced a major church schism in his youth observed that "as usual, personalities [were] intruding."[28]

The shifting balance of power from older, untrained leaders

to younger, educated ones strongly influenced the schisms of the 1960s. In 1964 Lebanon's young pastor, Millard Osborne, became editor of *Missionary Evangel*. In his editorials he wrote about the need to keep basic principles of belief but to adapt practice to keep pace with the times. He condemned faultfinding and criticism and increased the definition of foul language to include hateful and injurious words. He thanked God for older, experienced ministers but reminded them that they must earn the respect of younger ministers. He mentioned self-righteousness and lack of love within the PCC, wondering if love was not more needful than sound doctrine. Some PCC leaders thought he was intentionally needling the conservatives and requested that he stop writing editorials. But he continued until he moved from Oregon in 1970, preferring open communication to closed silence.[29]

It is understandable that older ministers or those with little formal training could feel threatened, particularly when the newcomers brought new ways of studying the Bible. They looked beyond the King James text to consider literary forms and historical and cultural contexts. They talked about Hebrew or Greek texts and which English versions were most accurate. The customary practice of taking the King James Version as God's clear and complete Word to his people was thus in danger. The power of the older leaders was decreasing Some of their long-held teachings about Christian conduct were deemphasized or disregarded and their interpretations of the Bible were being challenged. Thus, their grief and pain need surprise no one. Feelings of personal rejection mingled with their defense of the faith.

Denominational trends provided them little comfort. Mennonite colleges and seminaries and publications all seemed to be in line with the young pastors from east of the Rockies. Their own young people, too, returned from Mennonite colleges with similar modern ideas. Even the visits to Oregon of respected denominational leaders such as J. C. Wenger and Paul Erb did not bring reassurance to those who saw no alternative but to leave the conference. Erb, after being in Oregon in 1968, wrote to a bishop who had withdrawn shortly before. He expressed regret that they did not meet on this visit and wondered if the few points on which they disagreed would seem that important when they sat down together in heaven.[30]

The two groups thought and spoke in differing styles. Communication seemed impossible. For the one group, to question a time-honored belief was heretical. For the other, valid beliefs could withstand honest questions. The one group acknowledged only one way of rightly understanding the Bible, leaving little room for another point of view. The other approached the Bible reverently, but with study skills unfamiliar and threatening to the first group, and requested that those who differed in interpretation still respect each other. The one group vigorously defended their position as a biblical "contending for the faith." The other considered such strong statements judgmental, lacking in love, and divisive. Accusations and rumors darkened the picture, causing individuals from one congregation whose pastor led the Concern Group to ask younger ministers in the conference if they believed in the resurrection, the blood atonement, and the inspiration of Scriptures, because they had been told over the pulpit that the younger men did not. One of the accused thought such statements so absurd as to hardly merit a response.[31]

As Bible Mennonite Fellowship began a schedule of annual conferences, speakers gave reasons justifying their separation. One spoke of the apostasy, deception, and false teachings within the PCC. He considered that the BMF had not left the conference, but the conference had left them by departing from its own discipline. Another speaker emphasized that God is the author of division. An out-of-state preacher referred to unspecified church leaders who were preaching false doctrines. Persons who did not support the BMF found such statements appalling.[32]

Neither side was free from fault, as a thoughtful, mild-mannered layperson sympathetic with the BMF noted in reply to an observer at the first annual fellowship meeting. The sympathizer thought that while the BMF might give the impression that it was the herald of truth and that the PCC was far out of line, one might get the same kind of picture from the observer's critical questions. Frequently we are guilty of that which we condemn in others, he noted. Having worked on similar committees on both sides, he judged that neither side was getting to the basic issue: that carnality seemed about as evident on one side as the other, with both lacking genuine Christian love. Even so, he noted a genuine spiritual interest and concern on both sides.

The striking thing to him was that people could be so discriminating about the faults of others and so blind to their own. He wrote of the tendency to read into what other people say things they may never have intended, and he expected that the more educated should be more able to overlook such deficiencies in the less educated, otherwise the value of education would be contradicted. "An offended brother is harder to be won than a stalled ox," he wrote, and he supposed that some persons must confess to helping offend others. The real issue enabling me to help my fellow Christian, he concluded, is not whether I am right and my brother is wrong, but whether I am yielded and filled with God's Spirit so there is no controversy in my heart with anyone.[33]

Angry rhetoric, even if righteously angry, released words that could be recalled no more than could feathers. People on both sides created the flutter.

During the 1960s, as the lines were being drawn, ministers Max G. Yoder and Harold Hochstetler emerged as men in the middle. Younger than the older leaders but older than the young ones, both were men of the West who had come to the conference as young men. Both had been called to the ministry from within conference congregations, not from outside the conference. Neither was a trained, professional preacher, though Hochstetler did complete a college study program in several stints after his ordination. Both had roots in families or congregations sympathetic with the BMF, though they both brought openness and acceptance to newer ways of working and to younger, trained leaders. Each had served as conference moderator for several years. Their leadership and church statesmanship helped provide stability and renew confidence within the conference amid the turbulence encircling the schisms.[34]

Few were able to straddle the line and keep a foot in both camps. Marcus Lind, another man of the West from his childhood, was one who did. A longtime worker in the PCC, Lind was older than Yoder and Hochstetler. Unlike most of the leaders in the Concern Group, he had professional training. He had been a schoolteacher for much of his adult life and taught at Western Mennonite School until he retired in the winter of 1975-76. He shared many of the concerns of the BMF, and its leaders were his dear and respected friends.

Though Lind sympathized with them, he did not lead or follow them in their withdrawals. From 1955 to 1970, he served on the conference executive committee all but four years, five times as moderator. During the 1970s others provided conference leadership, but he continued to participate faithfully in conference sessions. Although he moved increasingly in more conservative circles and occasionally spoke at BMF conferences, he remained in the PCC through 1976.[35]

The conflicts of a church schism may leave permanent scars, but people can and do experience God's healing touch. After the schisms, relationships among Oregon Mennonites could not be the same as in former years, but people among them were committed to nurturing respect and love even in the aftermath of the painful rending of the conference. And people did find a new peace after the division. In fact, Marcus Lind believed that afterward there was more peace and unity between the conference and fellowship people than before they parted ways. Respite from the earlier conflict brought a sense of relief, an opportunity to focus on needs and challenges that had been neglected earlier. Two organizations also permitted more persons to serve as leaders. As the pain of the initial rent healed, persons in both organizations began to establish new levels of contact with earlier co-workers and friends. And although they did not agree on how to understand the authority of the Bible, both groups continued to acknowledge the Bible as authoritative.[36]

For the PCC, the 1970s began as a period of attempted stabilization amid efforts to respond biblically to unprecedented change. With the implementation of the conference minister model of oversight in 1970, with the denominational restructuring in 1971 and its emphasis on congregations, and with the development of interconference denominational regions, the 1968 constitution soon became outdated. Frequent amendments preceded a major, low-keyed revision in 1976.

New issues and new approaches to old emphases vied for attention. Worship, evangelism, the Holy Spirit, race relations, family life, divorce and remarriage, war taxes, world hunger, and related issues came to the foreground in conference sessions and other meetings. Urbanization and increasing affluence brought new ways of understanding how to live one's faith daily. The place of women in the church was emerging as an issue by 1976, but how the conference would accept women's spiritual gifts remained unclear.[37]

Changes in ways of thinking and working also became evident. Goal setting became common. An emphasis on improved communication introduced new ways of speaking and acting. Modern educational and psychological lingo and activities became common in the church, as persons gave input more often and sermons or speeches less frequently. Workshops, role play, group process, and other types of interaction attempted to involve people more fully in the thinking and decision-making. Along with the varied issues and ways of working came questions about identity. Whereas earlier generations of Mennonites had emphasized sacrificial self-giving, in the 1970s a societal emphasis on self-fulfillment slipped into the church. More people began to question their personal identity and how to feel satisfied and happy about themselves. Harold Hochstetler, 1975 conference moderator, referred to a "continuing identity crisis with its painful feelings of irrelevance." He thought the first priority for his listeners ought to be "[affirming] one another as brethren," but he also called for "responsible involvement in various activities" of the day.[38]

Influential persons in the PCC, both ordained and lay, helped the conference respond to the new issues and adopt the changing procedures of the 1970s. Pastors coming to congregations from distant states contributed immeasurably to the conference and its needs, and several completed a decade or more of service in Oregon. But after a time, all moved east for further study or new assignments. Three long-term pastors left their congregations in 1970: David Mann (Albany), Roy D. Roth (Logsden), and Millard Osborne (Lebanon). Paul Brunner completed nine years at Zion in 1975. Two of the congregations called pastors from east of the Rockies. Nelson E. Kauffman, retired long-term worker with the Mennonite Board of Missions, served Albany as interim pastor for two years before James M. Lapp of Pennslvania became Albany's pastor in 1972. John P. Oyer from eastern Colorado came to Zion in 1975. Other congregations called Oregon men in 1974: Alfred Burkey to Logsden, and Richard Headings to Lebanon. Both had previously been teachers and Headings had attended seminary. Gifted pastors in a number of congregations offered strong leadership, but major stability and continuity in the conference came from Max Yoder and Harold Hochstetler, the pastors who had emerged in the 1960s as the men in the middle. They would continue as pastors and conference leaders well beyond 1976 and eventually retire in their native West.[39]

Although no congregations joined the conference in the 1970s before the 1976 centennial year ended, several which had emerged earlier became member congregations later. Several families in central Oregon began meeting together for worship and fellowship in 1974. By 1976 Lynford Hershey was accepted by the conference as pastor of this soon-to-be-organized Ranch Chapel congregation near Culver. Early in the 1970s independent mission work began among Spanish-speaking people in Woodburn. Eventually it resulted in a conference-related congregation there.

Conference membership reports in the 1970s reflected several emphases. One concerned evangelism, mission, and growth. After the 1970 drop to 1,935 members, a steady gain throughout 1973 suggested that evangelism and mission effort had succeeded somewhat. That year the membership reached 2,073, including 156 members in Mexico, the result of mission efforts there. The next year the membership of 1,917 showed a loss of more than 150 members, but it reflected a second emphasis, on a more accurate reporting of members. Attempts to face issues openly and communicate more clearly, calls to increasing commitment, and efforts by some congregations to clarify the meaning of church membership cleared their membership books of persons who no longer participated. In 1976 the PCC had 1,898 members in twenty congregations plus Mexico, where there were ninety-eight members. The three Idaho congregations had 292 members, the seventeen in Oregon, 1,508.[40]

■ ■ ■

By 1976 many changes had come to the PCC in its fifty-five years since AM and OM congregations had merged in 1921. The tensions of the 1920s had opened springs of differences which fed underlying currents of disagreement and dissension. Sometimes the undercurrents merged with calm waters and at other times they drew people toward opposite banks. Concern for sound theology in the 1930s purged the conference of heretical views and suppressed questions. Persons who could not contain their questions or subscribe to the approved theological positions usually left.

Maintaining sound theology in the 1930s smoothed the way for the fortitude and fervor of the 1940s. Conference congregations held fast to traditional practices even while expanding into institutional and mission programs. As the institutions grew and mission congregations emerged, and as more Mennonites adopted attire and ways of life common in the larger society, deviations from the conference discipline produced a lively ferment in the 1950s. Differing convictions among Oregon people about the authority of the discipline, amplified by an influx of energetic, trained young pastors, contributed to the schisms of the 1960s. In the early 1970s, the conference was experiencing a new stability. Though somewhat shaky at times as new issues bombarded it, the new stability rested on a broad unity of commitment to Christ as members of the Mennonite church, with individuals working out the details in their small or large communities of faith. The new unity fostered relationships of respect and love and gave the authority of biblical interpretation earlier claimed by the conference to congregations and, to a larger degree, to individuals.

During the first century of (old) Mennonites in Oregon, the tension between individualism and the church community, between personal rights and church authority, though relaxed at times, generally held tight among PCC members. Even though individuals in earlier years had ventured into forbidden pursuits, they acknowledged the authority of their church community to define the terms of their participation in it. When they sinned against God and defied church standards, confession and repentance restored them to the church. By 1976, individuals were still defining authority in terms of the church, but the church was not so much its preachers as it was all its people.

At the same time, individuals claimed far greater authority for their own standards and practices than Mennonites of a century earlier had done. Often loyalties were divided between the church community and competing collectives created by employment, recreation, nationalism, or militarism. Yet, in the midst of increasing individualism, "intentional" communities, both in the church and in larger society, sprang up. The perpetual pull for PCC Mennonites between individualism and their church community reflected the paradox that only within the community, the body of Christ, could they really be individual disciples of Christ.

Chapter 6
Smaller Mennonite and Related Groups in Oregon

Other Mennonite groups, in addition to the largest group of merged Amish Mennonites (AM) and (old) Mennonites (OM), also settled in Oregon. Of the Swiss Mennonites, a small group remained unaffiliated. Most joined Waldo Hills/Emmanuel, which affiliated with the General Conference Mennonite Church (GC). Some of the Russian Mennonites, too, became GC. Mennonite Brethren (MB); Evangelical Mennonite Brethren (EMB); Old Order Amish (OOA); Church of God in Christ, Mennonite (Holdeman) (CGC); and Brethren in Christ (BIC) were among Oregon's other small groups. A few later, unaffiliated congregations had historic relationships to the OMs.[1]

For most of the groups, their sense of community was congregational. But they also related to regional or denominational organizations. Some practiced congregational autonomy, vesting authority more in local bodies of believers than in regional conferences or denominational policy. Other groups relied more heavily on visiting denominational leaders, who promoted commitment to distinctive practices or emphases. Those more conservative in practice emphasized more the claims of their church community than did the less restrictive groups, which allowed more individualistic expressions of faith. At the same time, however unconsciously, most groups also accepted elements of competing theologies or movements. All groups had to consider the degree to which such competing collectives as well as individual ideas and practices would be subject to or allowed to supersede those which the church community held as biblical.

Swiss Mennonites

Oregon's first Mennonite settlers in 1876, Christian C. and Magdalena Wenger and John and Elizabeth Lichty, were Swiss

Mennonites, so known because they or their families had emigrated directly from Switzerland to Ohio without living for a generation or more in the German Palatinate. Those who came to Oregon in 1877 included families or individuals named Geiger, Geiser, Neuenschwander, Lichty, and Steffen—all from Wayne County— and the John Heyerly family from Allen County. This totaled fourteen Mennonite members, according to Wenger. Apparently not all who came were baptized members. A number of single men did not become Mennonites. Within ten years, others named Mueller, Beutler, Biery, Beer, Beugli, Dapp, Amstutz, Blosser, Gerber, Sutter, and Steiner joined the community. In 1889-1890, another group of families came, some of them from France and southern Germany. Some of these family names were Ramseyer, Rich, Wenger, Martins, Roth, and a large Gerig family. In 1896, Jacob, Joseph and Chris Riegsecker—AMs from Archbold, Ohio—went to Oregon to look for gold but worked instead in a prune orchard. Two were later buried in the Swiss Mennonite cemetery. Other family names, before or soon after 1900, were Herr, Sommers, Hofstetter, Kauffman, Moser, Meyers and Welty. Some earlier settlers may have lived from their birth at Sonnenberg in eastern Ohio or in another conservative, established Swiss Mennonite community in America. Many, including most of the 1889-1890 group, had immigrated recently and settled briefly in less conservative communities in Ohio, Kansas, Michigan, Indiana, or Wisconsin before moving to Oregon.[2]

The Swiss Mennonites settled east of Salem in what became known as Dutch Flats or in rolling hill country near Silverton. This area may have attracted them because it was much advertised as the American Switzerland. The community, known as Switzerland by 1883, was given its own post office about five miles southwest of Silverton in 1887. Ten years later the name was changed to Enger. A year later, to avoid confusing it with Eugene, it was reportedly the Mennonites who renamed it Pratum.[3]

Life for these people had both joys and disappointments. Mrs. Sam Beutler was so elated to discover the first apple in their young orchard that she kissed it. Gottlieb Meyers carried a basketful of eggs to Salem to sell, then had to carry them home again because he found no market. They would have broken had he taken them by wagon on the corduroy road. Young Peter Steffen said that the only way he could look out from his home was straight up—timber blocked his view all around.[4]

Christian C. Wenger, writing soon after the earliest Mennonites arrived, desired most an organized church with a minister. He felt that their greatest need was a minister and feared that without one they would be "scattered." He trusted, however, that the Lord would send those who would preach "his word in truth," and he pleaded that any minister visiting Oregon would not forget to stop by. In March 1879, GC missionary S. S. Haury and itinerant minister J. B. Baer stopped briefly in Oregon, en route to Alaska. But perhaps they were not the sort of Mennonites Wenger had in mind.[5]

Wenger had also written to elders of the Apostolic Christian Church (ACC) in Lewis County, New York, another religious group with Swiss origins, inquiring about their beliefs. In 1879 ACC elder Peter Virkler traveled across the continent just to visit Wenger, and Wenger and his wife became the first in Oregon to accept baptism in the ACC. This church, led by Samuel H. Froehlich, had begun in 1832-1835 in Switzerland. Dissatisfied Mennonites composed one group in the first congregation, at Langnau in the Emmental. In 1847, under the ministry of an associate of Froehlich, Amish Mennonites in Lewis County, New York, began the first ACC congregation in North America, and a year later Swiss immigrant families founded a congregation at Sardis, Ohio. By 1860, during C. C. Wenger's youth, an ACC elder had established a congregation in Wayne County, Ohio, where Wenger lived. There families divided over whether to stay Mennonite or become Apostolic Christian. In many other areas, including Illinois, which became the American center of the group, ACC leaders proselytized Mennonites.[6]

What attracted Wenger away from his Mennonite faith, soon after he moved to Oregon? More than did the Swiss Mennonites, the ACC emphasized a warm piety and a definite salvation experience. Baptism by immersion was a central doctrine. With Wenger yearning for preaching services and wanting to practice his faith conscientiously, the ACC elder who visited Oregon ahead of Swiss Mennonite bishop C. B. Steiner won Wenger over. After Wenger's "repentance and baptism, he severed all connections . . . with the Mennonite church," according to Ernest K. Werner, an Apostolic spokesman. Other early Swiss Mennonites worshiped with the Apostolic people occasionally, or even regularly for a time, and some joined. Several, including 1876 immigrants John and Elizabeth Lichty and an infant child, were buried in the Apostolic Church cemetery, but family tradition says that Lichty and his son

Alexander,, who also attended services, were not ACC members.[7]

The developing relationship between Oregon's Swiss Mennonites and the emerging ACC congregation greatly concerned Mennonite bishop C. B. Steiner of Wayne County, Ohio. He made his first visit to Oregon in the fall of 1880. Perhaps on that visit he ordained Christian Geiger as minister and organized a congregation. Steiner visited Oregon again in 1883 and 1884, baptizing persons both times, including John Beer, age twenty-five, in 1884. Several days later he ordained Beer as minister, Christian Geiger as bishop, and Peter Neuschwander as deacon.

After his 1883 trip, Steiner planned to move to Oregon, and in March 1884 he sold his farm for $2000, two-thirds of what he had paid for it in 1856. But the buyer backed out of the bargain, and in March 1885 Steiner resold it, this time for only $1500. Perhaps he thought he could recoup his losses by buying comparatively inexpensive land in Oregon. However, the need of Oregon's Swiss Mennonites for stronger spiritual leadership probably motivated him more.

In April 1885, Steiner, almost sixty years old, his wife, Catherine, and most of their unmarried and married children moved to Oregon. The Mennonites Steiner ministered to were scattered geographically. Those unable to buy the more expensive, developed land had to buy or rent less-developed land, six, ten, twelve, or more miles from other Mennonites. Meeting to worship in a pre-automobile era with primitive roads was a major undertaking, and they first met monthly, in homes. Later they met biweekly.[8]

The Swiss Mennonites gradually grouped according to conservative or progressive views. The influx of families in 1889-1890, which included minister John Rich, strengthened the progressive element. Rich immediately stepped into leadership apart from Steiner and his fellow ministers. In the fall of 1889 he obtained permission to use a German Reformed building in the neighborhood, vacant because dwindling membership had caused the congregation to disband. At first Rich preached there monthly, later twice a month, walking the ten miles from his home in Salem. Lutherans and Reformed people joined the progressive Mennonites for their services. For a few months the conservative group, becoming known as the C. B. Steiner Church, also used the building. Rich asked to take turns preaching with Steiner, Geiger, and Beer, but they refused because they regarded Rich as too liberal. In 1890, the Steiner group invited the progressive Mennonites to attend their Good Friday service, called a "Discipline Meeting." At the close of the service, the bishop read a paper outlining church regulations which among other things forbade Sunday school, singing school, and the wearing of mustaches. The progressive group could not accept such restrictions, and a clear break occurred. The more liberal group began meeting for services every Sunday, rather than biweekly. About two months later they organized the Waldo Hills congregation.[9]

The C. B. Steiner Church with its ten families resumed meetings in their homes for several years. Those who lived farthest away often came to the host home on Saturday evening. Women and children slept on beds on the floor, and the men in the barn. There were two services on Sunday, morning and afternoon, with the host family serving a light lunch at noon. Each family brought its own German songbook, with singing before and after the long sermon. Once, about 1892, when services were to be held at the Peter Neuschwander home in Brooks, the food for the Sunday lunch mysteriously disappeared during Saturday night. Discarded and scattered containers in the field between the house and the nearby railroad tracks pointed to the probability that some transients ("hobos") had helped themselves to a good supper. So two young men went to Salem on Sunday morning to buy food.[10]

The Steiner Church had fraternal relationships with OM and AM congregations but remained unaffiliated. (Old) Mennonite David Garber visited in 1899 and convinced the congregation to observe foot washing at communion services. The women wore black prayer caps, a sort of scarf tied under the chin. A few years later an elderly widow from this group who married a man from the Fairview AM congregation had to take off her black scarf and wear a white covering before she could commune there.[11]

Between 1893 and 1895 the Steiner group built a meetinghouse one-and-a-half miles from Pratum on an acre of land donated by John Heyerly, Sr. But they did not use it long. People called it the Cemetery church, because it was beside the cemetery which both Mennonite groups used. Their number decreased when a few joined the Waldo Hills congregation. Several, including John Heyerly, Jr., and his wife's family, the Peter Neuschwanders, moved to Linn County and joined the AM congregation there. About the time Steiner died in 1903, the remaining families moved to Clackamas County about twelve miles east of Hubbard. Also about that time, between 1900 and 1907, they tore down their building, and the Waldo Hills congregation took over the cemetery. The C. B. Steiner Church then again held monthly services in their homes, using the German language and Swiss dialect, with special instruction for new members before baptism but still with no Sunday school. Besides bishop Geiger and minister Beer of their own group, visitors who preached for them at times included Peter Christner and Mose Miller. Geiger died in 1913, Beer in 1928. After Beer's death, the remaining members disbanded and united with Zion (at Hubbard) and congregations of other denominations.[12]

General Conference Mennonite Church (GC)

Oregon Mennonites had only loose relationships with the General Conference Mennonite Church (GC) before the 1890s, though most early settlers who became GC had GC contacts in the Midwest or Great Plains before coming to Oregon. While those east of Salem were mostly Swiss Mennonites, those who settled at Dallas were largely Russian Mennonites of the immigration that began in 1870s. Three of Oregon's four GC congregations that began in the twentieth century, before 1976, had roots in OM congregations. Although the GC denomination allowed greater individual freedom than the OM church did, GC people in Oregon also relied on community support and guidance from their congregations and conference.[13]

The more progressive Swiss Mennonites, with John Rich as minister, invited John B. Baer, the GC traveling preacher, to help them start a Sunday school and church. On Pentecost Sunday, May 25, 1890, after having meetings for a week or more, Baer organized the Waldo Hills congregation at Pratum. Some of the thirty-two persons considered to be charter members joined several years after Waldo Hills organized. Some family names were Amstutz, Beutler, deVries, Gerber, Gerig, Herr, Meyer, Muller, Rich, Sommer, Stauffer, Steffen, and Steiner. Several had previously belonged to the Reformed Church and were baptized as adults before becoming members. Rich did not continue long as pastor, because in 1894 he accepted rebaptism (immersion) from Pastor Kliewer of the German Baptist Church in Salem. This was a German-speaking Baptist group, not the German Baptist Brethren, or "Dunkers," who later took the name Church of the Brethren. The church register noted that "this second baptism" would not "help him any

Wayne A. Steffen

The Emmanuel Mennonite congregation in front of their meeting-house, about 1931. Some continued to attend forty-five years later.

concerning his salvation" and that Waldo Hills no longer recognized Rich as member and elder. Soon after, elder Jacob Schrag from the Emmaus congregation at Irving visited Waldo Hills and helped the congregation adopt Johannes Moser's church ordinance as their constitution. Three days later, on December 16, 1894, Schrag ordained Peter Gerig, Jr., one of their own members, as minister. Gerig had a meager education and keenly felt his lack of preparation for preaching, but he accepted the call as from God and served faithfully until his death in 1909.[14]

Waldo Hills soon outgrew the German Reformed meeting-house and in 1904 constructed their own building. At that time they took the name Emmanuel Mennonite Church. In 1966 they dedicated a new educational unit and in 1970, a new sanctuary.[15]

Several strong leaders who served Emmanuel for extended terms provided continuity and stability. After Gerig died, S. S. Baumgartner from Kansas came in 1910. He had attended the Halstead (Kansas) Seminary preparatory school, shortly before Bethel College opened as its successor, and had taught German school in

Kansas. When he resigned from Emmanuel in 1925, the membership was 122. John M. Franz, the next pastor, had previously served Zion at Polk Station, near Dallas. He, like Gerig and Baumgartner, served fifteen years before he resigned. During Franz's tenure, membership again doubled, to 250 in 1940. Though he had attended the Fundamentalistic Moody Bible Institute in Chicago, he strongly supported the GC denomination and its institutions. The next several pastors served shorter periods of time. During Wilbert A. Regier's longer tenure of eight years, membership reached its height, 284 in 1948, 224 of them resident members. The congregation updated its membership soon thereafter and dropped some thirty names. When Allan R. Tschiegg became pastor in 1958, a new period of stability and growth began. He was the first pastor in almost two decades to serve longer than ten years, and during his ministry, Emmanuel regained some of its earlier losses. Beginning in 1973, pastors served only short tenures until 1976, when membership was 265.[16]

Although Emmanuel's charter membership of thirty-two dou-

Rufus M. Franz

John M. Franz (1884-1971), Emmanuel pastor 1925-1940; also pastored Grace (Dallas) and Grace (Albany); served the PDC (GC) as minister-at-large and in other capacities. (1950 photo)

bled several times in about fifty-five years, it reached a plateau by the mid-1940s beyond which it seldom moved in the next thirty years. In 1944 the membership was 264; in 1976 it was 265. In the years between, it was occasionally slightly higher and often substantially lower. Perhaps families had fewer children than in earlier years. The congregation experienced no major crisis or division. Interest in congregational program and missions continued. And a sizable building program began in the late 1960s.

With about half the families still engaged in farming in the early 1970s, did young people leave the farm and community? Did pastors during those three decades emphasize a Fundamentalist, individualistic faith and witness that diminished the essence of Mennonite community, discipleship, and peace? Were other evangelical denominations considered equally as acceptable, or more so, than the GC church? Most of the pastors after John M. Franz supported Fundamentalist Bible schools with interdenominational emphases rather than denominational colleges and seminaries that promoted a distinctive Mennonite understanding of biblical discipleship. Claims of the Mennonite faith community weakened under the call to individualistic faith experiences and mission programs.[17]

A few years after Swiss Mennonites began to settle east of Salem, Russian Mennonites identified in Oregon as Schrag Mennonites settled near Dallas. They had Swiss rather than the Dutch ancestry of most Russian Mennonites. After a few years of hardship in South Dakota, five families moved to Oregon in November 1882. Other Schrag Mennonites, including families of Gering, Graber, and Kauffman, arrived within a few years. They soon learned that they had settled on poor farmland, not suitable for grain crops. In the late 1880s most of them sold their farms and moved temporarily to the Germantown addition of Dallas before moving to Lane County between 1890 and 1892.[18]

Poor farms were not the only trials for the Schrag Mennonites. Illness and death added sorrow to disappointment. The story of the Joseph and Barbara (Graber) Schrag family has become legendary among their descendants. Shortly after they arrived in Oregon, their daughter Lizzie died, at age four. Later, Joseph became almost blind from cataracts and was unable to work. Barbara took in washings to eke out a meager living. In 1888, while Mary, age eighteen, was on her deathbed with tuberculosis, two-year-old Nellie died. Soon after, following a twenty-four hour coma, Mary told her family that she had been to heaven and had seen Nellie and other family members, some of whom she had never known in life. When she had asked to see Jesus, they had told her that she could not until she tasted death, but that one day soon, at two o'clock, they would come for her and take her to heaven with them. Just before her death, as the clock on the mantel struck two, Mary spoke of seeing them come. Several days later, Joseph Schrag died, making three deaths in the family within two weeks.[19]

Records give few hints about the spiritual life of the Schrag Mennonites during their early years at Dallas. Over four years after the first families arrived, Christian Kauffman was ordained as minister on April 30, 1887. Elder Jacob R. Schrag moved from South Dakota to Oregon the following year. Though he lacked theological training, he delivered well-prepared sermons fluently. Probably the group first met in homes for worship services. Perhaps they did not build their small frame meetinghouse until they moved to town. Soon after, they dismantled and shipped it by rail to Lane County.[20]

The Schrag Mennonites began moving to Lane County in 1890 and quickly established a new community. At least six families purchased portions of a large tract of land, owned by C. W. Washburne, between Alvadore and Irving, small towns a few miles northwest of Eugene. Washburne, a prominent farmer near Harrisburg who was also a land speculator, purchased the Polk County properties of several Mennonites who bought portions of his land. By 1892 the last Schrag Mennonites had left Dallas. After building dwelling houses, they rebuilt their meetinghouse near Clear Lake, on Goodman Road, and took the name Emmaus Mennonite Church. The children had school for a time in the Jake Graber home, around the large dining table. When more children reached school age, the Mennonites built a one-room school, secured a teacher from town, and had school in the English language. In the next years persons from the Swiss settlement at Pratum and some of Low German heritage from Dallas—named Waltner, Unger, Becker, Welty, Steffen, and Steiner—settled nearby. They probably lived there only a short time.[21]

The two-thousand-acre Washburne Estate was flat, with a heavy growth of ferns. People called it Fern Ridge. A few oaks and small fir trees were scattered over the land, which was no more productive than their Dallas farms had been. Discouraged by their poor, weedy crops, the Schrag Mennonites listened gladly to glowing reports from young Jacob and Daniel Krehbiel of wonderful wheat land in Adams County, Washington. Elder Schrag and two other men scouted out the land in Washington to verify reports of homesteading possibilities before several families moved there by covered wagon in 1899. In 1900 the remaining families left Lane County, almost all of them moving to Washington, where they established the Menno Mennonite Church. David Unger and his wife, the former widow Barbara Schrag, moved back to Dallas with her daughters. Already one, Anna, had married Ben Emmert from Lane County's nearby AM congregation, and J. D. Mishler's son Jim was courting and later married Carrie, the second one. Younger daughters later married OM men.[22]

Before leaving for Washington, the Emmaus congregation sold their meetinghouse to the Alvadore Christian Church, which used it fifteen years or more before including its materials in a new building in town. When the Mennonites left Lane County, they could not know that in later years some of the land they had farmed would become part of the dammed-up Fern Ridge Reservoir, and some, part of Eugene's Mahlon Sweet Airport, with motorboats and jet planes shattering the peace of their quiet, if unproductive, acres.[23]

Other Russian Mennonites, GC, MB, EMB, and CGC, had started moving to the Dallas area in 1889 or 1890, before the Schrag Mennonites moved to Lane County. The first three groups twisted a common strand that left their beginnings intertwined.[24]

The largest group of new settlers, with GC connections, settled in the Polk Station-Smithfield area about three miles northeast of Dallas. They were from different areas of Russia than the Schrags, and their ancestry was largely Dutch or north German. The Peter Redekop, Wilhelm Vogt, Franz Kliewer, Jacob Wiens, Cornelius Hiebert, and Gerhard Braun families were among the first of twenty-five or more to emigrate from Manitoba, Canada, to Dallas in 1889-1890. Other Manitobans with several of those family names also moved to Dallas, as did Penner, Bergen, Dyck, Unger, Quiring, Esau, Loewen, and Peters families. A number may have been or became Mennonite Brethren. Some families—including Gerber, Warkentin, Becker, Siemens, and Rempel—had immigrated to other parts of the United States before moving to Dallas. Soon after Franz Kliewer purchased a farm, he donated land for the Polk Station school, which opened in October 1890. Oregon's mild climate and reports of productive farmland had attracted those from Manitoba (and perhaps others), but even productive land did not offer the quick wealth which some claimed that others expected. Doubtless other factors contributed to dissatisfaction among those families from half a dozen or more Manitoba villages. Within several years, a majority of the Manitobans left Dallas.[25]

The group of families that remained at Dallas met with greater success than did the Schrags. In 1893 the editor of the *Dallas Itemizer* wrote of visiting several of their farms. One, Abram Enns, had purchased seventeen acres from John Ellis and planted it in prune trees. Between the rows of small trees grew a variety of garden vegetables. The editor thought that "perhaps no area of ordinary ground in the country is being made to produce so good [sic]." Two Bekker families were poultry farmers, selling turkeys in Portland for from five to six dollars per dozen, and one, Abraham, patented a gopher trap and sold them for two dollars each.[26]

The first Mennonites at Polk Station probably worshiped with the Schrag Mennonites in their church house in North Dallas until the Schrags shipped it to Lane County. Later they met for worship in the Polk Station schoolhouse located on the Kliewer place. Traveling minister Baer visited them in 1893. Early MB families who settled not far away, near Salt Creek, had their own small congregation for the short time they lived there. But new MB families who began moving to the area about 1893 later joined the Polk Station Mennonites for worship services.[27]

Into the Dallas Mennonite community came Gustav Schunke from Salem, state missionary for the German Baptist Church. Baptists had strongly influenced Mennonite Brethren from their inception in Russia, some thirty years before, particularly in such doctrinal teachings as baptism by immersion. Baptists also affected MB church polity. In North America, too, Baptist theology and practice continued to attract some MBs. Without a Mennonite minister among the Dallas MBs and GCs, the timing was right for such outside influences. Late in 1895 the MBs invited Schunke to preach for them. After he had daily meetings there for a week, the Salt Creek people invited him to come one week of each month. Schunke wrote that he "made Salt Creek a permanent mission station, although no Baptist brethren" lived there at the time. Soon, if not from the start, he used the schoolhouse the Polk Station Mennonites used. They, too, participated. Attendance was good and several were converted. On his fourth visit, early in February 1896, twenty-nine young people gathered at the home of

Isbrand Peters and formed a youth society. They chose Schunke as president.[28]

Division came when a number of young people requested that Schunke baptize them. Mennonite Brethren people wanted Schunke to continue as their leader and establish a German Baptist church. However, the Polk Station Mennonites opposed the idea. On a Friday afternoon in April 1896, when Schunke arrived at the schoolhouse to hold a previously scheduled meeting, he found it locked. Franz Kliewer, who usually unlocked the school and made a fire in the stove, was friendly. But, he said, one of his boys, looking for some cattle up in the mountains, had the key in his pocket. Schunke decided that the Polk Station Mennonites no longer wanted his services. Without joint Mennonite support for Schunke, the MBs withdrew from the Polk Station Mennonites.[29]

Church affiliation and mode of baptism may have been focal issues which caused the two Mennonite groups to separate. The MBs felt a close kinship with the Baptists; the Polk Station Mennonites did not. Both Baptists and MBs considered immersion the only acceptable form of baptism, and Schunke promoted immersion for young people and even rebaptism for adult Mennonites who had not been immersed. The Polk Station Mennonites objected to that. No doubt they had heard about, discussed, and opposed the recent rebaptism of Mennonite elder John Rich of Waldo Hills, by German Baptists in Salem. When the Polk Station Mennonites cut off relationships with Schunke, they were without his energetic leadership and the support of the MB families. But someone assumed leadership in their Sunday school and in planning group business meetings to discuss their building needs, their services, their rules and practices. In May 1896, they participated as a Sunday school in the newly formed Pacific District Conference (PDC) of the General Conference Mennonite Church.[30]

Traveling preacher J. B. Baer strongly influenced denominational development in Oregon. After organizing Waldo Hills in 1890, Baer returned to Oregon several times in the next years for preaching visits. He planned the May 1896 meeting at Pratum, which organized the PDC. J. J. Balzer of Mountain Lake, Minnesota, one of several denominational leaders who accompanied Baer, served as secretary. He wrote of their meeting on the "peaceful shores of the quiet Pacific Ocean," which was actually sixty miles farther west. The conference included a mission and children's festival, a Bible conference, and a Sunday school convention, as well as business sessions. Waldo Hills layman D. J. Steiner directed a thirty-five-voice choir of members from the three Oregon groups.[31]

These sessions marked the small beginning of the PDC. At the closing business session, Waldo Hills at Pratum; Emmaus at Irving, which soon moved to Adams County, Washington; and Onecho at Colfax, Washington, formed the conference of about seventy members, affiliated with the General Conference Mennonite Church. Its purpose was "to promote fellowship, . . . to cooperate in the spreading and establishing of the Kingdom of God" and to support the work of the denomination. The PDC appointed P. R. Aeschliman of Colfax, Washington, as minister-at-large, to promote intercongregational relationships and to visit scattered Mennonites who did not live near a Mennonite congregation. The Polk Station Sunday school near Dallas could not become a member until it organized as a congregation a few months later.[32]

Several months after the PDC organized, the Polk Station Mennonites organized the Zion Church (the record book did not include Mennonite in the name) on December 19, 1896, with the help of Aeschliman. They did not have a minister, but chosen persons read from books of sermons. The record book did not specify the number or names of charter members. Some family names mentioned in the church register through 1911 are Bachman, Bekker (Becker), Braun, Diehm, Dyck, Friesen, Gerig, Graber, Kliewer, Neufelt, Peters, Quiring, Reddekopp [Redekopp], Reimer, Rempel, Rose, Schrock, Siemens, Stump, and Warkentin. People moved in and out. The 1911 membership was thirty. Isaac Dyck donated a plot for a church house, which they completed in 1898.[33]

Ministerial leadership in the first ten years was neither continuous nor long-lasting. H. A. Bachman from Kansas served several years and also taught a German school. Late in 1902 Zion elected Isaac Dyck as minister. Two years later P. R. Asechliman ordained him, on December 31, 1904. A short time later, after a scandal briefly touched his family, Dyck, though innocent, offered to resign. The congregation refused his offer, yet he began to receive criticism, and in 1908 Zion called in PDC officers to force Dyck to resign in peace and leave the church. He died a short time later, on December 5, 1908, at age forty—some said of a broken heart. Years later, persons who knew him remembered him as a good man and an excellent pastor.[34]

The next pastor, chosen a year later, had the longest tenure of any in Zion's history. In December 1909 they chose from their membership John P. Neufelt, who served over nine years until he resigned, partly because he could not preach in English as the congregation requested during World War I, and partly because some members were dissatisfied with his sermons and attended only Sunday school, not preaching services. In his closing prayer after he resigned in April 1919, he asked for God's blessing on the church and forgiveness from the members for his failures. The Neufelt family and other Zion members soon joined the Bruderthaler (EMB) congregation near Dallas. Ministers in the next two decades served from two to six years each.[35]

Already in the mid-twenties, some Zion members lived and worked in the town of Dallas. Attendance at services in the country was often poor. On March 11, 1928, Zion voted to hold services in town for six months. If ten members joined during that time, they would continue to meet in town. The membership increased by more than ten, and on October 7 the group voted twenty-three to three to remain in Dallas. But some people soon decided to return to the Zion meetinghouse at Polk Station. They felt that farm life and a rural church provided the best atmosphere for Christian living. The division demoralized those who stayed in town. They scattered and for a time worshiped with other denominations. But layman Nick Neufelt and former pastor John M. Franz encouraged the scattered people to regroup, and they began to meet again for services. Some family names were Goossen, Linscheid, Neufelt, Roupp, and Schrag.[36]

In the next several years the townspeople made decisions about a meetinghouse which precipitated an even more serious breach of fellowship with the country people and required PDC conciliation. Early in 1930 Zion members were encouraged to enter their names in a new membership book, apparently to make official the congregation's move into town. But the country people resisted. A June 1930 deadline was later extended indefinitely for members who remained in the country. In February 1932 the townspeople voted to close the Polk Station church. After they purchased a house on Jefferson Street for $300 and put Nick Neufelt in charge of remodeling it, they decided in August to install in it the windows of the country building. By September, persons who still wanted a church at Polk Station filed a suit against the members meeting in town. Conference leaders came in November to attempt a reconciliation. Persons from the town group promised to "forget the past and extend the Christian brotherly hand of welcome" to the country people. They asked "but one thing," that the country people would "worship and labor" with them "in harmony as fellow workers in the kingdom under the present reestablished order." That order was as members in the town meetinghouse.[37]

The PDC conciliators also considered conflicts concerning Gerhard Baergen, who had come from Montana as pastor in December 1929. Earlier actions had built up to a crisis between pastor and people which brought a series of resignations, excommunications, and reversals of some such actions. To clarify roles, the conciliators defined the pastor's responsibility as the spiritual edification of the people, the board's as the material welfare of the church, with all to work in Christian cooperation.[38]

In spite of the November 1932 appeal from the town group to the country group, the two did not soon come together harmoniously. Because incorporating and organizing as a new congregation cost less than changing Zion's incorporation papers so it could do business in town, the town group organized Grace Mennonite Church in Dallas on August 5, 1933. At that time Grace agreed to a distribution of specified church funishings to the Zion people. During these official proceedings, about half of Zion's members joined Grace. In the next years, hard feelings softened, and by the end of 1939, Zion had disbanded and most members had joined Grace. Although severe tensions had surrounded the transition and legally they were separate organizations, in essence Grace was an extension of Zion and in later years dated the organization of Zion as its beginning.[39]

Baergen's term as pastor ended shortly before Grace organized and acquired a new pastor. His problems at Dallas included more than a divided congregation. Some members suspected, perhaps correctly, that Baergen wished their congregation to become Baptist. Upon leaving Zion, Baergen did become pastor of a Baptist congregation. The first pastor of Grace was Herbert E. Widmer, who had grown up at Albany in an OM family and only several years before had become part of the new GC congregation at Albany. He served at Dallas from the summer of 1933, when Grace organized with about two dozen members, until April 1939, when he took a pastorate in Bloomfield, Montana. To help the struggling new Dallas congregation, the PDC provided a financial subsidy for pastoral support for several years. The membership increased to fifty-seven in 1938.[40]

Providing and furnishing a town meetinghouse caused early hardship and later challenges. During the 1930s, paying only three dollars per month on the $300 purchase price of the Jefferson Street building was difficult. The "Workers' Exchange," a small paper published by the PDC, noted in November 1934 that Rufus Franz, a Mennonite teacher in the local high school, had recently paid off the debt on the piano. In the late 1930s Grace constructed a new building on the site of the old one, and in the 1960s they built an educational building first, then a sanctuary, on East Ellendale Road.[41]

The growth which began during Widmer's tenure accelerated in the next years, after Homer Leisy from Salem came as pastor. Leisy took charge in June 1939 and encouraged the people to complete their building. Four months later, on October 15, 1939, the same day that he was ordained minister and elder, the congregation dedicated the new building and received forty-five new members. With Leisy's encouragement, more Zion members united with Grace. Families who moved from the Midwest and the dustbowl of the plains during the 1930s—including family names such as Balzer, Dick, Duerksen, Fast, Franz, Janzen, Kliewer, Thiessen, Toews, and Wiens—also joined Grace. An unnamed eulogizer considered Leisy an unusually influential evangelist, due to his "speaking ability, his salesmanship, and his ability to draw religious cartoons." Leisy also recognized that people needed to be active in the church and promoted a full program of choirs, orchestra, women's and youth groups, Bible study and prayer groups, teacher

Vivian Schellenberg

Homer (1894-1948) and Bertha (Roth) (1896-1951) Leisy. He served the Grace Mennonite congregation at Dallas 1939-1948 during its "Golden Age."

training sessions, revival meetings, and mission outreach.

By 1942 the congregation had become debt-free and self-supporting. Leisy died on June 10, 1948, after a brief illness. He had pastored the congregation just a few days short of nine years. The membership had grown to 331. No other subsequent pastor served Grace as long as Leisy. His tenure was the congregation's golden age of harmonious relationships and growth. The next several pastors served short terms and membership fluctuated downward by as much as forty.[42]

A period of moderate growth during the tenure of Harold D. Burkholder was followed by a time of dissention and division. Burkholder, who had earlier written a history of the PDC, published in 1951 as *The Story of Our Conference and Churches,* resigned as president of the Fundamentalist-leaning Grace Bible Institute (GBI) at Omaha, Nebraska, to become pastor at Dallas in 1955. He served about five years before returning to GBI. The membership high of 372 came in 1960, the year Burkholder left. Waldo J. Flickinger from Ohio became pastor later that year. By 1964 some of the members were dissatisfied because they thought Flickinger lacked dedication to the denomination and the PDC, which had supported Grace financially in the 1930s and early 1940s. Other members, however, strongly supported Flickinger. Hostilities erupted and several members were excommunicated, despite unclear charges. Efforts by GC and PDC committees did not bring reconciliation, and the two groups polarized. Flickinger resigned in 1965 and in January 1966 organized an Evangelical Free Church about two miles east of Grace Mennonite, with fifty-one of its fifty-eight charter members coming from Grace. During these turbulent years, membership dropped to 293 in 1966.[43]

Several capable leaders helped rebuild the strife-torn congregation, including Olin Krehbiel, a respected leader of denominational stature, and layperson Ray Frey, congregational chair. Ted Fast, a former MB missionary to India, came as interim pastor in 1970 and stayed on as permanent pastor through 1976. Grace, with a membership of 315, by then largest of Oregon's GC congregations, was then essentially the size it had been at the end of its golden age in the late 1940s just before Leisy's death.[44]

The congregations at Pratum and Dallas were Oregon's only PDC congregations for thirty-five years, except for Emmaus at Irving before it moved to Washington. In 1900, a few OMs in Oregon also had wanted to join, according to P. R. Aeschliman. J.

D. Mishler and L. J. Yoder, while still in Lane County, had attended the PDC sessions in 1896, with floor and voting privileges. Mishler, particularly, who soon had a daughter-in-law from Emmaus, apparently respected the PDC people highly and attended several annual sessions. Perhaps after George R. Brunk I from Kansas organized Hopewell and Albany as congregations in the distant Kansas-Nebraska Conference (KNC), Mishler wished for closer fellowship with nearby congregations in the PDC. Brunk later charged that Mishler had favored a withdrawal from the KNC. But something held Albany and Hopewell in the OM fold. Had they joined the PDC, Oregon Mennonite history would have carved a far different course to 1976.[45]

Other congregations, in California, Washington, and Idaho, soon joined the PDC and took their turns at hosting the annual sessions. Being scattered over such a large geographical area brought difficulties. Delegates might travel up to 1,200 miles to attend conference. But meeting together encouraged both delegates and the host congregation so much that they continued to meet annually.[46]

The 1908 conference, held at Dallas, initiated a ministers' conference and an evangelization committee. (A name change later made it a home missions committee.) The evangelization committee was to do city mission work and supervise the minister-at-large. In years following, additional responsibilities included helping organize congregations, assisting congregations with internal problems, and providing financial support for struggling congregations and mission efforts. Four of Oregon's six congregations received financial assistance.[47]

The PDC (GC) differed from the PCC (MC) in various ways. The PDC never considered itself a "law-making" body, but an advisory one. It was to unite congregations for joint work and to assist scattered settlements. Congregations were to "stand on a Scriptural confession of faith" and "adhere to the doctrines generally accepted by the Mennonites," such as believers baptism, nonresistance, church discipline, and refraining from oaths and membership in secret societies. While the PCC required specific standards of attire and conduct, the PDC referred mostly to general principles. This permitted more personal freedom and a more liberal approach to living as followers of Christ. Individual independence often prevailed over conference conformity.[48]

At the time of the PDC's annual sessions in 1931, only two of its sixteen congregations were in Oregon. Two more, at Portland and Albany, organized immediately following. Two would join within the next twenty years: Calvary at Barlow in the 1940s and Sweet Home just before the 1951 conference sessions.

The PDC congregation in Portland was the last of three Mennonite congregations to organize there. General Conference Mennonites, like OMs and MBs, had lived in Portland since the late nineteenth century. Like the MBs, most of the GCs lived in a German district in the city, though the Mennonite groups had little contact with each other. The GC families worshiped with other German-speaking churches—Baptist, Lutheran, or Methodist. The PDC considered beginning a mission in Portland for eight years or more before Miss Catherine Niswander, who had worked in a Chicago mission church since 1914, arrived to help begin a work there at the request of the GC Home Mission Board. She opened the mission in a store building at 833 Alberta Street on December 16, 1928. Although the planners wanted this mission church to attract Mennonites in the city, Miss Niswander intended that it should also attract people in the neighborhood, and she decided that services should be in the English language, not German. The following summer the mission moved to a rented meetinghouse at the corner of NE 23rd Avenue and Sumner, owned by the Norwegian Congregational Church. Later the board purchased the building.[49]

Taking the name of the community, on June 29, 1931, Alberta Community Mennonite Church organized with eleven charter members. Some family names were Bartel, Gunn, Hicks, Krug, Leisy, Niswander, Peck, and Zook. Five were neighborhood girls who received baptism and six came by letter. Miss Niswander, as her co-workers called her, had built up the Sunday school to an enrollment of approximately eighty-five. Being the only full-time worker she essentially served as superintendent, doing everything except the preaching. S. S. Baumgartner, who then lived in Portland, at first alternated preaching between Portland and Dallas, before taking a pastorate at Monroe, Washington, in 1929. After that, ministers from the Baptist seminary or Portland Bible Institute preached when visiting GC ministers could not be there. Niswander continued in her earlier role even after Albert Claassen came as first pastor. In 1937, in spite of her desire to stay in Portland, the GC Home Mission Board transferred her to Philadelphia. Baumgartner, retired from his Washington pastorate and again living in Portland, wanted a student-minister to help him with the preaching. Keeping Niswander would have made the staff unafford-able.[50]

A succession of pastors served Alberta. Membership and attendance fluctuated from time to time. Several pastors in the early years attended Western Baptist Seminary (there was then no Mennonite seminary), and several in the 1960s were associated with Western Evangelical Seminary. Although Niswander had worked mostly with children, her successors, Edmund J. Miller and his wife, Christine, reached out to adults as well. In slightly more than two years they left due to ill health. By then attendance had tripled or more and membership was forty. Perhaps the membership peak was 105, in 1951, when Clyde Dirks resigned because of illness after six years as pastor. About ten years later membership dipped to thirty-eight. In 1955 John and Jeanne Zook, a doctor-nurse couple from the congregation, were ordained as missionaries and began to serve in Africa under the GC Foreign Mission Board. After a low in the early 1960s, attendance and membership again increased during Nobel Sack's interim pastorate of most of ten years. Because of overcrowding, the congregation relocated in a purchased Evangelical United Brethren building only four blocks from their previous location.[51]

When Elmer Friesen arrived from Houston, Texas, in June 1971 to be permanent, full-time pastor, the Alberta community was rapidly changing from a white, middle-class neighborhood to a low-income black ghetto. Fewer and fewer community people attended services. Members who lived in the community moved to other parts of Portland or even away from the city. Some formerly active persons became inactive. Young people in a voluntary service unit worked in the community and brought enthusiasm and renewal to the congregation, but they could not stem the trend toward becoming a suburban church. The congregation purchased a site in East Portland at 196th Avenue and Glisan Street and with much volunteer labor constructed a multifunctional building which they began to use in July 1975. After they moved from the Alberta district they changed their name to Peace Mennonite Church. In 1976 about half of the sixty-six members were nonresident. Most of the active members were new to the church, young, with below-average income for the area. They were excited about being an emerging congregation in an area with potential for growth, and they were committed to Anabaptist concepts of the gospel and the church.[52]

Elmer Friesen

Pastor Elmer Friesen (1918-), guiding the plow in the 1975 groundbreaking for Portland's Peace Mennonite congregation, formerly Alberta Community Mennonite Church. Inset: Elmer Friesen.

Three of Oregon's PDC congregations, Waldo Hills/Emmanuel, Zion/Grace, and Alberta/Peace, had historic GC connections even before they organized. Oregon's other three PDC congregations, Grace at Albany, Calvary, and Sweet Home Community Chapel, began at the initiative of persons who had earlier left OM congregations in the 1930s and 1940s.

The impetus for organizing Grace Mennonite Church in Albany came from George Kenagy and his extended family, who left the Albany OM congregation because of a dispute over life insurance. Related issues were attire and musical instruments. Several Emmanuel members living in Albany joined the Kenagys. On June 29, 1931, the same day Alberta in Portland organized, Grace organized with twenty-one charter members. Some family names were Erb, Funk, Kenagy, Rieser, Stauffer, and Widmer. They purchased the Grace Presbyterian Church building at East Fourth and Main, a beautiful old building requiring frequent costly repairs. W. Harley King came from Quarryville, Pennsylvania, to be the first pastor. He and the next two pastors all resigned because of health problems. The era of most prosperity and growth came during the tenure of P. A. Kliewer, who came from Bluffton, Ohio, and served from 1941 to 1949. Membership rose steadily to 128 in 1949, just short of the peak of 131 in 1951. After the December 1946 annual meeting, the congregation hired Ruth Jantzen as a church worker for a short time. She later married Earl Roth and they served as missionaries in Africa for many years.[53]

Problems of division, finances, and morale began in 1952 when fourteen members withdrew because pastor Henry Dalke refused to perform the marriage of a member to a person not professing Christianity. Most joined local Baptist or Evangelical United Brethren congregations. The following year some Grace members wanted to drop the word "Mennonite" from their name, since occasionally people confused them with Albany's OM congregations, Twelfth Street and Fairview. But this change did not occur. Something about pastor E. J. Peters caused extreme dissatisfaction in 1954, and he did not complete his three-year term. The problem must have contributed to the loss of seventy-two members in 1954, leaving only forty-two. After the massive drop, membership did increase again, but never to its former level. Financial problems became severe when several families moved away. On November 10, 1968, the congregation of fifty-seven members disbanded. The majority joined the Evangelical Church of North America. Others joined another PDC congregation. Two were charter members of the OM congregation at Corvallis.[54]

Calvary Mennonite Church at Barlow organized on August 6, 1944, a few months after minister Paul N. Roth and about sixty-five members left Zion (OM) at nearby Hubbard. Before the charter membership closed early in 1945, sixty-two persons joined Calvary. Some family names were Banker, Berkey, Burck, Conrad, Egli, Hartzler, Heyerly, Hondrick, Hostetler, Jones, Kauffman, King, Lackey, Miller, Morris, Roth, Reznicsek, Schumacher, Stanley, Stutzman, Stuwe, Troyer, Wheeler, and Yoder. Calvary soon purchased the Barlow Christian Church building and enlarged it several times before constructing a new, larger building on the Aurora-Lone Elder Road in 1972. With the new building, the address changed to Aurora.[55]

In its thirty-year history before 1976, Calvary had two ministers who served more than a decade each. It experienced steady growth in membership. The first pastor, Paul Roth, served twelve years until October 1956, when he took a pastorate in Carlock, Il-

Mrs. Paul Roth, Jr.

Paul N. (1900-1970) and Velma (Burck) (1904-1984) Roth, minister at Portland (MC) and Zion (MC) congregations before he started Calvary (GC). (1956 photo)

linois. He also served a short interim in the early 1970s. The second long-term pastor, Harry Howard, served from 1960 to 1973, when he declined to accept another term. By the mid-1960s, Calvary had become a community church in its composition, though it continued as a PDC congregation. Members came from more than fifteen denominational backgrounds and from several national heritages, with a wide variation in educational and economic levels. Gerald Mendenhall of the Kansas Yearly Meeting of Friends, who came in March 1974, continued to serve in 1976. Chester Kauffman, formerly a minister at Zion and Meadowbrook, a mission church started by Zion, became minister of visitation at Calvary in August 1976. Membership had grown from fifty-one in 1944 to 270 in 1976.[56]

The PDC congregation at Sweet Home officially began as a mission outreach, but persons who in 1945 had withdrawn from the Sweet Home OM congregation initiated the idea. They did not support conservative practices of their former congregation and had joined Grace Mennonite Church in Albany, but they found it difficult to participate there because they lived almost thirty miles away. A large, recently opened sawmill brought many people to the Sweet Home area, and the PDC evangelization committee considered it an open mission field. Even though a few PDC families participated, the committee wanted this to be, as they said, not necessarily a Mennonite church but rather a mission work which introduced people to Jesus Christ as their personal Savior. The committee called Alfred Schwartz from Monroe, Washington, to serve as pastor. Within a month after the Schwartz family arrived in February 1949, they opened their home for Sunday school, church, and, in the summer, vacation Bible school. In 1950 the mission dedicated a concrete block chapel and later added an annex.[57]

Within several months the somewhat shortsighted focus on bringing individuals to a personal decision for Christ, but not necessarily to a Mennonite (or another) church, presented a dilemma when persons requested baptism and membership. If the mission was not a congregation, where would converts become members? The dilemma itself illustrated that salvation includes not only receiving Christ as personal Savior but also becoming part of his body, the church. The evangelization committee recommended a temporary stopgap, that converts be baptized and accepted into "the fellowship of believers" until the group organized. On May 30, 1951, the Sweet Home Community Chapel organized, and after eight persons were baptized on June 10, there were thirty-one charter members. Some family names were Brewer, Burkholder, Elliot, Emmert, Miller, Parker, Robertson, Schwartz, Shoemaker, and Wiens.[58]

In the next years the congregation experienced ups and downs in membership and morale. During the pastorate of Peter Peters, 1957-1963, membership increased to eighty-eight, to dip to twenty-eight in 1967. The congregation considered disbanding until one couple heard Larry Sloan preach at the local Assembly of God and invited him to preach at their chapel. Six weeks later the congregation invited him to be their pastor. Sloan agreed to an interim arrangement that became permanent and stretched out through 1976. Gradually membership increased. The congregation outgrew its building and in 1972 moved into the Assembly of God building which they had purchased the year before. Beginning in the late 1960s, they ministered to countercultural young people whose way of life included deviant attire, long hair, and drugs. Some who found Christ became active in the congregation, serving on the church board, as teachers, as leaders of services, and in various types of community outreach. Membership seesawed in the 1970s, from a low of 55 in 1975 to a high of 174 in 1976.[59]

After 1900 Oregon had a minority of PDC congregations. In 1976, the state had only five of the PDC's twenty-one congregations but 30 percent of the membership, (963 of approximately 3,250). Nonetheless, Oregon became the official headquarters of the conference when the PDC incorporated in Oregon about 1940 in order to transact legal business after purchasing a parsonage in Portland. Occasionally Oregon men served as president or treasurer of the PDC, and Oregon people regularly served on committees and other positions. Three persons from the Portland congregation and one from Dallas edited the PDC publication, which began in 1929 as the "Workers' Exchange," a mimeographed newsletter. The publication later appeared in printed form ten times annually as "The Messenger," and, finally, as a bimonthly insert in *The Mennonite*. Christine Miller edited the periodical in 1943-45; Clyde Dirks, 1950-52; George A. Fast, 1953-1968; and La Vernae J. Dick, 1973 through 1976.[60]

The PDC emphasized fellowship, mutual encouragement, and cooperation for home missions more than nonconformity to worldly society. In general the PDC and its member congregations tolerated a wide diversity of theological perspectives, although one Washington congregation did withdraw in the 1960s because of theological disagreements. By the mid-1970s some people in the PDC sensed a growing restlessness under the surface unity. Questions arose about power and whether the home missions committee should control more than three-fourths of the annual $36,585 budget. Most conference officers were clergy, even though laypersons were often nominees. Attendance at annual sessions was decreasing, especially if held in a small congregation on a geographical extremity of the conference region. Whether congregational autonomy and tolerance of differing "nonessential" beliefs would allow for continuing fellowship and cooperation among PDC congregations would be tested in the second century of Mennonites in Oregon.[61]

Mennonite Brethren

Before 1976, MB congregations developed at Portland, Dallas, Salem, and Eugene, but the one in Portland did not survive. Portland and Dallas related to other regional MB conferences until the Pacific District Conference (PDC) (MB), comprised of congregations in Washington, Oregon, and California, organized in 1913. Even before the PDC organized, the MB general conference considered Oregon as a mission field. The PDC home mission committee (later board) also regarded Portland and certain other MB efforts in Oregon as mission work and offered direction and assistance.[62]

Minister Heinrich Helzer (Henry Hoelzer) and his family were among Oregon's first MB families, moving from Sutton, Nebraska, to Portland in 1886. Perhaps he started a congregation soon, as more families settled in Portland. By 1892 there were twenty-two members; by 1895, thirty-eight. In 1893 and again in 1901 and 1927, the congregation filed articles of incorporation. During much of its existence it was viewed as a home mission. By 1916, and for some years following, there was both a mission and a congregation, with the two merging in 1930. One was located on Sixth Street [Avenue]. Many in Portland were Volga Germans with Lutheran background, first-generation MBs from North Dakota and Nebraska, who joined because of missionary efforts. In the early years in Portland discord caused problems. According to MB archivist Kevin Enns-Rempel, perhaps this was due in part to Seventh-Day Adventist influence, perhaps to tensions between the Volga Germans and the ethnic MBs. Some family names were Cook, Dill, Fast, Friesen, Heinrich, Helzer, Huwa, Koch, Martens, Nachtigal/Nightengale, Pauli, Popp, Reisbich, Ross, Sauer, Schnell, Schwindt, Singer, Sittner, Urbach, and Wittenberg. They located in Albina, where other Germans had settled, some of them in an area near the present Emmanuel Hospital. Membership remained low, with thirty-seven reported in 1912, ten in 1926, and wide fluctuations in surrounding years. In 1937 there were twenty-four members.[63]

After Helzer's death in 1904, the congregation lacked strong resident leadership. For some years Dallas ministers preached regularly at Portland, as often as every other Sunday—Peter C. Hiebert in 1907-1908 and Heinrich S. Voth in 1909-1915. A Voth daughter remembered that they always went to the nearby home of a church family, Mr. and Mrs. David Nightengale, for Sunday dinner. Mary Martens, a single woman from Saskatchewan, was then serving as a city missionary doing home visitation. Peter Heinrich, a single man, was a lame baker who regularly sent a long green box with two layers of cookies home with Voth after his weekend in Portland. For many years before Heinrich moved to California in 1929 he was listed as a Portland leader in the PDC yearbooks, often with an ordained preacher or two and a deacon. But the congregation always struggled.[64]

Erma Neufeld

Family of Frank F. (1871-1949) Friesen and Mary (Wiens) (1880-1952), a widow Neufeld when she married Frank. Back: Frank Neufeld, Marie Friesen, Ann Friesen, Ann (Enns) (Mrs. F. F. Friesen, Jr.). Front: Elizabeth Neufeld, Frank Friesen, Sr., Mary Neufeld, Mary (Wiens) Friesen, Anna Neufeld, F. F. Friesen, Jr., later ministered at the Portland Sixth Street MB congregation.

Urbanism and financial problems contributed to the demise of the Portland congregation. Even among other German-speaking people, mission outreach in their community never prospered greatly. And adapting to the urban culture brought considerable stress. The responses of young people to cultural change in the larger world produced a crisis in the congregation, with a loss of members, especially in the 1930s. Finances were inadequate to support strong leaders. The work nearly ceased in 1932, revived in 1933, then ended by 1938. Most members then were older people. They were advised to join the Dallas congregation, some sixty miles to the southwest. When the PDC sold the church property in 1939 a report noted that those funds were then "available for a new work" in Portland. But in 1940 the committee for home missions reported that they had not found an opportunity for such a work. Instead, the PDC loaned the money to the new congregation emerging that year in West Salem.[65]

In 1890 MBs, including farmers Peter Hiebert and Elias Bergan, began to move to Polk County near Dallas. Others named Peters, Beier, Voth, and Friesen soon moved to the area. In 1891 elder Heinrich Voth of Minnesota visited, helped them organize, and appointed Henry Voth as leader. But elder Voth felt that this was a temporary settlement and, as he expected, some families soon left Oregon. During this time, however, new MB families moved to Dallas, including Jacob Buhler and family from Adelsheim, Russia, in 1893. Some felt that the "Kirchliche" Mennonite families had lost their strict Mennonite faith. (*Kirchliche* [or "churchy"] refers to the main group from which the MBs divided in Russia in 1860.)

Peter Wedel, MB missionary, conducted meetings at Dallas for several weeks in 1895, and a few more families joined the group. But others moved away, and, as the previous section noted, the MBs worshiped with the Polk Station Mennonites until the joint group disbanded over whether to support German Baptist missionary Gustav Schunke. Schunke, with several MB families comprising seven members, and perhaps a few other people, organized a new congregation which filed articles of incorporation on May 18, 1896, for the First German United Mennonite Baptist Brotherhood of Polk Station. In everyday terms, it was Salt Creek Baptist Church. Isbrand Peters donated five acres of land and the small group constructed a church building.[66]

In 1905, twelve MB families, including those who left the Baptist congregation and others who began moving to Dallas in 1904, organized the North Dallas MB Church. Family names of the twenty-four charter members included Abrams, Beier, Buhler, Fleischman, Friesen, Goertz, Nachtigal, Ratzlaff, and Toews. Jacob Toews was elder. They built a small meetinghouse about five miles northwest of Dallas, diagonally across the road from the Salt Creek school, hardly one-fourth mile south of the Baptist meetinghouse. Early leaders, in addition to men from within the congregation, included young Peter C. Hiebert (1907-1908), who later helped organize Tabor College in Kansas and chaired the Mennonite Central Committee for thirty-three years; and Heinrich S. Voth (1909-1915), son of the elder Voth who visited Dallas in 1891, later a respected Canadian evangelist and denominational leader.[67]

Voth and his assistant P. H. Berg held services in the town of Dallas on Sunday evenings for MBs as well as for EMBs who lived there. Most of them were recent arrivals from Canada and from east of the Rockies who did not have transportation to their country meetinghouses. In 1917 the group began holding regular services in Dallas. After a revival, when their number increased, they asked the North Dallas congregation either to move the church building to Dallas or to release the members living there so they could organize a city church. The members were released with God's blessing, as Berg recalled years later. When the town congregation organized, it meant considerable loss for the one in the country with a membership of about eighty. In the next years, as roads and transportation improved, more persons transferred to the town congregation. On January 7, 1923, North Dallas disbanded and the Dallas congregation received the remaining twenty-five members.[68]

The MB Church in Dallas had organized on December 21, 1919, under the lay leadership of D. A. Peters. Some family names were Berg, Friesen, Hildebrand, Kroeker, Peters, Regehr, Reimer, Wiens, and others. They elected Peters to continue as leader, with P. H. Berg as assistant. The new congregation used the Seventh-Day Adventist building until they constructed a meetinghouse on the corner of Washington and Hayter streets in 1920. In 1934 they erected a larger structure on the same site and later remodeled it twice. Membership growth in the 1920s came from the merger of the country and town congregations, from an influx of MB families from other states and Canada, and from evangelistic services conducted by J. D. Hofer of near Reedley, California, and William Pietsch, a Baptist minister. On a May Sunday afternoon in 1926, more than forty young people received baptism in the cold LaCreole Creek. Growth in membership in the 1930s came in part from MB families from Montana and Nebraska moving to Dallas. During the time Jacob J. Toews from Canada served as pastor (1940-1943), he updated the membership roll, with the consent of the council, and dropped inactive and nonresident members.[69]

After World War II, both growth and separations occurred. Growth came when MB families from other areas moved to Dallas. In 1951 approximately half of the members were rural people. A steady upward trend in membership continued until 1956 with a reported peak of 363. In the mid-1950s a few members withdrew and joined a Baptist congregation in Salem. Discouragement and difficulties later resulted in more losses. In 1972 five families named Braun, Buhler, Paul, and Schmidt withdrew. With a lay leader named Don Denlinger and others in the community, they

Evelyn Boese

*Abe A. Loewen (1912-1980), first
pastor at West Salem/Kingwood
MB Church.*

formed the Dallas Community Church. In 1976 the MB congregation reported a membership of 206, up from 195 of two years earlier. Stan Lyman was pastor, Glenn Makin, associate pastor.[70]

In 1913 MBs started a church at Woodburn and two years later moved to Donald, near Newberg, to disband the same year, 1915. During their short time at Donald, H. S. Voth ministered there.[71]

A few Mennonite Brethren families, members at Dallas, lived in Salem by 1940 and wished for a congregation there. Encouraged by N. N. Hiebert, a well-known denominational leader and evangelist then living in Oregon, they bought land for a building, began meeting regularly, and organized the West Salem Mennonite Brethren Church on October 13, 1940. Including pastor Abe A. Loewen and his wife, Agnes, who came from Nebraska about a month later, family names of the twenty-seven charter members were Balzer, Beier, Buhler, Duerksen, Esau, Fadenrecht, Guenther, Harms, Hiebert, Loewen, Pankratz, and Willems. Many had originally come from North Dakota and Minnesota. The congregation frequently expanded their building in the eleven hundred block of Elm Street. Later they constructed a new building, remodeled the old building, and built a large activity center.[72]

Impressive growth in their first decade preceded a severe

loss in the 1950s, followed by another period of growth. In the 1940s, membership increased by ten times. As the congregation reached out to persons of non-MB background, they decided in 1948 to change their name to Kingwood Bible Church. At that time they also decided to accept nonimmersed members of other Mennonite churches who wished to join. In 1953 membership dropped from 274 to 164. Sixty or more who left started the West Salem Baptist Church. During the fourteen-year tenure of pastor Leonard Vogt, the congregation again grew rapidly and steadily, from 179 in 1960 to a high of 411 in 1974. Vacation Bible school and occasional spectacular events became a valued way to reach children for Christ. A Kids' Day celebration in 1969 included a parade, a float, free food, and a television clown who gave an invitation to receive Christ. Counselors using Billy Graham follow-up materials worked with those who responded. Ralfe Kaiser came as pastor in August 1975. The membership for Kingwood in 1976 was 402.[73]

The Mennonite Brethren congregation in Eugene began as a mission church of the PDC. It was unique among MB congregations because of the widely varied background of the core group of families. A few had lived in Eugene for several decades and had

The Leonard Vogt family. Back: Leona (Kleiver) and Leonard (1925-). Front: Philip, Dwight, Dewayne, Grace. Vogt pastored Kingwood during its peak of prosperity.

worshiped with the Evangelical United Brethren (EUB). But they were not entirely comfortable with some EUB doctrines. The eight to ten families who began meeting in 1962 wanted to be Mennonite, and Dan Goertzen, executive secretary of the PDC home missions board, helped tip the balance toward the MBs instead of another Mennonite group. He indicated that the PDC would be willing to provide a minister, his initial financial support, as well as financial help with a building.[74]

The congregation organized on September 13, 1964, under the leadership of Harold Schroeder, an MB pastor fresh from Conservative Baptist Theological Seminary in Denver. Thirty-four persons, named Doerksen, Franz, Goerz, Hiebert, Hooley, Janz, Kroeker, Martin, Paschall, Sather, Schneider, and Schroeder, joined before charter membership closed on January 10, 1965. Less than half were of MB background. Others had been GC, OM, EMB, German Baptist, or Methodist. They soon constructed a building at Harlow Road and Honeysuckle Lane in northeast Eugene and later completed a social hall. Soon after they purchased the land, they adopted the name North Park Community Church, Mennonite Brethren. They wanted to be a missionary church instead of propagating an MB congregation and hoped people would be more attracted if they had no denominational name. Some members and most pastors moved through the congregation rather rapidly. Membership fluctuated when persons completed studies at the University of Oregon or changed employment. In 1975 it reached a high of eighty-eight before the 1976 report of eighty. Don Mac-Neill, who became pastor in 1972 and continued in 1976, served longer than any previous pastor.[75]

The three Oregon MB congregations were a small minority of the thirty-three congregations in the PDC in 1976. Most were in California, with a few in Washington, Oregon, and Arizona. PDC membership was 7,266, with 688 in Oregon. Mission outreach was a primary denominational focus, and for that purpose some congregations deemphasized their Mennonite roots. Although the MB Biblical Seminary was established in Fresno, California, in 1955, many MB pastors took their training elsewhere. In all three Oregon congregations, the pastors in 1976 of non-MB heritage, had been trained in other-than-Mennonite seminaries, and had earlier served Baptist congregations. Mennonite Brethren historically had emphasized "brotherhood-consciousness and church loyalty," but according to MB historian, J. A. Toews, by the early 1970s this sense of community was being undermined. He noted that "inroads of American individualism as well as . . . modern inter-denominationalism" had weakened its historic position. The challenge for Oregon's MBs would be to renew a biblical sense of community that could modify the individualism that threatened it.[76]

Evangelical Mennonite Brethren

In 1890 the first Bruderthaler moved to Oregon (where in 1940 they took the name Evangelical Mennonite Brethren) (EMB). They were so few that they worshiped with the Polk Station Mennonites (GC) for about two decades. After the large Bruderthaler family of Solomon Ediger moved from Inman, Kansas, to Dallas in 1910, and several other Ediger families soon followed, the group organized as a congregation in 1912 and chose Solomon Ediger as pastor. More families arrived, and in 1916 the congregation constructed a building one mile east of Dallas near Oak Villa. After World War I some families moved to Dallas from Chinook, Montana, because of drought. Some came from other states and provinces, including several former members of the Church of God in Christ, Mennonite (Holdeman) (CGC), in Canada. One, David Thiessen, excommunicated because he owned a phonograph, intended not to join another church. But influenced by his father-in-law, the friendly people, and conversion in revival meetings, he changed his mind.[77]

There was occasional dissension but the congregation grew in spite of it. By 1924 it outgrew the country meetinghouse and constructed a new facility in town on Miller Avenue. Membership then totaled about one hundred. Some family names were Dick, Duerksen, Ediger, Frey, Friesen, Funk, Hamm, Neufelt, Peters, Quiring, Rempel, Schroeder, Thiessen, Unruh, and Wiens. Concerned for their youth, the congregation provided religious and social alternatives to the movies, ball games, and other worldly entertainment in town. In the early 1930s, David Thiessen and his class of high school boys, including his son Alfred, enrolled in a Moody Bible Institute correspondence course. Thiessen also offered Sunday afternoon recreational and musical activities, at his home. Pastor Jacob H. Quiring did not approve of some of Thiessen's activities and in 1932 the Thiessens and a few other families withdrew to start a congregation in Salem. About this time several other families also withdrew and joined a small Christian and Mis-

Dallas EMB Church

Dallas Evangelical Mennonite Brethren church, largest congregation in the denomination. (Photo likely from the 1950s)

sionary Alliance congregation in Dallas. But others, including families from Meade, Kansas, who wanted to escape the red dust storms, moved to Dallas and joined the Bruderthaler.[78]

With the coming of D. P. Schultz as pastor in 1941, new growth and prosperity began. Most Salem members returned to Dallas. More community persons of non-Mennonite heritage joined the congregation, and again they outgrew their building and constructed a new facility, just around the corner on Howe Street. The 1976 membership of 507 made Dallas the largest congregation in the EMB denomination, about one-eighth of the total membership. Pete Unrau, who came in 1969, continued as pastor in 1976, with Randy Benson as youth pastor.[79]

The first Salem EMB congregation, which included families named Dick, Doerksen, Friesen, Funk, Hamm, Nickel, Thiessen, Unruh, and Wall, organized in 1933, but it was short-lived. David

R. Doerksen, a leader in the movement, lived in Salem. Most if not all of the other families lived in Dallas and drove to Salem only for services. They bought a small church building and parsonage at 17th and Chemeketa in Salem. For a while attendance was good and the congregation prospered, with the membership reaching seventy. But the group was unable to survive the Depression years, and their primary reason for leaving Dallas—dissatisfaction with the pastor—dissolved when D. P. Schultz became pastor at Dallas. The group disbanded in December 1941 and sold the property to Mormons.[80]

A second Salem EMB congregation was the result of the long-held vision of Mennonite families who had settled in Salem after World War II and in the late 1940s began midweek meetings. Most were GC; a few, EMB. Neither the GC nor the EMB congregation at Dallas at first encouraged them to start a church. But eventually the EMB congregation offered support and assistance. Several months after Frank C. Wiens, of Luton, Iowa, came as first pastor, the Liberty Gardens Bible Church organized in July 1958 with seventeen members named Ediger, Olson, Reimer, Schultz, Warkentin, and Wiens. The next year they began using their multi-purpose building at 304 Hrubetz Road in South Salem, completing the facility some years later. During the pastorate of Wayne Deason (1970-1975), membership grew from thirty-seven to seventy-five. However, quite a few members left when he did, and the 1976 membership was forty-seven. Interim ministers served Liberty Gardens the remainder of 1976.[81]

Old Order Amish

Whether Gideon Lantz and Levi J. Yoder, 1876-1877 settlers at Hubbard reported to be Amish, were actually Old Order Amish (OOA) at the time they moved to Oregon is not clear. If so, within a few years they joined the Amish Mennonites (AM). The Joseph Meyer named was apparently a Swiss-born Catholic who had joined the Amish at Needy, perhaps about 1878, when he married Jane Keck, who had been raised by an Amish family. He became an Amish preacher, perhaps the first in the settlement. Later he joined the Apostolic Christian Church near Silverton. Daniel D. Miller of Middlebury, Indiana (not the later Indiana leader so named), who came in 1878 was without question OOA. Other families who settled in neighboring groups near Hubbard and

Ken Berkey

Home of Amish entrepreneur Isaac S. Miller (1838-1918), built about 1890 near his sawmill and tile factory. One of the better houses of its time, its main floor had a movable partition between two rooms to provide a large space for Amish services.

Needy (however briefly and probably not all at one time) included at least twenty-eight families before 1900. Some of their family names were Beiler, Borkholder, Christner, Deetz, Kauffman, Kramer, Kreider, Miller, Schrock, Swartzendruber, Weirich, and Yoder. Most were related to other families who came to Oregon. Few who stayed remained Old Order Amish. Some moved back and forth several times between Oregon and other places. Jacob K. Miller ("Oregon Jake Miller"), an 1879 immigrant to Oregon who became known as the "movingest Amishman," lived in Oregon three times before he died in Delaware.[82]

Few records tell of Oregon's early Old Order Amish church life or the ordained men (reportedly seven). Perhaps Joseph Meyer had been ordained before 1879, when he wrote of "the small congregation" at Hubbard. In 1880 bishop Jonas J. Kauffman and family of Douglas County, Illinois, moved to Oregon. Kauffman and his wife, Rachel, were the first permanent settlers who remained Old Order Amish in Oregon. With each filing a land claim, they obtained 320 acres, and family tradition says they hired Chinese workers for about twenty-five cents a day to clear the heavily timbered land. This was at a time when Chinese workers in salmon canneries earned $1.00 to $1.50 per day. On the other hand, it seems the Kauffmans were comparatively well-to-do and had a reputation for offering hospitality. For decades the first Schrag Mennonites remembered Rachel's gracious kindness as she hosted them in her large, two-story frame house upon their arrival in 1882. Kauffman, as only OOA bishop at Needy/Hubbard, served over twenty-five years, until he died in 1907. With Old Order Amish families moving in and out frequently, their numbers were never large. The 1890 U.S. Census reported twenty-five communicant members at Hubbard, thirty-two at Needy, perhaps near the membership peak.[83]

Before long, individualism among Oregon's diverse Old Order Amish families threatened their church community. However, what may seem to onlookers to have been petty quarrels were usually serious attempts to apply their faith to the small particulars of everyday life. Old Order Amish shunned pride in any form as a mark of worldliness and held forth humility as a primary virtue. But countless details essential for faithful living assured small differences which caused separations. With religious problems being the "underlying process" in Amish migration, according to sociologist John Hostetler, OOAs from various communities brought ideas and practices which did not mesh together well in Oregon. Differences between layman Daniel D. Miller and bishop Kauffman apparently contributed to their problems. Miller was a reader, writer, teacher, and traveler. By 1881, perhaps before, with Miller's strong support, the OOAs of Oregon had a German Sunday school to teach the German language as well as church doctrines. Reports in 1884 and 1886 told of a German school which Miller taught. In 1889 Miller moved to Kansas, possibly because he differed with Kauffman about the values of education. So far as is known, neither the Sunday school nor the German school continued after Miller moved away. Another problem was the influx of AMs and OMs into the Hubbard area. Some of the Old Order Amish feared they would lose their young people to these less conservative groups, and their concerns were well founded. Young people and middle-aged folks, too, including descendants of both Miller and Kauffman, later became members at Zion or another AM or OM congregation.[84]

The combination of church problems and a depressed economy caused many Old Order Amish to move away from Needy/ Hubbard. During the Panic of 1893 (a depression which lasted four years), Oregon land that had earlier sold for $80 and $90 an acre was now selling for $25 to $35. Prices paid for farm products dropped, too. Some OOA families weathered the depression and encouraged people from east of the Rockies to come to Oregon, because for anyone who could afford it, attractive farms were now available cheaply. Yet some families left for other states. By 1895 others were moving some forty miles west to Yamhill County, near Whiteson and McMinnville. In early 1898 about eleven families, with twenty-six members, remained in the two Oregon Old Order Amish settlements. In the next years the Needy OOAs continued to lose strength. By 1906, some had joined the nearby Zion AM congregation, and the OOA membership had dwindled to twelve. After Jonas J. Kauffman died in 1907 they had no resident leader. By 1920 more had joined Zion or moved away, leaving only Rachel Kauffman, who died in 1922 at age ninety-two. Both Jonas and Rachel were buried in the Zion cemetery.[85]

Like the Needy/Hubbard Old Order Amish, those who lived in Yamhill County, near McMinnville, had divisive problems. Three times Amish settled there, then moved away.

The first OOA settlement in the McMinnville area survived less than a decade. In 1896 four OOA families moved from Needy to Whiteson, south of McMinnville, and others, including minister David C. Schrock, followed in the next several years. A correspondent wrote of the pure air that allowed one to see Mt. Hood sixty miles away by moonlight, of trout-filled rivers, and of fertile soil in which vegetables grew to perfection. Two Old Order Amish bishops, Daniel Beachy of Arthur, Illinois, and Eli E. Bontrager of Shipshewana, Indiana, visited the Oregon OOAs and ordained Tobias T. Yoder minister in 1898 and bishop in 1899. But a bishop, a minister, and productive land did not insure success as an Old Order Amish church. In 1902 preacher Schrock moved to Geauga County, Ohio, and bishop Yoder moved to Custer County, Oklahoma. By the end of 1904 most of the remaining families had moved to Ohio, Michigan, and perhaps other states.[86]

The second settlement of Old Order Amish in the McMinnville area began in 1906. Most of them had previously lived in Oregon or were relatives of Oregon people. Four ordained men served the group at one time or another in the next six years. For some of the families, Amity was their address. Amity, meaning peace and friendship, had received its name decades earlier when a teacher had reconcilied two opposing groups regarding the location of the school. The nearby OOAs had serious disagreements, too, but they lacked a conciliator. Some objected to the bishop's visiting a saloon in a large city far from home, and his expectation that no one would learn of it. Another person called for forgiveness, love, and leaving old grudges behind. Within months, several families sold their farms, and one or more moved to Illinois. By the end of 1913, bishop David Y. Miller and six other families, all related to him, moved to Salinas, California. Seven families remained in Yamhill County, but without a minister they could have no church, so they had Sunday school instead. Bishop David J. Plank of Arthur, Illinois, provided bishop oversight for several years and ordained Alvin M. Beachy as minister in 1915.[87]

Meanwhile, the California settlement lasted less than a year. Several families moved to other states and then back to Oregon. Before preacher Dan Miller returned he wrote a letter to Beachy, the new minister, asking if the people would allow him to come back. The Oregon people extended forgiveness, and by the end of 1916 Dan, brother to former bishop David Miller, moved back to Oregon from Thomas, Oklahoma. The Miller father, "Oregon Jake Miller," after denying rumors that he planned to return to Oregon, moved back to Oregon by 1919 as did bishop David Y. Miller, Jake's son. Between their leaving Oregon in 1913 and their return six years later, they had lived in California, Virginia, Delaware, and Montana.[88]

The second settlement in Yamhill County lasted longer than the first one, but again problems eventualy caused its dissolution. In 1921 Daniel E. Miller, who had been ordained bishop in Oregon several years earlier, moved to Rusk County, Wisconsin. The following year, preacher Alvin M. Beachy moved to Somerset County, Pennsylvania, and bishop David Y. Miller, brother to Dan, moved to Delaware. Again the group was without a minister, and more families moved away in the next years until all had left by 1930.[89]

By 1935 the third and final movement of Old Order Amish to the McMinnville area began. Two preachers, Mose Yoder and Menno Swartzentruber, and their families were among the first in the new settlement. By the late 1940s, twenty-three OOA families lived there. Bishop Eli J. Bontreger of Shipshewana, Indiana, ministered to this group semiannually for some years and ordained Mose Yoder as bishop in 1939.[90]

While in many ways these Old Order Amish were similar to other Amish churches, in other ways this was a more liberal community than most. Like most Old Order Amish, they wore traditional Amish attire, used horses and buggies for transportation, and had biweekly preaching services in German followed by a simple meal. But unlike most Amish, they had German-language Sunday school on alternate Sundays, with adults using the Bible and children using lesson books. Before 1940 they had electricity in their homes. Preacher Sam Weaver, who came in 1945, did not agree that electricity or refrigerators should be used, but electricity was in, and it stayed. They also took a more liberal position on shunning, or the ban, applying it only to members guilty of such sins as divorce or adultery and not to those who merely joined another church.[91]

Their diversity brought problems. Already in the mid-1940s, bishop Mose Yoder moved to Iowa after Samuel A. Weaver and Ben M. Slabaugh moved to Oregon. They were ministers, but had caused problems for their bishop in Michigan when they put forbidden rubber tires on their tractors. By the late 1940s bishop Bontreger of Indiana heard reports of disunity in the McMinnville Amish church. Again he visited the group several times, the last probably in 1951, when he was eighty-three. Besides performing three weddings in the first eleven days, he picked berries and beans for commercial growers. Unfortunately, he found a "very bad two-sided condition in the church, caused by distrust, backbiting, suspicion, and slander." Working with the church several weeks, he helped restore peace and ordained Menno Swartzentruber as bishop. But decline set in. Several ministers and other families left and in the next ten years membership dropped from forty-seven to sixteen. In those years some, including several of the bishop's children, joined nearby Mennonite congregations.[92]

Disagreement about various changes caused the eventual division of the group. By 1960 eight families, one widow, and one single woman comprised the small congregation. When the bishop and the minister went east for a time, four families and the single woman purchased automobiles. They hoped that when the ordained men returned to Oregon they would accept this change. But they did not. In December 1961, Swartzentruber moved to Sarasota, Florida, and Weaver to Kentucky. The two remaining families without automobiles also located in Kentucky.[93]

Those families who remained in Oregon now considered themselves Beachy Amish. They invited former minister Ben M. Slabaugh to be their shepherd. He was by this time a bishop at Garnet, Kansas. About the time he moved back to McMinnville the group began meeting in the old Briedwell School just west of Amity instead of in homes. However, the congregation did not prosper. In the spring of 1973 Anna Weirich, widow of William Weirich, joined the Mennonite church at McMinnville. Others also joined Mennonite congregations. In 1976 only two or three families and a single woman continued to meet for biweekly preaching, with Sunday school on alternating Sundays, all in German. But those few remaining Oregon Amish would soon lose their identity.[94]

Church of God in Christ, Mennonite (Holdeman) (CGC)

Three Holdeman groups settled in Oregon, but only the last survived through 1976. The first arrived in 1890 from Kansas where, after emigrating from Russia, they had joined John Holdeman's church and lived about fifteen years. In Oregon they settled in northern Polk County near Perrydale, about ten miles from Dallas. Some family names were Unruh, Ratzlaff, Giesbrecht, Esau, Boese, and Schimmelfeming. Elder John Holdeman visited them in 1893 and ordained Samuel Boese to the ministry on November 23. In 1902, due to the Panic of 1893 and economic hardships that followed, the group dissolved. Some moved to Linden, Alberta, Canada.[95]

The second group, the Jacob G. Loewen extended family, moved from Winton, California, to Lane County, a few miles south of Eugene, in 1945. Farmers and loggers living north of Creswell, they established the Cloverdale congregation with Loewen in charge of the weekly services held in the homes. Through their witness several local men were converted and became baptized members. The 1950 membership was thirteen. But contrary to the hopes of the Loewen family, no more Holdemans moved to the area, and after ten or twelve years the small group left Oregon.[96]

In 1957 families in the third group began moving to Scio, northeast of Albany, an area with relatively inexpensive farms and friendly people. There they organized the Evergreen congregation. They came from the Winton and Livingston congregations in Merced County, California, because of urban pressures there from Castle Air Force Base with its screaming jets. Family names were Becker, Loewen (several of them), and Toews, all from California except one from Langdon, North Dakota. In the next years others joined them. In 1959 Edward Jantz, a minister at Winton, moved to Scio. Through 1975 he continued to be the only minister there.

The congregation held services first in their homes, later in the Pioneer Queener schoolhouse, and finally in a church building they constructed in 1960. In 1973 its membership was ninety-five and Sunday school attendance totaled 155. For this, as with other Holdeman congregations, maintaining church standards of plain and simple living and reaching out in mission work, both very important to them, were like tugging at both ends of a rope. This called for a congregation large enough for members to have easy access to each other and provide support and fellowship, a security for current members and an attraction for new ones.[97]

Brethren in Christ

Almost nothing is known about the earliest Brethren in Christ (BIC) people in Oregon. Early in 1893 Samuel Zook, a respected BIC bishop and leader from Kansas, visited four members who lived in Oregon and preached in two Sunday services. When these people arrived, where they lived, and how long they stayed is unknown. An Oregon tent meeting in 1918 apparently did not produce lasting results. There was no link between these efforts and the BICs who later established congregations at Grants Pass and Salem.[98]

Benjamin M. Books, a BIC minister in the large Upland congregation in California, provided the vision and vigor that started both the latter Oregon congregations. In 1944, not content to be one of many preachers when people elsewhere had no minister, Books and his wife, Priscilla, moved from Upland to Grants Pass. A few BIC families already lived in that area. At first they worshiped with other denominations such as the Nazarenes, but soon they began to meet together regularly for prayer and fellowship. Books considered Grants Pass a good place for a BIC congregation. Although both "plain people" and "a holiness class" of people lived there, no church combined the two emphases. The denominational home mission board supervised the early Grants Pass work and soon appointed Books as mission pastor.[99]

About the time in 1945 that Books, a carpenter, constructed a building two miles west of Grants Pass on the Redwood Highway, the group organized under the name Redwood Country Church. On July 1 it began having regular services. In 1970, after enlarging the first building several times, the congregation completed a new building. At that time more than two hundred attended Sunday services. Books served approximately four years before moving to near Salem about 1949. Other pastors served before Sam Hollingsworth became pastor in 1976. Though the congregation maintained ties with the larger denomination, it considered itself a community church and deemphasized its BIC affiliation.[100]

Labish Village, the area then seven miles north of Salem where Books moved about 1949, had no church and appeared to be a needy community. Apparently a few BIC families then lived at Salem and participated in the home mission that Books started. In 1951 he constructed a building and two years later added to it. While his strengths were in carpentry and preaching, Priscilla's gifts were in relating to people personally, in their homes. They served at Labish village until about 1960.[101]

The Labish congregation did not become large. In 1973, Labish Village was a disadvantaged, run-down community of five hundred people, many with low incomes, many Hispanic or black. Attendance at services was about sixty-five but only seventeen were members. Arthur Cooper pastored the entire community and performed countless acts of love and caring, but the people had little incentive to participate in a traditional church program. Into this place of obvious need came the "Labish Tentmakers," young people from elsewhere who volunteered their services in the church and community while supporting themselves. They brought new energy and enthusiasm as they taught Sunday school, directed children's clubs, helped with nutrition and sewing classes, worked in community camps and schools, improved homes of elderly persons, and motivated neighborhood clean-up and development. They gave fresh hope to the community, the church, and to Arthur Cooper, who continued as pastor in 1976.[102]

Unaffiliated Mennonite Groups

In the mid-twentieth century through 1976, a number of Oregon congregations considered themselves Mennonite but did not participate in the PCC or another Mennonite denomination. Several had begun as mission stations of PCC congregations. Others had withdrawn from the PCC. Some of them related to the Bible Mennonite Fellowship.

One congregation began as a mission Sunday school which Zion started near Silverton. After Zion people began to work there in a union Sunday school in 1937, one girl, Anne Tolmsoff, born in

Russia of Molokan parents, was converted. She joined the Menno-nite church, and served in various Mennonite congregations in the next years and after her marriage to Tim Strubhar. When a local supporter moved away, the Sunday school closed but the Zion chorus regularly presented a Christmas program in the community. In 1947 Zion began a new effort in the Silverton hills with summer Bible school and in 1949 it started a Sunday school with Edward (Kelly) Kenagy as superintendent and newly ordained minister. The school used a Grange hall before occupying the new brick building in 1953 that Zion helped build. At that time the group took the name Chapel in the Hills. By 1955 average attendance was in the upper seventies. Kenagy had been an enthusiastic worker at Zion and in the PCC, but he felt a strong tension between Mennonite expectations and reaching people with the message about Jesus Christ. He did not want distinctive Mennonite practices, probably those relating to attire, to smother the fresh-ness and vitality of new Christians. When in 1961 the PCC invited the Chapel to join, Kenagy declined. The PCC was then too con-fining for his congregation. By 1960 the Chapel in the Hills had become a community church without a denominational identity. In 1976 Kenagy was still its pastor.[103]

Another congregation began in 1948 as a mission effort of Zion, when members held a summer Bible school and then began a Sunday school in the Meadowbrook schoolhouse. It was in a pleasant foothills community near the Cascade Mountains about five miles northwest of Molalla. Naomi Strubhar was one of the most influential early leaders there until her death in 1956. In 1949 Zion appointed minister Chester Kauffman to take charge of this growing work. Within two years attendance reached the nine-ties and there were seventeen converts, most of them joining other denominations. Kauffman's emphasis was on winning souls to Christ, not necessarily to the Mennonite church. After Zion built an impressive brick-and-block meetinghouse for Meadowbrook in the early 1950s, more attended services.[104]

In August 1958 Meadowbrook Mennonite Church organized with thirty charter members. Some family names were Counts, Emmert, Hamilton, Kauffman, Mengershausen, Obelander, Pratt, Ratzloff, Schultz, Weaver, and Wyatt. Ten transferred their mem-bership from the nearby Molalla Mennonite Church, which had dis-banded in 1951. Members at first were largely persons with Men-nonite heritage who wanted to remain Mennonites. Within a few years community people who were not interested in being Mennonites joined Meadowbrook. In 1964 all who participated in the congregation became eligible to vote in business meetings, and eventually they had no official membership roll. Though some favored joining the PCC, others preferred another denomination or none at all. Meadowbrook remained a community church, and after Kauffman resigned in 1964, seminarians from Western Evangelical Seminary or Village Missions served as pastors. Harold Maycumber was pastor in 1976. By then, Meadowbrook, with only seven Mennonites, was Mennonite in legal name only.[105]

Mission work which Sheridan began a few miles southeast in the small town of Ballston, population 200, became a congregation much later. After a summer Bible school there in 1936 and biweekly services for a few months after, the work ended until 1947. That summer Sheridan had another Bible school in Ballston, with evangelistic meetings led by James Bucher, followed by regular services. People responded well for about a decade, and several accepted Christ and became faithful workers in the Mennonite church, including Helen Kaltenbach, who later served as a missionary in Mexico with her husband, Maynard Headings. Attendance peaked around sixty or seventy in the late 1950s.[106]

In spite of declining community interest and attendance in the 1960s, LeRoy Cowan, a seventy-one-year-old Sheridan minister who preached frequently at Ballston, organized the Maranatha Mennonite Church there in October 1965, with twenty-two charter members. Family names were Cowan, Evers, Kaltenbach, Kennedy, Krehbiel, Lehman, Marner, Neal, Nisly, Stockton, and Zook. This was, in essence, a break from Sheridan, whose officials did not participate in the service, although some members were from Sheridan. Cowan took a more conservative stance, though interpersonal relationships may also have played a part. The group cleaned up the site and completed a building which another denomination had begun years earlier. Maranatha did not join the PCC but maintained relationships with Harrisburg, Porter, and Tangent of the Northwest Fellowship of Unaffiliated Conservative Mennonites. Cowan continued as pastor through 1976 in spite of declining health, with an assistant or two most of the time. The membership doubled to forty-four by 1970. But in the next years some moved away; others died. Some who left may have chafed under Cowan's tight rein. By 1976, with seven of only ten members being from the Cowan family, the future of Maranatha seemed uncertain.[107]

A short-lived congregation in Portland formed when James Bucher, mission worker among the Jews, and Joe H. Yoder, superintendent of Portland's Rock of Ages Rescue Mission, began services in the Bucher home in southeast Portland in 1968. They called it the Berean church and intended that it provide a church home for the mission workers, converts, and I-W men and their wives. Primarily, it served people who preferred a more conservative fellowship than Portland Mennonite Church offered. Jonathan Zook, Bethel bishop, officially organized Berean, probably late in 1968 or in 1969. Family names of the ten charter members and one added later were Brown, Bucher, Dow, Ebersole, Peterson, Ross, and Yoder. Three were Rescue Mission converts. A few nonmembers also attended services. Joe Yoder was the designated pastor; James Bucher, copastor. Berean did not affiliate with any denominational organization and survived less than a decade. In 1973, they began using the Rescue Mission hall for services because of the Buchers' failing health. By the end of 1976, with both ministers ill, Berean disbanded.[108]

People who withdrew their support for the PCC organized the Bible Mennonite Fellowship (BMF) late in 1967 (see chapter 5). Ray Mishler served as chairman; Lloyd Kropf, vice-chairman; Melvin Paulus, secretary; Ralph Shank, treasurer; and Dan L. Gingerich, fifth member. Membership was open to congregations or individuals who supported the doctrinal statements, constitution, and discipline of the fellowship; who shared in its work and finances; and who applied for membership and were approved by the executive committee and the delegate body. None of the seven congregations that had withdrawn from the PCC by 1969 joined the BMF except Bethel, shortly before it disbanded. Rather, individuals provided the framework for the fellowship. And even individual membership did not develop as the early constitution implied it would. The BMF never had a complete list of members but rather continued as a loosely formed fellowship.[109]

Participants at the first annual meeting in November 1968 adopted a confession of faith and a constitution, but some persons who took part in later meetings did not agree to all of the details in the discipline. Although they all agreed about leaving the PCC, wide differences among them on such items as attire produced problems, as had happened while they were still in the conference. The fellowship supported Jewish mission and rescue mission work in Portland—both former projects of the PCC mission board—and mission work in northern British Columbia and in Mexico. The Women's Service Committee of the BMF provided fellowship and service activities for women.[110]

Although withdrawal from the conference did not unify the seceding congregations as some leaders had hoped, some members from most congregations continued to participate in fellowship meetings and activities in 1976. In addition to persons of Brownsville, Hopewell, Fairview, Sheridan, and Church in the Wildwood (which had not yet officially withdrawn from the PCC), persons from Arizona, Montana, and British Columbia also participated in the BMF. Officers in 1976 were Lloyd Kropf, moderator; Roy Hostetler, assistant moderator; Ralph Shank, treasurer; and Clarence Gerig, secretary.[111]

■ ■ ■

The intertwining of individualism and community among Oregon's Mennonite groups, both within and among congregations, presented as much complexity as a kitten tangled in knitting yarn. Where the strands of individualism ended and the skein of church community began depended upon the arrangement of the parts and the influence of outside communities, ideologies, or other forces. The congregations with official ties to a denomination varied in the degree to which they as local bodies and their members as individuals related to their conferences. Some congregations without denominational affiliation related to other like-minded congregations, particularly if they had earlier been part of a conference. At times they may have felt cut off from the larger skein from which they had earlier come. The several congregations with a community church status emphasized an individualistic religion more than a community of faith. Though some congregations with denominational affiliation also focused largely on an individualistic faith, most professed a degree of community with their denomination.

Chapter 7
Related Mennonite Groups in Neighboring States

Through geographically organized conferences, most Oregon Mennonites related to congregations in neighboring states. This contact influenced their faith and mission and gave them a denominational identity. When they met together for worship and fellowship, adopted doctrinal positions, and supported conference mission efforts and institutions, they experienced a partnership in a larger community of faith. Their conferences gave them a community broader than their individual congregations.

This chapter will briefly introduce Oregon's neighboring congregations in the MC Pacific Coast Conference (PCC) and GC Pacific District Conference (PDC), which authorized the writing of this history. It will help place Oregon's PCC and PDC Mennonites in the context of their larger relationships. The two conferences were not equally represented in Oregon. The PCC at times included congregations in California, Montana, and, through 1976, in Idaho. But Oregon congregations were always a large majority. In the PDC, except for the earliest years, the Oregon congregations were a minority. In 1976, most were in Idaho, Washington, California and Arizona. The MBs, EMBs, and other Oregon groups await inclusion in comprehensive histories of Mennonites of neighboring states.

The format for this chapter will be:

Name, location, conference, date
(date of organization, to disbanding/withdrawal [D/W], when applicable)
    1. Membership survey (beginning; high; 1976 report, or D/W)
    2. Leadership survey (beginning; 1976, or D/W)
    3. Other information

Blaine
Lynden
Newport
Monroe
Deer Park
Kalispell
Seattle
Rathdrum
Creston
Schrag
Spokane
Moses Lake
Ritzville
Warden
Lind
Colfax
WASHINGTON
Pasco
Almota
MONTANA
Ariel
Columbia
Portland
Salem
Eugene
IDAHO
Caldwell
Dubois
Boise
Nampa
Minidoka
Aberdeen
Hammett
Filer
Twin Falls
OREGON
OCEAN
CALIFORNIA
NEVADA
Corning
Reno
Rio Linda
Sacramento
Winton
Atwater
Dos Palos
Fairmead
Fresno
Reedley
Dinuba
Woodlake
Terra Bella
Adelaida
Estrella
Paso Robles
ARIZONA
Shafter
PACIFIC
Los Angeles
Phoenix
Chandler
San Diego
Escondido
Tucson

LOS ANGELES AREA

1 Lancaster
2 Pasadena
3 Whittier
4 Santa Fe Springs
5 Downey
6 Orange
7 Pomona
8 Upland
9 Victorville

Locations of Oregon-Related Mennonites

in the

PACIFIC COAST CONFERENCE

and

PACIFIC DISTRICT CONFERENCE (GC)

before or in 1976

Hope Lind

Washington

In 1878 Jacob and Magdalena Kauffman, Amish Mennonites, earlier of Lee County, Iowa, moved by covered wagon from Kansas to Almota in southeastern Washington Territory, on the Snake River in Whitman County. Most Mennonites arrived a few years later, after railroads opened the area for easier immigration. In 1889, AM bishop Jonathan P. Smucker of Indiana visited about twenty scattered members in this area. Most had emigrated there from Davis County, Iowa. The Kauffmans and perhaps other AMs later became charter members of the first Mennonite congregation in the state, at Colfax.[1]

Onecho Mennonite Church at Colfax (GC), 1893-1963

1. 19; 155 in 1961; 151.
2. Paul R. Aeschliman; Charles Lyman.
3. The congregation organized as First Mennonite Church of Colfax, worshiped with the Methodists for many years both before and after organization, and adopted Onecho as its name in 1954. Influenced by Fundamentalism and Scofield dispensationalism, its people protested the PDC's emphasis on social and political concerns and withdrew in 1963.[2]

Menno Mennonite Church at Ritzville (GC), 1900

1. ?, about 13 families; 181 in 1971; 169.
2. J. R. Schrag; Nick Kassabaum.
3. The Christian Krehbiel family from Germany were the first Mennonite settlers in Adams County in the early 1890s. Schrag Mennonites from Lane County, Oregon, moved there in 1899-1900. For some years elder J. R. Schrag was postmaster for the Menno post office, located in his home, across the road from the Graber country store. After worshiping in homes and the Menno schoolhouse, in 1908 they completed a nearby meetinghouse. In the 1930s many families left because of crop failures. In the 1940s pastor Edmund J. Miller's teachings on stewardship motivated generous giving for many years, several times the per member giving of most PDC congregations.[3]

Salem Mennonite Church at Ruff (GC), 1910-1937

1. 32; ca 60 in 1920; 24.
2. Menno ministers, including John Waltner, M. J. Galle.
3. Settlers from South Dakota settled west/northwest of Menno in 1902-1903 on undeveloped railroad land. They built a meetinghouse in 1918, eighteen miles west of Menno. Some families left in the 1930s depression. The remaining members disbanded and joined Menno in 1937.[4]

Congregations at Monroe (GC), 1918, 1944, 1971-1974

Five Mennonite families from Kansas and Oklahoma moved to Monroe, in Snohomish County, in 1911.

First Mennonite Church of Monroe, 1918-1971
1. 33; 119 in 1969.
2. J. M. Franz; Frank Ewert, 1970.
3. In 1944 a group withdrew and organized:

Mennonite Country Church, 1944-1971
1. 21; 63 in 1958; 43.
2. J. L. McNabb; Herbert Major.
3. In 1971 forty-three members merged with First Mennonite to become:

Monroe Community Chapel, 1971-74
1. 127; 134 in 1972.
2. Riley Rinks; Riley Rinks.
3. In 1974 the congregation withdrew from the PDC, to become an independent, unaffiliated congregation. It was not a unanimous decision; some members wanted to retain conference affiliation.[5]

Spring Valley Mennonite Church at Newport (GC), 1928

1. 16; 89 in 1958; 61.
2. J. J. Kliewer; George Leppert.
3. Mennonite refugees from Russia settled in the area in

1922. Mennonites from Kansas, Oklahoma, and Texas moved there soon after. Some settled on railroad land. The PDC subsidized Spring Valley for several decades.[6]

First Mennonite Church at Deer Park (GC), 1937-1943

1. 18; 26 in 1939; 17.
2. M. J. Galle; ?
3. Russian Mennonite refugees from Harbin, China, settled in the area in 1929-30, between Spokane and Newport. Soon members moved to Newport and Lynden, Washington, and Dallas, Oregon. The congregation disbanded in 1943.[7]

Glendale Mennonite Church at Lynden (GC), 1945

1. 22; 107 in 1968; 90.

2. F. D. Koehn; Merle Kauffman.

3. Early in the 1940s, Mennonites settled near Lynden, a few miles from the Canadian border. Seven families were from Deer Park, Washington. Seven or more were from Kansas, Oklahoma, Montana, California, and Mexico. The neighboring MB congregation, Blaine, attended the dedication of Glendale's building in 1945 and gave $250. A schism occurred in 1971, after a vote of confidence in the pastor failed and some older members left. The remaining group united under a new pastor.[8]

Warden Mennonite Church at Warden (GC), 1956

1. 11; 52 in 1973; 51.
2. Wilbur Schmidt; Frank Horst.
3. Former members of Menno had earlier lived near Warden, but many had left in the 1930s. With the coming of irrigation in the 1950s, Mennonite families located there again in 1954 and years following. Warden organized with the blessing of nearby Menno. People of other religious backgrounds participated at Warden.[9]

Columbia Basin Mennonite Church at Pasco (UM), 1967

1. 15; 64 in 1974; ?
2. Verle Stutzman; Verle Stutzman.
3. In 1961 PCC families began moving to a developing region north of Pasco. The congregation did not align with either PCC or Bible Mennonite Fellowship and remained unaffiliated. It requested counsel from both Verl Nofziger, who withdrew from PCC, and PCC leaders, and supported PCC mission efforts and Western Mennonite School. By 1976 community people participated more, and the emphasis had moved from traditional Mennonite expressions of faith to a more charismatic, nondenominational position.[10]

South Seattle Mennonite Church in Seattle (GC), 1968

1. 21; 62 in 1976.
2. Milton Harder; Loren Friesen.
3. Families began Sunday school in their homes. After a brief period of growth, economic and personal problems impeded progress. Members' scatteredness over the large city was a hindrance. The PDC subsidized the congregation, and a voluntary service unit supported peace and social concerns. Most original families left in the early 1970s, but others joined.[11]

California

California had both transitory and permanent Mennonite settlers. Johannes Dietrich Dyck was one Mennonite who followed the gold rush to California, but after ten adventure-filled years in Western United States, he returned to Prussia in 1858. Occasionally a family genealogy mentions other such prospectors. Urias Kreider of Elkhart County, Indiana, moved to San Diego County in 1876, hoping his health would improve. But two years later he died there, at age twenty-five. A decade later, in 1887, Henry Rees of Ashland, Ohio, settled in Pomona. He became a member of the Upland (GC) congregation, organized some fifteen years later. Between 1896 and 1906, GC congregations organized in three areas with large, new concentrations of Mennonites. After this, no continuing PDC or PCC congregations organized in California until

1954, except two in Los Angeles. Several experienced division or regrouping. At least eight congregations in the first four decades of the twentieth century did not survive until 1976.[12]

Some California congregations changed conference affiliation. In 1948 the PCC released its distant congregations in California and Arizona, at their request, and they organized the South Pacific Conference (later, Southwest Conference) (MC). Their summaries in this chapter will usually cover only the years they were part of the PCC. PDC congregations which organized in the 1960s and 1970s also became members of the MC Southwest Conference (SWC).[13]

Congregations at Paso Robles (GC), 1897, 1903, 1904

Recent immigrants began to settle in southern California in 1896, in the Paso Robles area. Elder Jacob Hege of Wisner, Nebraska, and other south German families settled on wheat country to the east, near Estrella. J. E. Claassen of Beatrice, Nebraska, and other north German families from West Prussia, including minister A. J. Wiebe, preferred the Godfrey Ranch area near Adelaida, northwest of town. Dialects and customs differed but all worshiped in High German.[14]

San Marcos Mennonite Church of Paso Robles, 1897-1903
1. ca 40; ca 60.
2. Jacob Hege; Jacob Hege.
3. The group first met in homes or a school, then built a meetinghouse in 1898 on the San Marcos Ranch near Chimney Rock, closer to Godfrey Ranch than Estrella. The Estrella group soon began to meet in an adobe building in their area. Cultural differences and traveling distances contributed to division, and the congregation dissolved in 1903.

First Mennonite Church of Paso Robles, 1903
1. ca 25; 201 in 1970; 150.
2. Jacob Hege; Herbert M. Dalke.
3. The congregation first organized as the Mennonite Church of Estrella and later adopted the name First Mennonite Church. They met on alternate Sundays in the town meetinghouse and a country schoolhouse until automobiles made traveling to town easier.

Second Mennonite Church of Paso Robles, 1904-1967
1. 39; 132 in 1947 and 1956; 110.
2. F. F. Jantzen; Benno Toews.
3. The congregation first organized as San Marcos Mennonite Church. In 1911 they moved their building to Willow Creek and took the name Willow Creek Mennonite Church. Later they adopted the name Second Mennonite Church. When their building burned in 1967, most members merged with the 100 members of First Mennonite, making a combined membership of 198.[15]

First Mennonite Church of Upland (GC), 1903
1. 18; 362 in 1948; 207.
2. Michael M. Horsch; Kenneth J. Peterson.
3. Henry Rees, 1887 settler at Pomona, wrote glowing reports which attracted Mennonite families to this citrus-growing region. After a large drop in membership when Earl Salzman resigned as pastor in 1951, the congregation never regained the former numbers.[16]

First Mennonite Church at Reedley (GC), 1906
1. 25; 627 in 1950; 508.
2. H. J. Krehbiel; Leo L. Miller.
3. In 1903 Kansas and Minnesota GC families began moving to Reedley in the San Joaquin Valley. They organized just one year after MBs organized a Reedley congregation. The influx of families moving to Reedley and family birth rates increased their numbers. By 1930 Russian Mennonites had come by way of Harbin, China. In the 1950s there was internal division over the theology of a controversial pastor and over the Korean War.[17]

Immanuel Mennonite Church in Downey (GC), 1918
1. 34; 299 in 1951; 197.
2. M. Horsch; Donald McClintock.
3. By 1906 GCs in the Los Angeles area met in homes for worship. The GC home mission board sponsored the River Station Mission in Los Angeles in 1910, with E. F. Grubb of Ohio as superintendent. The board wanted the mission to reach not only the un-

saved but also scattered Mennonites, which required German preaching. Grubb resigned. Horsch, from Upland, took over the work and organized the congregation. It later changed locations twice, adopting the name Immanuel Mennonite Church with the 1924 move. When it moved to Downey in early 1950s, dissension divided the congregation. A group withdrew and began the Bethel congregation at nearby Santa Fe Springs (see later section). Immanuel recovered and membership frequently reached the 240s.[18]

Calvary Mennonite Church in Los Angeles (MC), 1920-1948

1. 42; 140 in 1926; ca 100.
2. J. P. Bontrager; H. A. Wolfer, moved to Oregon 1948.
3. By 1903 MCs lived in Los Angeles and suburbs. They began a Sunday school in 1916, first in Pasadena, moving several times to other Los Angeles locations. This was a mission station, supervised by the PCC mission board, MC Board of Missions and Charities, and/or the two jointly. Sometimes the congregation was at variance with the PCC over standards in the PCC discipline. It adopted the name Calvary Mennonite Church in 1942 and joined South Pacific Conference in 1948.[19]

Extinct Congregations (MC and GC), 1909-1935

For several decades beginning early in the 1900s, scattered Mennonites settled in California communities, some without established congregations, others with short-lived organizations. Some maintained relationships with their Mennonite group; others did not. Some stayed for long periods of time; others soon moved elsewhere.

Victorville (MC), 1905-1906
Minister David Garber, Nampa, Idaho, moved to Victorville in 1905. Though he hoped to found a Mennonite colony there, about a year later he moved to La Junta, Colorado.[20]

Dinuba (MC), 1909-1916
1. 17; 22 in 1911; 1.
2. E. C. Weaver, deacon, left 1913.

3. The first MC families moved to Reedley in 1905, then to Dinuba, and soon organized a Sunday school. Most families later moved to Oregon in search of cheaper land. Only Delilah Sharer remained in 1916.[21]

Corning (MC), 1911-ca 1916
1. ?
2. Emanuel Stahley.
3. Families from Idaho and Pennsylvania settled at Corning, beginning in 1907, and organized a Sunday school in 1908. Families began moving away even before Oregon ministers partially organized a congregation in 1911. Only V. L. Schrock and wife remained in 1916.[22]

Escondido (GC), 1912-1934
1. 19; ?
2. Herman Janzen; H. D. Voth.
3. Mennonites built a meetinghouse at Escondido in 1911 and organized in 1912. Some families soon moved away. Sunday school was discontinued in 1930 and they held services only monthly. The congregation dissolved in 1934.[23]

Woodlake (GC) near Reedley, 1915-1929
1. 18; 3 families in 1929.
2. H. A. Bachman; ministers from First Mennonite, Reedley.
3. Mennonites helped transform virgin land a few miles southeast of Reedley into productive orange groves. They disbanded in 1929. Some joined First at Reedley, some another denomination.[24]

Terra Bella (MC), 1917 (informal)—after 1942
1. 16; 18 in 1919; 13 in 1930; ? in 1940s.
2. Emanuel Stahley; Luke E. Weaver.
3. The first families moved to Terra Bella in 1909, but some soon left. Stahley moved there from Corning in 1916. They had a union Sunday school in a schoolhouse for about 20 years and organized as a mission station in 1919. The group disbanded after 1942.[25]

Shafter (GC), 1918-1919, 1934-1964
1. 1918, ?; 23 in 1934; 100 in 1947; 50.
2. Herman Janzen, 1918; A. G. Schmidt, 1934; Kenneth Ross.

3. After some of the first families left, remaining members joined other denominations. They regrouped in 1934. The PDC provided financial assistance several years in the 1960s. The congregation disbanded in December 1964, when Ross left, and began meeting with the Shafter MBs in January 1965.[26]

Dos Palos (GC), 1930-1934
1. 30 families.
2. Daniel Gerig.
3. Mennonites moved to this area where a new irrigation project was to be developed. About 100 attended services, but the promised irrigation water did not materialize and families had to leave. The congregation disbanded in January 1934.[27]

Fairmeade (GC), 1920s, and Lancaster (GC), 1940s-1957
GC families lived at Fairmeade in the 1920s. In 1922 they joined the First Church at Reedley but continued to live in the Fairmeade area for some years. Six families were worshiping with MBs there in 1946. Nine families settled on farms near Lancaster by the mid-1940s and revived an inactive community church with the understanding that it would remain a community church to benefit the several denominations represented. The PDC funded the work for some years but discontinued funding in 1957.[28]

Congregations at Winton/Atwater (MC), (GC), 1931, 1940, 1966

Even before the 1931 (MC) and the 1940 (GC) congregations organized, CGCs and MBs had settled at Winton and organized congregations. Later, CGC people joined the MC and GC congregations.[29]

Winton Mennonite Church (MC), 1931-1960s
1. 23; 74 in 1933; 75 in 1946.
2. John P. Bontrager; John P. Bontrager in 1948.
3. After a Mrs. Koppenhaver, a convert of the Kansas City mission (MC), moved to Winton in 1925, Mennonite preachers visited her and held meetings there. Other MCs soon settled there and at first worshiped with the CGCs, then met separately and organized in 1931. Problems after 1933 reduced membership by a

third, but they recovered by the 1940s. Winton hosted the meeting which organized the South Pacific Conference in 1948.[30]

Bethel Mennonite Church (GC), 1940-1960s
1. 32; 93 in 1950; 13 families in 1960.
2. D. B. Hess; George Dick.
3. In the late 1930s GCs moved to area and worshiped with Presbyterians for several years before and after organizing. Their membership included people from the "Koehn Church," which minister Joel T. Koehn had organized in the 1920s after being excommunicated from the CGC. Severe problems twice regarding the meeting place divided them in 1951. The withdrawing group called a former pastor and the Bethel pastor resigned. When Bethel had no pastor, MC ministers sometimes preached.[31]

United Mennonite Church (GC), 1966
1. 65; 84 in 1970; 50 in 1975.
2. Merle Unruh; Robert R. Dalke.
3. Both the MC and GC congregations struggled to survive in the early 1960s. Sharon (MC) (Winton Mennonite, renamed) broke apart after the minister divorced his wife and married a young woman from the congregation. Bethel (GC) was struggling financially and people from both groups united. Membership fluctuated. United was a member of the PDC but not of the SWC.[32]

Congregations at Pomona/Upland (MC), 1934, 1942

Most MCs in the Upland area, from 1907 and after, joined the Los Angeles (MC) congregation rather than Upland's GC or BIC congregations. They wished for a congregation nearby and organized:

North Pomona Mennonite Church (MC), 1934-1942
1. 29; 32 in 1942.
2. James Bucher; James Bucher.
3. Sixteen Upland area MCs did not join because they did not support Bucher, who had earlier been involved in church trouble in Indiana. Problems occurred in 1939 when PCC bishops used the lot and ordained Jacob S. Roth minister instead of the nominee with three times more votes. At the recommendation of PCC bish-

ops, Bucher and Roth moved (to Oregon) because of indiscretion in the work, and the congregation dissolved.[33]

Seventh Street Mennonite Church (MC), 1934-1948
1. 25; 88 in 1948.
2. William Jennings; Sherman Maust, 1948.
3. This was first named Alpine Mennonite Church. Some charter members came from North Pomona, others were Mennonites previously uncommitted to a California congregation. They moved to new building in 1947 and adopted the title name. In 1948 they joined the new South Pacific Conference.[34]

Robla Mennonite Church near Sacramento (MC), 1953-1958

1. 16; 29.
2. Orrie D. Yoder; Merle Kropf.
3. Five Mennonite families from Oregon moved to the Sacramento area in 1952 to open a rescue mission sponsored by the PCC Mission Board. They soon organized a congregation. In 1958 the board closed the mission. It encouraged the families to stay in California and build a congregation from the community, but all returned to Oregon in 1958.[35]

Mennonite Community Church at Fresno (GC), 1954

1. 41; 158 in 1970; 123.
2. Peter J. Ediger; Floyd Quenzer.
3. GC families in Fresno first met informally in 1952.[36]

Bethel Community Mennonite Church at Santa Fe Springs (GC), 1957

1. 37; 78 in 1966; 56 in 1974.
2. Lyman Hofstetter; Fred Buckles.
3. A group from the Immanuel Mennonite Church in Downey, who called themselves "Group B," withdrew for unspecified reasons in 1956 and located in Whittier. Their address later became Santa Fe Springs.[37]

Orange Mennonite Fellowship (GC, MC), 1972

1. 10; 23 in 1975; 16.
2. John Kreider; John Kreider.
3. Missions committees of the PDC and SWC discussed beginning a witness in Orange County for several years before John and
Verlene Kreider began a house fellowship and community outreach
in September 1969. Of the charter members, only Kreiders had
Mennonite heritage. In 1976 four families had left, three for distant communities, one for a larger fellowship. Additionally, problems in relationships, economics, and differing ways of experiencing the Holy Spirit put the congregation's future in question.[38]

Idaho

It appears that few Mennonites moved to Idaho before colonization began and congregations organized. The George Hostetler
family moved by team and wagon from Missouri to Rathdrum, Idaho, near Spokane, Washington, in the late 1880s. About a year later
they moved to Hubbard, Oregon. Except for Nampa, where
irrigation was already making the Boise River Valley productive,
most Mennonites who settled in Idaho pioneered on undeveloped
land of sagebrush and rabbits, even into the 1930s. In general,
they came because of the promise of irrigation, and they helped
develop areas along the Snake River into productive communities.
Those who settled in dryland farming areas did not establish continuing congregations.[39]

First Mennonite Church at Nampa (MC), 1899

1. 28; 175 in 1976.
2. David Garber; Max G. Yoder.
3. Oregon Short Line Railroad offered colonization incentives
in Idaho. Mennonites first organized the Antioch Mennonite
Church, and later named it Nampa Mennonite Church. In 1963 it
became First Mennonite Church. A city mission existed in a
separate location about five years in the early 1900s, administered
by the denominational mission board; Christian Scientists,
Mormons, Adventists, and Russellites (Jehovah Witnesses) made inroads among the Mennonites, and some joined such groups. Nampa
began mission Sunday schools and a Christian day school in the

1940s. E. S. Garber, Nampa bishop in the 1940s and 1950s, was influential in Oregon.[40]

Congregations at Aberdeen (GC), 1907, 1912-1929

Mennonites from Kansas and California settled on the new Aberdeen-Springfield irrigation project near American Falls, along the Snake River, in 1905-1906.

First Mennonite Church at Aberdeen, 1907
1. 36; 384 in 1944; 340.
2. Jacob Hege; Lowell Gerber, interim.
3. First named Salem Mennonite Church, it took the name First Mennonite after moving to the town meetinghouse. In 1928 some families withdrew and helped start the Assembly of God Church in Aberdeen. A group which left about 1909 preferred using the German language and organized:

Emanuel Mennonite Church, 1912-1929
1. ?; ca 75, 1929.
2. Jacob Hege; John Toevs.
3. This was a rural group a few miles west in a dryland farming area. With Toevs in failing health, the group disbanded and accepted the invitation to rejoin First Mennonite.[41]

During those twenty years, in spite of differences, the two congregations worked together. Their ministers served Mennonites at Minidoka and Dubois. Aberdeen Mennonites contributed to their larger community, in business, agricultural extension work, medicine, education and other endeavors.[42]

South Nampa Mennonite Church (CC) 1908-1911, 1918-1927

1. ?; 37 in 1910; ? in 1918; 61 in 1926.
2. Lee Lantz; Menno Niswander in 1911; Lee Lantz, 1918-1926.
3. Early settlers, Ulrichs (1902) and Riessers (1904) from Illinois, did not join Antioch (MC). With minister Lee Lantz, they organized the South Nampa Church. Some members came from Antioch. South Nampa was a member of the Central Conference (CC)

of Mennonites (with congregations in Illinois and neighboring states), which joined GCs in 1946. Alkaline soil caused Lantz and others to leave, and the group disbanded in 1911. When drainage ditches improved the soil, Lantz and others returned. Lantz revived the congregation in 1918, partly to shelter member COs in World War I. Too far from the CC to receive needed moral and spiritual help, it disbanded again in 1927.[43]

Filer Mennonite Church (MC), 1914

1. ca 22; 108 in 1950; 65.
2. Samuel Honderich; Royden Schweitzer.
3. Beginning in 1911, Mennonites from Pennsylvania, Ohio, Illinois, Nebraska, and Oregon settled in the area. Honderich served over 50 years, often with other ministers, the longest tenure for any PCC minister. Two groups withdrew in the 1950s and organized Faith and Highland (see later sections).[44]

Bethel Mennonite Church at Dubois (GC), 1916-1919

1. 40; at most, 51 couples, 13 singles, plus children.
2. No resident pastor; Aberdeen ministers and others served.
3. Beginning in 1913, Mennonites from Kansas, Oklahoma, and Aberdeen homesteaded near Dubois. The Mennonite population reached almost 270. MBs lived in the area and worshiped with Bethel, though MB preachers came for special meetings. A small group, called the "Klane Gemeente," lived in an outlying area. Irrigation water did not become available, and farmers could not withstand the drought in 1919. The congregation disbanded, and most returned to former communities.[45]

Indian Cove Mennonite Church at Hammett (UM), 1935-1976

1. 19; 80 in 1957; 61.
2. Amos M. Shenk; Amos Shenk (son of A. M. Shenk).
3. It organized as a PCC congregation. Low land prices in a developing irrigation district along the Snake River attracted Mennonites to the area as early as 1926, but most did not arrive until the early 1930s. The congregation emphasized a strong sense of

the Holy Spirit's presence in their personal and corporate lives, an influence on Oregon PCC Mennonites. More of a community church than most PCC congregations, in 1976 it decided to withdraw, though apparently it did not inform the PCC for several years.[46]

First Mennonite Church of Caldwell (GC), 1947-1962

1. 15; 42 in 1955; 31.

2. Menno Kliewer; Menno Kliewer.

3. Mennonites from Nebraska and Oregon moved to southwestern Idaho in the early 1940s and joined former South Nampa (CC) members who remained in the area. Problems included influences from several cults, such as Jehovah's Witnesses and "Armstrongism" (Worldwide Church of God), which one extended family joined. Some feared the Armstrong group would try to take over the Mennonite meetinghouse. Limited employment options also contributed to low morale, and the group disbanded in 1962.[47]

Faith Mennonite Church at Filer (GC), 1955-1968

1. 19; 38 in 1963; 12.

2. W. Harley King; Frank Horst, 1967.

3. The group first met in homes in 1954. Most had withdrawn from Filer (MC) due to a complex set of factors, including tensions similar to those in the PCC in 1950s. In the 1960s, some moved away. Others left for larger churches. Too small to call a pastor, the group disbanded in 1968.[48]

Highland Mennonite Chapel at Twin Falls (UM), 1960-1964

1. 30 in 1962.

2. Clarence A. Horst; Bill Virgin.

3. This was another group which withdrew from Filer (MC). Issues included Filer leadership, pressures on mission station converts to conform to traditional Mennonite practices, and experiencing the Holy Spirit. They were offered and desired PCC membership, but records do not show official membership. Discord developed, and some members left. A pentecostal minister, rejected as

pastor in another state, took leadership at Highland and effected a quasi-organization that illegally appropriated the bank accounts. Doubtless some participated unwittingly in his reorganization. In 1964, the legal board closed and retained the books, effecting the official disbanding of Highland. The new group used the building a year or more before selling it and sending the money to a Mexico missionary with Mennonite connections.[49]

City Acres Mennonite Church at Nampa (MC), 1963-1974

1. 20; 28 in 1969; 12.
2. Robert E. Garber; Robert E. Garber.
3. City Acres Mennonite Church began as a mission Sunday school of Nampa (MC) in 1943. All charter members had Mennonite heritage. Community people participated and some were baptized but not as members of the Mennonite Church. It was more a community church than most Mennonite congregations. Located in a less desirable residential area which was becoming industrialized, with more Hispanic families and no members qualified to work with them, City Acres disbanded. The members transferred to First Mennonite, from where most had come.[50]

Montana

Most Mennonite groups in Montana did not have close relationships with Oregon Mennonites. For a few years, one in western Montana was an exception.

Mountain View Mennonite Church at Kalispell (MC), 1913-1923

1. 20; 61 in 1919; 36 in 1923.
2. Jacob Roth; Daniel D. Kauffman in 1923.
3. Beginning in 1903, a few Oregon Mennonites moved to the beautiful mountain valley at Creston, near Kalispell. Others came from Nebraska and Iowa. Mountain View joined the PCC in 1916. Several Mountain View leaders moved to Oregon congregations, including deacon Chris Snyder. The congregation requested release from the PCC in 1923 because of its great distance from other

congregations. In 1976 it was a member of the (MC) Northwest Conference, earlier named Alberta-Saskatchewan Conference.[51]

Arizona and Nevada

Mennonites (GC) first moved to Arizona in the late nineteenth century to begin mission work among the Indians. Although scattered Mennonites of several groups lived and worked at various locations in Arizona in the early twentieth century, no continuing congregation organized before 1946. Arizona Mennonite congregations related to Oregon Mennonites through the PCC and PDC.

Congregations at Phoenix (MC) (GC), 1946, 1964

Sunnyslope Mennonite Church in Phoenix (MC), 1946-1948
1. 15; 45 in 1948.
2. Joe H. Yoder.
3. Joined the new South Pacific Conference in 1948.[52]

First Mennonite Church in Phoenix (GC), 1963
1. 16; 81.
2. Donavin Diller; Ernest Neufeld.
3. Phoenix GCs began meeting in the early 1960s. They informally organized before December 1963, or perhaps January 1964.[53]

Congregations at Tucson (Joint GC, MC), 1973, 1975

By the late 1960s, a few Mennonites were living in Tucson. The PDC and SWC began working jointly in 1969 to secure pastoral leadership for the group. It began as an informal house fellowship. Some participants intended that the congregation there would be a house church. Nathan Oglesby came as pastor in 1973. He, with his wife, Debbie, and Mr. and Mrs. Elster Wallace, Debbie's parents, had in mind a second church model. The Wallaces purchased a church building and Oglesby began services there in September 1973. They became:

Evangel Mennonite Church (GC, MC), 1973
1. ?; 73 in 1976.
2. Nathan Oglesby; Nathan Oglesby.

3. They followed a traditional model of services, community outreach, and "soul-winning" programs. Not clearly accountable to the joint committee of PDC and SWC which provided support, their future was uncertain in 1976.[54]

Tucson Mennonite Fellowship (GC, MC), 1975
1. 12; 9.
2. Eli Miller; Don and Cathy Lichti.
3. Mennonites who did not join Evangel continued meeting as a house fellowship, with lay leaders. In 1975 they applied for admission into the two sponsoring conferences.[55]

Other congregations

Another inter-Mennonite church-planting effort began at Chandler, a few miles south of Phoenix. What started as a weekly Bible study in the mid-1970s emerged in September 1976 as the Koinonia Fellowship with nineteen charter members. Far to the northwest, at Reno, Nevada, a small Mennonite congregation began relating to the PDC and SWC in 1975, but it did not survive long.[56]

■ ■ ■

One cannot know Oregon Mennonites (MC and GC, in this chapter) apart from their conferences, their larger faith communities. These relationships influenced their positions and decisions on a variety of issues and activities. Non-Oregon congregations in the PCC exerted a strength of influence out of proportion to their numbers. The influence of Oregon Mennonites was less strong in the PDC, though a number of Oregon persons had major responsibilities in the conference at various times. Though Oregon's PCC Mennonites provided the primary sustenance for their conference efforts, most of Oregon's PDC congregations probably would not have survived without their conference. All but two received financial support from the PDC at one time or another.

Geographically, the PDC covered a larger region than the PCC did, except for the years when Idaho, California, and Montana congregations were PCC congregations. Nonetheless, through their conferences, individuals and congregations had primary connections with their denominations. In their annual fellowship and worship, in their mission efforts and institutional programs, they could narrow the gap between the sense of community that bound them together in a Mennonite form of the body of Christ and the individualism which focused mainly on personal inner faith and piety.

For all of the Mennonite and related groups in Oregon and neighboring states, their uprooting and planting did not produce a well-ordered garden of perfect individuals laid out in faultless church communities. Often these Mennonites disagreed on how to live the practical details of their faith. At times differing theological emphases which came from outside their Anabaptist heritage produced stress in their church communities. Usually when they quarreled about theology or practice, it was because they cared so deeply about their faith. In spite of thistly divisions that threatened to choke out the flowering and fruitbearing individuals, many Mennonite communities not only survived but flourished. Their larger vision led them to nurture their own members in order to strengthen their church communities and to sow new fields with the good news that Jesus and his body, the church, care about all humanity. In their own and nearby neighborhoods, even in other countries, their larger vision motivated them to establish and nurture communities of loving, caring people who gave of themselves to meet human need.

PART II
The Larger Vision

The uprooting and planting of Mennonites and related groups in Oregon produced a melange of beliefs and resultant actions. At times unlovely weeds intruded among desirable blossoms and fruit. Even so, Mennonites believed life was a sacred trust from God. The way they lived minute by minute and day by day partook of eternity. Nothing was trite or unimportant. Yet, beliefs differed, filtering through imperfect persons and producing a picture that included shadows and separations amid the light and unity Mennonites experienced in Christ.

For Oregon Mennonites, their larger vision focused on living faithfully in spite of such differences. They emphasized a quality of spiritual life intended to bring individuals into the warmth and brightness of Christ's presence, both in spirit and in the family-like circle of the church community. Such faith, they believed, would enable individual and church to minister to the larger community and world, to meet and help people with needs and hurts. The inner experience and the outward movement were two sides of the same larger vision. One without the other was incomplete.

As the larger vision moved from inner experience to outward expression, Oregon Mennonites preached the gospel and started churches. They sent dried fruit to hungry people in India and provided farm tools for displaced Mennonites in South America. Although Oregon Mennonites attempted to preserve and adapt their unique heritage, both Christian and secular influences and movements in the larger world touched and changed them. But for many, nonresistance and working for peace with positive acts of constructive service and ministry remained a primary witness to their faith. In their institutions of mercy, they met immeasurable human need.

Their varied ministries in the larger world and their nurture of the personal commitment to Christ which motivated them remained together, twin foci of their larger vision.

Chapter 8
Oregon Mennonites Nurturing Their Faith

During the first century of Mennonites in Oregon, their larger vision included the essence of their faith. With one eye they focused on belief and practice, lighted by their spiritual awareness and personal relationship with Christ. With the other eye they focused on spiritual and physical needs outside their own communities and how they might serve in their larger neighborhoods and world. The two foci merged as their larger vision.

To nurture faith, (old) Mennonites, particularly, emphasized distinctive beliefs and practices. For most Oregon groups, the Sunday school and sermons from their own and visiting preachers were primary sources of nurture. The substance and methods of nurture often intertwined with tensions between individualism and community, as well as the church community's competition with other theologies or ideologies. Both Sunday schools and preachers reflected several theological strands of thought that touched Mennonites. Revivalism, Fundamentalism, innovative perspectives on biblical prophecy, and holiness and Holy Spirit movements all influenced Oregon Mennonites. They fostered a religious individualism that paralleled increasing individualism in secular society, even while many Mennonites attempted to subject it to the authority of their particular church community.

Preachers, both resident and visiting, usually chose what essentials of faith they would proclaim and nurture. Until the mid-twentieth century, OM preachers were largely untrained men from within the congregation who possessed leadership ability. In the PDC (GC), some early ministers had professional training, for instance, P. R. Aeschliman, who was appointed minister-at-large in 1896. He had studied two years at Halstead Seminary in Kansas before he settled at Colfax, Washington, and ministered tirelessly to Oregon congregations.[1]

Even in the early years outside influences touched Oregon

Mennonites. Orie Conrad was baptized by a Methodist circuit rider because the Conrad family lived outside a Mennonite community at the time. But Orie later became a faithful Mennonite worker. In the early 1900s Zion young people at Hubbard often attended evening services at the neighboring Brethren church, which they considered a rather lively place. This caused Zion to begin its own evening Bible meetings for youth. Some Zion people objected at first, including one mother who said she would rather her two young daughters went to the moving picture show.[2]

The Sunday school, which often preceded the organization of a congregation, was perhaps as important for the opportunities it offered the laity to develop leadership skills as for the nurture it provided the pupils. Hilda Reist, historian of the Western congregation, considered Sunday school "the hot-bed of the church." There, as in their home vegetable gardens, women as well as men could plant, weed, and harvest. Sarah Lohrentz Wiens, a missionary widow at the Dallas MB church, taught a class of rowdy boys no one else could handle, some of whom later became influential MB leaders. Minister Omar G. Miller remembered that it was Fannie Weaver Yoder, Hopewell Sunday school teacher, who invited him to accept Christ. Harrisburg, which did not begin Sunday school until about 1918, was for some years an exception. There the ministers were usually in charge of both preaching services and Sunday school, on alternate Sundays until about 1933, though lay leaders also helped.[3]

Sunday school conventions or conferences improved the effectiveness of the Sunday school. From its first session in 1896, the PDC (GC) included a Sunday school convention. Oregon's AM and OM congregations held their first Sunday school conference jointly in 1904. Speakers presented talks or essays (in AM/OM circles, usually men "gave talks" and women "read essays") related to the problems and challenges of the Sunday school. The topics included such issues as whether it was "advisable" for a superintendent "to read long chapters and lengthy prayers in opening exercises." Later, such meetings gave way to other types of organization or program, such as Christian Workers' Conference or teacher training classes.[4]

Revivalism

Revivalism was one significant influence on Mennonite

groups, denominationally, and in Oregon. Revivalistic preaching methods and emphases brought new energy and excitement to Mennonites accustomed to a quietly contained religious experience. It held out both the familiar and the new. Familiar was the emphasis on individual choice of faith and commitment. New was a more emotional experience, warming the heart more than uniting community. It privatized faith and tended to isolate salvation from the church. Faith became equated with a deeply personal relationship with Jesus, accepting his redemption, and thus avoiding hell. Most Mennonites continued to emphasize righteous living as a result, but faith become more individualistic and less communal. Thus, Mennonites at times wished to baptize a convert only in relation to a private Christ, apart from membership in his body. The PCC affirmed in 1951, however, that baptism "incorporated the applicant into the visible church."[5]

Mennonite revivalists, usually fluent of speech and with a flair for drama, attracted whole families. Some preachers included Bible lessons and children's meetings before the evening's evangelistic sermon. Singing was always integral to the service. End-time preaching about the imminent return of Christ and the need to be ready for his coming sometimes frightened persons into accepting Christ. But Otto Bier of the Dallas MB congregation observed that such emotionally laden conversions "were nonetheless real . . . perhaps more so than some made unemotionally and uncharged."

Some preachers might have been accused of manipulating children or being unduly persuasive during the "invitation," which usually was accompanied by revivalist gospel songs at the end of the sermon. Still all were deeply concerned that their listeners have a right relationship with Jesus Christ. Many congregations scheduled revival meetings annually or more often to provide for an ingathering of their children and youth. Revivals became a time when children in the church and sometimes unchurched neighbors decided to follow Christ and join the church. The result was especially impressive when a man too drunk to walk to the front left the service a sober, changed person. Often one evangelist served several neighboring congregations. S. E. Allgyer of Ohio was one who in his youth had matured under a Methodist revivalist, but he also emphasized Mennonite distinctives.[6]

Often accompanying revival meetings were programs for teaching the Bible and distinctive Mennonite beliefs, called Bible conferences, schools, institutes, or normals. Among OMs, Bible con-

Cliff Lind

Congregations often prepared cards or fliers to announce revival meetings and Bible conferences.

ferences were more educational and inspirational and less evangelistic in method than were revival meetings. When congregations combined them, two ministers usually shared in the preaching and teaching. General Conference Mennonites had a Bible conference as part of the first PDC meetings in 1896. Themes and sometimes lively discussion focused on the care and nurture of the people in their pioneer settings, with frequent "Amen!" responses. In the 1930s, the PDC encouraged its congregations to hold "protracted or revival" meetings "with particular emphasis upon Bible study." The Bible schools, normals, and institutes that began in 1920 (PCC) and in 1938 (Dallas GC, MB, and EMB congregations) were more institutional in nature. The PCC school continued a few years, then terminated, to be revived and restructured as Western Mennonite School. The Dallas school evolved into Salem Academy.[7]

Urie Kenagy kept a careful record of possibly the first Bible conference held at Zion (AM), December 24-29, 1906, inclusive, with morning, afternoon and evening sessions. C. R. Gerig of Fairview and L. J. Miller from Sycamore Grove in Missouri were the instructors. Sessions covered such subjects as the fall of man, restoration, law and grace, faith, love, hope, the personality of the Spirit, baptism, communion, foot washing, the devotional covering, marriage, anointing, nonresistance, nonconformity, "noninsurance," "nonsecrecy," self-denial, and the power of the Holy Spirit. Each evening the instructors responded to a question box before the sermon. Some of the questions related to "taking likenesses" (photographs), the tithe, the wearing of gold, outreach by being friendly, requests for explanation of specific Bible verses, use of tobacco and liquor, hairstyles and the prayer covering for women, clothing styles, and musical instruments. The speakers often gave many Scripture texts to explain their teaching position. On the subject of obedience, for example, L. J. Miller used at least twenty-seven references.[8]

Although in earlier years Oregon Mennonites engaged mostly Mennonite evangelists, revivalists from other traditions influenced them also. One was Charles Price, associate of the flamboyant, sensational Aimee Semple McPherson, who founded the International Church of the Foursquare Gospel. Fairview members attended the Price meetings and some even served as ushers, in spite of bishop Gerig's firm stand against those meetings. Members of the town church also attended, including sons of bishop Lind, who said nothing about whether or not to go. In his meetings Price emphasized that all the money taken in at the meetings would go to "Sister McPherson's" church, except the last offering which would be for him. One observer remembered the healing ceremonies as "quite a performance," in which Price would "almost fall over with some of the people." A Mennonite man, "healed," put away his glasses, only to need them to read at a later prayer meeting and attribute it to his lack of faith.

The Price meetings resulted in the organizing of a Foursquare Church in Albany. They also precipitated discord at Fairview because members had attended the meetings. Some Fairview members left and joined the Foursquare Church; others joined Albany Mennonite. Also, several times in the 1920s the Dallas MB congregation invited W. E. Pietsch, a Baptist evangelist. By 1941 Grace Mennonite at Dallas was participating in a city-wide evangelistic campaign with eight other churches. By the 1950s and 1960s, various Mennonite congregations frequently participated in

Roland Jantzi

The Western Mennonite School campus was the site of the Hammer revival campaign in 1954.

city-wide campaigns or such a noteworthy event as a Billy Graham crusade in Portland.[9]

Revival tent campaigns were spectacular Mennonite events common in the 1950s, when Oregon's OMs hosted three major Mennonite tent evangelists. The Brunk Brothers Revival (George R. Brunk II, evangelist) in 1953, the Hammer Tent Revival in 1954, and Myron Augsburger's Crusade for Christ in 1956 all received wide publicity and attracted large crowds of people from Episcopalians to Old Order Amish, in addition to Mennonites. Many experienced God's presence in permanent life changes of purpose and direction. Oregon reporters attributed conversions and renewed commitments to prayer and Holy Spirit movement. It appears that tent crusades fulfilled their purposes in Oregon in that one decade. Brunk and Augsburger returned to Oregon from time to time, but without their tents. Hammer's contributions were cut short when in 1957 he took his own life on the South American mission field.[10]

By the 1960s, revivals were giving way, in most Oregon Mennonite congregations, to Christian life conferences and other forms of nurture. The emerging charismatic movement, however, kept alive some of the experiential, emotional qualities of revivalism.

Mennonite Fundamentalism

Fundamentalism, a theological influence that touched most Oregon Mennonites, grew from a primary concern to defend certain "fundamental" doctrines against the assaults of the modernists. It competed vigorously with Mennonite community in its historical and theological aspects, even while it promoted increased individualism. Several other strains of Christian thought and experience helped define or mingled with Fundamentalism. Two that developed a hold on Oregon Mennonites, premillennial dispensationalism and Holy Spirit movements, will be discussed later in this chapter.[11]

One impetus for Fundamentalism was Charles Darwin's theory of evolution. Along with Christians from other traditions, most Mennonites considered evolution a threat to biblical faith. Protecting their children and youth from exposure to the pernicious theory became one motive for establishing or promoting attendance at church schools. In the decades of the teens and 1920s more than sixty PCC youth registered at the Mennonite school at Hesston, Kansas. General Conference Mennonites read rebuttals to evolution in *The Mennonite*. One reason MB and GC people began the Salem Bible Academy in 1945 was to protect their young people from the influence of "atheistic teachers" who may have taught evolution.[12]

Another impetus for Fundamentalism was the threat from a new method of studying the Bible: the literary-historical approach. This approach challenged conservative, orthodox views of authorship and sometimes the nature and divinity of Jesus himself. Christians of widely different traditions joined to defend the reliability of the Bible and in 1919 adopted nine Christian fundamentals as "standards for evangelical orthodoxy." Their statement emphasized that the Bible was "verbally inspired by God" and that "man was created in the image of God." It endorsed the Trinity, the virgin birth of Jesus, his substitutionary death, his resurrection, salvation by faith, and bodily resurrection of all people to a state of everlasting blessing or punishment. Their statement also held to the "personal, premillennial, and imminent return" of Christ.[13]

What might be called Mennonite Fundamentalism developed as a parallel movement with distinct variations, largely within the OM denomination. Like Fundamentalism, however, it was not a totally unified movement. Many Mennonites felt an affinity with Protestant evangelicals who advocated social reform and meeting the simple needs of people, physical or social as well as spiritual. Some Mennonites supported what they called a fundamentalist position but really wanted only to conserve traditional Mennonite beliefs and practices. Other influential Mennonite leaders began to promote a more creedal religion than Mennonites had earlier known. They clearly outlined "doctrines of the Bible"—prescribed beliefs and practices often dubbed Mennonite fundamentals—which they supported by Scripture references. When Fundamentalists outlined their fundamentals, Mennonites adopted or adapted the doctrines as necessary to fit Mennonite beliefs. Two fundamentals which Fundamentalism overlooked were nonconformity and nonresistance. The MBs, EMBs, and some GCs did not modify Fundamentalism as much. They needed fewer corrections and additions. Mennonite Fundamentalists often adopted the strident, militant rhetoric common among Fundamentalists in place of a quieter or humbler demeanor more characteristic of earlier generations of Mennonites.[14]

One person largely responsible for the new focus on doctrines was Daniel Kauffman, OM preacher, writer, and editor. A logical thinker, committed to understanding and teaching the Bible, he organized subjects by questions and answers, articles and ordinances; and in 1898, he produced a book of Bible doctrines. Through several revisions, with other Mennonite leaders advising and assisting Kauffman, the book continued to be a systematic statement of belief and expected practice in the denomination for more than half a century. Although Kauffman did visit Oregon on occasion, his greatest influence came indirectly, through his voluminous writings and the many other evangelists who adopted his doctrinal statements and preached them with conviction and fervor. But his influence was even broader than the scope of his books. As editor of *Gospel Herald* and its short-lived predecessor, *Gospel Witness,* for almost forty years Kauffman came weekly in print to the homes of Oregon Mennonites—at a time when the printed page was much more compelling and authoritative than it is for the current generation.[15]

Mennonite fundamentals now offered a way of fitting many parts (doctrines) together to make a whole (the Christian life). In Kauffman's introduction to his 1898 book of doctrines, he grouped them in three categories: the plan of salvation, general Bible doctrines, and ordinances and restrictions. Baptism, communion, foot-washing and marriage were ordinances taught in the 1632 Dordrecht Confession, the confession Mennonites had regarded as their official statement of doctrine until then. In addition to these, the ordinances now included the prayer head covering for women, the holy kiss, and anointing with oil. The "restrictions" were nonconformity, nonresistance, nonswearing of oaths, nonmembership in secret societies, and not going to law. Kauffman expected "every properly enlightened child of God" to "esteem these ordinances and restrictions as a God-send . . . a privilege to observe." Of the restrictions, nonconformity to the world, "by far the most important," included being transformed by a new mind, purity from sin, temperance, honest business dealings, truthful speech, and refraining from politics, worldly amusements, and pride. But the longest section dealt with adornment. Kauffman acknowledged "instantly [meeting] a chorus of objections" when considering attire, which is the reason he gave it lengthier coverage.[16]

Mennonites had shunned costly apparel and emphasized that members should wear simple, plain clothing. But focusing on nonconformity as a doctrine was part of the new Mennonite Fundamentalism. Already in sixteenth-century Europe, when the Strasbourg Discipline insisted that Mennonites were to wear nothing "for pride's sake," humility was a basis for plain clothing. Linking humility and attire continued through the centuries, though humility faded in importance while the nonconformity which called for distinctive attire advanced as a Mennonite fundamental. For some OMs, it became a preoccupation. Early in the twentieth century a crusade began for a *uniformity* of plainness, which was a new approach for (old) Mennonites.[17]

While it was Kauffman who organized Mennonite thought into doctrines, George R. Brunk I promoted a new practice, uniformity in attire, which influenced large segments of the OM denomination, including Oregon. When he attended a holiness meeting in Kansas, men without neckties impressed him with their spirituality. He soon made the necktie a Mennonite issue and began a crusade to rid Mennonite men of that superfluous item of attire. Hoping to stop "the drift" toward immodest or elaborate attire, he also promoted particular styles of clothing. *Uniform* and *plain* were key words. In some areas, especially in the East, this included the "plain coat" (buttoning to the neck and without lapels) for ministers and for laymen who would wear it. For women the standard became the plain bonnet and "cape dress" (dresses with a particular style of short, waist-fitted cape). Kauffman and many other leaders endorsed and promoted this new emphasis on uniformity.[18]

Brunk's teaching on nonconformity was, of course, not limited to attire, although attire was often the point of greatest friction. Already in 1899 when he first visited Oregon, he set things in order, so he thought, in spite of "crowds" at Hubbard whom he described as "a sin-hardened, dancing, gambling, Sunday-breaking set." During a subsequent visit in 1902 he discovered women at Hopewell wearing hats and refusing to wear the prayer head covering, until he again restored order. Within fifteen years his crusade against the necktie influenced the PCC to include neckties as the first of a list of itemized articles which a resolution banned as "fashionable adornment." Though none of the PCC disciplines named the necktie among the restrictions, pulpit teaching produced results. By the 1920s and 1930s, none of the ordained men and a minority of laymen in the PCC wore the tie. A reverse trend accelerated among the laity soon after World War II, and later among ordained men, but in 1976 several congregations which had withdrawn from the PCC still forbade the necktie.[19]

The crusade for uniform attire did not meet with such wide acceptance in Oregon. Although most PCC ministers and a few laymen began to wear the plain coat, its staunch supporters never managed to include that literal specification in the PCC discipline after the AM/OM merger. Rather, the disciplines called for ministers to wear "plain clothing" or noted that the plain coat was the "general practice" in the denomination. Though a few ordained men of AM heritage wore a common lapel coat without a tie, most ministers wore the plain coat and considered it obligatory until the 1960s. The cape dress for women received little attention in Oregon, but several PCC disciplines required or urged the "plain bonnet or hood, conforming to the shape of the head," compatible with the "devotional covering." Some Oregon preachers promoted both the cape dress and the bonnet, and in several congregations a majority of women wore the cape, bonnet, or both, but neither became standard practice throughout the PCC.[20]

Mennonites who emphasized attire equated church authority with biblical authority, which intensified the issue. While Fundamentalism emphasized correct beliefs and individual faith above discipleship and church community, Mennonite Fundamentalism not only took particular biblical teachings literally but also believed the Bible called members to live in submission to the church. Though in essence all members comprised the church, in practice the ordained leaders were the church who interpreted the Bible. Authority emerged within the district conferences, which gradually developed specific regulations regarding behavior of members. Conferences, in turn, answered to the denominational general conference in which Kauffman and Brunk were influential leaders.[21]

The joint authority of the Bible and the church motivated conscientious Mennonites to observe what the church taught as biblical. Preachers often included the stipulations of the PCC discipline and even additional details, presenting them as the "all things" that Jesus had commissioned his disciples to teach. Keeping the "all things" demonstrated the ties between being and doing. It reflected the closeness of one's relationship with Christ. In contrast to earlier teachings which had linked attire to humility, the teaching now said that outward appearance portrayed inner piety—an intimate union with Christ. Though emphasized more than most, it was only one of many compartments of life that demonstrated separation from the world, holiness, and obedience to God—the characteristics of Christians who had experienced salvation. In his "West Coast Echoes" Omar G. Miller of Bethel referred to "the old bromide that secondary things" were not "essential to salvation. Well of course they are not," Miller agreed. "Any intelligent person knows that. They are the result of salvation." Leaders widely concurred that attire had nothing to do with receiving salvation, with "getting saved." The blood of Christ saved, but obedience to the Word *kept* one saved. So for many Mennonites, regulated attire became a way of "staying saved." It was one clearly visible, easily identifiable mark of being not conformed to the world, as a favorite text (Rom. 12:2) put the issue. It defined the limits and provided a secure boundary.[22]

By the 1950s change had begun to erode PCC authority as vested in the executive committee and bishop body. Although PCC Mennonites continued to regard the Bible as authoritative for their faith and life, the methods and polity of interpretation were chang-

-ing. Some church leaders and scholars were studying the Bible in its original languages, in relation to its culture and history, in light of its purposes and literary forms. This allowed changes not only in many practices which nonconformity had earlier encompassed, such as attire, but also in the locus of authority.

The perception of the church which interpreted the Bible was changing also. It was becoming less the ordained leaders by themselves and more they in consultation with the laity. Throughout much of the OM denomination, including the PCC, authority was being redistributed between the bishop's pulpit and the people's pew. In spite of a renewed emphasis on community which this process emphasized, it might be questioned whether in many cases it differed much from Fundamentalism in that regard. It was possible for it to become a way to rationalize placing a private relationship with Christ above a relationship with him in the community of his body.[23]

Mennonite Fundamentalism focused on more than nonconformity and nonresistance. It, like the larger Fundamentalism, accepted the Bible as final authority in the sense of "plenary and verbal inspiration," although the Mennonite version was even more inclusive. But making precise pronouncements about biblical authority was new for the (old) Mennonite general conference and its regional conferences. For Oregon's early PCC Mennonites, like their denomination, the authority of the Bible was simply understood, the source of all other teachings. Not until well into the twentieth century did they formalize their stance about the Bible. Even then, the words *revealed* or *inspired* were precise enough for PCC constitutions.

Within their denomination, however, Brunk and John Horsch, a leading OM scholar in the early decades of the twentieth century, were among a group who vigorously and repeatedly attacked Modernism, as they understood it. They insisted that the words *plenary* and *verbal* must describe the Mennonite understanding of biblical inspiration and persuaded Kauffman to include them in later revisions of his books of doctrines. Brunk and a committee of Virginia Mennonites, where he lived after moving from Kansas, prepared "the Eighteen Articles of the Fundamentals" which the denominational general conference adopted in 1921, with slight modification, as "Christian Fundamentals." On their own terms the Mennonite Church had joined the Fundamentalist movement, though they did not regard themselves as Fundamentalists "with a capital 'F.'"[24]

Maintaining Mennonite Fundamentalism required constant watchfulness. Just when Brunk thought he and his associates had chased Modernism out of the church, new hazards appeared. Calvinism, with views of predestination and sin alien to historic Mennonite doctrine, was making inroads among Mennonites. By the early 1930s Brunk was giving what Ohio evangelist B. B. King described as "thundering messages" against it. One Calvinistic teaching which Brunk consistently exposed and opposed was "unconditional eternal security." Nondenominational Fundamentalist Bible schools, such as Moody Bible Institute (MBI) and Bible Institute of Los Angeles (BIOLA), and such publications as *The King's Business* and *The Sunday School Times* as well as the *Scofield Reference Bible*, promoted this position. Brunk and his associates who contributed to the periodical Brunk published, *Sword and Trumpet* (S&T), attempted to educate Mennonites about such errors. Some Oregon Mennonites were among S&T readers.[25]

The Calvinistic doctrine of eternal security—the idea that once saved, a person cannot lose salvation regardless of actions—did not represent traditional Mennonite belief. But countless Mennonites attended MBI or BIOLA or read publications supporting Fundamentalism in general and eternal security in particular until the doctrine found pockets of Mennonite acceptance. General Conference Mennonite congregations in Oregon heard this teaching in the mid-1950s when H. D. Burkholder, former president of Fundamentalistic Grace Bible Institute (GBI), was pastor at Dallas. In one instance a small group of people from Calvary at Barlow who were attracted to Burkholder's teachings on eternal security asked him to hold Thursday evening Bible studies and prayer meetings in their homes. The meetings created tensions at Calvary, however, because many with recent ties to Zion (OM) still opposed the eternal security doctrine, as Zion did. Paul N. Roth, Calvary's first pastor who had led the group from Zion, resigned, and Nobel V. Sack, a teacher at Western Evangelical Seminary in Portland, began serving as interim pastor.[26]

Although early PCC constitutions simply assumed the authority of the Bible and did not state a position about it, at least one of Oregon's early PDC congregations made a formal statement. The 1896 constitution of Zion (GC) at Polk Station held to "the whole Bible, both Old and New Testaments, including all sixty-six books," as being the "only revelation for our belief and the only guide book for our lives." But they did not spell out details as the

PCC did. The only reference similar to MC nonconformity restrictions stated that members "shall flee worldliness, especially dancing." Attire received no mention, nor did it ever become a major issue in GC congregations. Fundamentalism unevenly influenced the GC denomination, as well as its Oregon congregations, so that by mid-twentieth century distinct differences appeared within. The PDC retained a more conservative statement about the "divine inspiration and the infallibility of the Bible" but even that was not enough to prevent two Washington congregations from withdrawing in the 1960s and 1970s. Emmanuel at Pratum regarded the PDC and the denomination as theologically liberal but did not withdraw until after 1976.[27]

Like their larger denominations, Oregon's MBs and EMBs moved toward Fundamentalism. Mennonite Brethren, who did not shy away from Fundamentalist terms as some GCs did, held to the Bible as "verbally inspired." Their historian, J. A. Toews, judged that Mennonite Brethren were "more susceptible to Fundamentalist influence than any other Mennonite group." Probably the EMBs were a close second. Their mid-twentieth century confession referred to "all Scripture, the Old and New Testament, [as] the only inerrant inspired Word of God." They, too, placed few unbending restrictions on attire and did not spell out nonconformity to the extent that OMs did.[28]

Oregon's Mennonite and related groups differed also in patterns of discipline and authority. The MB conferences were authoritative for their congregations, though they seldom used this authority to make stipulations about attire. Holdeman congregations were subject to denominational leadership and the people followed prescribed patterns of attire. The BIC denomination had councils which functioned somewhat as MC conferences did and emphasized some of the same aspects of attire, with similar patterns of development and change. Other groups, such as the GC, the EMB, and the Old Order Amish, were congregational in discipline. In spite of the distinctive ways of life and the generally uniform attire of the OOA, practices did vary from group to group.[29]

Fundamentalism attracted Mennonites largely because of the authority it accorded the Bible. This theological position won over many Mennonites who might otherwise have guarded more carefully their own theological concept of church community as the body of Christ. Though it overlooked such historic Mennonite and biblical practices as nonresistance and nonconformity, variously interpreted among Mennonite groups, it reinforced some Mennonites' regard for the Bible as their reliable guide. Most of Oregon's Mennonite groups adopted or adapted other key points of Fundamentalism also, besides those relating to the inspiration and authority of the Scriptures and to the life and work of Christ. Many made dispensational premillennialism a key to understanding the Bible.

Dispensational Premillennialism

This heavy label designated a system of biblical interpretation that became one strain of thought mingling with Fundamentalism. Premillennialism, an ancient but not predominant Christian theory, derived from a literal interpretation of biblical passages about Christ's thousand-year rule on earth in relation to his second coming. The newer dispensationalism was an intricate, elaborate theory which usually divided human history into seven distinct eras of time, or dispensations. Its proponents emphasized a faithful remnant of individual believers, separate from the world, not necessarily tied to the institutional church. C. I. Scofield, a close friend of D. L. Moody, systematized dispensationalism and invested it with authority. In 1909 he published a Bible in which he embedded his interpretation through copious notes: the *Scofield Reference Bible.*[30]

Historically, Mennonites have generally favored amillennialism, also called nonmillennialism, which interprets the thousand-year reign of Christ as figurative or symbolic instead of literal. Yet premillennialism, both in its classic and its later dispensational forms, left its print on Mennonites. AM bishop Jacob C. Kenagy (1821-1894) of Missouri's Sycamore Grove congregation was especially interested in prophecy and was rumored to be a premillennialist. Perhaps other AMs and OMs of his generation had similar leanings. However, A. D. Wenger claimed to be the first (old) Mennonite to teach premillennialism. He and several other young Mennonite men adopted that view while studying at MBI in the 1890s. When Wenger visited Oregon in 1897, one of his five sermons at Hubbard may well have included premillennialism. A few months later he lectured at a Bible conference at Johnstown, Pennsylvania, on "Unfulfilled Prophecies." John S. Coffman considered this a "somewhat new" treatment, "by no means the generally accepted view of the Mennonite people." Nevertheless, some other young, influential Mennonites soon supported and promulgated premillennialism, including S. G. Shetler, who had sat in Wenger's lectures at Johnstown. J. B. Smith, another ardent premillennialist, taught at Hesston College, where many Oregon young people attended.[31]

Others who influenced Oregon Mennonites toward premillennialism (although not necessarily with all the dispensationalism) included Wenger's brother-in-law George R. Brunk I, John Thut, and C. F. Derstine. After Brunk moved from Kansas to Virginia, he began to publish S&T in 1929. Avowedly conservative, "Devoted to the Defense of a Full Gospel," according to its masthead, it promoted premillennialism as part of the full gospel. Omar G. Miller, PCC minister accused of being sympathetic with Modernism in the early 1930s, was an early and faithful subscriber to S&T. Other Oregonians, too, read it. Some, including Orrie D. Yoder and Marcus Lind, in later years, contributed to it. George R. Brunk II, wearing the premillennial mantle of his father, spoke in Oregon at a 1953 prophecy conference at Western Mennonite School as well as on other occasions. Thut, of Harper, Kansas, lectured on prophetic subjects in Oregon congregations for about three months in 1934. The Bethel correspondent reported that Thut's messages "were greatly appreciated by all who attended" (although the Bethel bishop Fred Gingerich was himself an amillennialist). Clayton F. Derstine, a noted Mennonite evangelist and enthusiastic premillennialist, visited Oregon several times in the 1920s and 1930s. He impressed one young listener at Albany in 1936 with his "hellfire" preaching, "but people were saved!" In 1939 he held a three-week evangelistic tent campaign in Portland, including sermons on "The World's Greatest Coming Event," "Two Great Prophetic Dreams . . ." and "The Signs of the Times (Socially, Politically & Religiously)," in addition to topics relating to salvation and Christian living.[32]

Premillennialism never became an official PCC position. Although some Oregon leaders did not accept it, it probably became the dominant view in Oregon. Soon after World War I Zion bishop Amos P. Troyer asked one of his members not to circulate a paper advocating premillennialism. G. D. Shenk of Sheridan and leaders in the nonconference Harrisburg congregation were also amillennialists. But the premillennial interpretation which MBI students introduced to the denomination attracted many Oregon Mennonites. Glenn Whitaker, who served as superintendent of both the Portland and Los Angeles missions, attended BIOLA, a premillennialist school. Mrs. Emmanuel Kenagy of the Albany area received a premillennial magazine in the 1940s called *Prophecy Monthly,* edited by Keith L. Brooks. In 1944 Orrie D. Yoder of Bannock, Ohio, who had been ordained a few years earlier in Oregon, asked in an article in S&T if Christians could "be humble enough to believe . . . our Lord's solemn predictions *literally* . . .?" Fifteen years later, back in the West, Yoder referred to an "extreme 'spiritualizing' of prophetical Scriptures" by some persons at a denominational board meeting who had disapproved the "more literal views" of others.[33]

Some elements of dispensationalism intermeshed with premillennialism in Oregon. Both visiting preachers and Oregon's own ministers promoted specific teachings about "the rapture and the appearing" and the prominence of "a Jewish remnant," which were parts of dispensationalist teaching, not of historic premillennialism. The interest in and support of Jewish evangelism, and dispensationalist interpretations of modern Jewish developments in the Middle East also indicate its infiltration into their premillennialism. Many at Porter expressed appreciation for the lectures of S. J. Miller of Michigan in 1942 on a "Bible Dispensations Chart." Jacob Kauffman, pastor at Blaine, in 1960 gave messages on the different "Dispensations," which the people found "edifying and instructive." At Logsden, in the early 1970s, the midweek study focused on Bible prophecy with dispensationalist Hal Lindsay's *The Late Great Planet Earth* and the Bible as resources. Mennonites in Oregon, as elsewhere, bought and used the *Scofield Reference Bible.*[34]

By the 1960s, the historic amillennial position again received support in the PCC, along with the premillennial view. The 1963 conference, with the theme "The Lord Is Coming Soon," included speakers of both persuasions. But those with differing millennial views did not always respect the opposite position or trust each other. When Marcus Lind and Ray Mishler planned a prophecy conference in the late 1960s, PCC secretary David Mann urged that they let the PCC sponsor it and include resource persons of both viewpoints, to correct ideas which "grossly misrepresented" what amillennialists believe. However, congregations began to withdraw from the PCC before such a conference happened, taking along many vigorous proponents of premillennialism. Those who remained were generally more tolerant of, or open to, a differing view.[35]

Not all of Oregon's more traditional conservative Mennonites held to premillennialism, however. G. Richard Culp was an early teacher at Western Mennonite School who later trained as an osteopath. In the 1970s he practiced at Harrisburg, where he also attended Harrisburg Mennonite Church. Culp wrote *Bible Studies in Prophecy* and published it in 1971. In three hundred pages of persuasive but nonemotional writing, Culp carefully and systematically set forth biblical teaching and thoughtful arguments for the amillennial position. He referred to the antichrist not as a particular individual but as "the spirit of opposition to Christ." Apostasy was a "falling away from the faith at various times throughout the entire Christian era," not just a modern failing. He repudiated the "secret 'rapture' " of the church, discussed Jewish evangelism in light of dispensational teaching, and disputed J. B. Smith's interpretation and methods as presented in a commentary of the book of Revelation published posthumously in 1960 and widely acclaimed by many conservatives. Bible Mennonite Fellowship premillennialists could not understand how a conservative like Culp could so "misuse" the Scriptures. Meanwhile, Culp asserted that amillennialism was the "historic Mennonite position" still held by conservatives who had not been largely touched by "theological movements."[36]

Dispensational premillennialism also touched Oregon's smaller Mennonite groups. Among GCs, premillennialism was never the official denominational position, but according to historian J. C. Wenger, it did have "considerable influence." Some ministers became "outspoken dispensationalists." Early PDC leaders such as John M. Franz and P. R. Aeschliman held the amillennial view, but more pastors were coming from Fundamentalist Bible institutes. According to Rufus Franz, premillennial dispensationalism was a somewhat controversial issue in Oregon for a time. Most Oregon congregations accepted it. Pacific District Conference (GC) annual sessions, however, emphasized evangelism above eschatology, which merited no sermons or talks in annual programs, at least from the mid-1940s onward.[37]

Proponents taught dispensational premillennialism in congregations, however. An unidentified correspondent noted in the late 1930s that Homer Leisy, a popular evangelist, gave two "timely" messages at Grace in Albany "with the help of his charts." Church

worker Helen Thiessen reported in 1940 that Leisy brought revival
to Grace at Dallas with his teaching that in "these days of apostasy
and tribulations . . . the Gentile age is drawing fast to a close." In
1943, Emmanuel's new pastor, J. H. Turnbull, began a series of lessons on Revelation, "using a large chart to aid in the exposition."
At the same time, Grace in Albany studied the seventy weeks in
the prophecy of Daniel. J. J. Regier, while pastor of Grace in
Dallas in 1950, preached a series of sermons on "The Church in
View of the Tribulation." Several years later at Emmanuel, H. P.
Fast of Reedley, California, used a chart to illustrate his messages
on "God's Plan in the Light of Prophecy."[38]

Oregon's smallest Mennonite groups varied in their views of
millennialism. Denominationally, the MBs and EMBs generally
adopted its dispensational form, though not officially. In Oregon,
the Dallas EMB congregation sent students to, and received pastors from, the premillennial GBI. Probably Oregon's MB ministers
in earlier decades, like MB ministers at large, acquired Scofield
Bibles. They may have been among the many who historian J. A.
Toews said "were tempted" to regard Scofield's " 'footnotes' as
equally inspired with the biblical text." Many MB young people
from Dallas attended BIOLA. Multnomah School of the Bible in
Portland exerted a similar influence. Old-timer Otto Bier wrote
that the MB congregation "always welcomed" strongly dispensationalist Bible teachers of denominational stature, such as
Wm. J. Bestvater, H. F. Klassen, and P. E. Penner, as well as Baptist evangelist W. E. Pietsch. Occasionally someone presented
another view, as did H. S. Voth, who wondered "if in the final con-
summation the Lord would indeed follow [their] charted direction." The BIC denomination officially endorsed premillennialism
early in the twentieth century, but the Old Order Amish and CGCs
held to amillennialism.[39]

Dispensationalism found such ready acceptance largely because it upheld the authority of the Bible and taught salvation by
grace. However, one detail which most Mennonites did not accept
was Scofield's assertion that the Sermon on the Mount primarily
"gives neither the privilege nor the duty of the Church." Rather,
they accepted Christ's teachings in Matthew 5-7 as normative for
daily life and a primary basis for the practice of nonresistance.
Nevertheless, the teachings may have eroded Mennonite ethics.
The correlation between Mennonite groups influenced by dispensationalism and those with large percentages of young men who

entered armed services is not totally consistent. Other factors also influenced young men's choices. Still, dispensationalism can be considered an influence away from nonresistance.[40]

Experiencing the Holy Spirit

Another strain of thought that often fused with Fundamentalism was a new interest in the Holy Spirit. The holiness movement required a second, decisive experience of the Holy Spirit after one's initial conversion. This "second work of grace" was often called sanctification. It could be a dramatic event. By the end of the nineteenth century people in some revivalist traditions were experiencing it as "the baptism of the Holy Ghost." What came to be known as the Keswick movement emphasized "fillings" rather than "baptism" of the Spirit. In varying degrees all elements of the holiness movement focused on a deeply felt experience of consecration to Christ, victory over sin, and dedicated Christian service. These emphases helped produce the modern missionary movement. Influential proponents included Hannah Whitall Smith, author of *The Christian's Secret to the Happy Life;* C. I. Scofield, who taught that this was the dispensation of the Holy Spirit which had begun at Pentecost; and Charles G. Trumbull, editor of the popular *Sunday School Times* who also promoted dispensationalism among his wide reading audience which included Mennonites.[41]

Pentecostalism, a split in the holiness movement, was more emotional and less theologically precise. It emphasized speaking in tongues as evidence of Holy Ghost baptism. Not until the mid-twentieth century did many mainline denominations respect and accept the Pentecostal denominations which had emerged. As speaking in tongues gained acceptance in older denominations, new labels appeared. Old-line Pentecostals dubbed the newer advocates "Neopentecostals," who in turn took the name "charismatic movement" for themselves (although not everyone in this stream of Spirit experience accepted that label personally).[42]

The emphasis on Holy Spirit experience reached Oregon Mennonites early and continued in varying intensities through 1976. The holiness movement brought new vitality and strength and fostered growing commitment to Christ and the church. But objections came to what some regarded as emotional excesses and the teaching of a second work of grace. "Progressive sanctification," a somewhat new doctrine for Mennonites, was the descriptive position Daniel Kauffman's 1898 *Manual of Bible Doctrines* held forth. It implied growth in the Christian graces and perhaps ambiguously combined it with instantaneous sanctification, even while cautioning against a second work of grace. In 1895 and 1900 Western District AMs passed resolutions noting that a believer received the baptism of the Holy Ghost when receiving forgiveness through faith in Christ, and that "making a loud profession of holiness" was not edifying.[43]

The holiness movement first came to Oregon likely from Kansas and Ohio. The Kansas-Nebraska Conference, suffering stress and division, passed resolutions in 1899 and 1900 favoring the baptism of the Holy Ghost as a second definite experience following conversion. They recommended that bishops offer "a special prayer" when baptizing converts, imploring that "they might receive the Holy Ghost" if they had not already done so. Some conference leaders were not comfortable with this holiness language. Apparently George R. Brunk I, then of Kansas, did not use it. Rather, he taught a "progressive holiness" instead of a second work of grace, a holiness that produced obedience because God "gives the Holy Spirit to them that obey Him." Brunk also opposed *The Sunday School Times*, along with other publications which promoted an incomplete "Gospel fundamentalism." The differing messages from the conference resolutions and Brunk perhaps created more uncertainty than conviction among Oregon's (old) Mennonites.[44]

A more direct influence on Oregon Mennonites came from members who moved to Idaho and Oregon from the young Bethel Mennonite Church at West Liberty, Ohio. By the turn of the century "waves of unsound doctrine rolled high and roared loud" around West Liberty, a correspondent reported. Precipitating contention at Bethel were some members who had attended a rousing revival at a Quaker meetinghouse in the community. They had responded to altar calls and had come to favor a second work of grace. Leaders of denominational renown, including Brunk, came on request to help the congregation in this crisis, which members carried in their memories for many years after.[45]

Out of western Ohio came people who influenced Oregon thought and life. About the time of the Bethel crisis, David Hilty, Bethel's first minister, moved west, where he served at Nampa, Idaho, and (for a short time) Albany. A son-in-law of Hilty, John P. Bontrager, a charter member of Bethel, moved to Idaho about the same time as Hilty and within a few years was ordained as minister and bishop at Albany. About the turn of the century, Ben B. King "experienced a definite infilling of the Holy Spirit under the ministry of a Quaker woman," his obituary noted. After studying for a time at a Quaker school in Cincinnati he united with Bethel in 1902 and two years later began a long tenure of mission service at Ft. Wayne, Indiana. He ministered in Oregon in 1907 and again in the early 1930s.

Though Ben B. King's reputation as an evangelist and an ardent Mennonite Fundamentalist did not suggest any unusual Holy Spirit emphasis, the effectiveness of his evangelistic ministry was later attributed to his early experience of the Holy Spirit. His holiness influence may have been mostly indirect, through his daughter and son-in-law Carolyn and Fred Augsburger, who contributed to charismatic renewal in Oregon and elsewhere in a later generation. Amos M. Shenk, another minister son-in-law of Hilty, and layman David H. Kauffman both moved to Nampa soon after Hilty did. Kauffman was from the Bethel locale in Ohio, although whether he was ever a member there is not known. Shenk had lived at Elida, also in western Ohio, and at Osborne.[46]

Did Hilty and his sons-in-law leave Ohio to escape opposition to the holiness emphasis or to have more freedom to promote it elsewhere? If so, they were not the first Mennonite dissenters to move west. Possibly Hilty was among those who initiated the earliest discussions of the Holy Spirit in the PCC. In 1906 the first sessions which were held in Hilty's home community at Nampa. One question that arose at this session was, "Should believers be taught to seek a definite experience of the baptism of the Holy Ghost?" The approved resolution stated that "all ministers" and others "having the baptism of the Holy Ghost, teach and encourage everywhere that believers seek a definite experience" of such baptism. Bontrager was a moderator and Hilty and Shenk were on the resolutions committee, a committee which normally exerted considerable influence.[47]

In the next few years sermons and resolutions oscillated between positions of the second work of grace and those of a progressive growth in holiness. In 1907, E. Stahley and L. J. Yoder said "the work of the Holy Spirit" was to convict, comfort, give power, reprove, direct, drive away enmity and create love. Was this offered as a gentle corrective to the previous year's resolution? In 1910 S. E. Allgyer of Ohio and Albany's Bontrager were moderators. Hilty and Shenk were again on the resolutions committee. One question discussed was, "How shall we seek baptism of the Holy Ghost?" The resolution referred to it as a "long promised blessing of God" and resolved to "teach the people to seek for and expect it, meet conditions and ask in faith believing."

Again a corrective followed the next year, when John Blosser of Ohio preached the conference sermon. He considered "the great need" of the church to be "Holy Spirit power." The secretary succinctly noted sermon points: "Holy Spirit baptism received at time of conversion. By one Spirit all baptized in one body. Holy Spirit given once for all. One baptism many infillings. Special infillings for special service. Baptism received on three conditions: repentance, faith and surrender. Fulness [sic] of blessing received on condition of yielded life."[48]

In the next decade, "baptism of the Holy Ghost" terminology receded. After Hilty suddenly died of apoplexy in 1914, Holy Spirit emphasis disappeared from conference reports for almost ten years.[49]

The likely impetus for the PCC resolutions about the Holy Spirit in the early 1920s is not clear. The 1922 resolution in part restated the 1899 Kansas-Nebraska Conference statement almost verbatim, noting that the "baptism with the Holy Ghost is as necessary to be obtained as conversion" and that every believer should "seek and tarry" for a "definite experience." D. F. Shenk of Sheridan, E. Z. Yoder of Zion, and Chris Snyder of Oregon's Bethel, earlier of the KNC, were on the resolutions committee. Possibly David H. Kauffman, a Bethel lay delegate, may have lent encouragement from behind the scenes. Certainly he cast his vote for it. Formerly of Ohio, then of Nampa, in 1912 he was among the pioneers of Oregon's Bethel congregation before moving some twenty years later to the Indian Cove congregation in Idaho. Orrie D. Yoder, in a 1962 memorial tribute to Kauffman, characterized him as "perhaps a rather silent, but diligent servant." He noted Kauffman's "concern that more honor and place be accorded to the Holy Spirit" and that he "was often rather held in' disdain for his views because they were considered too extreme." Another possible influence may have been the earlier-mentioned 1922 Price revivals at Albany.[50]

Was the PCC resolution two years later yet another reaction to a previous resolution? In 1924 an unnamed speaker discussed "The Inter-relation of the Church and the Holy Spirit in Bringing the Message of Salvation to the World." The accompanying resolution, drafted by committee persons S. Honderich of Filer, D. B. Kauffman of Zion, and D. F. Shenk of Sheridan, lacked a distinctive Pentecostal tone. It recognized "the Holy Spirit as the personality of the Triune God who *indwells . . . every believer . . . guides us into all truth . . . gives us power . . .* and should be sought for according to Luke 11:13." In the Luke passage Jesus said that as a father gives bread to a son who asks, so will the heavenly Father give the Holy Spirit to those who ask.[51]

The differing emphases on the Holy Spirit contributed to problems in the PCC in its first two decades, when some persons left congregations in disagreement over holiness, divine healing, and sanctification. After 1924 the issue receded. Reference to Holy Spirit baptism, unusual for Mennonites of that time, was absent from PCC resolutions in the next few years, which referred instead to Holy Spirit direction or leading, to Holy Ghost power and humility. Ministers' meetings included topics such as the "unique power and authority of the Holy Spirit in the message of the minister" or "victorious living." But the Pentecostal movement among PCC Mennonites had lost visibility for a time.[52]

Although PCC resolutions after the mid-1920s did not endorse Holy Spirit baptism, the holiness movement continued to influence congregations, particularly Sheridan and Indian Cove.

Sheridan was a primary seedbed for Oregon's later charismatic movement. It emphasized a spirituality which urged members to be "different," comparatively more faithful in following Christ and open to the Spirit. In the estimation of a former member, revival methodology became "the driving force" in the congregation, which had "a fairly emotional side to its personality." It called the people to renewed inner experience. However, traditional patterns limited outward response and rejected Pentecostal expression. By the 1930s, reports from Sheridan of members going "deeper in . . . Christian experience," prayer and fasting for "more power in soul-winning," and "deeper consecration" indicated the developing character of Holy Spirit experience. Sheridan ministers often gave altar calls at regular services, as evangelists did at revivals. Sheridan's historian recorded that meetings might last until midnight or even two o'clock in the morning, when "a penitent soul at last found peace and forgiveness." In 1944 a momentous revival led by C. Z. Martin of Mountville, Pennsylvania, merited a detailed report to *Gospel Herald,* which told that the

"Holy Spirit fell like a blanket on the audience." It told of "blessed results" (about one hundred confessions and reconsecrations); illness, an anointing service, and God's healing touch; and the "marvelous presence" of God and "the power of His Spirit."[53]

The PCC's Indian Cove congregation in Idaho emphasized the Holy Spirit more distinctly and intensely than Sheridan did and with Pentecostal expressions that Sheridan did not endorse. Although a newly developing agricultural tract first attracted Mennonite settlers to the area, some who moved there from Nampa beginning in 1930 may also have wished for a freer experience of the Spirit than approved of at Nampa. In 1914, just before David Hilty's sudden death, S. G. Shetler attempted to correct erroneous sanctification teachings there which had taken two members to a Pentecostal group. Several from Hilty's family who later moved to the Cove, among them Amos M. Shenk, continued their patriarch's apparent interest in experiencing the Spirit. One theme running through Cove correspondence after its 1935 organization was a strong sense of the presence of the Holy Spirit in their personal and corporate lives.

After Shenk other later ministers at the Cove, including his son Amos and Paul W. Miller, also displayed a stronger interest in Holy Spirit gifts and on healing, miracles, and tongues than did most other PCC ministers. Miller wrote in 1946 about the need of "men sent from God, filled with His Spirit," to experience "identification with Christ in death, burial, and resurrection" and to provide an "intense spirit of evangelism." Miller moved in, Oregon circles at various times, as when he had revival meetings at Sheridan in 1953 before moving in 1972 to Oregon, where he assisted in leading an emerging charismatic movement. Visiting speakers at the Cove, such as Gerald Derstine of Florida, Mark Landis of Minnesota, and East African missionaries also nurtured the Cove's emphasis on the Spirit.[54]

Elsewhere within the conference other persons were experiencing the Holy Spirit in new ways. Already in 1948 Claud Hostetler, minister at the Portland mission congregation and editor of the PCC periodical, *Missionary Evangel,* wrote about the need for unity among those *true* believers who desired to see new and different "manifestations of the Holy Spirit." Missionaries who had experienced revival in Africa had visited both Idaho and Oregon, bringing many blessings and leaving "a fire . . . kindled." At subsequent informal "fellowship" meetings, many participated and "keenly felt" the Spirit of God. Hostetler urged participants in future meetings to "come praying and seeking" and to "leave 'self' at home." In 1954, Hostetler attributed one of Portland's best summer Bible schools in many years to "the presence of the Holy Spirit."[55]

These undercurrents of greater emotion and a more Pentecostal expression of the Holy Spirit began rippling the surface of the PCC stream of thought. At the 1952 conference Ray Mishler of Sheridan discussed whether spiritual gifts of 1 Corinthians 12-14 are for today, and if so, how they are manifested. (He probably did so as a caution against excesses.) Ernest Bontrager attributed the effectiveness of the Brunk brothers' 1953 tent campaign in Oregon to their "complete yieldedness to, and appropriation of, the power of the Holy Spirit." But the Pentecostal emphasis on speaking in tongues had split the larger holiness movement. George R. Brunk II and his brother and partner Lawrence would soon part ways regarding the baptism of the Spirit. And Oregon Mennonites also were beginning to differ, but cautiously.[56]

In the 1950s, language referring to Holy Spirit baptism again surfaced in conference-wide meetings, and distinctly Pentecostal patterns emerged within groups of people. By the early 1950s several Mennonite couples who had experienced the baptism of the Holy Spirit were meeting occasionally for prayer and speaking in tongues. The Western Mennonite School faculty sponsored a Bible conference in the fall of 1954 on "The Nature and Work of the Holy Spirit." Speakers, all from the PCC, represented various understandings of the way the Spirit works in twentieth-century Christians. Paul Miller of the Cove spoke three times, Max Yoder of Sheridan, twice. The others spoke only once. The concluding session's theme was "Sanctification and Baptism of the Holy Spirit." Speakers defined it, identified who needed it, and instructed how to obtain it. Some participants would have understood that the believer receives the Holy Spirit at conversion and that tongues are not a normative aspect of the Spirit's presence. Others promoted and experienced a special postconversion Spirit baptism and speaking in tongues, though they may not then have given public testimony to it. But the differing understandings and experiences produced dissension. The Tangent correspondent thought, in the late 1950s, that the PCC could save itself a lot of trouble if it would hold to "its historical doctrinal position" on the "second work of grace" and gifts of the Spirit.[57]

Even during the years of greatest tension regarding the specifics of nonconformity, which contributed to PCC division in the 1960s, ministers' meetings focused twice on how to practice the presence of the Holy Spirit. Many leaders clearly wished their people to experience the Spirit in biblical ways. But interpretations differed. Yet congregations which later withdrew from the PCC did not cite differences regarding the Holy Spirit among reasons for leaving.[58]

Although Sheridan, the Oregon seedbed of Holy Spirit awareness, did not officially support the Pentecostal emphasis on a special Spirit baptism or speaking in tongues, the sown seed sprouted and grew in individuals who later left Sheridan for service elsewhere. It continued among their children and in daughter congregations, bearing the fruit of varying contemporary expressions of the Spirit. Already in the mid-1930s, a few members, including deacon Will Beachy, who wished for Holy Spirit experiences which Sheridan did not offer, left Sheridan and joined the Assemblies of God. Minister Max Yoder left Sheridan in 1955 with a vision for beginning a congregation in Grants Pass. Respected and used by both groups, he became a bridge between those preferring a more traditional experience of Spirit presence and those desiring a Pentecostal expression. His son Allen contributed actively to charismatic renewal in Oregon. The Church in the Wildwood, started in the early 1950s by Sheridan members as a mission, often "felt the Spirit's presence" in physical healings and spiritual reconsecrations, Wilma Nisly noted. By the 1970s, if not earlier, Logsden and McMinnville, also started in the 1950s by Sheridan members, were nurturing distinctive emphases related to the Holy Spirit. In other congregations, too, persons supported such emphases. If they did not have roots themselves in Sheridan or Indian Cove, they related with people who did.[59]

By the early 1970s charismatic prayer meetings were being held in Mennonite homes in the Willamette Valley. To provide an opportunity for the groups to meet jointly for fellowship, teaching and worship, several persons planned a meeting at the Corvallis Mennonite Church in 1973. A committee composed of Richard Fahndrich, Paul Miller, Roy Miller, Mervin Berkey, Joe Yoder, and Allen Yoder, and their wives, and Lester Yoder, planned subsequent meetings and sponsored the first "Rejoice" in 1975. It became an annual weekend conference with speakers of various denominations from all over the United States and Canada, focusing on various aspects of the work of the Holy Spirit in the individual and in the church. Although some persons feared that the charismatic emphasis of "Rejoice" could become divisive in the PCC, Paul Brunner, secretary, noted in 1975 that it "need not be so," but could be one of "many varied programs" to serve needs and result "in a stronger brotherhood throughout the congregations." He challenged PCC Mennonites to "trust one another and seek the Holy Spirit's blessing in this as in . . . other activities." Including as speakers such respected leaders as Harold Bauman of a denominational board and Max Yoder of the PCC helped give integrity and stability to "Rejoice."[60]

Oregon's smaller Mennonite and related groups brought varying understandings and emphases to Holy Spirit teachings and holiness of life. Early in the twentieth century, the BIC denomination officially endorsed a two-step salvation in holiness form: first, experiencing the new birth and, later, receiving sanctification, which their statement defined as an experience "obtained instantaneously and subsequent to the new birth." The CGC and OOA did not lean toward the holiness movement. For the CGC, "newness of life" included the new birth and holy living expressed in every aspect of life, in "purity, humility, modesty," and other such Christian attitudes and qualities, according to historian Clarence Hiebert. Historian John A. Hostetler noted that the Old Order Amish stressed such attributes as "inner surrender, yieldedness . . . and residing quietly in Christ," not as instantaneous acquisitions but achieved "in a resolute walk through life in a redemptive community."[61]

Among Oregon's other Mennonite groups, GC, MB, and EMB, Holy Spirit emphasis was largely that of the Keswick-Scofield "practical concept of 'power for service,' " as the leading scholarly historian of Fundamentalism, George Marsden, has described it. They endorsed the evangelistic zeal of the Bible institute movement, which offered practical training in evangelism and mission work for lay leaders. The Pentecostal-charismatic movement touched all of these groups, but apparently received less attention among them than among OMs.[62]

The PDC (GC) at times focused on the Holy Spirit in annual sessions, and members here and there reached toward Pentecostal experiences. All papers and discussions at the 1930 conference centered around the theme "The Holy Spirit," and M. J. Galle's presentation included an extensive outline from the *Scofield Reference Bible.* In 1947, Wilbert A. Regier, pastor of Emmanuel at Pratum and member of the PDC evangelization committee, reported that wherever he went, he found Pentecostalism "making its bids for Mennonite people and always finding those willing to follow." The theme in 1949 related to Holy Spirit power in the life of the church and individual. In 1967, the PDC (GC) adopted resolutions about the Holy Spirit as leader and enabler and called for congregations to develop "in experience and in thought a clearer concept of the Holy Spirit" and "an atmosphere" in which Spirit leading could "become more dominant." This hinted at tensions such as Calvary experienced in the mid-1960s when a number of people became involved in the charismatic movement. Eventually most of them withdrew from the congregation.[63]

Within the EMB and MB congregations, too, undercurrents of the holiness movement surfaced at times. About 1920, Sol Ediger, first EMB leader at Dallas, and some followers withdrew and started a Christian and Missionary Alliance Church, a holiness denomination. About a decade later, missionary to China J. J. Schmidt, who served the EMB congregation as pastor during his furlough, taught the baptism of the Holy Spirit. The Dallas MB congregation highly regarded BIOLA as a training center for its young people, and R. A. Torrey, dean, exerted a "most profound" influence upon all PDC (MB) congregations, Otto Bier noted, "in spite of" his teachings about the baptism with the Holy Spirit. In later years, most PDC congregations felt the charismatic influence. But the PDC rejected the second work of grace and held that speaking in tongues should be optional, not required, and that after one receives the Holy Spirit at the time of the new birth, subsequent "fillings" can occur.[64]

■ ■ ■

Mennonites, through their first century in Oregon, held personal salvation and commitment to Christ and the church as their foundational priority and gave high priority to the nurture of their faith. The Bible showed the way and revivalism provided new methods. Teachings about the Holy Spirit often merged with premillennial dispensationalism to inject not only spiritual renewal but also, in some cases, more rigid requirements for holy living. End-times preaching provided impelling incentives to follow Christ, if his call to faithful living was not itself enough motive. The Fundamentalist movement, which Marsden regarded as "a subspecies of American revivalism," developed parallel to the holiness,

Pentecostal, and dispensational movements. Fundamentalism nurtured a spiritual individualism that produced new tensions in the community of faith, competing as a theological movement with the Mennonite understanding of church community. Fundamentalism also articulated basic biblical doctrines that appeared threatened by Modernism. Primary was the declaration of the inerrancy of Scripture, the umbrella under which all the other emphases mingled. But the nurture of personal faith and church commitment was, by itself, incomplete. It was only one part of Oregon Mennonites' larger vision. Another focus of that vision was outward, toward mission and service in their neighborhoods and elsewhere in their world.[65]

Chapter 9
Oregon Mennonites in Mission and Service

Just as most Mennonites accepted revivalism as a means for nurture and renewal, so they also joined the missionary movement, which was closely related. They envisioned bringing unsaved persons to Christ and the church, but they also wanted to meet other human needs and relieve suffering. In mission outreach as well as in their nurture efforts, the balance between individualism and their church community was often uneven. Mission focused on saving souls, emphasizing the relationship between the individual and God. Yet community expectations, often intermingled with Western culture, could influence whether the newly saved stayed with a Mennonite church community or joined a different faith tradition. (Old) Mennonites who defined the divine-human relationship in terms of both doctrine and practice emphasized the community's requirements for new Christians more than did the smaller groups who allowed greater individual autonomy. In all groups the ethnic identity of their church community could be an unintended barrier for new converts from outside the ethnic fold.

At first, denominational mission boards considered Oregon's isolated and emerging small groups of Mennonites as mission fields and sometimes financed visiting preachers from east of the Rockies. But Oregon Mennonites soon began to give as well as receive, to support both foreign and home missions nearby and elsewhere. They organized mission boards and committees. To present the gospel they used music, Sunday schools, summer Bible schools, literature, and radio. Women and girls, youth and men organized for witness and service. Portland became a main arena for mission work, but rural communities and other countries, including Mexico, also provided both familiar and novel settings.[1]

From its beginning, the PDC (GC) emphasized home and foreign mission work. Its first conference in 1896 began with a mission festival and divided its offerings between the GC home and foreign missions. In the early 1900s P. R. Aeschliman promoted missions, both to unite and strengthen PDC congregations and to provide financial support for mission workers. In 1908 the PDC established an evangelization committee which in 1959 became the home missions committee. It became the PDC's most influential and powerful committee.[2]

The OMs, too, promoted mission work. Meeting at Hopewell in 1905, they resolved that leading "souls to Christ is the mission of every Christian." The "western field" they defined as "every city, village, hamlet, mining camp, lumberman's camp, and rural district" west of the Mississippi. When the PCC organized in 1906 it created a mostly lay mission board. By the 1940s the board was sponsoring several mission efforts in Portland and institutions elsewhere. Like the PDC's evangelization committee, the PCC mission board helped organize congregations. Usually, however, individuals or congregations initiated them.[3]

Dedicated Oregon preachers carried on early Mennonite mission work as they visited and preached for isolated Mennonites. Nonchurched people at times also attended such services. In the earliest years the preachers traveled by train, in buggy, on horseback, or on foot, not deterred by accidents caused when animals wandered onto the rails, or by roads that were a muddy paste in one season and a dense carpet of dust in another. When going to Bethel for services, Zion (AM) and Hopewell preachers would "horse and cart" on such wretched roads as far as they could, then tie the horse to a fence and walk the rest of the way. Sometimes they walked the whole distance, six to ten miles. P. C. Hiebert and H. S. Voth, serving the North Dallas (MB) congregation in the early 1900s, preached frequently, sometimes biweekly, at the Portland (MB) congregation.[4]

While preachers traveled to isolated communities or small congregations, the laity at first shared in mission work mostly by supporting the efforts financially. As early as 1897 the Fairview Sunday school planned three collections annually for the (OM) Chicago Mission. One of their subsequent offerings totaled $1.75. Zion (GC) at Polk Station decided in 1905 to hold an offering for the PDC minister-at-large treasury. The following year they began to contribute the requested $1.00 per member.[5]

Quarterly mission meetings, which the AMs and OMs began in 1911, promoted mission work. These were all-day affairs with strong lay participation. They included children's meetings;

sermons, talks, and essays; offerings for designated mission efforts; and, beginning in the 1920s, "special" music in addition to congregational singing. In the first several decades women not only prepared the noon basket lunches for their husbands and families; they also read essays, gave talks, led singing, took minutes, and led children's meetings. However, by the 1950s they usually did no more than arrange special music and lead children's meetings (still preparing the noon lunch, no doubt). Topics at the mission meetings included purposes, goals, and results of mission effort; necessary Christian qualities and disciplines; areas of need; and motives and calling. The mission meeting movement had developed independently of any board or conference and remained so to its end. Though it had no authority to act, it provided strong incentives for mission service through most of its continuation. In the late 1960s, with interest and attendance decreasing, the meetings were discontinued.[6]

Missionary Day programs, mission study books and courses, and denominational publications such as the OMs' *Gospel Herald* and *Christian Monitor* also promoted mission interest and support. During the depression of the 1930s an article by Orrie D. Yoder insisted that Mennonites could not "afford *not* to . . . preach and witness for [Jesus] among all nations." They could not afford not to evangelize the Jew, not to give money, not to "believe, practice, and teach the 'all things' commanded" by Christ. Ferne Whitaker of Portland wrote about the importance of appealing to varied interests of different classes of people who needed the gospel message.[7]

Oregon's smaller Mennonite groups also promoted missions. They welcomed missionaries on furlough and held mission rallies and conferences. Emmanuel (GC) and perhaps other sister congregations held quarterly missionary programs in the 1930s. At the Dallas MB congregation, ministers frequently gave an altar call to invite persons to dedicate their lives to Christian service as missionaries, with evident results. Members served in both foreign and home missions. Liberty Gardens (EMB) read missionary letters every Sunday to acquaint the people with mission needs and to solicit prayer support.[8]

Both the PDC (GC) and the PCC established publications that helped promote mission interest and efforts. About 1927 PDC field secretary C. F. Mueller began sending an occasional newsletter to conference workers. Several years later Emma M. Ruth expanded it, named it "Pacific District Workers' Exchange," and served as its editor for about fifteen years. In 1959 it became *The Messenger*. La Vernae Dick was editor in 1976. In 1944 the PCC mission board began publishing the *Missionary Evangel*, a four-page quarterly. Paul E. Yoder, an early editor, asked for prayer that it might be "a real instrument in stirring up a hot spirit of evangelism." In the next decades its size and scope enlarged. John L. Fretz was editor in 1976.[9]

Congregational Outreach

One goal of missions almost as important as saving souls was to involve the laity in the effort. Though a few lay members served on conference mission boards or committees, their greatest opportunities came through congregational outreach.

Music was one medium which Oregon Mennonites used in reaching out to the unchurched or to lonely or needy people. Most congregations assembled groups to sing on the streets, at hospitals

Dallas EMB Church

The Dallas EMB choir sang for Sunday services which were broadcast on radio. Nels Friesen directed the choir for years. (Photo probably from the 1950s)

and homes for the aged, at migrant camps, jails, rescue missions, and other institutions. A congregation's choir or chorus not only sang in worship services but also gave programs at other churches, community centers, schools, or penal institutions. Zion's chorus paved the way for the opening of two mission stations, Meadowbrook and Chapel in the Hills. The Dallas EMB choir sang regularly as part of the Sunday morning service, which the congregation broadcasted on radio for a time. Men's, women's, and junior choirs, and quartets, trios, octets, and sometimes instrumental ensembles, all provided a way for the participants to witness to their faith in a universally loved medium, music. It was an attractive way to encourage members to engage in mission outreach. It afforded social interaction as well. At the same time, members nurtured their own faith and developed skills that helped enhance congregational music.[10]

The Sunday school was another method of mission for Oregon Mennonites. Sunday school rallies, rewards for children who brought new attenders, a church bus to pick up children—all were attempts to reach children and their parents through the Sunday school. A congregation might set a goal such as Kingwood (MB) did in 1966: to increase the average Sunday school attendance by 15 percent during the next year. Beyond the Sunday school of the home congregation, another method was to start a mission Sunday school in a nearby community. In 1912 the PCC "[granted] power to any qualifed Bro. or sister in good standing in church to organize Sunday Schools as needed." Beginning in the 1930s, denominational (OM) leaders I. W. Royer and J. D. Graber promoted the idea of "every congregation an outpost," at least a mission Sunday school. Half of the PCC's Oregon congregations which organized after 1950 began earlier as mission Sunday schools (often in connection with summer Bible school). Large numbers of the laity, women and men alike, participated. Oregon's MB, EMB, and GC congregations also worked in Sunday school outreach, but they more often cooperated with such organizations as the American Sunday School Union than did MC congregations. Such Sunday schools did not organize as congregations of a Mennonite group.[11]

In the 1940s and 1950s summer Bible school was a popular method of mission outreach among all of Oregon's Mennonite groups. Several began a decade or two earlier. The Portland Mission had its first summer Bible school in 1924—among the first in the denomination. Five years later, three women—Anna Snyder, Florence Kauffman, and Alice Rogie—started one at Bethel, "with the consent of the ministry," Snyder noted, and at the urging of minister Sam Shrock. Annual expenses for Bethel's first six years of Bible school varied from ninety-two cents to five dollars. Bethel considered it largely a ministry to non-Mennonite children. Anna Snyder promoted summer Bible schools in rural communities for many years and acquired the reputation of being a pioneer in the movement. By the mid-1900s larger congregations were often holding several Bible schools a summer in neighboring communities, some of which developed into mission Sunday schools. By the late 1960s, to meet competition from berry or bean farmers who hired young pickers, congregations frequently held evening instead of morning Bible schools.[12]

Some Oregon Mennonites became concerned about workers in nearby migrant camps. People from the EMB and MB congregations at Dallas promoted Sunday school and other ministries with migrants in nearby hop yards. For fifteen years Hopewell members worked with migrants near Woodburn, first with a summer Bible school and a tent revival, then with a Sunday school. The Spanish language of the migrants produced a barrier of such proportions that Hopewell eventually discontinued the work. A severe Columbus Day storm in 1962 destroyed the schoolhouse they used and forced the closing a bit earlier than planned.[13]

A few Oregon Mennonites reached out briefly to American Indians. In 1941 Hopewell had a Sunday school for about fifty Indian children at the Chemawa Indian School north of Salem. A few Siletz Indian children were among those who first attended Sheridan's Sunday school at Logsden in 1950. In the 1960s, Harrisburg helped in a joint mission work among the Indians of Topley Landing, British Columbia. But such ministries were brief.[14]

Some Oregon Mennonites joined an interdenominational movement to distribute gospel tracts and other Christian literature. Stories abounded about persons who had found Christ through a tract. From the 1920s into the late 1940s, S. E. Roth of Woodburn operated a "Gospel Tract Mission" to "supply prisons, hospitals, missions, and the needy poor" with free tracts, calendars, and Bibles. In the 1930s, short of funds, he appealed to *Gospel Herald* readers for help in giving "the unadulterated Gospel of free salvation" to all he could possibly reach, who included "many thousands of people in many lands and in many languages." If necessary, he was willing to sell his "little home" to meet obligations.

Orrie D. Yoder, in occasional articles in the 1930s, promoted "literary evangelism" or "colportage work" by which Mennonites would sell or distribute free Christian literature wherever possible. He especially encouraged travelers to the (old) Mennonite general conference, meeting at Turner, Oregon, in 1937, to display mottos with Scripture verses in automobile and train windows and to hand out tracts and Scripture portions at filling stations, train depots, and on passenger trains. He also suggested tossing tracts out of the car window while passing "the poor highway traveler, hopelessly plodding along . . . [and the] many highway laborers."[15]

Reaching out with the printed page took several forms adopted by lay and ordained persons alike. From congregations of Oregon's various Mennonite groups, young people and adults who often went two-by-two passed out tracts on city streets and in door-to-door visitation. People placed and stocked tract racks in public places. *The Way*, a monthly OM tract paper, also became a popular item to distribute or send on a church mailing list to community people. Though this method of outreach became less common in the 1960s, even in the 1970s some Oregon Mennonites continued to hand out tracts or New Testaments. In the 1970s the PCC promoted a new method of print outreach, known as Bookrack Evangelism, coordinated by a denominational agency. Individuals would receive permission to place a bookrack in a grocery store, laundromat, or other public place and stock the rack with paperback books for sale with a Christian message. Eugene Garber of Sweet Home (OM) and later Amos Schmucker of Fairview, with PCC mission board backing, promoted and supervised this ministry in Oregon. In 1973, such workers had placed 4,160 books. Several bookracks were eventually discontinued because the workers had moved away. The following year the PCC discontinued this effort and sold their racks and stock to the Successful Living organization, their strong competitor.[16]

In almost all Oregon Mennonite congregations women's groups strongly and consistently supported mission and relief efforts, whether for local, national, or foreign needs. Besides sewing clothing and making quilts and comforters, they also prepared used clothing for distribution. They sent dried fruit to overseas missionaries, gave money and materials for local community and church needs, scrubbed, painted, and decorated in such institutions as mission churches, homes for the aged, and parochial schools. They

Kathryn Yoder Miller; names from Margaret Shetler

The Zion sewing circle in 1945. They pushed church benches together to make room for their quilting frames. Starting at far left and going clockwise around first quilt (name of husband in parenthesis): Vinnie (Loney) Yoder; Elsie (Alvin) Hooley; Freda (John) Gahler; Edna (Edward) Kenagy holding Darlene; Mary (Jess) Troyer; Dorothy Louise Gingerich; Em (William) Kenagy; Mabel (Chauncy) Kropf; Nellie (Sam) Miller; Varda (Harvey) Brenneman; Malinda (Jake) Hershberger; Elfie (Dan) Widmer; Alene Widmer. Emma Belle (Amos) Lais at sewing machine. Second quilt, starting at left and going clockwise: Olive (Lewis) Garber; Fannie (Clarence) Shrock; Polly (Harvey) Kropf; Tillie (Abe) Jones; Lydia (John E.) Gingerich; Mabel (Uriah) Roth; Mattie (Daniel B.) Kauffman.

also visited the elderly, handicapped, lonely, and ill.

Emmanuel formed its women's missionary society in 1907. The Dallas EMB women began meeting in 1912 to sew and gather food for the needy, attempting to hold their costs to one-third of the donations, leaving two-thirds to send to foreign work. Women of Zion (AM) organized the Zion sewing circle in 1918 amid the careful scrutiny and supervision of the ministry and other Zion "brothers." They established a rather sophisticated organization, including the usual officers, three committees, and a general manager who was a man, John Gahler. Membership was open to women, of course, and to "any brother in good standing . . . by virtue of [being] head of the home and upon request of the circle." Zion women became known for their fine quilting. By the 1970s they frequently demonstrated this reviving art at a large department store in Portland and at the nearby Ox Barn Museum at Aurora. In 1973 they began quilting workshops, to teach quilting and also to witness to the Mennonite faith.[17]

To help girls develop an interest in mission efforts, women organized girls' sewing circles. The circles raised money to support missionary work and also provided purposeful activities, social interaction, and instruction in sewing and related arts for those who may not have learned at home. In one case, at the Dallas MB Church, the girls' missionary society, which Sarah Lohrentz Wiens organized, was the forerunner of the Ladies' Mission Aid. An early project was making a quilt, which won a prize at the county fair. In later years, girls' groups became auxiliaries or clubs, or took another name and style. In most of them, missions remained one focus. Sponsors in the Western congregation (and perhaps others) invited boys to participate as well.[18]

From the beginnings of their organizations, Oregon women in all the Mennonite groups included a time of devotion or Bible study in their meetings. By the mid-1900s they expanded their focus and service activities. They encouraged women to read good books and Mennonite publications and offered help to strengthen homes. They began Bible study groups and invited community women to attend. They taught Good News Clubs, a program developed by Child Evangelism, in release-time Bible classes. Women, and men, too, began boys' and girls' clubs and included crafts and social activities along with biblical teaching. In some ways clubs were similar to earlier girls' sewing circles. But they often focused more on the children themselves, many from unchurched homes, as objects of mission, and less on contributions *to* missions elsewhere.[19]

Young people, with the encouragement and help of their elders, gradually developed their own mission and service organizations. By 1920 Oregon's PDC (GC) congregations had Christian Endeavor societies patterned after an interdenominational movement that included both nurture and training for service. A few years later, after visiting at Dallas and Pratum, C. F. Mueller referred to the "host of earnest-minded young folk" as "a very encouraging sign," particularly in their response "to meet the needs of the day." Christian Endeavor at Grace (Albany), in 1947, as part of the personal work emphasis, had its young people going in groups of two or three in house-to-house witnessing, giving out Gospel of John booklets, tracts, and invitations to attend church services.[20]

In the PCC, youth organizations developed later. By 1942 Clifford Strubhar of Zion, after receiving the hesitant approval of the ministry, initiated an earning project. It was for his class of teenage boys, although men as old as forty also worked in the bean field. They earned $240 for relief and mission work in France, Mexico, Arkansas, and South America. The next year they amended the constitution to permit the girls to help also. Within several years other Oregon youth groups began similar projects. Crops and income varied from year to year, subject to the whims of weather, wandering cows, or other agricultural perils. In the 1950s, congregations merged the missionary projects with literary societies, which had organized as early as the 1930s for social, educational, and religious purposes. The outcome was a new denominational organization, Mennonite Youth Fellowship (MYF). Albany had the first MYF west of the Rockies, organized in 1950.[21]

Men's organizations usually were not as common or lasting as were women's organizations. Nonetheless, some made significant contributions to mission outreach and other needs. In the PDC (GC), Emmanuel began its men's organization in 1935. Oregon's other GC congregations also had men's groups which took the name "Mennonite Men," whose primary activity was raising money for such mission projects as buildings for small PDC congregations; medical supplies for John Zook of Portland, headed for Africa as a missionary; seminary scholarships; and MCC projects. By 1976 all of Oregon's PDC men's organizations had dissolved.

Some other Mennonite groups also had occasional men's organizations. Liberty Gardens (EMB) organized one in 1965 to provide fellowship and to hold occasional retreats. Among PCC congregations, Albany men organized in 1953 to provide emergency aid in disasters and to do mission outreach. But in the late 1960s they discontinued the men's fellowship, having become active in the nationwide Mennonite Disaster Service (MDS). From the late 1950s into the early 1970s, several other PCC congregations began men's groups, often loosely organized, to provide fellowship as much as to work in service or mission outreach. Often they did not survive long. For all congregations, MDS provided opportunities for service in major disasters. Conference and congregational committees for service and mission presented other needs and offered as many outreach opportunities as the men could respond to. Perhaps, too, the men did not need or value the fellowship aspect of a group as much as the women did, although not all women's groups survived, either.[22]

Radio broadcasting was another method of outreach that a few congregations used in the 1950s. The Dallas EMB congregation broadcast its entire Sunday morning service. Shorter programs which others sponsored usually included a men's quartet and an evangelistic message. Edward (Kelly) Kenagy and a Zion quartet began the "Peace in the Valley" radio program early in 1953, and Fairview's Gospel Messengers quartet and Ivan Headings started a radio program a few months later. The next year Albany began a radio witness, and in 1955 the Gospel Messengers and Allen Erb started a program over a Newport station in relation to the Logsden mission. "Peace in the Valley" continued through much of 1955, though apparently none of the programs stayed on the air for many years.[23]

Portland

Congregational outreach efforts were often far-reaching and effective, but some mission work needed conference support. In Portland, Mennonite mission work exemplified such cooperation. Like the MC mission, the MB and GC missions and congregations needed substantial financial assistance and occasional administrative oversight. But it seems their conferences did not exercise the level of authority the PCC did. Though MBs had both a congregation and a mission in Portland for some years, the denominational MB board considered that early congregation a mission (and the one at Dallas, too) and sent preachers to Oregon to serve both congregations. The PDC (MB) board of home missions related to the Portland mission until it disbanded about 1938. The GC mission which began in Portland in 1928 and organized as a congregation in 1931 was the last of the three Mennonite missions to be established in the city. Both the denomination and the PDC (GC) promoted it. The PDC provided financial and other support most years through 1976, but like the MB mission, the relation of the Alberta/Peace congregation to its PDC differed in scope and quality from that of the PCC to its Portland mission work. Al-

berta/Peace had a greater autonomy, equal with its sister congregations in Oregon.[24]

A succession of committees and much talk preceded the final
successful beginning of (old) Mennonite mission work in Portland.
A few OMs lived there before the turn of the century, but for
most, the city was more a place for mission work than for normal
living. Beginning in 1906, committees surveyed the need and
looked for a location for mission work but did not start one. In the
face of this inaction, minister John F. Bressler and his wife moved
from Hubbard to southwest Portland in 1907 and started a mission
Sunday school on Hood Street. It attracted up to seventy-five persons but closed after a year because Oregon's congregations did
not unitedly support it. Again talk and committees abounded, and
in the April 1912 and subsequent quarterly mission meetings, practical people promised to furnish such "eatables" as bread, potatoes,
butter, eggs, and sugar for mission workers in Portland. Offerings
built up a mission fund.

A second attempt began in 1915 when the PCC (but primarily Hopewell ministers) began monthly preaching services in
northwest Portland. During the year this mission existed, five persons joined the Mennonite Church, including Henry A. and Mary
Wolfer, who were dissatisfied with the Baptist Church and requested rebaptism as Mennonites. Henry Wolfer later served many
years as a Mennonite minister and bishop. Certainly one handicap
in this second effort was lack of a resident leader. Apparently, like
the first effort, it did not have a broad base of support. None of
the named ministers who served were from the Zion or Fairview
AM congregations.[25]

Not until after the (old) Mennonites and Amish Mennonites
merged in June 1921 did they successfully establish a mission in
Portland. A year later the PCC mission board decided "to establish
a Gospel work in Portland as the Lord may lead." Chris Snyder,
C. R. Widmer, and J. B. Mishler, appointed to the local board of
the Portland Mission, invited Allan Good, who had earlier served at
the Mennonite mission in Kansas City, to serve as superintendent.
Good and his wife, Fannie, arrived in September 1922 and in
November opened a mission on Savier Street between 22nd and
23rd Avenues, only several blocks from the location of the second
short effort. They rented two old buildings which the city fire
department condemned within ten years. The ground floor of the
first building became the mission hall. The second floor served as a

Kathryn Yoder Miller

Allan (1882-1942) and Fannie (Miller) Good, first superintendent and matron of the Portland (Old) Mennonite mission.

dormitory for young Mennonite men working in the city. The superintendent's family, other mission workers, and young Mennonite women working in the city lived in the second building.[26]

Although the Mennonites wanted to reach the unsaved in Portland, they also wished to to provide a church for Mennonite young people who were taking jobs in the city. "Working girls" at first did housework in homes of the well-to-do. By the 1940s they worked as secretaries or in hospitals, factories, or stores. Young men, too, found jobs in Portland. Some of these young people supported the mission with both funds and fervor. Within six months nine were each paying $5.00 a week for board, room, and laundry, which provided the mission with money for rent and utilities. They also helped in the mission program. In 1925 J. A. Heatwole of La Junta, Colorado, considered many of them to be "real efficient soul-winners" in this "soul saving station." With their "consistent lives and loyalty to the doctrine of Gospel simplicity and uniformity in attire" they shone "as lights in a dark city."[27]

Throughout the year conference congregations supplied weekly provisions of food and sewing circles sent clothing. Sometimes supplies from the country arrived late, but Muriel (Ethel) Snyder remembered Fannie Good as a wonderful cook who could prepare appetizing meals out of "practically nothing." She could also make meals stretch for "the many unexpected guests who arrived just at lunch or supper time." Her husband "always said that when there was nothing to eat, they would stick their heads in the empty flour barrel and pray, and the Lord would supply." Apparently even the hardest of times never brought such destitution. A large garden just across the street provided vegetables as well as exercise and fellowship for boarders, workers, and neighborhood children.[28]

Allan Good was the driving force in the work. He was zealous, ambitious, visionary, and innovative. People considered him a good preacher and teacher and an effective personal worker. His jolly disposition warmed his organizational and administrative skills and helped win friends in the neighborhood. Many loyal workers supported his ambitious program, which included two Sunday services, home visitation, weekly teachers' meetings, Bible studies, prayer meetings, jail services, occasional street meetings, summer evangelistic tent campaigns of several weeks, winter revival meetings, sewing classes for the girls, and other activities. Workers distributed hundreds of dollars' worth of Christian literature—new, used, and from the mission press. In 1924 Good started one of the early summer Bible schools in the (old) Mennonite Church. That summer he also began a fresh-air program for city children, in which they lived in the country for two weeks with Mennonite families. This grew to include, in 1929, the first camping program in the (old) Mennonite Church.[29]

Some mission efforts attempted to reach adults, but most of the mission program centered on children. By the mid-1920s, the mission was providing child care, full-time or by the day only, for orphans and children from poor families. All received religious instruction. The children's welfare program changed locations several times because of city licensing requirements and the eventual condemnation of the mission buildings. For almost two years beginning in 1926, the mission conducted a branch Sunday school on North Russel Street in East Portland. But lack of cooperation among workers produced stress at the mission. Attendance at the Sunday school dropped and the work closed in July of 1928.[30]

To house the program adequately, the property required attention and funds. When the mission board purchased the property and constructed a new mission hall, Good publicized financial needs throughout the the denomination. He sent twelve thousand "circulars" to two hundred Mennonite congregations, aiming "to get every Mennonite, as nearly as possible, to have a personal interest in this Soul Saving Institution." *Gospel Herald* carried reports of contributions, as much as $500 from the Eastern Mennonite Board of Missions and Charities and as little as fifty cents from each of several women. After the new building was constructed in 1927, receipts did not cover costs, and as the Goods traveled across the continent in 1930-31, he "sold" building blocks for twenty-five cents each to help erase the indebtedness. Still, financial straits plagued the mission. The Great Depression, which cast its pall over the national economy, discouraged contributions. In 1931 the rental income from the old mission buildings ended when they were razed.[31]

A bright new building served much of the mission program well, but the loss of the old buildings largely curtailed the children's welfare work. A vision of Good to expand such work brought abrupt changes. He dreamed of a small ranch to provide a self-supporting home for about ten children and planned to direct both the city and country programs. Apparently he began the paperwork for this purchase even before presenting his plan to the local board. The board and conference leaders refused his plan. In the deepening depression they preferred to erase the debt on the mission property before expanding, even though the proposed ranch might be clear of encumbrance. Nor did they want the superintendent to distribute his efforts between city and country. The "undivided service of a married couple as head" of the mission seemed necessary to them for "proper social relationships," given the flow of unmarried men and women workers in and out of the mission living quarters.

In April 1932, Good, not willing to accept the limits, stepped aside and ended nine-and-one-half years of dedicated, creative service. He had established the character of the mission program to its fullest. No later leader ever duplicated its scope. He innovated and saw to completion the development of property and facilities. His failure came, in the judgment of Robert Lee, an historian of the Portland congregation, when he attemped to expand the program without understanding the financial capabilities of the mission board.[32]

After Good left, hard times came to the mission. During

several years of decreasing conference support, due perhaps as much to dissension regarding Good's position as to the depression, cuts in the mission program eliminated the fresh-air and camping programs. The PCC and its mission board requested the mission not to ask for money from the board or its congregations, and the mission consolidated all its work and residences into the mission building, even enclosing inner spaces to make bedrooms for boarders. Henry and Lydia Yoder, longtime workers in the congregation, served thirty months while the board searched for a full-time couple. The Yoders, workers Viola Wenger and Sadie King, and other members of the congregation were doubtless the unsung heroes who kept the mission afloat during that difficult time. Though morale improved and conference support increased during the temporary leadership of Paul N. and Velma Roth, even acquiring the annual supply of firewood was difficult.[33]

During the leadership of Glenn and Ferne Whitaker, 1936-1939, conference support revived and brought debt liquidation, a new mission truck, and cord wood to last two years. Educated at BIOLA, Whitaker emphasized prayer, fasting, Bible memorization, and spiritual revival. He reestablished the camping program at a new campground on the Sam Miller farm near Hubbard and started children's sewing clubs and manual training classes. He also installed loudspeakers on the roof which carried singing up to ten blocks and brought both favorable comments and a complaint one evening about "too much racket."[34]

Other superintendents came and went and changes in the neighborhood began to affect the mission. During World War II, nearby shipbuilding and other war industries brought an increasingly transient group of children, including the first large group of blacks, who comprised about half the Sunday school. Workers attempted to attract people and meet needs with a neon sign, a kindergarten, and a home nursing classes. From 1947 to 1955, because of growing industrialization in the mission neighborhood, Claud M. and Nora Hostetler, the last superintendent and matron, promoted a "new" 35-passenger bus to bring in children from greater distances. In those days when people did not worry much about liability for overloading, the bus usually carried from 95 to 105 children. Once it carried 116.[35]

Many women and men assisted the leadership couples and implemented the programs they envisioned and promoted. During most of Allan Good's tenure, full-time staff included four single women and one single man along with the Goods. An occasional married couple worked in the child welfare program. Later, the auxiliary staff decreased to two single women. Many served only one year, others more briefly or part-time. Several women helped many years: Myrtle Miller (12), Viola Wenger (12), Sadie King (7), Rhea Yoder (5), Anna Snyder (4), and Bertha Troyer (3). The women provided stability in transitions between superintendents.[36]

In 1955 the PCC mission board terminated its thirty-three-year sponsorship of the Portland mission. Contributing to the decision were continuing changes in the neighborhood, city condemnation of the basement apartment in the mission building where the two women workers lived, Hostetler's resignation as superintendent, unsuccessful attempts to relocate the mission in a more promising section of the city, and changing concepts of mission in relation to congregation. In May 1956 the congregation adopted a new constitution and chose the name Portland Mennonite Church. Hostetler continued to serve as pastor until 1961. In the next two years, ministers from other Oregon Mennonite congregations brought messages and interim or temporary pastors served until Marcus and Dottie Smucker arrived in September 1963 to assume leadership.[37]

Beginning in the 1950s young Mennonites who settled in Portland brought striking changes to the congregation amid continuing traditions. In lieu of military service, they did alternative service in city hospitals. They worked in a predominantly black northeast Portland community in a Voluntary Service (VS) unit, trained for professions, and took jobs. They brought varied backgrounds and expectations and produced new tensions in the congregation, but added enthusiasm, energy, and an interest in experimenting with new methods of worship, service, fellowship, and discipleship. One focus unifying oldtimers and newcomers continued to be the concern for mission and service. Some longtime mission programs such as children's camp continued, although in 1956 the camping moved to Ralph Shetler's property near Scotts Mills. By 1970, Portland campers were beginning to participate in the program at Drift Creek Camp, which Mennonites were developing. For several years in the 1960s, the northeast Portland VS unit and some Portland members held a Sunday school and, later, worship services, in the basement of the unit house on Garfield Street. In this time of increasing civil rights awareness nationwide, Sunday school workers (often VS members) were excited about the challenge of interracial fellowship and sharing. However, in 1971 plans to develop a permanent work there failed as no permanent leader could be found.[38]

Increasing industrialization in northwest Portland eventually caused the congregation to move its worship and witness to another location. In 1969 the congregation purchased a used building at SE 35th and Main, a low-income residential community in the inner city. But the congregation maintained a witness in northwest Portland near the former building for several years, with a VS unit leading Bible studies, clubs, recreation, and other community services. At the new location, neighborhood needs became one major focus of mission outreach. In 1974 the congregation requested the VS unit to move to the more impoverished Sunnyside community in which the congregation was then worshiping and working. Smucker continued as pastor through 1976, except for a sabbatical year. Coming when the congregation had been on a maintenance program for months, he brought vision, sensitivity, and a new style of leadership that involved members more fully in choosing priorities and making decisions.[39]

Membership fluctuated over the years and in 1951 included such ethnic diversity as Chinese, Jewish, Russian, and Negro (later, terminology changed to "black"). One member, Robert Lee, was later ordained at Portland before he and his wife, Nancy, went to Japan as missionaries. In the early 1970s rapid growth brought a membership high of 157 in 1973. In 1976 membership was 147. By then major differences within the congregation were not so much ethnic or racial as generational, with almost 70 percent of the participants under thirty-five years of age. Also, participants represented several groups of Mennonite heritage and other denominational backgrounds and included persons with varied levels of education, income, adaptability, social concerns, and views of spirituality and discipleship. Mission focus had changed over the years, but commitment to mission remained a primary force in the congregation's life.[40]

The PCC mission board also sponsored other efforts in Portland, including work among Jewish people. Orrie D. Yoder, periodic Oregon preacher and early proponent of evangelization of the Jews, interpreted the charge Jesus gave to begin "at Jerusalem" to mean going "to the Jew first." As early as 1934 David H. Kauffman, then of Bethel and later of Indian Cove, acquired a mailing list of "many hundreds of Jews" and began sending

"Messianic literature" to them, according to Yoder. By 1936 Yoder was working independently among the Jews in Portland, as was Hugh Wolfer by 1941. In 1943 the board began supporting Jewish mission work, by prayer "and otherwise." Within several years workers included James and Fannie Bucher, although frequently they were away for evangelistic tours and other activities; Hugh and Ina Wolfer; and for a short time, Henry Wolfer. The workers attempted to gain the confidence of Jewish people, attended services in their synagogues, visited them in their places of business and homes, gave them Hebrew or Yiddish New Testaments, and talked with them personally about the Messiah. As a point of contact, Ina Wolfer studied Hebrew.[41]

With the passing of years, the Jewish community became more open and friendly, but few became Christians. The 1952 PCC sessions gave "a little time" for the "stirring testimony" of Sister Edith Evans, a Mennonite Christian of Jewish ancestry, but the report does not say whether her conversion occurred in Oregon or elsewhere. In the 1967-68 conference year, the year in which Wolfer died, the board suspended the operation of the Jewish mission. By that time Bucher was eighty, and what continuing work he did among the Jews may have been sponsored by the BMF. The turning of the Jews toward Christ for which the workers hoped, prayed, and waited never did occur. Most mission-minded people turned to other fields.[42]

Although it appears that Oregon's smaller Mennonite groups did not give much attention to work with the Jews, at least one congregation produced a missionary for them. In 1946 Lillian Beutler of Emmanuel (GC) began working among Jews in New York.[43]

Another effort which the PCC mission board supported was a rescue mission in Portland. Rescue missions, then found in all large urban centers, attempted to reach alcoholics and vagrants with the gospel and to rehabilitate them. On August 17, 1948, the board opened what soon was named the Rock of Ages Rescue Mission in downtown Portland, with Oscar and Louise Wideman of Sheridan as superintendent and matron. Guy and Mary Hostetler assisted the Widemans. With the help of ministers and singers from conference congregations, they held meetings four nights a week and served a light lunch afterward to all who attended. Unlike the Jewish mission work, the rescue mission could point to conversions and baptisms. So many men attended services that the hall which seated

Oregon Mennonite archival collection, courtesy of Millard Osborne

*Harold Reeder
(1902-1979), super-
intendent of the
Portland rescue
mission, passing out
sandwiches after a
service in 1964.*

eighty was crowded with 115. Sometimes men stood outside, where
loudspeakers carried the song service and the sermon. Later the
workers staffed a reading room next door, and for a time the mission offered beds for a few men.

One ambitious board project was to develop a donated acre-
age near McMinnville, forty miles to the southwest, into a country
home where converts could escape the skid-row environment,
regain physical health, experience loving relationships, and receive
spiritual nurture. Although small numbers of men did stay at the
farm for periods of time, the farm became too heavy a financial
liability for the board. In 1956 the board decided to convert it to
an old people's home.[44]

Over the years rescue mission personnel, location, and needs
changed, and support decreased due to differences of conviction
about how best to help the men of skid row. Many men had gone
forward for prayer, and some were converted and became members
of Sheridan or another Mennonite congregation. Although many
lapsed back into their former ways, some remained faithful. But
rescue missions in general were in trouble in the 1960s. A new
generation of vagrants often did not respond to rescue mission services as men had done earlier. In addition, the medical world had
come to regard alcoholism as a disease to be treated, not as a sin

to be forgiven and rooted out. A recurring question was whether rescue mission costs justified the returns. In 1967 the board decided to close the mission by March 1, 1968, unless the congregations then withdrawing from the PCC wished to operate it. The BMF accepted the board's offer and kept the rescue mission open through 1976, with Joe and Ina Yoder as primary staff, in spite of Joe's declining health. Probably Yoder never knew that after the Mennonites closed the mission two years later, shortly before or about the time of his death, a community group would operate it as a secular service agency and name it "Baloney Joe's" in his memory. It was an odd tribute to his quiet love that touched the lives of men who had showed up repeatedly through the years.[45]

Other Home Mission Efforts

By the early 1950s, some Oregon Mennonites wished to expand home mission efforts beyond Portland and interested the PCC board in beginning a rescue mission in Sacramento, California. The board appointed Joe Kropf, Merle Kropf, Lloyd Kropf, and David Hostetler for this work. All were laymen available on a self-supporting basis. All were present or former members of nonconference Harrisburg, and all were closely related to each other. Only mission rent and equipment would need to be covered by the board. With their families the four men moved to a rural suburb near Sacramento, remodeled a rented hall in the city, began services on April 11, 1952, and called their work the Rock of Ages Rescue Mission. Soon they established the Robla Mennonite Church and constructed a mission farm home as a halfway house for converts. Both laypersons and ordained men from Oregon assisted for periods of time, and California Mennonites also helped. Early in 1955 David Hostetler and Lloyd and Merle Kropf were ordained as ministers. But the distance from supporting congregations was too great and by the end of 1956 a shortage of workers became a serious problem. On March 15, 1958, the board closed the mission. Workers moved back to Oregon and served in emerging or young congregations.[46]

At mid-century, even with increasing numbers of Oregon Mennonites living in cities, the PCC mission board and many individuals still considered the city more a place for "mission work" than for developing a church community. In the late 1940s, Guy

Hostetler of California wished to locate in Salem and begin board-financed mission work there. But apparently the board felt the proposal lacked sound planning. It decided to "drop Salem mission work" for the time being. A decade later a Ben Vimont of Eugene wished for a Mennonite congregation there and informed the board of a vacant church building in neighboring Springfield. But nothing came of this concern, either. However, in the 1960s, with board counsel, Mennonites living in both cities started congregations.[47]

Beginning a summer service unit in 1950 was one way the PCC mission board attempted to involve young people in mission work while responding to seasonal needs. During ten summers and more, young people (and a few adults, too) taught summer Bible school and helped with children's camps in established and new mission efforts. They served in migrant camps at Stayton and The Dalles, teaching Bible school and offering child care and recreational activites. By the early 1960s more youths took summer jobs and fewer volunteered for summer service. The board's migrant ministry at Stayton ended in 1964, workers being from Oklahoma and Iowa, but not Oregon.[48]

At Yale, Washington, a small community about fifty miles north of Portland near Mt. St. Helens, a Bible school which the summer service unit held in 1951 initiated what became a year-round mission effort. Eldon and Lois Shetler and other helpers began Sunday school there and in several years the board financed a building at nearby Ariel. The work developed into essentially a community church, which caused problems because the board and PCC officials did not support Shetler's using "truly born-again" non-Mennonites as Sunday school teachers even though they agreed to teach the Bible as interpreted by the Mennonite Church and did not have voting power in matters relating to policy and discipline. Policy also required Shetler, who was licensed as a minister for the work, to wear the "regulation" coat, which he was willing to do in Mennonite circles but not in the mission community. Final resolution to the problems took several years. Finally, in 1956 the board released Shetler from conference and board administration. However, until 1959 it annually granted him the use of the building when it transferred the title free of charge to the Mt. Pleasant Community Church.[49]

The PCC mission board also sponsored a congregation at Vanderhoof, British Columbia, a young town of 1,200 people about five hundred miles north of the border. In the late 1950s, Ron and Barb Shenk and their family of Sheridan moved to a farm in the area and for several years worshiped with Sommerfeld Mennonite and Evangelical Mennonite Church families. In 1962 the board requested that bishop Ray and Elsie Mishler from Sheridan go to Vanderhoof for a year. In March 1963 Ray helped organize a congregation of seventeen charter members. About this time other Oregon Mennonite families moved there, including Merle Kropf, who became pastor, and the membership increased. The congregation established relationships with the BMF rather than with the PCC.[50]

The rural nature of the Vanderhoof congregation in its early years illustrates a concern which Oregon Mennonites (MC) had held for years. Writing in 1912 about "many neglected places . . . especially in the hilly regions where access is more or less difficult," Charles Mitchell told of persons who "do not hear the Word of God from one year to another." Most mission Sunday schools which Oregon Mennonites started in the next several decades were in rural communities. Anna Snyder, a charter member at Portland, who was later a member of rural Bethel, wrote in 1933 of the nation's millions of farm children who were "virtual pagans." For example, only one-third of the families who lived in a one-mile radius from one small Mennonite congregation were attending services. Modern transportation was intensifying the problems, because rural people were "no longer isolated from the temptations and vice of the cities as they once were." Anna's father, Christian Snyder, Bethel deacon, president of the PCC mission board from 1921 to 1944 and a continuing board member until his death in 1948, was a longtime advocate of rural mission work. His efforts and vision became reality when Ernest and Ida Bontrager came from Midland, Michigan, to Bethel in 1938 to serve in door-to-door contacts, visitation, distribution of religious literature, and cottage meetings. Even after they began the Porter mission Sunday school, they continued to work in the Bethel neighborhood for some years. Due largely to their visitation program, membership at Bethel peaked at eighty-nine in the early 1940s.[51]

In mission Sunday schools which organized as Mennonite congregations, a nucleus of ethnic Mennonite families often comprised the large majority of the membership. Working in a mission Sunday school permitted workers to express their dedication to Christ and at the same time be part of a popular religious movement. While the stated purpose was to reach the unsaved, some workers favored more progressive or, occasionally, more conservative positions than their home congregations endorsed. The Sunday schools and congregations located near sizable concentrations of Mennonites often included visionary or, at times, dissatisfied members from neighboring Mennonite congregations. Those at a distance often had more nonethnic Mennonite members and participants.

At times the PCC considered another rural mission effort which they called colonization evangelization. Groups of families would settle in a new community, organize a congregation, and give a gospel witness. Most rural Mennonite congregations actually began and functioned that way, but institutional recommendation and intentionality added a new distinction. For fifteen years, beginning in the late 1920s the PCC had a colonization committee, concerned primarily with Idaho, eastern Oregon, and Washington. This committee considered new agricultural [irrigation] projects, warned against unscrupulous land promoters, and promoted the spiritual welfare of settlers in such new areas. In the mid-1950s the mission board's Outreach Committee explored colonization possibilities in the Fort Rock area of central Oregon and recommended it in a lengthy report. But nothing developed there.[52]

Increasing urbanization after World War II contributed to the gradual decline of rural mission emphasis. In the 1940s and early 1950s, PCC congregations continued to hold summer Bible schools and mission Sunday schools in rural communities and small towns, but the urban world increasingly influenced thought and stimulated change among Mennonites and the people they reached. During the mid-1950s, as mission Sunday schools were becoming congregations, the PCC needed a new mission focus. It turned its primary attention to Mexico.

Oregon's GCs, MBs, and EMBs also reached out to rural peoples, and some of them worked with the American Sunday School Union or Village Missions in teaching and evangelism ministries in small towns or country communities. But with improved roads, school consolidation, and the pervasive influence of television, rural communities were no longer isolated from the larger world. By 1976 the idea of rural mission work had receded into history. Even though large numbers of some congregations continued to live in rural areas, most of them worked in towns and cities.[53]

Alongside postwar changes in the larger world, mission theory that called for "a mission outpost for every congregation" was changing. By the 1950s, J. D. Graber, OM denominational missions administrator, was emphasizing that saving souls and instructing new believers was not enough. The goal should include establishing a church—"more than a mere coming together of saved individuals," he said, but a congregation of "vital, witnessing" adult believers. In the next years, PCC mission stations organized as congregations. As a 1968 conference resolution encouraged, they and their mother congregations accepted new challenges as witnessing communities to offer "salvation, healing, and help" in a society "splitting apart" in delinquency, racial conflict, hunger, and poverty. With this new emphasis, the PCC mission board's role changed. Rather than directing details of a mission program it more often provided financial help for emerging or struggling congregations. In 1972 the board began giving partial financial support for Sam Hernandez, a former Mennonite from Texas whose vision was to begin Spanish-speaking churches in Oregon and south Texas. He wanted to help them become self-supporting like the Hispanic congregation he had established in Woodburn in 1964. In 1976 this was the second largest budget item for the board.[54]

The PCC mission board also supported several fellowships which would become conference congregations after 1976. The first, in Boise, Idaho, began in 1970 after Archie Janzen had interested the Nampa congregation in working in the Hyde Park area of Boise. In the next years the board assisted with finances and in 1976 was searching for a pastor who would arrive the following year. In central Oregon, sixty to eighty miles north of Fort Rock, a fellowship began in 1974, about a year after several Mennonite families moved to the Redmond-Prineville-Madras area. By the end of 1976 Lyn Hershey was pastoring the group and eight persons were preparing to become members of the soon-to-be-organized Ranch Chapel congregation.[55]

Like the OMs, some of Oregon's smaller Mennonite groups also gave new thought to mission theory. In the late 1950s the PDC (GC) examined its philosophy of sponsoring new congregations. Denominational leader Leland Harder's study on "Policy in Church Extension" had emphasized the mission character of every pastorate and congregation. Each congregation, "in a sense," was a "home mission congregation" helping to establish new "self-governing, self-supporting, and . . . self-propagating" congregations. None, however, began in Oregon. In the 1960s the MB denomination adopted a goal to double in the next ten years, the "Decade of Enlargement." Their PDC made winning people to Christ the top priority for congregations. It also charged its board of home missions to establish churches in areas where they could "be effective in presenting the good news of salvation and the Kingdom of God." The MB congregation in Eugene, organized in 1964, was an example.[56]

Foreign Mission Work

Oregon Mennonites also supported and served in foreign missions. In 1927 the Dallas EMB Church ordained and commissioned Mr. and Mrs. Loyal Bartel as missionaries to China. Other members of the congregation later served in Nigeria, Kenya, Zaire, Venezuela, Chile, and the Bahamas. The first missionaries from the Dallas MB Church were Mr. and Mrs. A. F. Kroeker, who began service in the Belgian Congo in the 1930s. Other members also served in the Congo and in India and Mexico. Dan and Eva Aeschliman from Emmanuel, going to South Africa, were among Oregon's first GC missionaries. Others in later years served elsewhere in Africa and in Nepal, India, China, Korea, South America, Spain, and Ceylon. Overseas missionaries from the PCC included Gladys Weaver (Becker), Florence Nafziger and Paul Conrad in India and Robert Lee in Japan.[57]

Missionaries who served abroad worked under various sponsoring agencies. Most of Oregon's MB and OM missionaries (except for PCC missionaries in Mexico) worked under their denominational boards. Oregon's GCs and EMBs often served with other boards or associations. Mennonites from Oregon who worked with the Congo Inland Mission (later named the Africa Inter-Mennonite Mission) included Allan and Selma Wiebe (EMB); Earl and Ruth Roth, Betty Quiring, and John and Jeanne Zook (all GC); and Harold and Joyce Harms (EMB). Oregon's OMs had fewer overseas missionaries than did the other groups. They emphasized more the local mission Sunday schools in which many members worked. Some, too, did not totally trust their denominational mission board. Perhaps another reason was that OMs had joined the modern missionary movement later than the GCs, MBs, and EMBs, who had emphasized missions from their beginnings.[58]

Oregon's OMs gradually developed a special interest in Central America and Mexico. By 1976 a somewhat complicated and ambitious mission effort conceived in the 1940s had branched out under several administering boards or committees, none of them churchwide agencies. During C. Z. Martin's revival meetings at Sheridan in 1944 and 1945, the evangelist spoke of mission needs among Spanish-speaking peoples. Max G. Yoder reported that this "stirred the fire" of interest which "had smoldered in the hearts of a few for a long time." Yoder had earlier come by this interest in part from his father, Hiram, who had located the family in southern Texas among Spanish-speaking people when Max was growing up. After Martin's challenge, several Oregon men made an investigative trip to Central America in 1947 on their own initiative and returned with deepened conviction that the gospel should be carried to the people of Nicaragua. They had in mind possible colonization along with mission work and, with Chris Snyder's encouragement, presented their idea to the PCC board. The board, however, showed little interest.[59]

Before long another investigative trip followed and an interested group organized the Mennonite Mission Board for Mexico and Central America, independent of, and more conservative than, the PCC board. They intended to begin a mission in the "Southland," but since they thought the PCC board should more rightfully do so they asked the board to consider it and to hold up a "high Biblical standard" as the work developed. Specifically, all the workers should "have a real born-again experience of salvation," wear the "regulation garb (brethren the regulation coat without the tie and sisters the plain bonnet and the cape)," and adhere to other specifics.

After due consideration the PCC board narrowly defeated a motion to accept responsibility for such a work *under its regular policy.* The independent board then proceeded as planned and Sheridan chose by lot (but did not ordain) Joseph and Adah Kropf and Eldon and Jessie Hamilton for the task. During language school in Mexico City, the Kropfs returned home because of Adah's health. But Hamilton was ordained at Sheridan in May 1952 for work in Honduras under the Eastern Mennonite Board of Missions and Charities, an agency in Pennsylvania. Oregon's independent board had dissolved and its constituency had appointed the Oregon Supporting and Advisory Committee for the Tocoa, Honduras, field, to assist in this cooperative venture.[60]

The new Oregon committee encouraged the PCC mission board to again consider Mexico and the peoples to the south. Max

Yoder reported for yet another investigative committee, noting new agricultural developments in Mexico due to irrigation and modern machinery. He suggested that "a number of consecrated families" might move there for self-supporting mission work. Admittedly, the language would be a barrier, and "clerical garb" and literature distribution were prohibited by law. Such laws were "winked at": his committee had "handed out much literature, even to policemen."[61]

By 1955 work in Mexico was under way, but not colonization. The mission board covered costs for Joe Kropf and Mark Emmert, who traveled the length and breadth of Baja California distributing Spanish-langage New Testaments, gospels, and tracts in many communities which had no gospel witness at all, "not even Catholic." They recommended several areas for a permanent witness. Six months later, Cecil and Faye Byers and Mark and Twila Emmert and their families were living and witnessing in southern Baja under tentative appointment by the board. The Byers family served there many years. Other families or individuals served for varying periods of time and frequency. After Cecil was killed in Arizona in 1970 in the crash of a crop-dusting plane, Faye returned to continue the witness in Mexico.[62]

The mission outreach in Baja California progressed rapidly, and at first the mission board supported and promoted the work. It offered unprecedented leniency, leaving the wearing of the regulation coat "to the discretion" of the workers and requiring only half the members of the local board to be conference board appointees. The work grew in spite of local opposition. Natives became Christians and missionaries received a burden to seek out "more of the Holy Spirit." The missionaries and local board, soon known as the Latin American Fellowship (LAF), worked in comparative independence from the PCC board.

At a May 1958 meeting the board decided to channel all funds for Mexico, unless otherwise specified, to a new work being planned, and in December 1959 the board discontinued its unsatisfactory "organizational relationship" with LAF. Doubtless Byers preferred the freedom accorded him by the LAF. But supportive Oregon Mennonites continued their strong, perhaps primary, financial support, and some who later moved into a nondenominational Pentecostal tradition also worked with LAF. Among them were Melvin and Emily Mishler, their son Robert, and his wife, Nellie. Mel Mishler also promoted and publicized LAF and raised funds. Without his leadership the work would not have developed as fully, in the judgment of Wilbert R. Shenk, an administrator of the denominational mission board. Though the PCC board discontinued financial support of LAF before 1960, it had moved full circle by 1976 when it budgeted $2,400 for a teaching ministry in Baja California.[63]

While the PCC board's relationship with the LAF was in transition, it began to negotiate with future workers who later began a work in northwest Mexico directly under board administration. The first appointees, James and Noreen Roth, visited the LAF missionaries and considered working with them. Byers was then still related to the PCC board. However, the Roths did not feel a call to Baja California, a stipulation Byers had placed on their joining his program. Roths emphasized that God had worked mightily in Baja, although they observed a need for teaching on "true prayer . . . on making everything we say meaningful." But they wished to establish a work somewhere on the mainland and hoped this decision would not cause "any unchristian attitudes" among the PCC board or constituency.

Late in 1959 Roths arrived in northwest Mexico and in 1960 settled in Ciudad Obregon, Sonora, where Maynard and Helen Headings soon joined them. Later workers included Vincent and

Maynard Headings

Maynard (1932-) and Helen (Kaltenbach) Headings and family, about 1964, during their early years as PCC missionaries in Mexico.

Marcella Frey, John and Doris Miller, and Raul and Vanita Tadeo, on long-term assignments. There were also short-term volunteers, but never more than four long-term couples on the field at one time. At a special delegate session in March 1966, the PCC approved the organization of the Mexico Church Conference. Soon native leaders emerged and became pastors.[64]

The division in the PCC that began in 1967 ultimately affected the mission work in Mexico. The three couples there at that time dealt with their own strained relationships and urged the PCC to do likewise—to confess and forgive, in order that division might be healed and that the work of mission witness need not be hindered. Congregations which withdrew from the PCC continued to support the mission work in Mexico with both personnel and finances. In 1970 the board established a subsidiary Mexico board to give all supporters representation. But when several missionary couples took extended leaves or terminated their services the Mexico work declined. Don and Elvina Zimmerman began serving late in 1975. In 1976 they with the Tadeo and Miller families were the workers under the board. Robert Lind, a short-term volunteer, was directing the school work of the Zimmerman children. Mexico Mennonite membership was ninety-eight.[65]

Though Oregon Mennonites focused largely on saving souls, they also contributed material assistance—locally, nationally, and internationally—to physical needs. They supported the work of Mennonite Central Committee (MCC) and similar organizations with finances, food, clothing, and other forms of assistance. In 1945 the PCC shipped approximately thirty-five tons of food to war-ravaged countries of Western Europe. In 1950 twenty-six heifers—twenty-one from Sheridan, three from Harrisburg, two from the McMinnville Amish—left Sheridan bound for Germany under the Heifers for Relief program and the U.S. government. Several Mennonite men accompanied the shipment.

From 1944 to 1951 women of the Calvary (GC) congregation prepared and shipped almost three thousand pounds of clothing, fifty-four comforters, sixty-two quilts, and over eighty kits and relief packages, besides almost $2,500 in cash. Probably every Oregon Mennonite congregation contributed goods, money, or both. Mennonite individuals, too, served as overseas volunteers with MCC or another Mennonite agency. John B. Franz of North Park (MB) was one of a number of Oregon Mennonites who taught in Africa in the mid-1960s. Mennonite Disaster Service (MDS), a new organization which began at mid-century in Kansas, coordinated the efforts of Mennonites to help people in times of flood, tornado, hurricane, earthquake, fire, and other disasters. By 1957 Oregon people organized an inter-Mennonite West Coast division of MDS, with Henry Penner as chairman, Clifford Kenagy as vice-chairman, and Lester Kropf as secretary.[66]

■ ■ ■

Like the fir forests and wild blackberry thickets so common in western Oregon, with their overlapping branches and tangled vines, so the emphases of Oregon Mennonites intertwined and crisscrossed. The nurture of their faith and their activities in mission and service came from the same roots. Although the degree and quality of emphases varied within and among groups, Oregon Mennonites were a people attempting to grow, sometimes struggling for light as in a crowded forest, sometimes thrusting out thorns along with proffered fruit.

The intertwining of roots and branches also extended beyond their historic Mennonite heritage. Some of Oregons Mennonites turned to other Christian traditions and left their Mennonite communities. A few who reached out in mission practiced and promoted an individualism incompatible with the mother church community, planted solitary roots, and developed unaffiliated community churches. Many emphasized faith and discipleship within their Mennonite conference community. During their first century in Oregon, as Mennonites intertwined their branches more and more with traditions which were not their own, most Mennonte groups changed certain emphases. Some did so quite completely.

Chapter 10
Oregon Mennonites in the Larger World

Although the first Mennonites who came to Oregon were among *Die Stillen im Lande* (the quiet in the land) they always related at least in some ways to their larger world. The few who settled in town met the world in their daily employment and neighborhoods. Even farmers, the majority, had to purchase equipment and market produce, talk with their bankers and neighbors, and live under the government of their land.

They knew that their contacts with others than Mennonites, unchurched or other-churched, could influence them. Thus they attempted to accept only what was useful and not unbiblical and to reject unscriptural beliefs or practices. But from their early years in Oregon, strong tension persisted between church community and individualistic compromise with attractions of other denominations and the larger world. No one can know how many youth from Mennonite families—and adults, too—put their individual inclinations or other ideologies above the claims of their Mennonite communities.

One family in Portland who had been Mennonite in Russia exemplified in the extreme the tensions between individualism and church community. Perhaps before Abe and Mary (Dyck) Isaak settled in Portland, about 1890, they came under the influence of anarchism. Anarchists opposed highly organized government and capitalism and were considered the most radical of labor groups. Most of America's anarchists were foreign-born. Several natives of Russia were well-known anarchist leaders, including Emma Goldman, who came to know the Isaaks. In Portland the Isaaks helped found an anarchist weekly, the *Firebrand*. But the paper was suppressed, its publishers arrested, and one colleague, H. J. Pope, imprisoned on charges of obscenity. The Isaaks then published *Free Society* and later moved to San Francisco and later still to Chicago, where they were suspects for a short time because of earlier contacts with the assassin of President William McKinley. In their case individualism and the claims of a conflicting collective snapped the threads that had connected them with the community of faith.[1]

Mennonites were not ignorant or without opinions about ideas and events in their larger world. They welcomed and even treasured such resources as the farmers' almanac. Joseph C. Hostetler, who lived at Needy by the late 1890s, had earlier written on the back of an 1858 German almanac that he would like to have it "after Grandpap is dead." Some views Mennonites quietly rejected. A. P. Troyer, bishop of Zion (AM), always had a herd of dairy cows, and he named all the bulls Brigham, one after the other. But Troyer never preached against Mormonism or other cults and his grandchildren did not understand until they were grown why the dairy bull was always Brigham.[2]

Mennonite historian Paul Toews used the images of "boundaries" and "nuclei" to envisage how Mennonites identified themselves in the larger world. To give themselves identity most groups tried to revitalize and strengthen their nuclei, or centers—the heart and essence of their faith. But all groups, especially in the early years, also clarified their boundaries, the distinctive limits for beliefs and behaviors. Biblical teaching influenced both nuclei and boundaries but did not produce uniform thought. Some groups emphasized the nurture of the nuclei to maintain boundaries. Others held that keeping the boundaries strong would preserve the nuclei. During their first century in Oregon, Mennonite groups set different boundaries and some groups maintained them more carefully than did others. But all groups allowed boundaries to move, whether little or much.[3]

Making a living by farming, as most early Oregon Mennonites did, required fewer boundaries than certain other areas of life, but circumstances forced some Mennonites to other work. Those who farmed usually established a reputation as good farmers. At Harrisburg the Amish Mennonites renewed depleted soil by planting clover and tilling the crop under. Bishop Daniel J. Kropf became known in the community as a successful farmer. His son Frank, who preferred carpentry but also farmed, thought he may have been the first mid-valley ryegrass farmer. Ryegrass later became a major seed crop in the Willamette Valley. Early Mennonite farmers with marginal or uncleared land frequently supplemented their meager incomes by working in lumber mills, rock quarries, and in other industries. Women took in laundry or did housework for well-to-do people in towns. Delilah Troyer, wife of the Zion bishop, did the doctoring for ten miles around her home near Hubbard, carrying her medicine case on the big bay horse she rode. Whether she received payment for her services is not clear.[4]

Though most early Mennonites were farmers, some became entrepreneurs with varying success. In 1890 Amos Conrad bought Tangent's general store and operated it and the post office until he bought a farm near Sandy eight years later. He moved in hopes of a better livelihood than his business provided during the "Cleveland depression" of 1893. By 1896 J. Z. Martin, formerly of Olathe, Kansas, was the proprietor of the Ohio House, apparently a Hubbard boarding house or hotel. A charter member of Hopewell in 1899, a few years later he forfeited his membership for unspecified reasons. In 1902 Katie Troyer thought she was marrying a farmer, but as soon as she and Amos Lais married, he bought a barrel of oil and a wrench, according to their son Ralph, and started a sawmill which became very successful. Unfortunately, the Hershberger sawmill of the 1890s in Lane County was a financial disaster that devastated and divided the AM congregation there.[5]

Isaac S. Miller, the 1880 Old Order Amish immigrant who bought a sawmill near Hubbard, developed a cluster of related businesses. With typical Amish thrift Miller used the mill's slab-wood by-products to fire the kiln of a small brick and tile plant which he built across the road from the mill. He also built a cider mill and did woodworking, tailoring, and blacksmithing. Besides all this, he sometimes sold bottles of "medicine," probably made from recipes later found in the mill books. In later years the mill ceased operation, but the brick and tile factory went from one Mennonite owner to other Mennonites. In 1976, as Needy Brick and Tile, it was a prosperous business with about fifteen employees, owned by Kenneth Berkey, Peter Berkey, and Keith Heyerly.[6]

Even before World War I some Dallas Mennonites began to move from farms to town to work in sawmills and other lumber-related industries. Such movement caused MBs to organize a town congregation in 1919, EMBs to build a meetinghouse in town in 1924, and Zion (GC) to begin Sunday school and services there by 1927. Toward the end of the 1930s families from such states as Kansas, Nebraska, Minnesota, and Montana joined the congregations at Dallas. A few farmed, but often former farmers found jobs in area industries. For instance, Oscar Franz of Grace worked as a handyman for a wealthy merchant's family, then took up painting

Oregon Mennonite archival collection

Isaac Miller's tile factory in 1909, shortly after his son Obed bought it. Later it became Needy Brick and Tile. Pictured: Obed Miller on wagon; Obed's sons Omar, Paul, and Nathan in order of age, in center; group in the back, neighbors.

until he began work in a sawmill. Ella Franz and other women worked in canneries. Children earned money picking strawberries, hops, and beans.[7]

The major transition from farming to other employment probably began later among Oregon's (old) Mennonites than among those at Dallas, but by 1940 fewer than half the PCC Mennonites were farmers. Some lost their farms during the depression, though a few benefited from generous creditors who waived payments until times improved. Implement companies sold Harrisburg Mennonites tractors in those years without a cent down. They knew they could expect payment when the farmers were able and felt that Mennonites were as good or better security than a bank. Already in the 1930s Emmert families of Molalla, later of Sweet Home, logged timber and hauled it to mills. Mennonites at Sheridan also worked in forest-related industries. As the lumbering industry expanded after World War II more Mennonite men took jobs in sawmills and related plants. Zion (MC) member Ivan Kropf's sawmill employed about twenty persons and had an excellent reputation. Other nonfarming Mennonites worked as carpenters, painters, teachers, nurses, butchers, and sales clerks. Some worked in factories, canneries, and offices. Still others owned their own businesses. Such a range of occupations was increasingly characterizing most Oregon Mennonite congregations and groups.[8]

Where young women should find employment was a question Ethel Reeser, herself a young women from Albany, considered in the late 1940s. Writing about the common practice of "Mennonite girls working as domestics in aristocratic homes in urban areas," she recounted her own experience as an employee catering to the luxurious laziness of her employer. She noted that consumption, materialism, and disrupted families and homes were common elements of urbanization. J. Winfield Fretz's 1940 study of Mennonites who had moved from farms to Chicago, showed that "a high percentage" of them were lost to the Mennonite church. Aware of this study, Reeser encouraged the kind of rural living that fostered nonresistance, mutual aid, the simple life, and New Testament teachings.[9]

But the vision of rural community as a cohesive base for witness and work did not last long. Most Mennonite farmers did not have money to provide a farm for each son, nor was there farming land for such expansion. Oregon's magnificent forests became a major resource and many Mennonites of most groups worked in forest-related industries. Other Mennonites went into business, service occupations, and the professions. By 1976, only in the conservative, nonconference Harrisburg, Tangent, and Brownsville congregations did the majority farm or work in farm-related industries. No Mennonite congregation of any group in Portland, Eugene, Sheridan, and McMinnville, or in rural mountain communities such as Logsden, Porter, and Blaine had any farmer in its membership. Most other congregations had a few. Fairview probably had the largest percentage, though still under half. Many Oregon Mennonites made their homes in towns or cities but many others chose the country as the better place to raise families even if they did not live by farming.[10]

The career status of Mennonite women was changing, too. In earlier years women had usually been homemakers who often worked with their husbands on the family farm. A few did housework for hire or occasionally took seasonal employment outside the home. In the decades after World War II, more Mennonite women took training and worked in traditional service professions, business, and industry. A rising standard of living often increased family expenses which a woman's income helped meet. Many women enjoyed their earning jobs, as well. By 1976, in most congregations, women worked outside the home or had gainful employment in the home, such as sewing, upholstery, writing, or other work. Numbers ranged from a very small percentage in some congregations to over half in several.[11]

Even from Mennonites' earliest years in Oregon, urban influences and pressures touched all of them—including the farmers. Earlier chapters have often mentioned nonconformity in attire. Other issues which the larger world presented to them included what language to use, whether to permit members to join secret societies or purchase life and other insurance, what technological innovations were acceptable, whether to vote and accept government aid, what recreation and personal habits were harmful, how to relate to labor unions, and divorce and remarriage.

Before 1900 most American Mennonites spoke a German dialect in their homes and used more or less the classic High German in church services. Whether to allow English in either place was perhaps the most intrusive and far-reaching issue they faced. For many it was a religious issue. They thought the church should be distinct from their larger world and the government, which used English. Using German would help their people remain separate

Church letter for members transferring to Zion (GC) from another congregation. German continued to be used well into the 1920s.

from surrounding culture and strengthen their nonconformity. However, this issue was not unique to Mennonites. Thousands of German-speaking Lutherans, Methodists, and Baptists also struggled with the issue, though for Mennonites the emphasis on nonconformity and nonresistance accentuated the issue.[12]

Of the Mennonite groups who came to Oregon, the Old Order Amish and Russian Mennonites used German the longest. Even the Beachy Amish conducted their worship services and Sunday school in German through 1976. The MBs and EMBs used German until World War II threatened and community pressures influenced them to begin using "the American language." Oregon's GCs did not keep the German language quite as long, but German was at first important to them. For a couple of years at the turn of the century, Zion at Polk Station had a German school. Zion switched to English for a short time near the end of World War I, when a vigilante committee came to a service in July 1918 and asked them to show their allegiance to the United States by having services in English. They continued to have business meetings in German. After the war they resumed worship services in German. Zion members who began meeting in town in 1927 and later organized Grace used English from the start. Even after switching to English for worship, several congregations kept a Sunday school class in German for some years.[13]

Oregon's (old) and Amish Mennonites made the change from German to English earlier, but some among them resisted the change. In 1896 a newcomer at Zion (AM) complained of not hearing an English sermon since leaving Missouri, months earlier. The newcomer also noted that some "even seem to think it wrong to talk English." Later Zion people, however, did not like a story in Shetler's 1932 history. According to the story, a fatherless child who did not know German was not allowed to repeat Scripture verses in English. Old-timers could not remember such an incident and felt it misrepresented Zion. If it did occur, perhaps it was when the primary purpose of Sunday school was to teach the German language.

At Fairview, by 1909, C. R. Gerig began to preach occasionally in English because some members of the C. G. Nofziger family did not understand German. A couple of years later several disapproving families transferred their membership to the more conservative Harrisburg congregation. After World War I, Gerig never again preached in German. By 1920, perhaps motivated by the war, the OM and AM congregations, except for Harrisburg, held most services in English. Harrisburg ministers preached in German most of the time until 1927, though English was acceptable for visiting ministers and when persons who did not understand German were present. The OMs accepted English from their beginnings, although especially at Hopewell German remained common if ministers spoke it more easily than English. By 1976 most Oregon Mennonites did not even understand a German dialect, but vestiges of influence remained in an occasional "Dutchy" expression.[14]

Whether Mennonites should join secret societies, or lodges, was not even a question among most groups before the mid-nineteenth century. About that time some congregations began to tolerate membership in lodges, and when Mennonites arrived in Oregon, it had become a live issue.

The Zion (GC) congregation took a strong stand against all such membership, extending the restriction to the Farmers Union in 1916. In the 1950s members voted by secret ballot not to accept as members an elderly couple who had insurance with the Masons. In 1968 the amended bylaws of the PDC (GC) modified the position to state that "membership in oathbound secret-societies" tends "to compromise the loyalty of the Christian to the Lord and to His church." (Old) Mennonites did not approve membership in secret societies, either. Hopewell organizers discontinued working in a union Sunday school because the superintendent was a secret order man. Later, in 1902, George R. Brunk I disciplined two Oregon men who had belonged to secret orders. All successive PCC disciplines prohibited or opposed membership in secret societies. Such membership was seen as "an unequal yoke with unbelievers." Furthermore, secret societies "employ hierarchical titles, require oaths, stand for organized secrecy, and may offer salvation on grounds other than faith in the Lord Jesus Christ."[15]

Oregon's other Mennonite groups also opposed membership in secret societies, some less strongly in later years. The EMBs and CGCs considered secret societies unscriptural and prohibited participation. In 1976 the MB denomination discouraged it, promoting instead "fellowship and brotherhood in the church." Mutual aid and close relationships in the Mennonite community of faith probably made secret societies less attractive to them than to persons without such closeness and fraternal concern.[16]

Insurance was another issue. Historically, Mennonites opposed commercial insurance. When illness, death, fire, storm, and accident struck, they simply helped each other. Mutual aid met all financial needs. When giving loans, the earliest Mennonites refused to accept interest. They cared for their own poor and elderly and gradually developed institutions for the aged, orphaned, and ill without family care. In America, barn raisings after a fire produced admiration and amazement within their larger communities.

But the industrial age caused twentieth-century Mennonites to reconsider earlier positions. The move from farming to the professions, business, and industry, made spontaneous mutual aid more difficult. Employees could not easily take a day off work to help a needy fellow member. Nor did they usually have the land investment that enabled them to provide for their widows. Many an earlier Mennonite farmer could clearly specify in his will that when he died his widow would receive a long list of necessities, including a place to live, the closest strip of garden space, three milk cows, and all the firewood she needed as long as she lived. Loaning money became a business matter, though often Mennonites loaned each other money at lower rates of interest than did lending institutions.[17]

Oregon Mennonites differed in their beliefs and practices concerning insurance. The Russian Mennonite groups accepted property insurance more readily than did the (old) Mennonites. By 1912 or earlier, Zion (GC) insured its meetinghouse for $450 with the German Mutual Fire Insurance Association. A decade earlier, in 1902, Brunk and Garber had forbidden OMs to insure buildings. They "allowed" participation in an unidentified Mennonite Aid Plan but did not recommend even that. Pacific Coast societies headquartered at Reedley, California—the Russian Mennonite center of the West—offered aid plans to help with property losses (1922) and burial costs (1941). But OMs did not share much in these plans in the early years. However, when loan agencies required insurance on homes Mennonites purchased with borrowed money, they had little choice but to purchase policies. By 1976, all the larger Mennonite groups accepted either Mennonite Aid Plan's property insurance or commercial plans.[18]

State laws requiring liability insurance for automobiles caused a dilemma for some of Oregon's OMs at mid-century, but several who hesitated learned by experience that compliance was better than liability in case of accident. A few years later liability insurance was no longer an issue for most Mennonites[19]

Life insurance was a larger issue for OMs than were other

forms of insurance. Honest Mennonites doubtless knew of the industry's well-earned reputation for corruption and greed that caused legislators to enact rigid controls on it. Even worse, they perceived life insurance as "trusting men more than God," as failing to provide for their own, and as "making merchandise of human life," to cite points outlined in Kauffman's 1952 *Doctrines of the Bible*. However, by the 1960s or earlier, Mennonites without a secure financial base who wanted to provide for their families in case of their death were quietly purchasing life insurance policies. About then the denominational Mennonite Mutual Aid was also preparing survivors' aid plans which provided the same type of protection and assistance. It emphasized not only protection but also biblical mutual aid among fellow Mennonites, an element missing in commercial plans. In 1976 only the most conservative, unaffiliated congregations and the CGCs taught against life insurance for religious reasons.[20]

Some Oregon Mennonites set boundaries between themselves and particular technologies of the larger world, at least for a time. Earlier chapters noted some Amish and Amish Mennonites who disallowed the telephone, electricity, and the automobile. One Fairview family who disapproved of automobiles transferred to Harrisburg, where most members, out of respect, waited to purchase automobiles until after the family left the congregation a few years later. These technological developments seem not to have been questioned much by Oregon's other Mennonite groups, who were satisfied with other forms of separation from the world.[21]

Two technological developments that did generate much discussion and precise statements among several Oregon groups were radio and television. In the 1920s some Fairview people who wanted radios transferred to the Albany (OM) congregation. In 1931, D. F. Shenk of Sheridan spoke of evil influences that undermined any good which radio might offer. But radios became increasingly common. In the 1950s about eight families left Harrisburg, partly because they wanted radios. By then, with television becoming a new issue, few Oregon groups taught against radio or even cautioned against questionable programs. Yet several did. Through 1976 Tangent required its members to "keep free from both" radio and television due to the worldly, subtle influences and erosion of morals on much programming. Other congregations such as Harrisburg held similar positions. The CGC denomination also banned radio and television.[22]

Television was an even larger issue than radio had been. In the 1950s the PCC received a committee report noting critical evaluations by surveys and such leaders of national repute as J. Edgar Hoover, director of the FBI. These surveys acknowledged that in addition to educational and "other unobjectionable" programs, much programming showed indecency, lawlessness, and violence as glamorous and desirable. In some MB circles television was "banned" for a time, as R. M. Baerg of Fresno noted. But by the early 1960s most MB homes had television. By 1976 educators, psychologists and other secular leaders were beginning to ask more questions about television. They were warning more loudly about its violence, explicit sex, and unrealistic expectations, and its influence on children's reading skills and life views. Ironically, by that time, most Oregon Mennonites accepted television with few reservations.[23]

Issues about how Mennonites should relate to the government were not always clear. Oregon Mennonites and their responses to war is the subject of the next chapter. Some of their decisions reflected their nonresistant position. For instance, the PCC stipulated early in the twentieth century that members not serve as jurors in cases allowing capital punishment, that they not hold offices requiring the oath or "carnal force in maintaining order," and that they avoid lawsuits. In 1908, whether or not PCC Mennonites should vote depended on circumstances. If "any evil in the land" were brought to the vote, "every Christian should quietly go and vote against it." Mennonites generally considered political parties "corrupt," but members of most groups served at the local level on school boards or in similar civic positions. In the late 1880s the MB denomination asked members not to participate in "the contentions of political parties," but permitted them to "vote quietly at elections . . . and for prohibition." Oregon Mennonites did not have a reputation for being politically active; yet among most groups by the 1960s and 1970s voting and civic involvement had increased.

Among the politically active were Clif and Lois Kenagy of Albany (MC), who helped draft and promote land-use laws to preserve farmland for agricultural production. Many Mennonites appreciated Oregon's U.S. senator Mark Hatfield for his advocacy of justice and peace issues. In 1976 Paul N. Roth, pastor of the Calvary congregation, was serving as mayor of the city of Canby and survived two recall attempts surrounding the city council's controversial firing of the police chief and a detective. Most congregations of Russian Mennonite heritage displayed both the national and the Christian flag in the church sanctuary.[24]

A major issue for PCC Mennonites, though not for most other Mennonite groups, was whether to allow members to accept various forms of state aid. Through the centuries deacons had administered alms funds established to help poor and needy members. In Oregon questions about accepting state aid recurred in the 1920s and 1930s. Most persons who taught against state aid were in the fortunate position of not having to rely on the sometimes inadequate charity of their families or a small congregation unable to provide full support. In 1934 the PCC declared one Nada Strong to be its dependent rather than that of Molalla. The next year the PCC instructed the deacons to appeal to the denomination to consider a churchwide plan to care for needy widows. Yet a decade later an Oregon leader feared that just such a new plan, Mennonite Mutual Aid, would become a life insurance company. In 1945 the PCC did recognize Mennonite Mutual Aid and encourage its support. But for some years the ideal of relatives and congregations providing for their own persisted. Through the 1940s PCC leaders continued to promote the church's scriptural responsibility toward widows and other needy persons, though in 1948 the conference conceded that members who accepted state aid "were not violating conference discipline."[25]

This was a boundary the PCC Mennonites could not hold much longer. The movement of Mennonites from farming to other occupations made support for needy relatives more difficult. The deacons' plan for church assistance simply did not guarantee adequate support. Increasing numbers of persons covered by Social Security benefits in the 1950s and 1960s gradually modified earlier opposing views. Business sense argued that if they paid into the system they may as well benefit from their investment. Even some more conservative congregations, such as Tangent, made it optional for members to receive Social Security retirement benefits.[26]

In their first decades in Oregon, all Mennonite groups set boundaries between themselves and certain types of recreation and personal practices common in the larger world. Early GC documents spoke against overindulgence in "strong drinks," dancing, and motion pictures. In 1947 Wilber A. Regier, Emmanuel pastor, lamented the open smoking he observed and reports of drinking he heard in a PDC congregation he visited in Washington. Members in his own congregation also smoked, but not openly, on the church grounds. Still, he thought it reflected negatively on one's spiritual life. In later years Oregon's GCs did not often name specific restrictions in their official documents. Oregon's MBs, too, disapproved of theater attendance, dancing, the use of tobacco and alcoholic beverages, and card playing—into the 1940s or longer for some practices. In the 1950s the EMBs also continued to ask members to avoid such questionable places and actions and to keep dress and conduct in line "with the high calling of a Christian."[27]

The PCC Mennonites itemized such restrictions in greater detail than did most other Oregon Mennonites. Especially in the earlier decades of the twentieth century, some of the laity and the occasional minister chewed or smoked tobacco or at times imbibed alcoholic beverages. Even some of the Hubbard grandmothers from Missouri smoked little clay pipes. But teachings against such practices surfaced early in the PCC's 1906 "Rules and Discipline." It discouraged the use of tobacco, "by precept and by example," and instructed that members "patronizing saloons" be censured. It also forbade attendance at theaters, circuses, picnics, "and all other places of worldly amusement." For almost half a century, revised documents included the same items. Although it relaxed a ban on picnics, which were soon perceived by most people as being harmless, the list grew to include moving picture shows, fairs, horse races, Fourth of July celebrations, operas, dances, poolrooms, card rooms, "buckaroos" (rodeos), public skating rinks, and arenas. Some people also considered swimming pools and ball games to be worldly. Although most PCC Mennonites in 1976 did not object to all such restrictions, the more conservative unaffiliated Mennonites continued to avoid most of them.[28]

In the nineteenth century increasing industrialization and the need for social and economic justice for workers produced the American labor movement and brought new questions for Mennonites. Clearly, capital and some businesses had abused their power and their laborers. The labor unions which organized had mitigated severe wrongs and brought reasonable wages and working conditions to workers. But by the time many Mennonites were entering industry, labor unions, too, were abusing power and a serious class struggle was emerging. Mennonites favored justice, but they questioned what constituted justice and, especially, the means to the end.[29]

During World War II union membership in Portland rose

enormously. GCs there struggled over the issue of union membership. But OMs considered it more comprehensively, as early as 1935, when eight-year-old Lois Catherine Evers of Sheridan wrote, "My papa works at the mill. We are having a strike out here in the West, but so far papa hasn't been laid off." At the 1936 PCC sessions, respected PCC leaders and denominational visitors Daniel Kauffman and T. K. Hershey drafted a lengthy position paper "on organized unionism, whether of labor or of capital." It promoted a neutral, peaceful position and instructed members to seek employment where "labor unionism is not a live issue." For a few years that seemed possible. But within a short generation PCC Mennonites varied strongly in their views. By the late 1950s, some totally rejected union membership while others accepted it without qualification. It seemed that many joined a union without inquiring about a third option, the official denominational position in which Mennonite employees arranged formal understandings which excused them from union membership. This option required their neutrality in case of a strike and permitted them to contribute the equivalent of union dues to union or other benevolent and welfare services.[30]

In the next years, Mennonite boundaries regarding labor unionism became increasingly blurred. Organized labor advanced into both the public and private sectors. Finding nonunion employment became increasingly difficult. It also became less important for Mennonites who were just then erasing other boundaries between themselves and the larger world. Fewer Mennonites continued to consider the issue relevant to their faith, except perhaps if a labor dispute resulted in a strike. Although a few people continued to avoid employment in unionized industry, by 1976 such employment was not an issue for Oregon Mennonites who no longer related it to historic nonresistance.[31]

Mennonites worked hard to maintain the boundaries protecting the sanctity of family relationships, particularly marriage. They regarded marriage as honorable, sacred, a commitment for life. Until the mid-twentieth century, most North American Mennonite groups approved marriage only within their own group. But inter-Mennonite marriages were frequent, especially in smaller, more isolated communities. Some young people married non-Mennonites. Mennonites did not permit divorce except for reason of adultery, though the occasional separation was generally allowed. Although OMs in some sections of the country allowed divorced and remarried persons to be members before 1900, a stricter position of non-acceptance emerged at about the turn of the century.[32]

By the mid-twentieth century, Mennonites active in mission outreach were reconsidering their position about divorce and remarriage. The Mennonite understanding generally was that if a divorced person's former spouse was still living, a second marriage constituted living in adultery. Persons who accepted the good news of salvation faced the bad news that because they were divorced and remarried, they could not become members of the congregation in which they had found new life. The options were to separate from the present spouse and live apart, or to go to a church that did not hold this position.

Christian families, too, experienced new stresses on their marriages. Urbanization, the dispersion of extended families and the support they offered, and influences of the secular world which openly accepted or even encouraged the breaking of a marriage increasingly bombarded Christian families. Within a decade or so, Mennonites themselves were experiencing more broken marriages. In 1976 Oregon Mennonites still held to the sanctity and intended permanence of marriage. However, all but the most conservative groups had cautiously changed their earlier position or were considering doing so.[33]

In the last few years of their first century in Oregon, Mennonites also considered other social concerns relating to their larger world. In the 1960s and 1970s some of them became strong advocates for civil rights. Occasionally, speakers, conference resolutions, and cross-cultural efforts promoted justice for oppressed minorities. In their conferences, as well as individually and in smaller groups, they focused on such issues as gun licensing, capital punishment, nonpayment of war taxes and support for a World Peace Tax Fund, litigation, alcoholism, abortion, sexuality, poverty, world hunger, and local land-use planning. Some of these issues, as others in this chapter, related to the general theme of nonresistance. Some were only beginning to surface by 1976 and would in the next years receive considerable attention.[34]

■ ■ ■

During their first century in Oregon, Mennonites moved in and out of their larger world in a variety of ways, sometimes fleetingly, often in patterns of increasing accommodation to change. They usually tested their movements in light of the Scriptures. Frequently they disagreed about the level of acculturation to sanction. Mennonites gradually accepted or adapted much from the perspective and practice of their larger world and made their own contributions as well. What Mennonites had to offer varied—from the salve that George Hostetler of Aurora recommended in 1925 "for its curative powers" to Mrs. Richard Boehr's 1971 exhibit of Chinese watercolor scrolls she had painted at the Capital Artists Gallery in Salem.

As Mennonites continued to search for a renewed sense of identity amid urbanization and affluence, they relied on few boundaries in comparison to a century earlier. For most, the church community was less restrictive and often overlapped other collectives or ideologies. In light of such indistinction, Paul Brunner in his 1975 conference sermon called for the kind of separateness "established by the unique ownership of God" which sets Christians apart "for His business." Brunner urged unity in the church and commitment to Christ. With such unity and commitment, community and individualism would be able to achieve a biblical balance within the larger world.[35]

Chapter 11

Oregon Mennonites and War

Oregon Mennonites who refused to participate in war and military service could look to a long history of precedents. For several centuries after Christ, his followers generally did not participate in military service. But in A.D. 380 when Roman emperors made Christianity the official state religion, the distinction between church and state disappeared and the church began to support or even initiate "just" wars. However, a few remnants of Christianity and occasional renewal movements rejected warfare. When the sixteenth-century Anabaptist-Mennonite movement stabilized, most members refused to bear arms.

Militarism in Europe was a major cause for the emigration of thousands of Mennonites from France, Germany, Switzerland, Holland, and Russia to North America. Mennonites believed that taking Christ as Savior meant following his example and teachings, practicing love in all relationships. The way of love, often identified as nonresistance, was the principle which guided their response to several issues the previous chapter considered. But conscription and wars tested their nonresistance intensely. At such times, loyalty to their community of faith conflicted with competing claims of their government. Individuals who diverged from their Mennonite community submitted themselves instead to the strident demands of the state.[1]

Challenges to nonresistance came not only from the state but also from the revival movement and the influences of Fundamentalism, which emphasized personal salvation or right beliefs above following Christ as disciples and his teaching in the Sermon on the Mount. For North American Mennonites well into the nineteenth century, the gospel of Christ, the gospel of salvation and the gospel of peace were all of one circle, descriptive but not separate.

Revivalism and Fundamentalism split the circle and laid it out in two tracks. Specific statements about God, the Bible, and salvation were "essentials." Nonresistance, the gospel of peace, was one of the "nonessentials" which Fundamentalists soon rejected completely. Mennonite leaders early in the twentieth century adopted the two-track approach to faith, though they included nonresistance among the essentials, even if not quite as essential as acknowledging the deity of Christ. Yet they, too, began more often to distinguish between being saved and being disciples. This distinction was one of the influences away from their historic practice of nonresistance.[2]

While revivalism and Fundamentalism were merging and infiltrating Mennonite circles, Mennonites were making a new life for themselves in Oregon. For most of them, nonresistance was then an important, identifying aspect of their faith. Zion (GC) at Polk Station noted in the first article of its 1896 constitution that one difference between the Mennonites and other evangelical churches was in their position about bearing arms or performing military service. In the spring of 1899, A. Yoder of Zion (AM) at Hubbard wrote of congregations in the Willamette Valley who worked "harmoniously with one another on the basis of non-resistance." It was a common element that joined them in fellowship.[3]

Although they regarded nonresistance as an important part of their faith, it appears that in their first decades in Oregon most Mennonite groups did not emphasize it greatly through teaching or conference resolutions. Occasional references to nonresistance in AM or OM conference reports or constitutions took it for granted as a pillar of their faith, but they did not examine it carefully to see if the pillar remained firm. Their sister groups of GCs, MBs, and EMBs emphasized evangelism and missions. Nonresistance, untested by war, received little attention. Denominational publications did promote nonresistance, but not strongly during peacetime or distant war. However, the U.S. entry into the First World War placed the issue squarely before them.[4]

During World War I the United States moved from official neutrality to fervent participation. Mennonites groped for freedom of conscience. Even while neutral, the United States sold "Liberty Bonds" to help finance a military buildup. Most Mennonites considered such support inconsistent with nonresistance, but some complied in the face of pressure which incuded threats and mistreatment. After the United States entered the war against Germany on April 6, 1917, hostility against Mennonites increased. The emotional fervor of the war caught up preachers in most American churches who echoed war propaganda and created their own militant gospel as well. Mennonite conscientious objectors became detested stumbling blocks on the road to the war the U.S. president said would end all wars. The Selective Service Act of May 18, 1917, provided a limited exemption for conscientious objectors by allowing them to serve in "noncombatant" roles. While confusion reigned for months over the specifics, consensus was forming among Mennonites that noncombatant service was unacceptable. They saw it as being clearly an essential arm of the military. Arrangements were later made for some conscientious objectors to be released for farm labor. Others went to France for relief work. The war ended before a Board of Inquiry had determined which of the conscientious objectors were really sincere and eligible for such alternative work.[5]

Under the pressures of World War I, Mennonite practice varied considerably. The Military Intelligence Division of the War Department surveilled and intimidated conscientious objectors, while the ambiguity of the Selective Service Act brought confusion and inconsistent administration in army camps. Some mistreatment occurred because the War Department lacked a clear policy regarding conscientous objectors, but eventually officers received orders to treat the objectors with tact and consideration in order to win them to military service. Mennonites had poorly prepared their young men to face conscription and the trials it would bring. However, in Mennonite historian Guy Hershberger's judgment, a large majority of conscripted Mennonites of all groups nationwide refused any sort of military service. A "substantial minority" accepted noncombatant service, and a few, combatant service.[6]

Oregon's Mennonites, it seems, paid little heed when the First World War broke out in Europe in 1914. Only after the United States entered the war in 1917 did the PCC officially acknowledge that a time of testing awaited them. A resolution admonished the draft-age "boys" of the church to "stand firm . . . and to acquaint themselves with the privileges" granted by the government. Mennonites, well respected in their communities, now became targets of scorn, intimidation, and even abuse. When Mennonites walked the streets of Dallas, people who met them spat. Newspaper editors incited their readers to support the war and oppose conscientious objectors. The *Albany Daily Democrat* regarded those who refused noncombatant service as being "too cowardly to fight, or too lazy to work, or too callous to heed the call of suffering and dying humanity." The *Hubbard Enterprise* referred to those who refused to buy Liberty Bonds as "the cringing apologetic contemptibles of the earth." In the *Harrisburg Bulletin,* the Red Cross chairman, in a rousing call to expend "every dollar and every drop of true Americanism" to defeat the German "military vampire," joined what sociologist Ray H. Abrams has called "atrocity mongers" nationwide. Such inflammatory rhetoric could incite a mob mentality, swallow men who were mostly reasonable, congenial persons in ordinary life, and vomit them back up as senseless and violent.[7]

After the United States entered the war the Hubbard and Albany area Mennonites lost favor in their communities. Those at Albany experienced less harassment. A few members of the Albany town church purchased war bonds, to their later regret. Fairview displayed a flag and did not make purchasing war bonds an issue. By the end of the war, Fairview was getting good press from the County Chairman of National Defense, who reported them "100 per cent loyal American citizens" in regard to the purchase of war bonds. Whether he represented them accurately is open to question. At Hubbard, the Whiskey Hill school district, with a large number of Mennonites, fell far short of its quota of war stamps. To placate the community, Zion displayed an American flag. Under pressure, some members bought war bonds. On one occasion the Harry West family left home to escape a mob. The three Zion young men who joined the army forfeited their membership. Few Hopewell members bought war bonds and some opposed the war quite openly. David Peterson, who researched Oregon Mennonite response to the war, learned that two Hopewell men "were run out of town." At Bethel, near Canby, most who were not Mennonites stopped attending services and so did some who were.[8]

Harrisburg's small-town newspaper noted that Mennonites contributed "very liberally" to the Armenian relief fund, but their later refusal to buy war bonds brought severe harassment. They were suspected of being German sympathizers, and those who ventured into town received verbal abuse. Sometimes at night, community men drove past Mennonite homes, yelling. On one occasion they fired bullets at buildings. Community zealots painted a yellow stripe around the Harrisburg meetinghouse and chained the double doors with a new padlock. Above the door they placed two flags and signs, one reading "CLOSED FOR THE DURATION OF THE WAR." Frank Kropf, who lived nearby, shattered the padlock with

Wilbur D. Kropf

Harrisburg meetinghouse, vandalized in World War I, destroyed by arson in World War II.

two blows of his hammer. The Mennonites continued to hold services as usual, but they did not take down the signs and flags until after the war ended. The yellow stripe remained so long that it became an embarrassment to the community.

One experience of bishop Daniel J. Kropf, as reported by sons who were present at the time, has assumed legendary proportions. Men from town went to the Kropf home, intending to tar and feather him if he refused to purchase a war bond. As Kropf left his house to meet the men, he told his family that the Lord would take care of him. Kropf offered to give the men money but said he would not buy war bonds. The men started toward Kropf, then stopped, turned and, inexplicably, left. Kropf felt that a supernatural power had kept them from harming him. Later one of the men said that they had seen a man dressed in white standing between them and Kropf.[9]

While Oregon Mennonites made decisions about whether to purchase "Liberty Loans," the army drafted their young men. Probably fewer than twenty went to army camps. Most went to Camp Lewis near Tacoma, Washington, where some received violent abuse. Intimidation and suppression of legal rights were common. Army personnel restricted a few to bread and water for several days. They ridiculed all the objectors and threatened most of them with imprisonment or even death. Elmer McTimmonds, after being rescued from hanging at Camp Fremont in California, was transferred to Camp Lewis. There army men forced him into the uniform and took him to a movie, against his conscience, though they could not make him watch it.[10]

Like McTimmonds, Orie Conrad barely escaped death in an army camp. For several weeks soldiers in the barracks subjected him daily to alternating hot and cold showers, which gradually got worse. He could still "feel" them sixty years later and considered them the worst torture he received. They "butchered" his hair and one Saturday morning took him out behind the barracks where he saw a rope slung over a tree. They asked whether he had any last words, then threw a sack over his head and the rope around his neck. Mounted police appeared shortly after and rescued the unconscious Conrad. From then on he received good treatment, but he spit blood for three days. The soldiers who hanged Conrad were court-martialed and Conrad was called as a witness. He did not harbor hatred or anger and did not want to testify against them, but a roomful of officers instructed him to simply answer their questions with a yes or no.[11]

Zion minister Edward Z. Yoder of Hubbard, as an appointee of a denominational committee, visited Mennonite men in Western camps several times, although certain community people strenuously opposed this ministry. He frequently corresponded with leading churchman Sanford C. Yoder of Iowa about his experiences. After a June 1918 visit to Camp Lewis he wrote that some of the men had accepted some form of noncombatant service. Those who had not "signed up" were in the guardhouse, being treated "fair" by then, despite earlier abuse. One had two bayonet marks on his "limb." Yoder had informed the officers that if such abuse continued he would report it. The officers assured him that no more injury would be "allowed to come on them."

By mid-July, the last Mennonites were released from the guardhouse and placed in quarters reserved for conscientious objectors. Sometimes officers tried to keep Yoder from visiting the men. Once he went to the same place five times before he was admitted. He wrote, "I got in all the same if it did take me two days. I made up my mind to get to them." Answering a call to Camp Fremont in California, he experienced similar problems. When he asked for Elmer McTimmonds, who was in the bull pen (prison), the officers told Yoder that McTimmonds was not there and asked what he intended to do about it. Yoder said he intended to stay until he saw McTimmonds. His persistence won out. He also ob-

Verna Birky

C.O. Detachment #1, Camp Lewis, Washington, in 1918. Most, if not all, were from Oregon. Back, left to right: Frank Hostetler, Homer Schlegel, John Kropf, Orie Conrad, Elmer McTimmonds, Charles Hamilton, Paul Snyder. Front, left to right: Chris Hostetler, Elmer Schultz, Jess Emmert, _____ Holderman, Lester Burkholder.

tained McTimmonds's transfer to Camp Lewis.[12]

Oregon's other Mennonite groups also had emphasized nonresistance little before the crisis of World War I. Many MBs, EMBs, and GCs had descended from Russian Mennonites, who had migrated largely because military exemption there was about to end. But perhaps the search for greater financial opportunities called for primary attention once they arrived in their new country. Here no war tested their nonresistance for several generations. Although their denominational confessions of faith upheld nonresistance, it did not filter down to Oregon congregations as a practice that called for much elaboration. Few records indicate their responses to World War I. Apparently they did not have treasured stories of experiences as conscientious objectors to pass down to succeeding generations. Most drafted MB men worked as noncombatants in the shipyards in Portland. Apparently none joined combatant ranks, though several "black sheep" among the EMBs did. Other EMBs, as conscientious objectors, did noncombatant service in the shipyards.[13]

E. Z. Yoder had occasional contact with "New Mennonites," who perhaps included men from Oregon's GC congregations. Yoder wrote of several GC ministers, one a "Baumgarden" (probably Samuel S. Baumgartner, then pastor of Emmanuel), who in April 1918 created quite "a stir" at Camp Lewis. Advised by a "Reickert of Kansas," a member of the Western District (GC) Exemption Committee, "Baumgarden" and the other ministers distributed "anti-war literature," some of it printed in German. Not surprisingly, this "didn't set very well" with the officers. The "boys were . . . given a good ducking" in the lake and the ministers ended up in the guardhouse with their young men.

They wired Yoder for help, but the Hubbard agent who took the message gathered a mob to prevent him from going. Someone who did not want the town disgraced by mob violence called the state attorney general at Portland, who advised Yoder to request help from the East. Perhaps this was the occasion when Yoder was warned to take the train from Woodburn instead of Hubbard, to escape gallows erected in Hubbard supposedly for him. Sanford C. Yoder of Iowa joined him and John P. Bontrager of Albany and together they visited Camp Lewis. But by then the "matter for the most part had settled itself."[14]

World War I, which showed North American Mennonites how ill-prepared they were to face conscription, also motivated them to educate and build convictions for peace among their members. Mennonite Central Committee (MCC), which in 1920 united several Mennonite relief committees, first offered aid to famine sufferers in postwar Russia. In the view of Mennonite historian James Juhnke, it also helped Mennonites regain acceptability in American society. In addition MCC promoted peace and helped strengthen the Mennonite conscience against warfare. Denominational Mennonite and inter-Mennonite peace organizations also promoted nonresistance. In the late 1930s, Mennonite leaders helped negotiate a plan for acceptable alternate service in case of future conscription. In Civilian Public Service (CPS), which evolved as a result, conscientious objectors could serve their country in work of national importance under civilian direction instead of serving under the military. In May 1941, several months after military conscription began in the fall of 1940, the first CPS camps opened.[15]

Although in the years between the wars leaders of Mennonite denominations promoted peace and nonresistance, this did always not carry over to individual congregations. Oregon's EMBs continued to give little attention to the issue of war and did not take a position regarding it. Many young people, influenced by friends from other denominations, did not develop convictions as conscientious objectors. During World War II, about half of the EMB-reared young men in government service entered the armed forces and most of the others were noncombatants. Five served in CPS.[16]

The PDC (MB) strongly endorsed CPS, but Oregon's MBs emphasized evangelism and missions more. Men who chose military service in the Second World War and those who did alternative service in CPS camps received equal blessing from their congregations. Many regarded noncombatant service as a nonresistant response. A majority of conscripted MB men in Oregon went into full military service. Six were in CPS. Dallas, however, attempted to meet its financial quota for support of CPS camps, though offerings often fell short. It did pay mileage for ministers who visited the CPS camp at Tillamook, on the Oregon coast. A young men's octet gave programs at CPS camps in Oregon. The West Salem congregation had two men in CPS but thought the government should operate the camps and, after the first year, claimed no responsibility for them, preferring, instead, to support the Red Cross. Yet when CPS men from LaPine in central Oregon presented a program at West Salem, the congregation gave a $10 check.[17]

In the PDC (GC), Field Secretary Emma Ruth promoted peace and nonresistance between the wars. During World War II the PDC focused on the issue annually. At a ministers' retreat in 1941, John M. Franz of Salem, who had barely escaped the noose in Montana in World War I, spoke on "the minister's responsibility in time of war." That year, a PDC resolution pledged "appreciation of and loyalty to the principle of non-resistance." Yet congregations did not meet their quota for support of CPS.

In 1942 the PDC educational committee encouraged members to visit camps, subscribe to camp papers, invite CPS men to speak in churches, and do such "practical projects as making camp kits, sending cookies, reading materials [sic], etc." Camp kits consisted of three sheets, two pillowcases, towels, needles, pins, thread, and a New Testament. Several carloads of young people from Portland visited the camp at Cascade Locks and gave a program there. At other times men from the camp visited the Portland church. When Dallas pastor Homer Leisy visited Cascade Locks, he took along an electric iron from the women's missionary society. Upon returning, he reported his good impressions of the camp. Emmanuel took monthly offerings for CPS and the women canned food, 478 quarts in 1945.[18]

In spite of PDC (GC) encouragement, many of its young men did not choose CPS. In Oregon, 15 percent took the IV-E position as conscientious objectors. Over one-third were in noncombatant service (I-A-O classification), and half were I-A, in full military service. But the pattern varied widely among congregations. From Calvary, which organized late in the war as a movement away from Zion (MC), half of its six inducted men worked in CPS camps, two were noncombatants, and one took the I-A classification. Grace at Albany, with partly MC heritage, had only one with IV-E classification, and Grace at Dallas had none in CPS. At Dallas more than half were noncombatants. At least one—probably most of them—worked in the shipyards in Portland.

At Emmanuel, pastor Daniel J. Unruh reported "a fine spirit of Christian tolerance" at a special busiess meeting in March 1942 to consider questions of war, the draft, and CPS, amid "wide divergence of opinion." They "recognized that above everything else" they needed "the guidance of the Holy Spirit in meeting the important personal issues." Such language, of course, encouraged individual rather than corporate decisions. Early in the war a number received farm deferments, but were later inducted. About three-fourths eventually went into full military service, but some went to CPS. At Alberta a sizable majority of inducted men had I-A classification and most others took the noncombatant position.[19]

Many of Oregon's GCs, MBs and EMBs took a neutral stance regarding nonresistance. Unlike salvation, it was not an essential, decision, but a personal one, a nonessential one. Having men in military service, whether as combatants or noncombatants, allowed them be both patriotic and evangelistic. Churches displayed a service flag and an honor roll for men in the armed services. At the end of the war Grace in Dallas had a "welcome home" service for the men returning from overseas. Pastor Homer Leisy preached a message entitled "Paul, the Commando for Christ." Arnold Regier, pastor of Alberta in Portland, observed that people who were not Mennonites sometimes seemed more open to nonresistance than some members of Mennonite heritage. Ministers and congregations helped provide spiritual nurture and recreation for 35,000 military personnel at Camp Adair near Albany, some of them GCs from elsewhere. The PDC newsletter reported that "some of the soldier guests were led to a saving knowledge of Jesus Christ."[20]

Rufus M. Franz

Rufus M. Franz, CPS administrator in World War II.

Though nonresistance did not receive strong support among Oregon GCs, some members practiced and promoted it. Rufus Franz, earlier of Dallas, became director of the CPS camp at Lapine, Oregon. He was a son of minister John M. Franz and a public school teacher in Eugene. The government official in charge respected Franz highly. Franz later became West Coast Regional Director of CPS. Pastor Arnold Regier of Portland had come from Kansas, where the peace position was strongest among GC Mennonites. He too supported that position and served on the Cascade Locks (Oregon) CPS camp board.[21]

Like Emma Ruth of the PDC (GC), PCC Mennonites increased their teachings on peace and nonresistance in the years between the wars. Beginning in 1925, young people's meetings on Armistice Day (November 11), or thereabouts, became an annual event, turning into two-day meetings occasionally in 1945 and after. They often focused on nonconformity, personal piety, evangelism, and missions, instead of, or in addition to, aspects of nonresistance. But this only indicated a concern to make nonresistance an integral part of their total life and witness. The very fact that the meetings were on Armistice Day was an implicit endorsement of nonresistance. Young people spoke on designated topics, with only the sermons assigned to ministers. In 1939, on the eve of World War II, the sole subject was nonresistance and peace.

In official Pacific Coast Conference sessions, nonresistance received infrequent attention until the Second World War loomed ahead. In 1938 delegates "heartily endorsed" the denominational position adopted the previous year, and a 1940 resolution reaffirmed nonresistance. Many Mennonites believed that a strict nonconformity helped preserve nonresistance and that laxity in nonconformity would threaten nonresistance. In general, the more conservative Oregon congregations had fewer men who joined the armed services.[22]

Oregon Mennonites received less harassment in World War II than in the previous war, but they did not escape untouched. John Lais of Fairview, who lived near Junction City, suffered when men at the sawmill where he worked stole his gasoline and broke his tools. Two employees in an Albany department store slandered and shunned a Mennonite fellow employee who refused to buy war bonds. Just after the Japanese attack on Pearl Harbor, the editor of the *Harrisburg Bulletin* asked his readers "not only to be on the alert against un-American activities, but also an un-American way of handling them."

However, in some quarters resentment smoldered because Mennonites refused to buy war bonds. When the Harrisburg church building burned to the ground on August 7, 1944, the Mennonites did not request an arson investigation. But many community people deplored the incident and the Christian Church in town even took an offering to help the Mennonites rebuild. The newspaper editor issued a stiff judgment, one the Mennonites themselves would never have considered making. He wrote that if, as some thought, the fire was not an accident, "the responsible party is bound to sizzle in the hereafter and should be sizzling right now."[23]

Mennonites in the PCC, some still struggling out of the depression of the 1930s, responded to World War II economics in various ways. David Peterson concluded that a "substantial minority" in Oregon congregations purchased war bonds in spite of government provision for Americans to purchase civilian bonds instead. Few worked in war industries, but some criticized sawmill workers, who, they thought, were indirectly aiding the war effort. Ministers advised farmers not to increase production during the war to avoid contributing directly to the war effort. Omar G. Miller in his "West Coast Echoes" warned that "blood money should never be used for personal benefit. And the extra dollars" resulting from a wartime economy had "the blood of millions on them."

Even so, high prices for farm products lifted farmers out of the depression doldrums and set them on firm financial footing. Some became the envy of their neighbors. Others, not wanting to prosper largely due to the war economy, increased their giving for relief purposes. One farmer, wishing to make an unusually large contribution to MCC anonymously, dropped a folded Cleveland bill in an offering designated for relief and afterward enjoyed hearing the congregational treasurer muse as to its possible origin. The treasurer did not surmise that the one-thousand dollar gift came not from one of the wealthier farmers but from one of modest means with a large family.[24]

In World War II many more Mennonites from Oregon were subject to conscription than in World War I. The first registration included men aged twenty-one to thirty-five, inclusive. Later the age was lowered to eighteen. One Fairview family had six young men drafted. In the PCC over half of the classified men received farm, logging or other deferments to work in an occupation their draft boards considered essential. Of the remainder, about 15 percent served as noncombatants, and over 16 percent in combatant service. Peterson's recent study indicates that in Oregon nearly three-fourths of the drafted men served in CPS.[25]

Most Oregon (MC) men in CPS worked in camps and detached service units in Montana, Idaho, Washington, and California, though a few went as far as Nebraska, Iowa, Illinois, and several Eastern states. They worked in soil conservation and other types of agriculture, forestry, national park maintenance, dam construction, mental hospitals and training schools. Some of them did dramatic work as smoke jumpers who fought forest fires. The PCC in 1941 appointed N. A. Lind to have spiritual oversight of its young men in CPS and continuously reappointed him to the end of the war. Other Oregon ministers corresponded with their CPS men and visited CPS camps located in Oregon.[26]

Men in CPS camps did not suffer widespread persecution as did conscientious objectors in the previous war, but they did experience varying difficulties and discouragements. Now and then surrounding communities resented them. But usually their hard work reversed criticism and produced acceptance or even praise. Civilian Public Service men in MCC camps received no wages, only small monthly allowances at best. Those with wives and children lacked means of support for their dependents. Local churches and

MCC contributed, and some married men moonlighted to provide for their families. Many wives took jobs, too. Institutional living in barracks was a test. The men lived in close proximity with many other men. Food items were rationed.

Their work was a test, too, much of it "made" work, rather than obviously needed. It was sometimes boring, occasionally challenging, often exhausting, and dangerously exciting for smoke jumpers. The wide range in ages of the men, conservative and liberal views, intolerance, and varying levels of Christian commitment and maturity called for mutual toleration. Gripers made life difficult for others who wished to serve in a spirit of love. Those who got into drinking, smoking, stealing, and questionable nighttime pursuits, or who were not interested in religious activities disappointed the campers who took their faith and nonresistant witness seriously. And CPS lasted a long time. Some men served for more than four years.[27]

But most Oregon Mennonites believed the values of CPS outweighed the difficulties. They noted opportunities for witnessing, spiritual growth, constructive service, education, recreation, and hobbies. They learned to solve difficult problems without specific help from parents and church leaders, and they made friends from other states and Mennonite groups. Their CPS relationships and experiences caused them to reassess their traditional beliefs and brought new understandings to their nonresistant faith. They promoted relief work and improved mental and public health. Government agencies, which at times initially hesitated to give work to CPS men, found them good workers and often requested more.[28]

Mennonite Central Committee administered three CPS camps or units in Oregon. LaPine, a large camp in central Oregon, operated under MCC about fifteen months, with the men clearing land and constructing a dam. Director Rufus Franz remembered years later that if he needed help of any kind, he just called Sam (S. E.) Eicher of the PCC. LaPine closed as an MCC camp at the end of 1943 because the government wanted to take over its operation. At Tillamook about twenty CPS men worked on dairy farms for fifteen months, ending in September 1946. The last MCC unit of CPS opened at the Veterans' Hospital at Roseburg, where twenty-four Mennonite men helped care for the mentally ill. Although relations between regular staff and conscientious objectors were sometimes a bit strained, the administrator said that he did not know what he would have done without the CPS men. This unit closed after less than a year, in December 1946.[29]

A number of men from Oregon's GC and MC congregations went to the CPS camp at Cascade Locks, along the Columbia River. The Brethren Service Committee and MCC jointly administered this camp which early in 1942 had over one hundred men representing twenty-eight denominations and creeds, and both religious and political conscientious objectors. About half had college or graduate training. (Half a dozen were from UCLA.) They included teachers, musicians, artists, and photographers, as well as farmers and laborers. Most of the Mennonite men were from Oregon and California. But the religious and political mix did not work well. Secular pacifists regarded the Mennonites as too conservative or as proud and judgmental, not accepting of secularists' views. Later in 1942 thirty or more Mennonite men transferred out of Cascade Locks to other CPS camps. By November 1945, only four Mennonite men remained.[30]

Mennonites contributed both money and material goods to help support CPS camps, but news items and PCC reports referred more often to material goods. In several roles S. E. Eicher of Fairview supported and guided the CPS program in the Northwest and cooperated with MCC, the Sisters' Sewing Circle, and others who supplied the camps with food and other necessities. N. A. Lind noted "unhesitatingly" that "no one man in [the] district rendered better service" to CPS men than did Eicher, "in a multitude of ways."

But without the women of the conference, Eicher would have been severely limited. Women sent cook aprons and caps, pot holders and tea towels, Christmas fruitcake and goodies, and above all, canned food. Several sewing circles canned hundreds of quarts of food. One alone sent almost two thousand quarts. The district's annual report early in 1945 showed that conference women had contributed a total of 11,706 quarts of vegetables, fruit, and jam. They also gave forty-nine quarts of lard and over five hundred pounds of dried fruit and vegetables.[31]

Even though PCC Mennonites emphasized nonresistance more between the wars than before World War I, it appears that their young men were not well prepared to meet the pressures of conscription in World War II. Less than three-fourths of their drafted men served as conscientious objectors, barely half from Albany and only 62 percent from Zion. One basic influence mentioned frequently by ministers was the quality of a young man's personal relationship to Christ and his level of understanding of biblical teaching on the subject. Other strong influences were urbanization, education, and age.

Peterson's recent study concluded that men engaged in nonfarming occupations and those who had attended high school were more likely to enter a branch of the armed services than were farmers or men with only a grade school education. And men who took up military service were, on the average, over a year younger than those who chose CPS. Similar patterns emerge from draft census records of GCs and MBs. Co-workers and high school peers as well as aggressively pro-war teachers undermined the nonresistant faith of Mennonite families and churches. This influenced (old) Mennonites to begin several high schools during World War II, though Western Mennonite School in Oregon did not officially open until shortly after the war ended.[32]

In contrast to many GCs, MBs and EMBs, Oregon's MC leaders took a strong stand for nonresistance. Men in OM congregations who joined the noncombatant or combat ranks knew their church membership would come into question, if indeed it had not already occurred. Some bishops routinely excommunicated them. Others took them out of good standing as members but kept in contact with them. Some thought the noncombatants were more misguided than in total error.

Parents and lay members also helped determine the quality of relationship with the young men in the armed services. The Zion sewing circle remembered their "nearly fifty boys in all parts of the world" in CPS camps and "in the service," with gifts at Christmastime and for their birthdays. Most of the boys sent letters of appreciation. Men whose ministers showed a spirit of redemptive love and forgiveness were more likely to return to their congregation in repentance and become reinstated as members in good standing than were men whose ministers shunned them completely.

Many who felt rejection and judgment from their church turned away in bitterness and later joined another denomination or none at all. Some observers believed that while the more liberal congregations had more men who entered the armed services, they may also have had a larger percentage who returned to the church after their discharge. Whether they all reentered with stronger convictions for nonresistance is not clear.[33]

Oregon's PCC Mennonites cooperated with MCC in CPS and relief work during World War II, but they were extremely uneasy about how this would affect their position on nonconformity. Conference leaders were "gravely concerned" that most CPS camp administrators were from other Mennonite groups. They wanted their young men to be in camps staffed with personnel who were "whole-hearted adherents" to their standards of nonconformity. But programs of such magnitude as CPS and even the smaller MCC could not easily accommodate exclusionist practices.

Many (old) Mennonites learned to appreciate new friends of more liberal Mennonite groups who had few if any restrictions about attire and behavior. True to fears, this did influence their opinions and convictions. Departures from PCC standards of nonconformity became increasingly evident, although certainly increased exposure to the larger world was also a significant influence. In 1947 the PCC requested that the denominational general conference (OMGC) sponsor its own relief work rather than continuing to cooperate with MCC. It said that affiliation with MCC took the "nature of an unequal yoke" which had caused many of their young people "to become confused doctrinally and weakened spiritually." The OMGC, however, approved continuing cooperation with MCC in "emergency types of work" which could "most advantageously be carried on together," though each Mennonite group would see to its own permanent institutional and mission work.[34]

Since much of MCC's work for years after World War II qualified as emergency work, strong cooperation among Mennonite groups continued. After the war, Mennonite relief workers assisted war sufferers with tons of food, clothing, bedding, and soap contributed by folks at home. They worked in reconstruction and health care and helped resettle Russian Mennonite refugees in South America. Oregon Mennonites contributed, too, with money, new and used garments, quilts, and comforters. Fairview sent four and three-fourths tons of farm implements to Reedley by truck for war refugees in South America. Not many Oregon Mennonites worked personally with MCC in the 1940s and 1950s, at home or abroad, but a few did, such as Luke and Verna Birky and Fannie Schrock from Fairview, Anna Snyder from Bethel, and Gladwyn Schmidt from Grace at Dallas.[35]

While many Mennonites worked with MCC simply from a desire to serve, a peacetime military draft nudged others into service. The CPS program was discontinued in March 1947 and conscientious objectors were deferred in a conscientious-objector category

Margaret Shetler

Anna M. Snyder (1896-1963) of Bethel, during her service with MCC in Akron in the mid-1940s.

until June 1951, when the draft was reactivated. During the interim, MCC and its constituent churches began a new emphasis, encouraging young people to give voluntary service in needy parts of the world as a continuing witness to Christian love and the way of peace. Mennonite men, including some who had served earlier in CPS, began reconstruction work in Germany under a new program called Pax (the Latin word for peace), which soon met alternative service requirements. Over a dozen Oregon men from several Mennonite groups served in Pax. In the 1960s and 1970s, MCC moved into third-world, often war-torn, countries. Oregon volunteers, men and women, served in such ways as agricultural development, health care, and education. Jon Snyder of Zion barely escaped death in civil war crossfire in the Belgian Congo.[36]

The 1951 alternative service format, which differed greatly from CPS of World War II, offered greater personal opportunities and called for fewer sacrifices. Usually it was not difficult for Mennonite men to receive the I-W classification, which permitted either voluntary service under a church agency or employment at an approved hospital or other service institution. A sizable majority of Oregon's PCC young men did alternate service until the draft ended in 1973. Some, living away from home and in a large city for the first time in their lives, stretched their ties with the church and sampled worldly pleasures. Many matured personally and spiritually. In the mid-1960s, counselors stepped up educational efforts and offered orientation programs to help young men understand options and choose wisely. Ministers tried to keep in touch with their men, and nearby congregations often provided a multifaceted ministry. Portland Mennonite Church and the PCC attempted to support Portland's many I-W men, who came from all over the United States, and to encourage them to relate to the church.[37]

After World War II, MC, GC, and MB leaders and conferences and committees increased their emphasis on nonresistance. They began to speak more of peace and service, enlarging and making positive the traditional concept of nonresistance. The PDC (GC) especially kept the issue before its people with its Christian Service Committee, which often had members who had earlier come from or had close relationships with MCs. But among the GCs and MBs particularly, Fundamentalism had taken a heavy toll on nonresistance. Some teachers and writers held that nonresistance is "not scriptural, but on the contrary, that the Christian has a moral obligation to go to war." In the judgment of GC scholar J. Winfield Fretz, such teachers and writers influenced GCs against nonresistance as much as local pressures did. John A. Toews, MB historian, noted that Fundamentalists, who "generally rejected nonresistance as a part of liberal theology" and did not distinguish between humanistic pacifism and biblical nonresistance, influenced MBs against the ethic of love and nonresistance.[38]

Oregon GC and MB congregations felt strongly the influence of Fundamentalism, but in some congregations the renewed denominational and conference teaching did reverse the trend away from nonresistance. By 1958 the number of PDC (GC) men who did alternative service after World War II had increased 16 percent, compared with a 20 percent increase denomination-wide. However, Oregon's GC congregations did not all reflect such an increase. After the draft resumed in 1951 Emmanuel men served only in the armed forces. Calvary and Grace (Dallas), however, had several men in overseas peace service, as well as some in the armed forces.

Among MBs, the percentage of men in alternative service did not change much over the twenty years after World War II ended. But during the Vietnam War it rose from about 32 percent in 1968 to about 58 percent in 1972. In Oregon's Dallas and North Park congregations, after 1969, about half of the young men chose alternative service. One of eleven from Kingwood was a conscientious objector. Some in the military service may have been noncombatants, although many MBs considered any type of military service as valid as alternative service. A Vietnam War veteran might show pictures to a youth group or speak of his experiences in a Sunday evening service with as much blessing as a conscientious objector might who had served in a peace assignment in Africa.[39]

By the mid-1960s, with United States involvement in the Vietnam War, changes were sweeping across the nation and the church. The war was not popular and did not generate the passionate patriotism common in the two world wars. While many Americans supported American involvement in Vietnam, others criticized their country's participation and refused to support it. Never before had historic Mennonite nonresistance, or elements of it, received such strong endorsement from other denominations and voices in American society. This doubtless helped some Mennonite men choose not to participate. But new applications of nonresistance appeared as well. Particularly on Mennonite and other college campuses, young men protested against even registering for the draft, seeing it as a first step in cooperation with the military. Some who had registered earlier burned or turned in their draft cards. Such Mennonite resisters felt that total noncooperation was the most consistent expression of nonresistance. In 1969 a group of young people in the PDC (MB) requested that the conference recognize noncooperation with Selective Service as a valid peace witness. The conference declined.[40]

In the (old) Mennonite church, major consideration of noncooperation with Selective Service occurred at Turner, Oregon. In August 1969 the denominational general conference met at Turner. A group of college students hitchhiked from Indiana to request official recognition of draft resistance as valid. Mennonites who for several decades had administered alternative, nonmilitary CPS and I-W programs were shocked at the idea that they had in reality been cooperating with the military arm of government. Many of them disagreed with this assessment and disapproved of draft resistance.

The appearance of the young draft resisters, nonconformed to the norms of either the Mennonite church or society at large, caused consternation as well. Oregon, with its mild climate and sheltered valleys, had already attracted a variety of countercultural people—the so-called hippies—and some of Oregon's Mennonites had little sympathy. Such persons were inclined to object to the

Oregon Mennonite archival collection, courtesy of Millard Osborne

Tim Beachy and Jonathan Lind talking with Sam Janzen at the Mennonite Draft Resisters' booth at (Old) Mennonite general conference at Turner, Oregon, in 1969.

long hair and casual attire of the draft resisters as much as to their draft resistance. However, the delegates approved a reaffirmation of the historic position on nonresistance and enlarged it to recognize noncooperation with Selective Service as also valid.[41]

The PCC position on nonresistance had shifted somewhat by 1970, when it encouraged pastors "to counsel thoroughly with young men" regarding Selective Service options. The statement noted the importance of understanding those who chose "nontraditional" positions—combatant, noncombatant, or nonregistrant—and encouraged congregations "to enter dynamic and redemptive dialogue" with members who did not accept nonresistance. Many PCC Mennonites opposed the Vietnam War but only a few men were draft resisters. Most PCC conscientious objectors during this era accepted alternative service as their witness to peace.[42]

Many of Oregon's EMBs accepted the militarism which Fundamentalists promoted, although a small number held to nonresistance. At Dallas, several boys in an OM family who joined the EMB congregation in the 1960s influenced others to become conscientious objectors. After 1964 a small minority performed nonmilitary alternative service. From Liberty Gardens, several men served in the armed forces following World War II. During the Vietnam War, two did alternative service and at least one served in the military.[43]

The three smallest Mennonite-related groups in Oregon had little visibility in their responses to war and peace. Only the Old Order Amish were present in Oregon in World War I.

Oregon's Old Order Amish community near McMinnville had few men of draft age during times of conscription. If any young men were drafted in World War I, classic Amish practice would indicate they were probably conscientious objectors. But during World War II, if draft census records are accurate, this Amish community had one man in full military service, one in noncombatant, and none in CPS. Perhaps this reflected the dissension and other problems which plagued the community during much of its intermittent existence. The census shows that most Amishmen who did not register as conscientious objectors came from comparatively small congregations, like the McMinnville group. But the McMinnville Amish in 1950 contributed two heifers for relief and reconstruction efforts in Germany.[44]

Records for Oregon's BIC and CGC congregations are few. It appears that BIC conscripted men served in all three categories—CPS, combat, and noncombatant—during World War II. Apparently some of their youth participated in peace education activities in the early 1970s, but their community church character suggests that nonresistance was likely not strongly taught or observed. The CGC position on nonresistance was clear. Historian Clarence Hiebert noted in 1973 that CGC men could not participate in military service and retain their membership. After Evergreen organized in 1957, their young men did I-W service at the Lebanon Hospital. The congregation also established a unit house in Lebanon for I-W men from other communities, who participated as members of the congregation during their time there. Some of them married Evergreen girls and stayed on in the community.[45]

■ ■ ■

Wartime experiences accelerated change among Mennonites, particularly in the 1940s and after—change in language, attire, occupation, education, recreation, worldview, and other practices and perspectives. Some men went to college after their CPS or I-W service, pursuing new interests and goals. Many who became lay leaders in their congregations held broadened views and were more willing to depart from tradition than some of their ministers wished. Men who returned to their home congregations after military service brought to their church communities even more diversity and fostered an increasing individualism.

In 1976 Oregon Mennonites held widely varying positions about nonresistance. Some supported the traditional position of only enough political involvement to preserve the privilege of alternative service. They regarded war as a permissive function of government for which they assumed no responsibility, either for its cause or its outcome.

Many Oregon Mennonites were talking about "the peace position" and attempting to move beyond a nonresistance that focused mostly on nonparticipation in war. They emphasized "shalom," the sort of peace that Mennonite missionary-theologian John Driver defined not as "mere tranquility of spirit or serenity of mind [but also] harmonious relationships between God and his people . . . characterized by justice." Some supported civil rights, rejected capital punishment, and refused to pay "war taxes" (the proportion of federal income tax allocated for military spending). More who became aware that poverty, repression, and injustice contribute to modern wars began to speak in the political arena as advocates for the poor and oppressed. Others, who were influenced by Fundamentalism, regarded nonresistance as irrelevant or even a hindrance to Christian living. For them, the gospel of peace was internal, private. Commitment to peace among the peoples of the world was a nonessential of the Christian faith, or else it included accepting the state's methods for achieving peace.[46]

At the end of their first century in Oregon, Mennonites differed widely in their convictions about war and peace. Those differences tightened the tension between individualism and church community. They also reflected the degree to which the state had successfully competed with the church for the primary loyalty of its members. How to respond in times of conscription was not the only question. How to work for peace in a world constantly at war and producing destructive capabilities beyond their worst imaginations also called for commitment and creativity.

As they entered their second century in Oregon, attempts to restore Christ's way of peace as one essential element of the gospel, even while building love and respect among Mennonites who separated the gospel of peace as a nonessential, would test the claim all of them made, that the Christian life is the way of love.

Chapter 12
Mennonite Institutions in Oregon

Oregon Mennonites established a variety of institutions. As they did, certain important elements of their larger vision—concern to nurture their own people as well as commitment to minister to the larger world—blended together. To nurture the faith of their young people and children, they organized schools. The hospitals and homes they started served their own people and also gave them a broader mission. Camps combined teaching and evangelism with recreation. Strong, gifted individuals—the visionaries who promoted and planned the institutions and the administrators who organized and developed them—had to remain accountable to the conference or churches that supported them and to the people who staffed them. For an institution to succeed and to meet the needs that motivated it, individualism had to yield in part to community, even while individuals assumed major responsibilities.

Education

In the PCC, many Mennonites valued education from a Christian perspective. In 1911 there was brief interest in beginning a school between Jefferson and Salem, and in 1920 a Pacific Coast Bible School actually opened. A local board planned and publicized the school as an opportunity for "more systematic Bible study" in a two-year curriculum. It would include "regular Bible work" as well as "vocal music, Sunday school normal work, personal work, and missions." In addition, it would include special lectures, a missionary conference and a ministers' conference. Beginning on December 13, its first three weeks were at Hopewell, the last three at Albany. Tuition was $1.75 per week, with board and room at reasonable rates. Students furnished their own stationery but could pur-

306

chase books at reduced rates. Tuition was free for anyone unable to pay.[1]

This first Pacific Coast Bible School was a satisfying success. The total enrollment of 115 exceeded expectations. Lloy A. Kniss of Johnstown, Pennsylvania, living in Oregon that winter, noted that in "a good spirit of scholarship," the Bible was "used to decide all questions" that arose. At least four young people committed themselves to serve in the anticipated mission in Portland. Of the thirty-six who completed the first year's course, sixteen were women. The members of the faculty were S. G. Shetler (who also served as principal), F. J. Gingerich, and M. H. Hostetler. Faculty received no regular salary, only the balance of tuition payments which remained after expenses were paid, prorated among them according to the amount of work each had done.[2]

Despite bright prospects and continuing plans, the Bible school did not soon become an annual event as anticipated. S. G. Shetler and his wife, Maggie, were slated to be two of the four

Sanford G. Shetler

Pacific Coast Bible School at Hopewell, 1921. Faculty: S. G. Shetler, front right; F. J. Gingerich, front left; M. H. Hostetler, balding, bearded smiling man, about third row from back, second from left.

instructors the second year, but then suddenly moved back to Pennsylvania, leaving the school bereft of S. G.'s organization and administration as its principal. The board struggled to revive the school and three years after the first successful term convened a second one, again at Hopewell and Albany. Attendance averaged about thirty, and fifty-four took all or part of the exams. Also, fifty persons "openly confessed Christ" at revival meetings held in several congregations in connection with the school. Beginning in 1925-26, schools operated four successive winters at several locations. The 1926-27 term began a four-year course of study, and persons completing it would receive credit for one full year at Hesston College. Enrollment ranged in the thirties and low forties. Freewill offerings in congregations and solicitation efforts financed the later schools.[3]

After completing the third of the four-year course in 1929, the faculty recommended that the board consider "launching" a nine-month school. Unfortunately, the result was instead the demise of the B ble school. Findings from questionnaires distributed to congregations early in 1930 convinced the board that the PCC was not yet ready to support a nine-month school. Further, sentiment strongly supported less "secular" study and "more of Bible" in Bible school work. What did this mean? Missions and Sunday school pedagogy were hardly secular subjects. Surely no Mennonites objected to the teaching of music. The only other secular course offered was English. Did the instructors promote innovative or unusual methods for missions and pedagogy, to which people objected? Had Bible school students assumed more leadership or shown more initiative in their local congregations than some ministers thought appropriate? Did some disapprove of possibilities for Hesston College credit? The report offered no details.

The board had not planned a Bible school for early 1930 because of the possibility of a nine-month school. In light of the questionnaire findings, the board recommended that the PCC "not require" it to now arrange a Bible school and instead urged congregations to "take advantage of Bible conferences, Bible studies, etc., as may be possible." The Pacific Coast Bible School had ended before completing its four-year course of study which would have earned students a year of credit at Hesston.[4]

In the next decade several congregations organized Bible schools, as the board recommended. Sheridan had a two-week one in the fall of 1937 and considered it so successful that it extended the 1938 session to four weeks. The class schedule covered a full day, from nine to four. The General Sunday School Committee of the Mennonite Church offered credits for the classes. Zion began a two-week school the day after Christmas in 1939 and another the following winter.[5]

In the meantime, probably in 1935, the PCC began promoting "young people's institutes," a teaching program which had recently developed in the denomination. Institutes were usually two- to four-day retreats with instruction, worship, discussion, and recreation. The institutes were first held in connection with PCC annual sessions, then for several years separately and at another location. In the early 1940s the Young People's Institute Committee, with expanded responsibilities, revived the Bible school format of two decades earlier. It endorsed a three-week school plan for congregations to use singly or conjointly. By the third winter, 1944-45, four congregations held five three-week terms, an impressive fifteen-week Western Bible Institute. Sixty-two men and seventy-six women enrolled. The school filled a need for many who had a limited education. Fifty-seven had not finished eighth grade, fifty-five had. Only twenty-five had graduated from high school and one from college.

The following year only Fairview had a Bible school, a two-and-a-half-week term. Congregational impetus for such institutes had waned and the institute committee judged that they had "filled the present need." By then the PCC was planning a nine-month school.[6]

While the PCC was providing Bible training for its people, other Mennonite groups in Oregon were doing the same. In 1926 the PDC (GC) initiated institutes, also called retreats, at Salem. Eleven persons registered and sixteen visitors participated in the first retreat. The members of the faculty were M. J. Galle of Aberdeen, Idaho; Harry Krehbiel of Lind, Washington; Anna Stauffer of Los Angeles; and L. J. Horsch of Upland, California. Of the next two retreats, the only Oregon person who attended was Catherine Niswander, in 1928, at Colfax, Washington. Soon after, the PDC began holding state- rather than district-wide retreats. Oregon's retreats began in 1941, at Silver Creek Falls, and continued at least through 1946. In the PDC (MB), organized Bible training first occurred in congregations. In 1931 Wm. J. Bestvater, former MB Bible school teacher and author of two German textbooks of Bible study, taught for eight weeks at Dallas, and in 1932 for six weeks. In both MB and GC congregations in the next years, pastors offered or arranged for Bible instruction on winter evenings and during vacations. However, both GC and MB young people frequently attended Fundamentalist nondenominational Bible institutes. In 1940, J. S. Dick, PDC (MB) home mission board secretary, questioned where to get future leaders if young people attended "schools of other confessions."[7]

The Dallas Bible School, later named Beacon Bible School, began in 1936 as an inter-Mennonite endeavor, intended for young people who had completed high school. Though the Dallas and Salem EMB congregations initially helped support it, the PDC (MB) claimed the school as its own for several years. Early instructors were N. N. Hiebert and Herman D. Wiebe (MB) and H. H. Dick (EMB). The first year twenty-seven students each paid $3.00 tuition for the four-month term. Several years later, Grace (GC) at Dallas and the new West Salem (MB) congregation joined in its support. By 1940, Homer Leisy (GC) was teaching in the school. The day students now numbered thirty and night students about thirty-five. In March 1941 eighteen graduated. In 1945 W. A. Regier of Pratum was commencement speaker for the last graduating class. By then the supporting congregations were planning a Bible academy.[8]

The Beacon Bible School dissolved into Salem Bible Academy and College, which began in the fall of 1945 with one hundred high school and fifteen college freshmen students. The school offered all courses required by the state, plus Bible subjects. In addition, it included evening schools with Bible doctrine classes in Dallas and West Salem, with approximately eighty attending at each location. John W. Ediger from Henderson, Nebraska, a graduate of Wheaton College, served as first principal of the new institution, heading an interdenominational staff of fourteen teachers. The second year the school added a second year of college, although it soon dropped the college and added seventh and eighth grades and became known as Salem Academy. At first the school used the West Salem MB building. A year later it began to develop a twenty-four-acre campus in the West Salem hills.[9]

Already by the second year, Dallas MB pastor G. H. Jantzen noted that the school was "entirely interdenominational in its organization and administration" and in its student body, too. Of the 120 students enrolled, thirty-five were MB, twenty were EMB, and three were GC. Seventeen were Baptist and the remainder consisted of Free Methodist, Friends, Nazarene, community church groups, and ten or more other denominations. In its tenth year, only fifty-nine of the 208 students were Mennonites of one group or another. By 1955 Salem Academy had become fully accredited by the State Department of Education as a standard high school. Although the student body and faculty continued to include Mennonites, the school's Mennonite ties loosened increasingly over the years. The school last reported to the PDC (MB) in 1956. Almost forty years after Salem Academy opened, Otto Bier, an elderly MB member from Dallas, believed that for "better or for worse, high school, whether public or private, was an amalgam serving to compromise Mennonite distinctives."[10]

Mennonites in the PCC tried to avoid that sort of compromise when they began Western Mennonite School (WMS) in 1945, the same year the Salem Academy opened only a few miles to the south. However, not all PCC people supported a Mennonite high school. One minister did not see how anyone could attend high school at all—whether secular or Christian—and be a Christian. Others who did want a school disagreed about whether WMS should work for accreditation or be a Bible school. But Oregon's new compulsory attendance law, requiring young people to be in school to age eighteen or until graduated from high school, caused the school advocates to work together. Wartime pressures also influenced their cooperation. They planned a five-year program that included Bible study about half-time during the first four years, with the fifth year devoted to "wholly secular courses." Those wanting primarily a Bible school could just skip the fifth year. However, the school was to be accredited, a PCC action which Omar G. Miller in his "West Coast Echoes" considered "a debasing compromise." Twenty-three students, all freshmen except one sophomore, attended the first year, in the unused Bellevue school building near Sheridan. They boarded and roomed in homes of Sheridan Mennonites. Marcus Lind of Oregon and Gladys Hostetter of Virginia comprised the faculty. The expectations and soon-to-be-written bylaws governing conduct and appearance were strict, in accord with PCC discipline and emphases of the late 1940s.[11]

Development of permanent school facilities was a long, arduous process. The school board accepted a donated, forty-four acre site ten miles north of Salem, somewhat centrally located but so far from Mennonite congregations that it would always be primarily a boarding school. The second year the school opened on its new campus in an unfinished rectangular "cracker box" which served as dining room, dormitory, classrooms, and chapel, as well as for all other purposes. At first students washed at the nearest outside faucet under a tree because there was no indoor plumbing. Eventually Oregon Mennonites completed the building and added others.[12]

Many changes occurred at WMS in the next years. The five-year curriculum soon lost favor. It became optional in 1951 and was discontinued shortly after. However, accreditation by the Northwest Association of Schools and Colleges did not occur until 1975. For several winters in the late 1940s and early 1950s a six-week "Special Bible Term" included Bible courses and classes in music, composition, English, public speaking, and various practical arts for persons unable to take the regular program. In a few years regulations for appearance and conduct relaxed, course offerings increased, and sports programs developed. Beginning in 1950, Oregon Mennonites welcomed WMS graduates who soon became leaders in the church. Yet in spite of all their dreams, the early visionaries could never have imagined that within four decades after they began their school, one of their graduates, Lee F.

Oregon Mennonite archival collection, courtesy of Millard Osborne

Western Mennonite School students Orval Larrew, Cheryl Cowan, and Leroy Kropf visiting with principal Glen A. Roth during 1966-67 school year.

Snyder, would be the first woman dean of a Mennonite college (Eastern).[13]

Western Mennonite School usually teetered between bare survival and minimum financial stability. As regulations and practices relaxed, families and congregations who wished to preserve more restrictive attire and other disappearing standards withdrew their support. Furthermore, not all PCC congregations felt a strong need for a Mennonite high school, particularly a boarding school. On the helpful side, students came from other MC conferences without a church school, including North Dakota and the Canadian West. Some foreign students and minority youth from American cities attended. Non-Mennonite students enrolled at WMS in larger numbers, partly because of the prevalence of drugs and other negative elements in public schools, although even Western also had to deal with such problems. From the mid-1950s onward, enrollment hovered around one hundred or a few more, except for two years, 1974-76, when it climbed to 144. The increased enrollment helped reduce financial pressures but taxed the boarding facilities. The fall 1976 enrollment was 116, with twenty-eight faculty and staff. Glen A. Roth was principal.[14]

In Oregon, only (old) Mennonites started elementary schools, except for the Amish and the Dallas Mennonites who had German schools a short time before or at the turn of the century. On September 7, 1948, Bethel started Oregon's first Mennonite elementary school with sixteen students enrolled and Lois Roth of Dayton as teacher. In 1958, at the end of the tenth year, two of the first year's first graders, Ordena Bond and Kenneth Snyder, along with transfer student Elsie Bucher, were the first high school sophomores to complete their training at the school. In 1959 Bethel and Hopewell formed a joint committee to administer the school, which moved it from the Bethel church grounds to the former Elliott Prairie public school building. In 1976, with fifty-three students in grades one through twelve, Dwight Strubhar was the teaching principal and Beulah Shank and Kathryn Schrock were full-time classroom teachers. Beulah Shank had acquired a reputation as an exceptional teacher with the gift of being able to motivate children to read.[15]

Several other congregations began elementary schools later, some offering high school as well. Harrisburg opened a school in 1952 which in 1976 had two teachers for the thirty students in grades one through ten. Children from Tangent also attended.

Porter began a school in 1967; Fairview and Winston, in 1975; and Sheridan, in 1976. The latter three schools used the Accelerated Christian Education curriculum, an individualized instructional program produced by a Fundamentalist nondenominational organization with a strong emphasis on patriotism. Enrollments in 1976 ranged from nine (Sheridan) to fifty-six (Fairview).[16]

Health and Welfare

Oregon Mennonites joined the larger Protestant missionary movement in promoting institutions of mercy when they established hospitals and homes to meet physical need and minister spiritually to patients and residents. Before they began such work in their own state, Oregon's PDC Mennonites (GC) knew about two such institutions in their conference, the Bethany Deaconess Hospital at American Falls, Idaho, and the tuberculosis sanitarium near Upland, California. In 1912 Aberdeen Mennonites opened the Idaho hospital, staffed largely by deaconesses, and operated it about a decade before it became a community hospital. The deaconess tradition traced back to Anabaptist or even apostolic times, with women, usually single, committing themselves to minister to the physically and spiritually needy. American (GC) Mennonites considered deaconess work as a form of home missions. Before the Idaho hospital opened, GCs had begun two Kansas hospitals where deaconesses served: Bethesda at Goessel (1899) and Bethel at Newton (1908). The California sanitarium, which opened in 1914, closed about seven years later because too few patients and Mennonite nurses came to the isolated rural institution.[17]

Mennonites (GC, MB, and EMB) at Dallas and Pratum founded the Salem Deaconess Home and Hospital, which four deaconess nurses opened with twelve beds in the former Capitol Hotel in December 1916. Later an occasional OM also served on the board of directors. Franz (F. B.) Wedel, the first superintendent, had earlier founded the society which began the Bethany hospital, even before he moved from Kansas to Idaho. From Aberdeen he had moved to Salem to head the new institution there. Later, Mennonites of all the Dallas groups salvaged bricks from a burned-down mill, cleaned them, and used them in constructing a three-story hospital. It opened with sixty beds.[18]

The Salem Deaconess Home and Hospital served the community for years. Eventually it outgrew its Mennonite base. In 1923 it treated 1,488 patients and performed 800 surgeries. It offered religious instruction and medical courses. For a time, it owned a farm and provided a home for needy old people and orphaned children. It also provided mission work for area Mennonite women, who would meet at the hospital for all-day sewing bees. In 1934 the hospital added a sizable south wing of three stories and another nurses' home. By 1945 Mrs. B. F. Wiens had ministered twelve years at the hospital, visiting hundreds of patients, speaking personally and praying with most of them. But charitable practices undermined its financial footing. In 1948 a new local board, consisting primarily of business people, endeavored to make the hospital pay its own way. By then it had about 100 beds. As administrator the board appointed Irwin Wedel, son and grandson of previous administrators, and renamed the institution Salem Memorial Hospital. In 1969 it merged with Salem General Hospital.[19]

In 1948, the same year the Salem/Dallas area Mennonites turned their hospital over to local business people, PCC Mennonites took over operation of a locally owned hospital in Lebanon. In 1917 several doctors had started a hospital in a "mansion" in the small town. In 1919 they moved to a more practical house on the corner of Ash and Second streets, which accommodated from six to eight beds.

In 1922 the Schuler sisters, Mary and Martha, recently graduated registered nurses, took over its management. The hospital became crowded in the next several years. According to one story, when the sisters returned home from shopping one day, they found an emergency patient in their own double bed and had to sleep elsewhere that night. In 1936 a group of doctors built a 36-bed brick hospital adjoining the old house. Then in the next decade logging and mill industries made Lebanon a boomtown. Population tripled to almost six thousand. Even more taxing, the Lebanon doctors had an excellent reputation which attracted patients from other areas. One year the hospital operated at 129 percent capacity and had 631 babies born in it. In the midst of all this, the Schuler sisters decided to retire.[20]

In a rather roundabout way, the PCC mission board learned about the search for someone to operate the Lebanon hospital. Investigations revealed that negotiations for taking over the management might be technical and complicated. In late December 1947, the board appealed for help from Allen H. Erb of La Junta, Colorado. Erb was a well-known Mennonite bishop who for more than thirty years had successfully administered a Mennonite sanitarium and hospital at La Junta. Erb traveled to Oregon and, with Sam Eicher and Dan Nofziger of the board's committee, met with the local physicians and key citizens. In mid-January 1948 the board accepted Erb's recommendations to take the responsibility. The final agreement that Erb negotiated called for the mission board to lease and operate the hospital beginning on July 19, 1948, with the community to construct a new facility as soon as possible.[21]

Erb moved to Oregon to become administrator of the hospital, and the next several years tested his statesmanship and skills. Eventually the new Lebanon Community Hospital opened for occupancy on August 15, 1952, under Mennonite operation. Negative community sentiment for a time had threatened both fund-raising and future Mennonite operation. Some community people feared profits would leave town or that Mennonite doctors would be given preference over other doctors. Community leaders emphasized that the new hospital would be nonprofit, open to any accredited physician and to patients of any race or creed.

When funds remained short at a critical juncture, Erb diplomatically leaked the news that the Mennonite administration of the old hospital had $20,000 in the operation fund that it would be willing to transfer to the hospital association, allowing it to engage a contractor. This gesture restored the confidence and good will earlier adverse publicity had tarnished and made possible a Hill-Burton federal grant which permitted construction to begin. Erb also proposed that the PCC mission board, inexperienced in hospital administration and tending toward paternalism, transfer the hospital operation to the denominational mission board. Erb's proposal was approved at the 1950 PCC sessions, although some Oregon leaders did not support the transfer. Omar G. Miller in his "West Coast Echoes" thought the PCC board "withdrew" because it "could not reconcile hospital regulation with Gospel principles."[22]

Lebanon Community Hospital as operated by the Mennonite church soon received well-deserved publicity and community acceptance. Several wings constructed later almost doubled the capacity of the original 53-bed unit to 101 beds in 1976. A fully staffed emergency room remained open round-the-clock. Erb retired in 1959 and moved to Kansas. Even while administrator, Erb also served as chaplain. Later chaplains were Millard Osborne and

Donald King. Charity Kropf became director of nursing when the Mennonites began operation of the old hospital in 1948. Both Kropf and Gene Kanagy, who succeeded Erb as administrator, continued in their respective positions in 1976.[23]

The children's home for which PCC Mennonites hoped stayed out of reach for years. A children's welfare committee (or board), first appointed in 1914, placed two Slatter children in the John Yoder home at Hubbard in 1916 and considered an offer of three acres of land and a small house in 1921. An offering at the April 1924 mission meeting became a "nest egg" fund for a children's home. But the board placed children only in private homes until 1929. Then it merged with the Portland mission local board in caring for needy children there for several years. In 1946 the PCC mission board took responsibility for a children's home in Nampa, Idaho, begun in 1939 by Viola Wenger, with partial support from the Nampa church. Gilbert and Iola Lind served as superintendent and matron for as many as nineteen children at one time. The local board purchased property, with plans to construct a building, but even then the count was decreasing. In 1950 the mission board discontinued the home. The era of children's homes was ending, as social service agencies preferred placing children in family homes rather than institutions. In keeping with that trend, an occasional Mennonite family provided foster care for needy children for varying lengths of time.[24]

Several Mennonite groups in Oregon established homes for the aged. They intended that such homes provide care in a comfortable, homelike setting for older members of their churches— persons without families able to care for them. But increasingly, others than Mennonites also came. Mennonite homes opened at Albany and Dallas in 1947. Coincidentally, both were dedicated on July 27.[25]

Long before that, as early as 1921, some PCC Mennonites had urged having an old people's home in the West. By 1941 a resolution spoke of growing concern because their "needy old people [were] largely dependent on county or other unfavorable sources for their support." In 1944 a committee (which included a Harrisburg member, because that congregation so strongly promoted an old people's home) began making plans. A year later the PCC made it the mission board's responsibility. The board agreed on a site near Albany instead of options near Harrisburg, Hubbard, or Sheridan.[26]

After churchwide solicitation of funds, construction began by 1946 with Frank Kropf of Harrisburg as chairman of the building committee and superintendent of construction. Oliver Schmucker donated a building site of seven acres, three and one-half miles southeast of Albany. What developed was a U-shaped building that would accommodate twenty-four residents. The visionaries saw the home as partially self-supporting, with gardens to provide vegetables and animals for meat and milk. A chicken house and a hog house were among the first buildings, and at one business meeting the board took an offering totaling $51 and instructed the treasurer to pay for a cow out of the equipment fund. In early 1947, as construction neared completion, the board found costs going $4000 above the planned $35,000, with furnishings and equipment to cost about $8000. Appeals for funds continued and promoters noted such useful gifts as "one hundred fine young hens."[27]

The Albany Mennonite Home opened in 1947 with Harold and Myrtle Reeder as superintendent and matron. Beginning in the 1950s the home added a new wing, cottages, and other improvements. In 1976 Henry Becker was administrator of the home, which had capacity of seventy-one residents receiving nursing and residential care and six apartments for independent living.[28]

After the idea grew at a Bible camp in 1946, the Dallas and West Salem MB and the Dallas EMB congregations sponsored the Dallas Home for the Aged. An October meeting at the EMB church furthered the movement. Soon there was a steering committee, then a board, chaired by Peter Pankratz. They first planned to construct a new building, but to save time the board instead purchased a property on the outskirts of Dallas. For $8500 it acquired five acres of land with a good old house which needed only a few alterations before the July 27, 1947, dedication and open house. On August 1 the home opened with four guests. A year later there were eight. A Mrs. Thiessen (GC) served as caretaker. On January 1, 1954, after the other congregations asked to withdraw from the corporation, the Dallas MB congregation assumed full responsibility and soon changed the name to Dallas Rest Home. That summer Herman D. Wiebe became administrator, assisted by his wife, Elisabeth. The home expanded in 1952, adding an L-shaped building. By 1960 the old structure had been razed and a new wing extended over that site. Subsequent additions raised the capacity to 115 in 1976, and the home offered both nursing and residential care. Like the Mennonite home at Albany, the Dallas home became a leading care facility in its community.[29]

In the 1950s PCC Mennonites established the Rock of Ages Mennonite Home near McMinnville, attempting to make the best of a previous failure. The Portland rescue mission farm and home did not serve well as a rehabilitation center for rescue mission converts, so the mission board decided to convert it into an old people's home for men who could pay their keep. They reserved several rooms for "worthy converts" from the rescue mission. However, before the opening, the board decided to accept both men and women. The home accommodated sixteen guests. The first two arrived soon after it received its state license in November 1956. Dedication services were on June 30, 1957. John and Elvina Ratzloff served as first superintendent and matron.[30]

In the next years the Rock of Ages Mennonite Home expanded services but did not prosper. A nursing wing in 1960 and later alterations increased the capacity to twenty-eight, but marginal financial operations and often inadequate staffing, due to low wages, jeopardized its survival. In October 1972, after the state required a costly sprinkler system to be installed by January 15, 1973, the mission board accepted a local board's recommendation that the home be closed by the end of the year. In the next months, wavering negotiations produced an agreement between the mission board and the Bible Mennonite Fellowship in which the home passed to the latter. In 1976, the Fellowship completed the extensive changes necessary for the home to receive state licensing for twenty-eight guests. It reopened with Ralph Holderman as administrator.[31]

The hospitals and homes which Oregon Mennonites operated combined compassion and mission. In all three homes for the aged, local or valley congregations conducted worship services. Staff members led in daily devotions or ministered to individual residents. On occasion, a resident might accept Christ as Savior and be baptized into church fellowship. Mennonite attempts to provide compassionate, high-quality care for residents helped renew their reputation from whatever tarnish may have remained from their refusal of military service.

Recreation

Early Mennonite camping in Oregon was a part of mission outreach. In 1929 Allan Good of Portland first took children away from their crowded urban environment for a week or two and provided outdoor living along with Bible instruction. Except for several years in the 1930s, this program continued through the 1960s. First the Erb brothers, then Sam Miller, and finally Ralph Shetler provided camp space on their woodlands or farms south of Portland. At a minimum, the camps included only the land to which Good and successors hauled tents, stoves, and other necessary equipment. At best, floors were constructed for tent foundations, and a "power line" was strung to the site. On the Shetler property, a kitchen-dining facility replaced an earlier cook shack. With few exceptions only Portland children took part in these camping programs, although in later years children from the owner's congregation usually attended, too.[32]

While camping for Portland children received wide support, youth camps for teens and young adults from other PCC congregations generated considerable caution and occasional opposition. The PCC and Christian Workers' Conference executive committees, with PCC bishops, planned the first weekend camp, held on the wooded WMS campus, July 8-10, 1947. However, controversy arose about a camp which the Willamette Youth Fellowship (WYF) officers and sponsors planned the next year for June 21-28 at Camp McGruder, a Methodist facility on the coast. The WYF was an unofficial organization for social and spiritual fellowship in which the youth of most PCC congregations participated. Respected churchmen Paul Erb, editor of the denominational organ, *Gospel Herald,* and John R. Mumaw, new president of Eastern Mennonite College, were speakers, and Erb was director. Even so, some PCC leaders remained distrustful. One bishop objected to the campground, pictured in a grove of trees on the attractive announcements, because of a biblical reference to groves where persons worshiped idols. The committee printed new programs, but questions arose also about recreation and adult supervision in a faraway campground. Only two congregations announced the camp and encouraged their youth to participate. Still, from fifty to sixty young people enrolled and weekend attendance approached one hundred—a bittersweet success for the planners.[33]

Youth camping continued to raise questions and concerns. Some PCC leaders wished camps to be held at WMS, but except for several years before 1956 or 1957 without youth camps, they continued at developed campgrounds at the coast or in the mountains. About 1967 the location shifted to Drift Creek Camp (DCC),

Cliff Lind

Elvon Kauffman singing with children at Drift Creek Camp about 1971.

a new Mennonite facility in the Coast Range. By 1975 attendance had become small, only thirty-one. Attempting to attract more youth, sponsors announced a retreat during Christmas vacation instead of a camp for 1976.[34]

Camping for juniors developed differently, at the initiative of several congregations. In the first years quite a few campers came from mission Sunday schools and non-Mennonite homes. But Mennonites valued the experience for their own children, too. Paul Yoder and people from the Albany congregation, with interested persons from Zion and Fairview, conducted a one-week summer camp in July 1951 at White Branch Camp, about sixty-five miles east of Eugene, just off the winding, scenic McKenzie Highway. Seventy-one children between ten and fourteen attended. Seventeen of the twenty-one who accepted Christ were children from non-Mennonite families. This junior camping program expanded in later years with over one hundred campers divided by age into two camps. In 1964 the junior camps moved to the new facilities at DCC and became an integral part of its program, usually with three camps each summer. By the mid-1970s children just out of third grade participated. Because of concerns among some people about whether the child evangelism approach to camping was right for the younger children, the focus had shifted before 1976 to include themes of biblical teaching appropriate to the age level of the various campers.[35]

Although Portland Mennonites had hoped that the new Alder Creek Camp on the Shetler property would "have a place on the map as THE camp in the green mountains of Oregon," within four years a grass-roots camping committee began searching for possible sites for another new Mennonite camp. They wanted a permanent camp site, bigger than the beautiful little campground near the Shetler home, one designed for institutional use. In the previous two decades, Mennonite camping programs and facilities had sprung up all over the country, and Oregon Mennonites joined the enthusiastic movement toward expanded programs and owned facilities.[36]

The unofficial group of interested Mennonites grew and in 1960 they organized the Mennonite Camp Association of Oregon, Inc., independent of the PCC. They chose a camping committee, which also became the first board of directors, composed of Claude Buerge, Orie Conrad, Ben Kenagy, Earl Kennel, and David Mann. The association decided on an unimproved site of twenty-five acres on Drift Creek, about eleven miles inland, by road, from Lincoln City. Drift Creek Camp developed slowly, but dedicated volunteers gradually cleared land, built an access road and a second bridge (after the first one washed out), and installed a power plant so that major construction could begin. Plans called for a large, three-story A-frame lodge, a caretakers' cabin, six cabins to accommodate twelve campers each, utility buildings, and play fields and hiking trails. Memberships and donations financed the construction and related loans. Individuals and groups contributed money, labor, materials and equipment.[37]

Drift Creek Camp began a summer camping program in 1964 and gradually developed its facilities for year-round use. The association sponsored junior and youth summer camps as well as occasional camps with such emphases as family, music, and fishing. The first several summers, with temporary facilities, camping was somewhat primitive. Construction of the lodge began by the fall of 1966 and within several years Mennonite congregations, Sunday school classes, and other church and family groups began to rent the camp for retreats and reunions. Lynford Hershey, with his wife, Jeanie, served as first camp director, from 1966 to 1970, and Amos and Maxine Stoltzfus were the first caretaker-business manager couple, beginning in 1970. After Cliff and Hope Lind directed junior camps for three summers, 1971-1973, the board hired Ken Roth as full-time director and acquired caretaker couples on a voluntary service basis. Roth and his wife, Myrna, served until August 1979. Dave and Marjorie Nafziger served as caretaker couple at the end of 1976.

By then use had gradually increased to include 3,665 campers in fifty-four groups, 183 days of the year. Among the groups was Operation Cop-Out, a program for juvenile offenders and emotionally disturbed boys which the camp and Lincoln County had first jointly sponsored and operated in 1974. It expanded in 1976 to include girls.[38]

Other Mennonite groups in Oregon also developed camping programs. Most congregations that withdrew from the PCC in the 1960s did not support Drift Creek Camp, but through the BMF they sponsored junior and youth camps at rented facilities. In 1941 Oregon's GCs started youth retreats, also called institutes, which included Bible instruction, recreation, and fellowship as did many camping programs. A retreat in the mid-1940s at Twin Rocks on the coast included Bible classes for both high school and college age people. Ninety-six persons participated. Such retreats continued into the 1950s or longer. GC camps (also called retreats) for children began by the early 1950s. Soon the MBs and EMBs joined them. Often they used Camp Tapawingo or Black Rock Camp, facilities in the nearby Coast Range, and for a time in the 1970s they rented DCC. Amanda (Yoder) Anderson of Portland, who may have participated in Portland's (old) Mennonite camping program as a young person, headed these retreats for many years in the 1950s and into the 1960s. Helen Thiessen of Dallas also served on the staff until she moved away in 1961. In 1956 the Dallas EMBs began to sponsor their own camps for juniors and youth.[39]

■ ■ ■

The institutions which Oregon Mennonites established all responded in some way to the culture or needs in their larger world. Schools protected students from its evils. Hospitals and homes dispensed mercy for its needy, along with medicine and security. Camps purposed to integrate teaching for the mind, salvation for the spirit, and recreation for the body, in settings of natural beauty where campers could be invited and strengthened to follow Jesus in the larger world. The institutions also drew Mennonites together into cooperative communities. Though individuals often stood out as innovators, supervisors, and supporters, they channeled their leadership through the sponsoring constituencies.

The larger vision for Oregon Mennonites continued to mingle their concerns for the spiritual nurture of their own people with their commitment to meet human need elsewhere in its varied forms—in mission and service, in daily contacts with their larger world, in efforts to promote peace, and in their institutions of education and mercy. Both elements of the larger vision offered possibilities for relating Oregon Mennonite groups to their larger denominations and to each other, and for turning strangers into friends.

PART III
The Ongoing Community of Faith

How Mennonites related their individual faith to their corporate commitment varied from group to group, from time to time. Even when individualism threatened a church community, Mennonites who worshiped and worked side by side formed local and overarching communities of ongoing faith. Within such communities as their larger denominations, Oregon Mennonites could clarify their identity and acquire resources enabling their local communities to grow in strength and commitment. Their larger vision was to equip their people with inner spiritual resources in order for them to offer their hands and purses to meet human needs. It helped them look over and beyond divisive differences, whether viewed as primary or petty, to continue as communities of sometimes vibrant, occasionally faltering, faith.

In their relationships with sister Mennonite groups and with congregations of other Christian traditions, Oregon Mennonites could test their understandings and discover and share common bases of faith and practice. Certainly such relationships posed risks. Frequently individuals switched loyalties to a different community. But those who offered their sister groups respect and fellowship often learned that the benefits outweighed the risks. Oregon Mennonites who participated on committees and other aspects of denominational life helped strengthen relationships between their congregations, regional conferences, and larger church bodies. Many Mennonites in Oregon also developed increasing respect for other Christian traditions, sometimes so much that their new tolerance jeopardized their commitment to Mennonite ways.

Mennonites and persons in related groups who migrated to Oregon in 1876 and succeeding years could hardly have dreamed of the changes which their faith descendants would experience in the years through 1976. Rapidly accelerating change by 1986, perhaps more change than earlier Mennonites had experienced in half a century, continued to challenge Oregon's Mennonites. Though groups differed in how they practiced their faith, all continued their commitment to follow Christ faithfully.

Chapter 13

Oregon Mennonites: Strangers and Friends

Oregon Mennonites' relationships, both among themselves and with others, ranged from estrangement and disagreement to friendship and cooperation. A few Mennonite groups remained relatively isolated and aloof from each other. Occasionally, deteriorating relationships generated new congregations, of the same or another conference or denomination. Oregon congregations withdrew from the PCC and before 1976 several congregations in neighboring states also left the PDC (GC). Yet most cooperated with other Mennonites at certain times and for particular purposes. Even the most reserved groups occasionally had such contacts. In the creative tension between individualism and church community, relationships could either disintegrate or strengthen.[1]

Sometimes two neighboring congregations developed a reputation for squabbling. Ervin Beck, a Mennonite college professor, learned of a Mennonite folk story passed around in Oregon. Someone asked what caused two particular congregations to be "in a state of feud most of the time." A member said, "Well, we really don't remember what it was, but we're not going to forget it!" A grain of truth nurtures such stories. Feelings of estrangement can pass from one generation to the next unless individuals exercise Christian love to transcend their differences.[2]

Between Conferences and Denominations

All Oregon Mennonites related to their larger church bodies, though some felt a closer kinship than others and such kinship varied in strength. Oregon's OMs relied strongly on their denominational general conference (OMGC) after it organized in 1898, and on the countless preachers who visited them. Often they based their own doctrinal statements and discipline standards on OMGC position papers. A few leaders of denominatonal stature pastored

Oregon congregations, and Oregon contributed a few major thinkers or theologians of its own to the larger denomination. Examples before 1976 included Millard Lind, Mennonite seminary professor and author, and Wilbert R. Shenk, Mennonite missiologist and missions administrator. Oregon people willingly served on denominational committees and boards. Their contributions to the larger church via such group dynamics dare not be discounted. Some Mennonites left Oregon to teach in Mennonite colleges or other Mennonite schools elsewhere, influencing younger generations of Mennonites. A few Oregon writers wrote for denominational publications. In spite of their small numbers, Oregon Mennonites may well have contributed proportionately as much to their denomination as have those in some states with much greater Mennonite concentrations.[3]

Though congregations which separated from the PCC in the 1960s had lost trust in the OMGC, the PCC reaffirmed its support for OMGC, which in a 1971 denominational restructuring became simply the "Mennonite Church" (MC). A new relationship formed western regional conferences into Region II. However, David Groh, editor of *Missionary Evangel*, noted great distances which prevented frequent fellowship, wide regional diversity in race and culture, and the lack of an institution or "large church agency around which to rally." Mission, Groh asserted, was the only cause strong enough to hold the new region together. In 1975 Stanley Weaver of Arizona began serving as Region II missions field worker to help mission agencies and congregations in the region become aware of opportunities for outreach and discover how to meet such needs.[4]

The new MC structure could not overcome Oregon's distance from denominational centers of thought and from the larger concentrations of Mennonites. Even in the jet age, distance isolated and insulated them more than eastern folks realized. Though church leaders occasionally flew to Oregon for a day or two of conferences and consultations, and Oregon Mennonites flew east to work on committees and boards, Oregon remained on the far edge of the continent. By the time the morning sun reached Oregon and roused people out of bed, eastern Mennonites were ready for their morning coffee break. Young people who drove across the country to attend a Mennonite college learned how far away Oregon really was. Pastors who moved to Oregon from east of the Mississippi discovered the vastness of the West and the smallness of Oregon's

Mennonite population. In 1974, James M. Lapp, pastor at Albany, envisioned the church occasionally sending an "apostle" to Oregon and other out-of-the-way places, someone who could "spend extended periods of time in a local area," perhaps two or three months, and help believers "reflect on who they are and where they are going." Oregonians themselves initiated such ministries, in modified form, and brought Paul and Alta Erb to Portland for over three weeks early in 1974 and J. C. Wenger to Portland, Zion, Salem, and WMS during the three-week seminary interterm in 1976.[5]

Mennonites who withdrew from the PCC in the 1960s and sympathetic others valued relationships with a larger group of like-minded people. In 1961, Harrisburg, Porter, Tangent, and the yet-unorganized Ballston congregation joined with several small congregations in Western Canada to organize the Northwest Fellowship of Unaffiliated Conservative Mennonites. This fellowship was not a legislative body, or a quasi-conference as the later Bible Mennonite Fellowship became, but a forum to exchange views and discuss issues. From the BMF, which organized in 1967, Lloyd Kropf and Melvin Paulus from Oregon spoke at the first annual nationwide Bible Fellowship Meeting in 1972, in Elkhart County, Indiana. Oregon speakers in later years included Maynard Headings, Jim Eigsti, Marcus Lind, and Dwight Strubhar. All participants wished to conserve elements of teachings and practice of earlier days which much of the Mennonite church no longer emphasized.[6]

Unlike OM congregations and their regional conferences, GC congregations were always basically independent in relation to their denomination. Desire for fellowship and commitment to mission formed the basis of their cooperation, in the spirit of the descriptive quotation, "In essentials unity, in nonessentials liberty, in all things love." Samuel F. Pannabecker, one of their historians, noted wide diversity in thought and patterns of life that this produced, including a "rather free borrowing" from non-Mennonite religious movements. This characterized Oregon's GCs, whose ministers often were trained in Fundamentalist Bible institutes. The ministers were men devoted to Christ, but their education tended to minimize a sense of church community, whether congregational or denominational, while they emphasized individualized religion. A member of the PDC evangelization committee wrote in 1948 that they were not particularly interested in beginning a Mennonite church in the Foster/Sweet Home area but rather in "doing real missionary work—helping boys and girls, men and women really find the Lord Jesus Christ." Such separation of salvation from the church community reflected their closer affinity with Fundamentalism than with the historic Mennonite vision of salvation within the community.[7]

But GC leaders continued to visit Oregon and often helped strengthen Oregon's relationships with the denomination. H. A. Fast, a Bethel College professor and writer on biblical teachings on peace, spoke on war and human conflict at the 1964 ministers' conference. At various times persons such as Orlando A. Waltner, the denomination's executive secretary, spoke and listened and interpreted denominational positions and concerns. By the mid-1970s, PDC president Elmer Friesen of Portland observed new loyalties developing in the conference toward Mennonite principles of faith. He thought that having more western Mennonites on denominational commissions helped to strengthen their Mennonite beliefs and relationships.[8]

Oregon's MBs were even more isolated from their larger church and its PDC. They were also a smaller minority in their church than were Oregon's GCs. Otto Bier of Dallas acceded some credibility to the charge that his congregation "had maverick tendencies regarding M.B. distinctives." However, he insisted that "close ties were always maintained with District and General conferences; and the M.B. confession of faith, generally, served the church as guide in faith and practice." Yet Oregon's MBs, in emphasizing evangelism and mission outreach, tended to downplay their Mennonite connections. Thinking that a denominational name was difficult to "sell," both the Salem and Eugene congregations chose names without it but retained their MB affiliation as a secondary identity. Nevertheless, Oregon's MB congregations participated in their PDC, and Dallas and North Park received significant assistance in their early years. Denominational leaders and educators helped nurture their relations with the larger church. Men of churchwide stature who served an Oregon congregation on a regular or interim basis included Lando Hiebert and Orlando Wiebe, professors at Tabor College, and Hiebert's father, N. N. Hiebert, a former missionary to India.[9]

Oregon's smaller groups also related to their larger churches, some more closely than others. The Dallas EMB congregation, largest in the denomination, had close ties with its larger body. So did Liberty Gardens. In 1976 the Dallas pastor, Pete Unrau, served as conference president. The EMB periodical *Gospel Tidings* and the annual July conferences and February workshops helped unite its members and congregations.

Oregon's two small BIC congregations were members of its Pacific Conference, and news items about them appeared occasionally in the BIC organ, *Evangelical Visitor*. However, both emphasized their neighborhood relationships as community churches.

The CGC (Holdeman) congregation at Scio was isolated from all sister congregations, the closest being hundreds of miles away. But simply to be Holdeman, with distinct attire and restrictive practices, required a strong sense of denominational identity. In addition, participating in denominational mission efforts and disaster service, ministering to young Holdeman men in alternative service in nearby Lebanon, and hosting and visiting others of their people from other states helped the Evergreen congregation feel a part of its denomination in spite of geographical isolation.[10]

All Mennonite groups represented in Oregon except the Old Order Amish provided literature for their congregations and families. They published at least an official magazine, and several published supplementary periodicals, curriculum materials, tracts, books, and pamphlets. Mennonites who used their own denominational literature were more likely to feel a close kinship to the denomination than those who used other materials. The Old Order Amish could rely on their oral culture.[11]

From their earliest years PCC Mennonites supported their Mennonite Publishing House (MPH) at Scottdale, Pennsylvania. However, they did not hesitate to object when they disagreed. Conference efforts in the 1930s to get MPH literature, especially *Gospel Herald*, into each home echoed through the decades into the 1970s. But at times persons such as Orrie D. Yoder lamented "questionable theories" in Sunday school materials, or in particular statements about prophecy. On one occasion, Millard Lind, a son of Oregon who was an MPH editor for some years, wrote something that greatly disturbed an Oregon reader. The reader thought that Marcus Lind, Millard's older brother, had written it. In a public meeting the person severely criticized Marcus. Marcus just listened and did not reply. Millard, across the continent in Pennsylvania, regarded this as brotherly love in action, particularly since the two brothers sometimes disagreed. By the early 1960s some congregations were turning to competing materials of smaller, more conservative Mennonite publishers or to nondenominational publications. But in the early 1970s all remaining PCC congregations in Oregon except Church in the Wildwood used at least one level of MPH Sunday school materials for grade school children, and most used the whole range.[12]

Oregon's GCs and MBs were also urged by denominational leaders to read their own group's publications. In 1942 when Arnold J. Regier was pastoring the Alberta congregation, it was the only Oregon GC congregation on the one hundred percent subscription plan for *The Mennonite*. The editor considered it "a sinful inconsistency" for Mennonite homes to have newspapers reporting on earthly kingdoms and not to have a church paper telling "about the work in 'God's kingdom.' " Promoting the paper helped. A year later, all of Oregon's congregations had at least some members receiving *The Mennonite*. As for Oregon's MBs, in 1940 fewer than one-fourth were reading *Christian Leader,* the denominational organ. Only one other state had a lower percentage. In 1948 a Dallas bulletin insert describing *Christian Leader* and promoting the reading of MB papers may have helped increase its use in that congregation. Oregon's three MB congregations all contributed news items to the periodical through the years, with occasional lapses of a year of more.[13]

Half a continent or more separated most Oregon Mennonites from their church schools, a handicap for young people who wished to study at a Mennonite college. But quite a few did, especially before the depression of the 1930s and in increasing numbers after World War II. Many who attended the academy or college at Hesston, Kansas, considered Hesston College "safer" than Goshen College in Indiana, in both theology and practice. Some graduated but many enrolled in non-degree programs which emphasized Bible training. Most Oregon Mennonites who attended Goshen were from the more liberal congregations. From the 1930s onward, official PCC support for Mennonite colleges was often qualified, punctuated with requests that the schools promote church dress standards and sound doctrine. A few students from Oregon's more conservative congregations attended Eastern Mennonite College (in Virginia), which maintained more restrictive dress standards than either Hesston or Goshen. By the 1960s all three colleges reflected liberal changes occurring within the larger church. This influenced some youth from withdrawing congregations to attend Rosedale Bible Institute at Irwin, Ohio, established by the Conservative Mennonite Conference in 1966.[14]

General Conference Mennonite leaders often urged Oregon young people to attend Bethel College (in Kansas), where, L. J. Horsch of California asserted, "earnest, conscientious" Mennonite youth could get a "thorough collegiate, yet Christian education" [sic]. But Oregon's GC youth more often attended BIOLA, Multnomah School of the Bible in Portland, or a secular Oregon college.

They were also more open to Grace Bible Institute (GBI) in Nebraska, which was an independent Mennonite school with a Fundamentalist orientation. The purpose of GBI was to train young people for full-time Christian service, but it was also a conservative reaction against perceptions of theological liberalism at Bethel. While GBI affirmed its stand "as true and loyal to the time-honored Mennonite doctrines," it accepted ex-military personnel as teachers. Several Oregon pastors, including Harold D. Burkholder and Frank S. Harder, worked at GBI before or after their terms in Oregon, or served on its board of directors. Most Oregon GCs remained distrustful of Bethel. In 1948 one pastor thought that Bethel was doing more to undermine the faith of GC youth than to help them find God's will for their lives. Nevertheless, now and then through 1976 one or two Oregon students attended Bethel.[15]

Some Oregon MB youth attended one of their colleges, Tabor (in Kansas) or Pacific (in California, a Bible institute which became a college in 1960). But more studied at Bible institutes or state schools. Early in the 1900s North Dallas young people started a common practice of attending BIOLA for two or three years. But Oregon MBs did not view Tabor and Pacific College with the caution and distrust that Oregon's MC and GC congregations had toward their colleges, even though Tabor, like Goshen and Bethel, had experienced conflict over religious viewpoints. Unfortunately for Dallas, most of its sizable number of students who attended Tabor or Pacific in the 1950s and 1960s did not return to Oregon, and Dallas lost some of its most gifted people.[16]

The EMBs, with a total 1976 membership in the United States and Canada of under 3,800 in thirty-two congregations, did not have their own school. Instead they cooperated with GBI and other Bible schools or academies. In 1974 three couples from the Dallas EMB congregation studied at GBI. But of the fifty-nine Dallas people studying beyond high school, half were in state colleges.

Most others were in Bible colleges or institutes and several were in liberal arts colleges.[17]

Between Denominations

In their early years Oregon Mennonites were perhaps more open to inter-Mennonite fellowship than were Mennonites in areas with larger Mennonite concentrations. Correspondence in the *Herald of Truth* indicated that Mennonites and Amish mingled frequently with each other and with more recent Swiss and Russian Mennonite settlers. At Dallas, the GCs, MBs and EMBs worshiped in shared facilities or with one of the other groups for varying periods ranging from a few months to a decade or more. Early in the 1900s, P. R. Aeschliman (GC) from Washington preached at Zion (AM), and J. P. Bontrager (OM) filled "appointments" at Emmanuel (GC) "for some time," according to Matilda E. Steckley. In the 1920s to 1940s, Zion and Emmanuel exchanged programs. Now and then an OM minister preached or an OM chorus sang in a GC congregation.[18]

It seems that Oregon's OMs had few if any contacts with MBs or EMBs until the 1950s or later. All were more exclusive than the liberal GCs whose founders had wanted to extend "the right hand of fellowship" to all Mennonite groups. But PCC Mennonites maintained close fellowship for many years with Harrisburg. Through the 1950s annual reports usually noted that Harrisburg ministers who attended were privileged to participate in conference work (speak and vote) as they chose. Harrisburg and some PCC Mennonites, too, had contacts with the BICs. In the late 1940s, a young woman at Harrisburg was receiving *The Sunday School Herald,* a weekly BIC paper. At least by the 1940s and into the next decades, young people from Zion and other Oregon congregations attended high school or college at Beulah (later Upland) College, a BIC school in southern California. Zion both lost and gained members from this association, when its young people married and joined the BIC or brought a BIC spouse to Zion.[19]

Among the Russian Mennonite groups in Oregon, relationships were usually more open and cooperative than between them and PCC Mennonites. Though differences did divide early MB and GC groups at Dallas, the relationships were reestablished within a decade or two. Recent immigration from Russia and concerns to preserve the German heritage combined with isolation to diminish the differences which had separated the Russian groups not so long before. All of them were fluent in the same German dialect, "Plattdeutsch," which contributed to open relationships. (Only Emmanuel's Swiss Mennonites lacked the Russian experience of Oregon's early GC, MB, and EMB groups.) Persons from all three groups attended each other's mission conferences, youth retreats, and other special events, and ministers from one group occasionally pastored a congregation of another group.[20]

Though World War II produced strain among PCC Mennonites in regard to inter-Mennonite cooperation, after the war, inter-Mennonite contacts in Oregon continued among GC, MB, and EMB congregations. It increased between PCC Mennonites and their more progressive cousins. On a congregational level, Zion and Calvary exchanged programs and speakers and shared special occasions. In 1973 Paul Brunner represented the PCC as a fraternal delegate at the PDC sessions and said that "barriers that might have existed in the past [were then] being broken." Inter-Mennonite mutual aid organizations such as Mennonite Aid Plan, headquartered at Reedley, California, helped develop fraternal relationships.

In the spring of 1975 the first Inter-Mennonite Festival of Praise at Salem attracted about one thousand persons. Twelve music groups from MB, GC, and MC congregations participated, and for later festivals EMB groups prepared special numbers. In fall 1975, Oregon Mennonites met at Western Mennonite School to hold the first northwest assembly of West Coast MCC. And Oregon's MC, GC, MB, and EMB congregations cooperatively celebrated the 1976 centennial of Mennonites moving to Oregon. Increasingly, Mennonites who had been strangers were becoming friends.[21]

Contacts with other-than-Mennonite denominations varied. The GCs, MBs, and EMBs were more likely to cooperate in mission Sunday schools, city-wide revival meetings, and vacation Bible schools. But in early years AMs and OMs also had worked in union Sunday schools, attended Methodist services when their community had no Mennonite congregation, and had gone to others' revivals. However, the PCC soon discouraged such relationships and in 1920 considered the "Interchurch World Movement . . . an abomination to the Lord," bringing "many false doctrines into the Church." Yet congregations continued to have occasional contacts with Protestant denominations and by the 1960s PCC congregations helped sponsor city-wide evangelistic crusades in Albany. In the next decade they cooperated with other denominations in peace displays and witness.

In more conservative congregations, Sheridan women participated in World Day of Prayer services with other church women, and Porter cooperated with the local ministerial association to sponsor released-time Bible classes in Estacada. Members of most Mennonite groups, including the BMF, attended Bill Gotthard's interdenominational, Fundamentalist Basic Youth Conflicts seminars in the 1970s. Apparently Northwest Fellowship Mennonites and CGCs did not participate.[22]

■ ■ ■

By 1976, many Oregon Mennonites were more open to relationships with each other and with other denominations than earlier. Mennonites had cooperated in relief work, mutual aid and disaster aid. Oregon GC and EMB missionaries who had worked together in Africa, alongside the MB field, and had sent their children to jointly sponsored schools became good friends. Jeanne Zook, one of those missionaries, judged that their home congregations were "at least vaguely aware" of the inter-Mennonite character of the mission work. The most conservative groups, however, did not participate in inter-Mennonite efforts and events, although even they cooperated at times with other denominations.[23]

With more openness to each other and to other denominations, some Mennonite groups emphasized more strongly than before their Anabaptist-Mennonite history and faith—particularly an enlarged focus on peace. Such emphases attracted persons from other traditions, some of whom became Mennonites. Other Oregon Mennonites became impatient with an increased Anabaptist-Mennonite emphasis and preferred a more Fundamentalist position. While still loyal to their church, they spoke more of the individual's personal relationship to Christ. Their emphases, too, attracted new members of other heritages.

In their second century in Oregon, expanding inter-Mennonite relationships and greater openness to other denominations would both nurture and test Mennonites in their concern to be more faithful to their biblical heritage.

Chapter 14

Following After Faithfulness

The story of Mennonites in their first century in Oregon reflects both their commitment to faithfully follow Christ and God's encompassing faithfulness to them when they failed. A strong cord of spiritual vitality, firmly attached to their faithful God, not only kept them alive but also contributed to their growth. Sometimes the cord wore thin. Frequently it frayed at points of tension. But its core strand of faith remained strong. All Oregon Mennonites agreed that personal faithfulness to Christ was essential but often they did not fully agree on what it meant to live in faith. Amid their disagreements, the independence of individualism frequently threatened community, which was basically a religious concept almost synonymous with the congregation, as Mennonite sociologist J. Winfield Fretz described it. A broad range of cultural and economic influences also helped to define and sometimes limit community. For Oregon Mennonites, attempts to keep individualism and community in balance tested their personal and corporate faithfulness to God.[1]

All of Oregon's Mennonite groups shared a common focus in the Bible as they attempted to live faithfully. They regarded it as God's Word, written and preserved through the centuries. From the Bible they learned of Jesus Christ who brought salvation for all people. In the Bible they found Christ's loving call to follow as disciples, though some groups defined discipleship differently than others. Controversies about the Bible—its reliability and inspiration, its authority and interpretation—erupted within larger Christian circles as Oregon Mennonites plowed land and built meetinghouses, made pickles and scrubbed floors. They listened to some of the quarrels and tossed them back and forth among themselves. At the end of their first century in Oregon they differed more about how to interpret and apply the Bible than at its beginning. But all continued to regard the Bible as authoritative.

Another focus common to most Oregon Mennonites, motivated by their desire to live as faithful disciples of Jesus Christ, was commitment to witness and mission. All except the Old Order Amish and the most conservative Amish Mennonites tried direct means to communicate the good news of Christ outside the Mennonite fold. Success, if measured by converts or new members, was irregular. Most preferred to gauge success by their degree of faithfulness in proclaiming the gospel, though the occasionally impressive numbers of new members were an obvious satisfaction. Denominational and other mission boards helped them witness in distant cultures and lands.

Commitment to service was another characteristic Oregon Mennonites held in common. Though they often served each other, caring for their own widows and orphans or combining work with pleasure at quilting bees and on butchering days, they served others, too. Wandering tramps knew the good and generous Mennonite cooks on their routes, and Mennonites carried food to neighbors at times of death of other crises. When a neighborhood house burned down, they made up boxes of bedding and clothing. They also responded to larger world needs with money, food, clothing, bedding, and even sons and daughters, who served needy peoples in their own lands.

Change of course created stress. Oregon Mennonites attempted to conform their lives to Christ and put biblical teachings into practice. But accelerating change continually challenged their judgments about what was unbiblical. Some challenges came from revivalism and related movements, but most Oregon Mennonites soon adopted the Sunday school and only a few held back from the modern missionary movement. Challenges from secular society made greater strains and influenced them to reconsider earlier precise definitions. Most persons along the way reversed their positions or simply accepted a particular practice they had earlier regarded as unbiblical. Such practices included having telephones, wearing wristwatches, buying auto liability insurance, participating in Social Security, and wearing wedding rings.

For many, such an about-face was multiplied time after time, as changing interpretations of the Bible allowed such accommodation to their contemporary culture. Whether a new interpretation or an accommodation to change came first also was an issue. Some who objected to such changes believed that only after forbidden practices became common did people look for a different biblical interpretation to validate the change. Persons on both sides of an issue might accuse the other of reading into the Bible what they wanted it to say.

Oregon's location in the distant West isolated its Mennonites, contributed to individualism, and handicapped them in understanding and sensing their connectedness with their larger church groups. Some who occasionally attended large meetings in the East were surprised at the size of the Mennonite communities there. One Oregonian who participated in the 1947 (OM) Board of Missions meeting at Atglen, Pennsylvania, wrote, "We saw many Mennonites and thought we could get acquainted with them; but soon found out we couldn't if we stayed there for several years."

Mennonites who traveled to the West from east of the Mississippi or from populous Mennonite communities in the prairie states also expressed surprise. Lester Hostetler, visiting the PDC (GC) in 1928, noted the immensity of distances between Mennonite congregations in the West and "found it necessary more than once to revise" the impressions he had "received from the study of geography in the common school." Later Oregon Mennonites who attended church colleges or had other associations with larger Mennonite centers got over their surprise at the many Mennonites in the East. They understood better their interdependence with their larger church. But Oregon remained a distant state and continued to isolate many of its Mennonites from their larger bodies.[2]

Oregon Mennonites were far from their denominational centers not only geographically but also relationally. They might simultaneously criticize leaders and institutions east of the Rockies and at the same time feel slighted by them. Paul Brunner, PCC secretary in 1975, expressed gratitude that the distance "in mutual trust" between the PCC and the larger church was lessening. But distance in both geography and relationships, as well as limited opportunities in small Western conferences, influenced some of the most gifted non-native pastors to move elsewhere after a time in Oregon. Its natural beauties, mild climate, and friendly people could not compensate for the distance from families and church opportunities across the Rockies or on the far side of the Mississippi. Still, Oregon had influenced them and their subsequent contributions to their larger church. Even after they left Oregon they helped strengthen bonds between Oregon Mennonites and sister organizations farther east.[3]

Distant relationships could and did exist also between conferences not so geographically far from each other. But people of the West often were "different," a quality that both evolved from and reinforced their distance. Joan Didion, a contemporary Western writer, observed that the West "is a different mirage altogether," still a frontier, a land of movers and independent people who disregard class distinctions and social expectations more common in the East. John Naisbitt, analyst of contemporary trends, referred to "a romantic frontierlike quality" of the West. Mennonites, more than ever a part of their larger culture in 1976, reflected this elusive quality, too. Even in the 1960s and 1970s Oregon Mennonites included the movers, persons who left families and friends in proper, well-organized Mennonite communities and found a quality of freedom and informality in Oregon they had not known before. The western mystique invited some Mennonites to be more independent than many of their eastern sisters and brothers might be, nourishing an individualism that diminished their sense of need for strong relationships with their larger groups. At the same time, an element of cultural and religious conservatism held others to traditional ways, even within a western mentality.[4]

Oregon Mennonites, reviewing the miracle of their first century of faith, could rejoice in God's faithfulness and humbly accept their unique spiritual heritage with respect and gratitude. Their history gave them a memory. It permitted them to build on truth of past generations, to turn from evident error, and to glimpse their connectedness with the past and their responsibility to future generations. While they remembered past failures and sins, the most humble could reflect that even in their full commitment to live in God's will, no one person or group among them could know the total infallible will of God. Individualism, which militates against humility, tended to lure Oregon Mennonites away from their memory and dim their learnings from history. A challenge for second-century Oregon Mennonites is to refresh their memory and review the distant past and dominant present with renewed Christian humility.[5]

In 1986, ten years after the Mennonite centennial in Oregon, as this history neared completion, separation between some Oregon Mennonite groups held firm but other groups had become more open to new or renewed relationships. Joint PCC and PDC (GC) sessions in June 1986 evidenced increasing fraternal relationships, and the majority of PCC delegates favored openness "to discovering any joint means of cooperation with the other West Coast Mennonite conferences," though several opposed it. The Peace congregation had joint membership in the PCC and PDC (GC).[6]

Both the PDC (GC) and the PCC lost and gained Oregon congregations after 1976. In 1986 only three of the PDC's previous five congregations remained as members. Emmanuel and Sweet Home Community Chapel had withdrawn. But a new congregation had begun in Clackamas. As for the PCC, of its seventeen Oregon congregations in 1976, Blaine, Cascadia, and Church in the Wildwood disbanded or withdrew within the following decade. But three small Hispanic congregations in Oregon joined the conference, the first significant intercultural development in decades. Of several other new congregations which also joined the PCC, only Ranch Chapel remained a member in 1986. None of the other Oregon Mennonite groups lost or gained congregations in those years.[7]

Several joint endeavors drew Mennonite groups together in new ways. The MCC Oregon Fall Festival, an annual benefit celebration which began in 1984, gathered support from most Mennonite and Brethren in Christ congregations, though most of the more conservative unaffiliated people did not take part. A few members of the Apostolic Christian Church east of Salem also participated. Several of the groups held joint conferences to promote curriculum materials, peace emphases, and service opportunities.

As Mennonites progress in their second century in Oregon, where will they find their identity? What will be their mission to Christianity and to secular society? Will their identity command their mission? Or will their mission and what they do in response to their calling give them their identity? Can they separate identity and mission? At times Oregon Mennonites will need to consider formally the source of their identity and the focus of their mission. Searching for identity can help individuals and communities sense anew their worth, but a person or a people can establish an identity only in relation to other persons and in the context of their history. Obsession with identity can cause persons to overlook the worth of another, just as obsession with mission can influence them to neglect their own worth and its nurture. Lewis B. Smedes wrote that promises establish a person's identity. A promise to pay a debt, be faithful to a spouse, or meet a church membership commitment gives identity and at the same time values the worth of another person or a people. Promises merge identity and mission. Most of the time, even while they sing together or wash the church windows, give money for missions or serve in soup kitchens, Christians will informally express their identity by the way they carry out their mission.[8]

Past experience and practice suggest that Mennonite identity will come in part from the balance between the individual and the community. Individual choice can degenerate into a self-centered individualism, a commitment to personal fulfillment at the cost of church and family relationships. On the other hand, community can reduce itself to an authoritarian order of legalistic obligation. Individuals who covenant together in the power of the Spirit of Christ and in mutual submission and shared responsibility can guard against both the secular individualism that threatens Christian community and the dogmatic regimentation that stunts Christian individuality.

Within their faith communities, Oregon Mennonites will need to define the roles and nurture the gifts of pastors and other servant leaders, including women, and to reinforce the responsibility of each member as part of the body of Christ. They will consider how to be a community of faith amid such changing family structures as broken marriages and within the limitations of time and energy when both parents of a family work outside the home. Questions about human sexuality will challenge their communities of faith. Mennonites will decide how to practice stewardship of their money—whether personal desire and convenience are more important than the church at worship and witness. And they will choose whether to respect or disregard the earth and its atmosphere for future generations.

Part of the Mennonites' mission will be to integrate salvation, peace, and wholeness (sometimes called shalom) with the needs of their neighbors, their country, their world. Their unique heritage calls them to proclaim a salvation that not only prepares the soul for heaven but also offers hope and healing for bodies and spirits broken by hunger, injustice, repression and war. They will consider changes that will strengthen their witness as they invite persons to faith. They will decide when to accommodate to and when to demonstrate against the claims of government. They will consider such issues as paying war taxes, participating in military forces, accepting or denouncing the nuclear arms race, and serving in government and other political activity. They will choose whether to support a civil religion which attempts to impose selected Christian values on a secular society by what may be unchristian methods, under the guise of Christian faith. And conversely, they will consider to what degree and by what means they will pressure government to espouse their own selected Christian values. They may question the differences between political liberals who decry militarism but endorse abortion, and political conservatives who protest abortion and support militarism. Some will respond to both dilemmas out of an awareness of the contributing greed, injustice, poverty, and despair that influences the issues. In their hospitals and institutional homes, they will face advanced technologies that require ethical decisions about the beginning and end of life, as well as its quality in between.

Increasing diversity among Oregon Mennonites will complicate their search for identity and their definition of mission. Intercultural relationships, particularly with Hispanics and Asians, will inject new challenges and insights. Developing urbanization and the entrance of more persons into the professional world will add other new complexities. Varieties of religious Fundamentalism and other theologies within and without the Mennonite world will continue to woo members of all groups. Changing worship patterns and types of music, especially changes growing out of the charismatic movement, may label or compartmentalize groups or congregations. Some will choose a faith that focuses on personal experience while others will emphasize a discipleship that concentrates on meeting human need. How leaders fill their roles and how they receive training will influence both congregations and conferences and produce additional diversity.[9]

Amid such diversity, what will prevent gross individualism from smothering church community? Can Mennonites who earlier based community on authoritarian biblical interpretations and cultural homogeneity construct a new base from the crumbling mortar of the old? In their search for a common bond to supersede such diversity, they may continue the trend among Mennonites which divides belief and practice into essentials and nonessentials. Association of local communities with their larger bodies will also help balance individualism and community.

In 1986 Mennonite historian Paul Toews appeared optimistic that Mennonites could retain their sense of community in spite of assaults against it. He observed that their lives were not as "corrosively individualistic" as those of many of their neighbors. Considering Mennonite community in its larger sense, he looked beyond the local context at the denominational and even global peoplehood. He found a predominantly religious value system, an appreciation of ethnic strengths, and a social cohesion through more-than-local Mennonite associations, especially those of conviction and service such as MCC. These qualities, he believed, could be "hedges" against a "continuing erosion of the communal elements of Mennonite life."[10]

Second-century Mennonites in Oregon who work faithfully to balance individuality and community will need open hearts, submissive spirits, and clear minds. Their faithful God will continue to work within their diversity to create a unified body of Mennonites and Brethren in Christ, as they come to him in humility, seeking forgiveness for their proud judgment of each other, and resolving to live together in the love of his Spirit.

Notes

Preface

1. The National Geographic Society map of U.S., Sep. 1987, gives U.S. population as 243,600,000; MY, 1988-89, 181, gives all U.S. Mennonite and BIC membership in 1987 as 232,012; *Oregon Blue Book*, 1987-88, 6, gives Oregon population in 1986 as 2,659,500; Oregon Mennonite and BIC membership, based on HL 1987 figures for ME V, was 4,545.

2. Henry Steele Commager, *The Nature and the Study of History* (Columbus, 1966), 86.

Part I

1. Joseph C. Liechty, "Humility: The Foundation of the Mennonite Religious Outlook in the 1860s," *MQR*, Jan. 1980, 5-31; printings include John M. Brenneman, *Pride Vs. Humility*, tr. from German by J. D. Wenger, quote from p. 3; *Pride and Humility, A Discourse Setting Forth the Characteristics of the Proud and the Humble. Also an Alarm to the Proud* (Elkhart, 1873); Daniel Kauffman's books on doctrine repeatedly included pride as a sin to avoid, in relation to attire.

Chapter 1

1. Dorothy O. Johansen and Charles M. Gates (J&G), *Empire of the Columbia* (New York, 1957), 343; HT, Apr. 1878, 68; May 1878, 85-86; June 1878, 102; HW, Apr. 1878, 65, lists the names of early settlers with greater accuracy; HL and LD interview with Grover Lichty, Aug. 18, 1976; survey of ACC cemetery; Marion County Deed Records.

2. Harold S. Bender, "The Anabaptist Vision," a classic statement first published in *Mennonite Quarterly Review*, Apr. 1944, since reprinted in many Mennonite publications including *The Recovery of the Anabaptist Vision*, Guy F. Hershberger, ed. (Scottdale, 1957), 29-54; see also Franklin H. Littell, "The Anabaptist Concept of the Church," and J. Lawrence Burkholder, "The Anabaptist Vision of Discipleship" in above book, 119-134, 135-151. Other sources include Harold E. Bauman, "Forms of Covenant Community," in *Kingdom, Cross, and Community* (KCC), John Richard Burkholder and Calvin Redekop, eds. (Scottdale, 1976), 118-130.

3. Foster Rhea Dulles, *The United States Since 1865* (Ann Arbor, 1959), 51.

4. Philip H. Parrish, *Historic Oregon* (New York, 1958), 37-38; J&G, 20, 29; Richard K. MacMaster with Samuel L. Horst and Robert F. Ulle, *Conscience in Crisis . . .* (Herald Press, 1979), documents early Mennonite responses to issues of war.

5. Gordon B. Dodds, "Oregon History," *Oregon Blue Book, 1983-1984* (Salem, Oregon, 1983), 400ff.; Mrs. Victor P. Morris, lectures on Oregon history at Eugene, 1972; Parrish, Chaps. XIII and XIV; J&G, 208.

6. J&G, 203, 254-257, 287.

7. J&G, 343, figures rounded; 378-381, 383.

8. Allan Nevins and Henry Steele Commager, *A Pocket History of the United States* (New York, 1956), 265; Lally Weymouth, *America in 1876; The Way We Were;* Lewis Paul Todd and Merle Curti, *America's History* (New York, 1950), 466-469.

9. Weymouth, op. cit.; HT, Apr. 1878, 68.
10. *Oregon Blue Book,* op. cit., 6, 224.
11. J&G, 359, quoting Bowles, editor of *Springfield News;* also 360; Marge Davenport, *Northwest Glory Days,* 45ff.
12. J. Denny Weaver, *Becoming Anabaptist* (Scottdale, 1987), synthesizes and interprets recent scholarship on Anabaptist/Mennonite origins and thought; see also Walter Klaassen, *Anabaptism: Neither Catholic nor Protestant* (Waterloo, 1973); *Mennonite Encyclopedia* (ME), 4 volumes (Scottdale and Newton, 1955-1959); J. C. Wenger, *The Mennonite Church in America* (Scottdale, 1966); Fritz Blanke, *Brothers in Christ* (Scottdale, 1961); C. Henry Smith, *Story of the Mennonites,* revised and enlarged by Cornelius Krahn (Newton, 1967); Cornelius J. Dyck, ed., *An Introduction to Mennonite History* (Scottdale, 1967, rev. 1981); William R. Estep, *The Anabaptist Story* (Grand Rapids, 1975).
13. Smith, op. cit.; ME, III, 586-587.
14. Dyck, op. cit., (1967), Chap. 9 and 145-147; Cornelius J. Dyck, "European Mennonite Motivation for Emigration, 1650-1750," *Pennsylvania Mennonite Heritage* (PMH), Oct. 1983, 2-9; John L. Ruth, *Maintaining the Right Fellowship* (Scottdale, 1984), 52-54; Jan Gleysteen, "Before Germantown" and "The Arrival of the Concord," MHB, July 1983, 3-4.
15. Dyck, *Introduction . . .* 147ff.; Wenger, op. cit., Chap. 8; also, regional histories such as Ruth, op. cit.; Frank H. Epp, *Mennonites in Canada, 1786-1920* (Toronto, 1974); Harry Anthony Brunk, *History of Mennonites in Virginia,* Vols. 1 and 2, (Harrisonburg, 1959, 1972); Grant M. Stoltzfus, *Mennonites of the Ohio and Eastern Conference* (Scottdale, 1969); J. C. Wenger, *The Mennonites in Indiana and Michigan* (Scottdale, 1961); Willard H. Smith, *Mennonites in Illinois* (Scottdale, 1983); Melvin Gingerich, *Mennonites in Iowa* (Kalona, 1974); Paul Erb, *South Central Frontiers* (Scottdale, 1974); Samuel Floyd Pannabecker, *Faith in Ferment; A History of the Central District Conference* (Newton, 1968); David A. Haury, *Prairie People; A History of the Western District Conference* (Newton, 1981).
16. ME; Dyck, op. cit., 225-226; Smith, op. cit., 395-396.
17. ME: I, 90-92, 93-97, 254, 700; III, 29; IV, 43-47; Dyck, op. cit., Chap. 13; Elmer S. Yoder, *The Beachy Amish Mennonite Fellowship Churches* (Hartville, 1987), esp. Chaps. 3-6 and pp. 76, 125.
18. Clarence Hiebert, *The Holdeman People . . .* (South Pasadena, 1973); Samuel Floyd Pannabecker, *Open Doors; A History of the General Conference Mennonite Church* (Newton, 1975).
19. J. A. Toews, *A History of the Mennonite Brethren Church* (Fresno, 1975); ME, II, 262-264; David J. P. Smucker comments on reading ms.
20. Wittlinger, Carlton O., *Quest for Piety and Obedience* (Nappannee, 1978), on the Brethren in Christ.
21. Hostetler, *Amish Society* (Baltimore, 1968), 310; Cornelius Krahn, "To Go or to Stay?" GH, Feb. 26, 1974, 174-175.
22. Peter Neuschwander obit, GH, Nov. 2, 1945, 599; HL and LD interview with Rose Roth and Bertha Kenagy, Apr. 9, 1974, at Albany; N. A. Lind, "An Aged Pilgrim," GH, May 4, 1945, 78; HT, Apr. 1878, 68; Lehman, *Sonnenberg—A Haven and a Heritage* (Kidron, 1969), 43.
23. Shirley Yoder, "Rue, Sassafras, Wormwood—The Medical Practice of Delilah Troyer," MsEv, Spr 1976, 11; HH, 6855, p. 535; info from Ethel Snyder of Zion.
24. Omar G. Miller, "A Story of Isaac S. Miller," nd, unpub., copy in author's possession; Edward Kenagy, "The Brick and Tile Industry," *Mennonite Community,* Feb. 1949, 24-27.
25. Krahn, op. cit.; La Vernae J. Dick, *Early Mennonites in Oregon,* Oregon College of Education, master's thesis, 1972, 32; Zion Church (Dallas) records, gathered by LD; ME, III, 647-648.

26. Orie Conrad letter to HL, Feb. 10, 1975.

27. HT: Apr. 1878, 68; May 1878, 86; misc correspondence in HT; congregational records and family genealogies; Conrad, op. cit.

28. Survey of correspondence in HT and reports of misc meetings.

29. Conrad, op. cit.

30. Frank H. Epp, "The Migrations of 100 Years and Their Meanings," GH, Feb. 26, 1974, 172.

31. J&G, op. cit., 249.

Chapter 2

1. HT: Sep. 1, 1883, 264; Oct. 15, 1883, 314; Aug. 1, 1888, 233; June 15, 1892, 189; HL telephone conversation with John Lais, Jan. 21, 1975; HL conversation with Edna Troyer Yoder, Oct. 30, 1966, in Eugene; S. G. Shetler, *Church History of the Pacific Coast Mennonite Conference District* (hereafter noted as CH) (Scottdale [1932]), 12.

2. J. P. Smucker travel journal in MCA; HT: Oct. 15, 1883, 314; Dec. 1, 1889, 362-363; Shetler, op. cit.

3. Shetler, CH; Lane County Deed Records; Amos Schmucker's history of Fairview and HL interview with Schmucker, Apr. 24, 1980, at Lebanon.

4. HT: June 15, 1888, 194; Aug. 1, 1888, 233; Dec. 1, 1889, 362; John Lais info; *The Twelfth Census of the United States, 1890 . . . Vol. 50, Part 7*, p. 490.

5. Barry Fix interviews with Simon Hostetler, Feb. 4, 19, 1976, at Hubbard, transcripts in Zion library.

6. HT: Jan. 1, 1891, 10; Jan. 15, 1891, 26; Feb. 1, 1891, 44.

7. Shetler, CH, 15, 18; HT: Nov. 15, 1891, 347; Margaret Shetler info.

8. Paul Erb, op. cit., 81-82, quoting from minutes for 1883, 1884; Ethel Snyder letter to HL, Jan. 15, 1977.

9. HT: Mar. 15, 1884, 91; Dec. 1, 1889, 362; Paul Erb, op. cit., 86; *Western District A.M. Conference Record . . .* (Scottdale, ca. 1911), 23 (hereafter designated as Record); Barney Fix interviews, op. cit.; Ethel Snyder info; analysis of Zion member who wishes to be anonymous, letter in author's file.

10. HL personal and telephone interviews with John Lais, grandson, fall 1972, at Junction City, and Jan. 21, 1975.

11. HT, Aug. 15, 1893, 258, says there were 49 members but other records support forty; Record, 10-13; Zion's 75th anniversary booklet, 12; Ethel Snyder letter to HL, Feb. 20, 1981.

12. Fannie and John Zook letters to Mattie Zook, May 16, 1896; to "Dear Sister and all good Friends," June 2, 1896; copies of letters in author's possession; punctuation added, spelling corrected.

13. Shetler, CH, 16; Ethel Snyder info.

14. John Zook letter to "Dear Father, Brothers and sisters," Dec. 19, 1895; ME, III, 399-400.

15. ME, IV, 750; info from: Ethel Snyder, John Lais, Wilbur Kropf.

16. Snyder, Lais, Kropf, op. cit.

17. Occasional notes in HT, 1880-1883; MHB, Apr. 1970, 5-6; Barbara Coffman, *His Name Was John* (Scottdale, 1964), 143-145; Don Yoder, "Trance-preaching in the United States," *Pennsylvania Folklore*, reprinted in *The Diary*, May 1981, 9ff.

18. ME: III, 157; IV, 543-544, 1110; MCD, 409; Pius Hostetler, *Life, Preaching and Labors of John D. Kauffman* (Gordonville, 1980), 27-29; Smith, op. cit., 158-161.

19. Erb, op. cit., 80-81, 394-396; A. Yoder letter to "Dear friends," Dec. 14, 1892, copy in author's possession; Ethel Snyder and John Lais info.

20. Kathryn Yoder Miller, "Edward Z. Yoder," unpub. ms., 1975, copy in author's possession; HL interview with Kathryn Yoder Miller, May 13, 1975, at Salem; LD interview with Ralph Lais, May 22, 1975, at Seaside.

21. MY membership summary, 1905-1954, by Clif Kenagy, in author's possession; MY, 1977, 56.

22. Shetler, CH, 28-29; ME, I, 310; Ethel Snyder info; HL interview with Milo and Martha Schultz, Apr. 23, 1980, at Molalla; GW, June 13, 1906, 168; CM, Sep. 1912, 671.

23. First Record Book of Bethel, in possession of Alvin Rogie in 1980; Shetler, CH, 29-31; GH: Apr. 11, 1912, 25; May 29, 1919, 157; MY membership summary; Omar G. Miller letters and info.

24. Info from Amos Schmucker, Fairview historian.

25. Ibid.

26. Mary Erb Gerig notes, originals in possession of Martha Gerig Eicher; Amos Schmucker info; Reminiscences of John Heyerly, Dec. 25, 1950, copy of transcript in author's possession; HL interview with Henry and Bertha Gerig, Apr. 9, 1975, at Lebanon.

27. Schmucker info; MY: 1965; 1977, 61.

28. HT, June 15, 1902, 178; Schmucker info; HL conversation with Dan Widmer, Apr. 19, 1975, at Salem; Jerry Brenneman, "Mennonites in Oregon . . ." unpub. ms., 1953, copy in author's possession.

29. HT: Dec. 1, 1897, 361; Jan. 1, 1899, 9; GH, Oct. 3, 1908, 426; Gerig, op. cit.

30. ME, IV, 543-544; Melvin Gingerich letter to HL, May 7, 1975; Paul Erb, op. cit., 394-396; DJH, 7733, 7752 and related entries; John Lais info; Edna (Mrs. Joe) Reber letter to HL, May 23, 1975; HL telephone interview with John Lais, May 20, 1975, transcript in Harrisburg folder; Hostetler, op. cit., 19, 28-29 as examples.

31. Info from Wilbur Kropf and Amos Schmucker.

32. Wilbur Kropf info; MY, 1977, 62; survey of PCC reports; Harold B. Barclay, "The Plain People of Oregon," *Review of Religious Research*, Spring 1967, 147.

33. Wilbur Kropf info.

34. Ibid.; DJH, 7752 and related entries.

35. Ira Headings letter to HL, May 12, 1975; Barclay, op. cit., 148-149; ME, IV, 358; PCC sec. files, 1950s; Wilbur D. Kropf draft, 9.

36. Lane County Deed Records; HT, Apr. 15, 1889, 121.

37. Shetler, CH, 12, 92; survey of HT correspondence; Lane County Deed Records; Luthy, *The Amish in America; Settlements That Failed, 1840-1960* (LaGrange, 1986), 214-217.

38. Shetler, CH; survey of HT correspondence; HL interviews: Ira Evers, May 1969, at Eugene; Edna Yoder, 1966 and 1967, at Eugene; Orpha (Mishler) Brenneman, May 1967, at Albany.

39. HT, Feb. 15, 1890, 57; survey of HT correspondence; Lane County Marriage Records; Orpha Brenneman quote about Christner; Mabel Conrad letter to HL, Jan. 11, 1977; Chap. 6 tells of the Swiss Mennonites.

40. HT correspondence; Peter Mishler tombstone at Oak Hill Cemetery, Eugene; John Zook letter to "Dear sister and all," May 31, 1896, copy in author's possession; MCD, 248-249.

41. HT, June 15, 1895, 184-185, 186; HL interviews with Ira Evers, John Lais, and others.

42. Survey of HT correspondence, incl. quotes: Oct. 1, 1897, 297; Nov. 1, 1897, 329.

43. HT: Nov. 15, 1891, 348; Aug. 1, 1896, 233; Aug. 1, 1897, 233; family genealogies; Lane County Marriage Records; HL and LD interview with John Lais, fall 1972, at Junction City, when Lais told of Ellie Eash, who left Pete Christner to go to Illinois with Noah Eashes; MCD, 101-02.

44. HT, Oct. 1, 1896, 291; MCD, 43, 210; M. L. Stutsman letter to Ernest E. Lehman, Aug. 26 [ca. 1972], copy in author's possession.

45. HT: July 15, 1898, 217-218; Jan. 15, 1899, 25; Aug. 15, 1899, 250; HL interviews with Orpha Brenneman, John Lais, Esther Fowler (granddaughter of Evers).

46. ME, IV, 190, 385, 543-544; Ira J. Headings information; Herman Hostetler letter to HL, May 31, 1975; info from Wilbert Kropf, Harrisburg bishop; John Lais info; Lorraine Roth, comp., *Family History and Genealogy of Magdalena Oesch and David Kropf* (Kitchener), Apr. 1969.

47. Record, 47, and survey of attendance reports; GH, July 1, 1909, 223.

48. Record, 9, 10; 1913, 5-6; 1917, 3-5; 1918, 6, 1919, 6; PCC Report, 1921; Shetler, CH, 57-60.

Chapter 3

1. HT: Mar. 1, 1895, 73; Nov. 1, 1896, 329; Nov. 15, 1896, 339; Aug. 15, 1897, 249; Erb, op. cit., 61; W. Richard Hassan, "Christmases Recalled 1895 to 1910," *Mennonite Heritage*, Dec. 1986, 37-38, 41-44, info about and from Florence Landis Schertz.

2. HT: July 15, 1896, 217; Sep. 1, 1897, 265; Aug. 15, 1899, 250; Oct. 1, 1899, 299; Dec. 15, 1900, 378; June 15, 1902, 178; J. C. Wenger, *Faithfully, Geo. R.* (Harrisonburg, 1978), 52-57; *Conference Record Containing the Proceedings of the Kansas-Nebraska Mennonite Conference, 1876-1914* (place and date missing from author's copy), hereafter known as KN Record, 106, 111, 117, 124; S. G. Shetler, "History of the Pacific Coast Mennonite Conference," MY, 1916, 25-26, Shetler quote.

3. HT: Aug. 15, 1899, 250; Oct. 1, 1899, 299.

4. HT: Oct. 1, 1899, 299; emphasis in source.

5. HT: Dec. 15, 1899, 378; Jan. 1, 1900, 4; Dec. 15, 1900, 378; June 15, 1902, 178; KN Record, 106, 111.

6. Shetler, MY, 1916, 28-29; HT, June 15, 1902, 178, Brunk quotes; reports of early PDC meetings, LD notes.

7. HT, June 15, 1902, 178.

8. KN Report, 124; Shetler, CH, 94; HT: Jan. 14, 1904, 21; June 16, 1904, 196; July 21, 1904, 236, Hamilton quote; Aug. 4, 1904, 252.

9. HT: Dec. 15, 1899, 378; Jan. 4, 1904, 21; "Account Book of the Mennonite Church," 7-8, in possession of Allen Schlabach in 1978; Shetler, MY, 1916, 28-29.

10. Shetler, CH, 20-21; Maynard Headings reply to HL letter of June 27, 1978; MY membership summary.

11. Shetler, MY, 1916, 26; Shetler, CH, 13, 18-20; Allen Schlabach talk at the Hopewell Historical Meeting, Aug. 12, 1978; HT, Sep. 15, 1901, 287; GH: May 27, 1915, 137; Nov. 25, 1915, 572; Nov. 30, 1916, 641; Sterling Roth reply to HL letter of Apr. 26, 1975; HL visit to Hopewell, 1978.

12. HT: July 15, 1897, 218; Oct. 27, 1904, 346; GH, July 29, 1926, 392; Shetler, CH, 52; Omar Miller talk at Hopewell Historical Meeting, Aug. 12, 1978.

13. PCC minutes, 1914, 9; GH: Jan. 21, 1915, 689, quote; Mar. 18, 1915, 816; Sanford G. Shetler, *Preacher of the People* (Scottdale, 1982), 155-196; 1932 publication date does not appear in Shetler's CH but in GH advertisements.

14. "Account Book . . ." GH: Aug. 5, 1904, front; Aug. 21, 1941, 454; June 5, 1956, 549-50; GW, Sep. 26, 1906, 408; Shetler, CH, 92.

15. HT: June 15, 1900, 185, Mishler quote; June 1, 1901, 170; Aug. 15, 1902, 249, for Detweiler spelling; Jan. 14, 1904, 21; Oct. 27, 1904, 346; Aug. 24, 1905, 268; GW, Sep. 26, 1906, 408, Kulp quote; info from John Lais; Shetler, CH, 52-54, 68, 71; GH: Jan. 21, 1915, 689; June 29, 1916, 232; Shetler, MY 1916, 26; Floyd Emmert talk at Hopewell Historical Meeting, Aug. 12, 1978.

16. HT: Apr. 1, 1897, 195; Aug. 1, 1899, 250; Oct. 1, 1899, 299; June 15, 1902, 178; Dan Widmer, op. cit.; Brenneman, op. cit., 29, 42; Shetler, MY 1916, 28;

Shetler, CH, 21; Luthy, op. cit., 214, 217. Ezra Burkholder and wife, Ada, said by Shetler to have lived in Eugene before moving to Albany and becoming charter members there, are recorded in Bethel Church records—she was received by confession 3-13-1921, he was baptized 2-17-24; his obit in Sep. 21, 1938, GH, 543, says he and Ada moved to Oregon in 1900. However, his daughter Grace (Mrs. Floyd) Emmert, b. at Peabody, Kansas, Dec. 1898, said in letter to HL, Apr. 24, 1984, she was eight months old when they moved to Albany.

17. Shetler, MY 1916, 28; notes by Katie Widmer Burck, provided for HL by Viola Kropf about 1975; GH: Sep. 16, 1909, 892; Feb. 20, 1909, 745; Sep. 16, 1909, 392; MsEv, July 1952, 12; Brenneman, op. cit., 38.

18. Claud M. Hostetler, "Biographical Sketch of Bishop John P. Bontrager," MsEv, July 1949, 1, 11-12, quote p. 12; GH: Oct. 26, 1911, page not noted; May 29, 1919, 152; Nov. 6, 1919, 584-5; Aug. 9, 1949, 789; HL interview with Floyd Whitaker, Apr. 9, 1975, at Albany.

19. Orpha Brenneman and Florence Shank at Albany's 75th anniversary meeting, Jan. 26, 1975; HT, Mar. 22, 1906, 94; GH, Apr. 29, 1915, 72-3; MY survey through 1977.

20. Shetler, MY, 1916, 28; GH, Oct. 26, 1911, page not noted; Orpha Brenneman at 75th anniversary meeting.

21. N. A. Lind memoirs, 250, 255-56, 266-277 1/2, in MCA; GH, June 23, 1921, 23; see Chap. 4 for details of friction.

22. Survey of KN Record, esp. 129-134.

23. PCC Reports in HT: Nov. 22, 1906; Nov. or Dec. 1907, 445.

24. Shetler, CH, 32-34, 93; PCC Report, 1914, 10; HL interview with Mary (Glick) Weaver, May 18, 1975, at Portland; Mary Weaver letter to HL, May, 1975; GH: Oct. 26, 1911; Feb. 25, 1915, 769; Jan. 13, 1916, 685; July 22, 1920, 333; Jan. 25, 1923, 847; June 14, 1923, 223; Firdale Church Record Book (Birky spelled Birkey in this source); Wilbert R. Shenk, comp., *Autobiography of Barbra Weaver Sharer with Family Record* (Elkhart, 1973), 14-15.

25. Shetler, CH, 34; Ray Kenagy story, told to HL, May 15, 1974, at Silverton; Mary Weaver info.

26. Survey of PCC records; Vernon Gingerich at Zion, Feb. 7, 1988; Omar G. Miller, "West Coast Echoes," July 1950 Suppl.

27. Parrish, op. cit., 194, tells of almost three times more autos in Oregon in 1922 than in 1917; survey of FA issues for several decades.

28. PCC Report, 1921, 1-5, quotes, 7.

29. John Lais info; survey of PCC Reports, incl. 1922, 7; 1923, 6; correspondence and reports in PCC sec. files; 1924 constitution and discipline in Shetler, CH, 73ff.

30. PCC Report, 1924, 6.

31. Survey of PCC Reports and PCC sec. files.

32. Info from Mildred Schrock, Sheridan historian; HL conversation with Wilbert Shenk, July 6, 1978; Shetler, CH, 37-39; GH: Sep. 28, 1922, 504; July 5, 1923, 284; Aug. 6, 1923, 409.

33. GH: Oct. 4, 1923, 440; Dec. 25, 1941, 833; Feb. 12, 1942, 977; Schrock info; letter from John Fretz to HL, Aug. 30, 1978; Shetler, CH, 37-39.

34. 50th anniversary program; GH, Jan. 31, 1924, 886, first quotes, reporter unidentified; Feb. 14, 1924, 935, Mishler quote; Mar. 10, 1938, p. 1069, M. W. Mishler article; Schrock info.

35. GH: Jan. 8, 1925, 809, quote; Aug. 20, 1925, 425; May 13, 1926, 126; July 29, 1926, 392; MY: 1926, 52; 1954, 80; 1977, 64; Schrock info; Ray Mishler info to Schrock; Shetler, CH, 37-39.

36. GH: Sep. 28, 1922, 504; June 14, 1934, 232; Oct. 17, 1940, 617; Aug. 28, 1956, 835; Apr. 18, 1961, 376; July 31, 1962, 688; MsEv: Apr. 1946, 5, 8, Oct. 1952, 16; Schrock info; survey of PCC Reports.

37. GH: Nov. 9, 1922, 628; Aug. 14, 1924, 404-405; Sep. 18, 1924, 484; PCC Report, 1924, 4; Robert Lee, "History of the Portland Mennonite Church . . ." unpub., Goshen College, 1958, 17, 45; Shetler, CH, 42, 95.

38. GH: Sep. 27, 1934, 557; Gerig, op. cit.; Lais info.

39. PCC Reports: 1930, 4, 7-8; 1931, 3; GH.

40. ME, IV, 704-708.

41. ME, II, 418-419.

42. ME, II, 418, 547; PCC Reports: 1925, 7; 1928, 3; 1932, 6; 1933, 6; 1934, 3; GH, Feb. 13, 1930, 947; info from Omar Miller; Report of Dec. 7, 1931, meeting of Exec. Comm. and Apr. 1, 1932, report of consultation with Miller, in PCC sec. files.

43. Survey of PCC Reports of the 1940s and 1950s; GH: Oct. 7, 1937, 589; Wilbert Shenk letter to HL, May 19, 1987; HH, 6894 and related entries, 538.

44. 1915 constitution, 12; 1924 constitution in Shetler, CH, 79; Albany Mennonite Church historical records; LD interview with Mrs. Elmer Widmer, Apr. 16, 1975, at Albany; LD manuscript of Grace Mennonite Church, 2; Floyd Whitaker, op. cit.

45. Ernest G. Lehman letter to HL, Apr. 10, 1980; Milo and Martha Schultz, op. cit.; GH: Aug. 15, 1929, 425; Sep. 12, 1929, 501, Henry Lehman quote; Sep. 8, 1938, 509; Mildred Schrock (Sheridan) info; Mrs. Joe Yoder letter to HL, May 5, 1980; Henry J. Yoder, "A Few Glimpses and History of the Molalla Mennonite Congregation," undated paper in Henry J. Yoder notebook, original in possession of Milo and Martha Schultz in 1980; ME, III, 724; Howard King talk at Hopewell anniversary meeting, Aug. 12, 1978; appeal of Molalla people to organize the congregation, in PCC sec. files.

46. Schultz info; GH: Sep. 8, 1938, 514, 517; Jan. 19, 1939, 897; Mar. 28, 1940, 1098; July 18, 1940, 341; Mar. 13, 1941, 1065; Yoder notebook; MY entries appear unreliable; Joe Yoder's annual pastoral report, 1941; E. Lehman letter.

47. MY survey, 1930-1940.

Chapter 4

1. Survey of PCC Reports and records in PCC sec. files, 1940s.

2. PCC Report, 1940, 6; PCC sec. files; HL interview with former members.

3. Robert Yoder, "History of the Zion Congregation," unpub., undated, in the PCC archives; PCC sec. files; Zion Membership Record Book, 44-45; PCC Reports: 1944, 6; 1945, 6; interviews with persons who wish to be anonymous.

4. PCC sec. files; PCC Reports: 1945, 6; 1949, 4; 1950, 3; minutes of Meeting of the Exec. Comm. and Bishops, Dec. 1-3, 1940, in PCC sec. files; Jason Schrock letter to HL, Apr. 30, 1981.

5. Unpub. ms. in PCC sec. files.

6. Survey of PCC Reports in the 1940s; 1940, 3-4.

7. Report of exec. meeting, Dec. 1, 1949, in PCC sec. files.

8. Membership records in the PCC sec. files.

9. N. A. Lind, "Sweet Home, Oregon," CM, Jan. 1941, 17; HL interview with Elmer McTimmonds, Feb. 27, 1981, at Albany; GH: May 30, 1912, 137; Oct. 24, 1912, 473; May 16, 1940, 153; info from Eva Emmert, 1974; Miriam Hooley, "History of the Sweet Home Mennonite Church," read at the Apr. 1980, fortieth anniversary celebration; N. A. Lind, Memoirs II, unpub., copy in author's possession, 39.

10. Lind, op. cit.; Hooley history; Church Membership book, which lists 43; GH: Aug. 22, 1940, 457, 460; Jan. 30, 1941, 940; ME, IV, 668; MsEv: Apr. 1951, 14; Oct. 1951, 13; Jan. 1952, 13; Eva Emmert and Eugene Garber info; PCC membership reports, in PCC sec. files.

11. Hilda Reist info.

12. Ibid.; MWR, Apr. 15, 1976, 5; MsEv: July 1952, 15; Spr. 1976, 15; ME, IV, 934; MY, 1977, 56.

13. GH: Aug. 31, 1945, 417; Dec. 17, 1946, 810; MsEv, Apr. 1949, 7; HH, 1716, 2474, 6800, 6855, pp. 146, 206, 531, 535; Ethel Snyder info.

14. Jerry Brenneman info; GH, Apr. 9, 1942, 40; 75th anniversary talks; pastoral files in PCC archives.

15. GH: May 19, 1938, 153; June 29, 1945, 240; Feb. 11, 1947, 996; June 1, 1948, 524; Bontrager info.

16. Survey of PCC Reports of the fifties.

17. Minutes of meetings, Dec. 1, 1949; Dec. 1-3, 1949; in PCC sec. files.

18. Report to the Ministerial Body, in PCC sec. files; emphasis in original.

19. PCC Reports: 1950, 6-7; 1951, 5; 1952, 5; 1953, 5-6; 1954, 3, emphasis added; minutes of May 16, 1954, and May 31, 1954, in PCC sec. files.

20. Melvin Gingerich, Mennonite Attire Through Four Centuries (Scottdale, 1970), 145-153; Steven L. Denlinger, Glimpses Past (Lancaster, 1985), 8-21, 81-91.

21. PCC Reports: 1952, 5-6; 1955, 2-3; 1957, 3; 1958, 5.

22. PCC Reports: 1951, 3; 1955, 2; 1956, 1; 1958, 5.

23. Melvin Schrock statement with Jason Schock letter to HL, Apr. 30, 1981; PCC sec. files, 1950; Gerig, op. cit.; PCC Report, 1950, 5; for further discussion of the holiness movement, one source is George M. Marsden, Fundamentalism and American Culture (New York, 1980), 93-101, and other sections.

24. Jason Schrock info.

25. Ibid.

26. GH, Jan. 6, 1938, p. 857; Dec. 7, 1939, 773; May 11, 1945, 112; Ernest and Ida Bontrager, "We Got More Than Huckleberries," unpub. ms., revised and updated from MsEv history of Porter, Jan. 1954, 1, 15-16.

27. HL interview with Olive Miller, July 20, 1981, at Estacada; Bontrager history and related info.

28. Bontrager history; GH: Apr. 23, 1942, 85, 89; Apr. 15, 1943, 57; Oct. 14, 1953, 601; Olive Miller info; Kathryn Yoder, "A History of Education Among the Mennonites on the West Coast," 1949, unpub. ms. in MHL at Goshen College; MsEv: Oct. 1951, 11-12; Spr. 1967, 15; Program info; Ernest Bontrager letter to HL, Mar. 26, 1981.

29. MsEv: Oct. 1955, 7; July 1956, 1, 16, "History of the Winston Mennonite Church" by Arlene Hostetler; Oct. 1956, 15; Ivan Headings letter to HL, Feb. 25, 1975, in East Fairview folder; PCC Report, 1953, 4; Roy Hostetler info; David Johnstone, "Winston," unpub. ms., prepared for Missions class at WMS, 1959, copy in author's file; Tim Zook info.

30. MsEv, Oct. 1955, 15; Headings letter; Zook info; Roy Hostetler info; MY, 1977, 64.

31. Rosalie Kentta, "Logsden Mennonite Church," MHB, Jan. 1958, 2; MsEv: July 1952, 10; Oct. 1956, 1.

32. Kentta, op. cit.; MsEv: Oct. 1950, 12-13; July 1951, 17; Oct. 1956, 2; survey of 1955 and 1956 issues; Wolfer appeal, copy in Logsden folder.

33. Info from Betty Dickason; MsEv: Jan. 1958, 13; Jan. 1959, 14-15; GH, Sep. 22, 1959, 787-788.

34. May Larrew's corrected copy of Blaine history, which was printed in MsEv, Oct. 1952, 1, 15-16; Loyd is the correct spelling; GH, June 11, 1946, 233.

35. Larrew info; MsEv: Apr. 1946, 5, 8; Oct. 1952, 16; Jan. 1954, 9; Spr. 1967, 12; Mildred Schrock info in Sheridan file; GH, Feb. 11, 1947, 996; June 10, 1947, 236; Apr. 6, 1948, 331; Aug. 12, 1952, 803; June 8, 1954, 549; MY 1977, 56.

36. Amon Birky, "History of the East Fairview Mennonite Church," unpub. ms., copy in East Fairview folder.

37. Wichita Eagle and Beacon, May 28, 1978, 2F; Birky, op. cit.

38. MsEv: Jan. 1953, 9, 12; Oct. 1954, 1, 15-16; July 1957, 10; Jan. 1959, 13;

July 1959, 10; Jan. 1961, 12; HL interview with Ivan and Ardis Bare, Jan. 17, 1982, at Lebanon; Birky, op. cit.; Ivan Headings letter to HL, Feb. 25, 1975; survey of MY records; HL interview with Harry and Edith Stauffer, Apr. 3, 1981, at Albany; Mildred Knuths info.

39. HL interview with Marjorie Nofziger, Apr. 14, 1980, at Lebanon, and other Nofziger info; Allen H. Erb letter "To Whom It May Concern," Jan. 24, 1956, copy in Lebanon folder.

40. Minutes of meeting, copy in Lebanon folder; Statement of Purpose, copy in Lebanon folder; MsEv: Sep. 1958, 14; Apr. 1959, 8-9; Oct. 1962, 12-13; Fall 1976, 18; Nofziger info, including scrapbook items and undated *Lebanon Express* photo and script; MWR, Jan. 4, 1968.

41. Nofziger info; MY 1977, 56.

42. MsEv: May 1958, 1, 16; survey of MsEv 1961-1969; Ralph Myers info; Record Book #1, 18-20.

43. Record Book #1, 5-6; Book #2, unp.; MsEv: Apr. 1957, 10; survey of MsEv, 1950s and 1960s; Ralph Myers info; MY, 1977, 56.

44. Naomi Sharer, "History of the McMinnville Mennonite Church," 1960, unpub. ms., copy in McMinnville file; Louise Wideman info; spelling according to Amos and Becky Eash; MsEv: Jan. 1958, 13-14; Oct. 1964, 8; Sum. 1966, 14; Win. 1968, 14; Spr. 1969; Win. 1970, 9, 15.

45. Wideman info.

46. MsEv: survey through 1976, incl. Oct. 1954, 11; July 1957, 1, 15-16; Win. 1969, 11; Michael Ruckert, "Plainview Mennonite Mission," May 15, 1959, term paper for Missions class at WMS, unpub., copy in file; HL interview with Perry Schrock, Jan. 17, 1982, at Lebanon.

47. MsEv: survey through 1976, incl. Jan. 1959, 13; July 1959, 15; charter list from Orie Conrad; MY: survey of membership; 1977, 56; Schrock info.

48. Jonathan Zook info; MsEv: July 1951, 14; July 1956, 15; Jerry Brenneman info, Albany file; Western file; Grants Pass file; John Lederach letter to Ethel Snyder, Sep. 11, 1974, copy in Zion file; survey of PCC reports.

49. Survey of PCC Reports.

50. Letters from Porter in PCC sec. files, June 1, 1958, and May 17, 1959.

51. Notes from Aug. 15, 1959, meeting of ordained men, in PCC sec. files.

52. Tangent letter, Sep. 20, 1959; "To the 1959 Session of the . . . Conference," from the Western Mennonite congregation, in PCC sec. files; 1953 Constitution and Discipline, 15; PCC Reports: 1959, 3-5; 1959, 5.

Chapter 5

1. Barclay, op. cit., 147-148; letters in the PCC sec. files from Merle Stutzman and Melvin Schrock of Tangent, Ernest J. Bontrager of Porter, J. A. Birky, and Willard L. Stutzman, between May 6 and May 27, 1960; Theron Schlabach letter to HL, July 15, 1988; Chap. 8 discusses how Fundamentalism influenced Oregon Mennonites.

2. HL conversation with Marcus Lind, Feb. 9, 1986, at Salem; author's experiences, memories and associations in the 1950s and 1960s.

3. MsEv, July 1955, 2, 14-15; Dolores Wolfer Baker info; history read at Oct. 28, 1979, dedication of church building; Lloyd Kropf info.

4. Baker and Kropf info; MsEv: Apr. 1959, 12; April 1960, 12; Oct. 1960, 10; notes from Barbara Garber diaries.

5. Wilma Nisly info in MsEv, Oct. 1957, 1, 15-16, and in response to HL queries, Jan. 20, 1981; MsEv: Apr. 1952, 14; Oct. 1952, 9; July 1953, 10; Jan. 1954, 9; Oct. 1955, 10; Oct. 1957, 15-16; May 1958, 9-10; Sep. 1958, 10; July 1964, 15-16; Oct. 1964, 12; Sum. 1965, 13-14; Spr. 1967, 15.

6. Nisly info; survey of MY records; PCC Report, 1976.

7. World Book 1964; HL memory; John Fretz info; MsEv, July 1961, 11.

8. Fretz info; MsEv: July 1964, 15; Jan. 1965, 15; Fall 1967, 15; MY, 1977, 56.

9. MsEv: survey of 1944-1976; some reports and histories mistakenly give 1942 or 1943 as the starting date; Miriam Hooley's history of Sweet Home, prepared for Apr. 1980 anniversary celebration; Lyle and Dorothy King info.

10. MsEv, Oct. 1963, 10, and other correspondence; King info; survey of MY records.

11. HL, congregational historian; notes from record book of first meetings, recorded by Wilma Kennel, in Eugene files; membership book records; congregational records.

12. HL info; congregational records; MY, 1977, 56.

13. Aug. 31, 1965, report of Bethany group to PCC executive committee, also minutes of meetings, letters, and statements in PCC sec. files; HL interview with Wilmer and Mary Leichty, July 21, 1981, at Albany; David Groh info; PCC Report, 1966, 3; MsEv: Spr. 1966, 11; Sum. 1966, 12; Fall 1966, 12; Leichty info; MY, 1969, 72.

14. Groh info; Leichty info; survey of membership records in MY; 1975 and 1976 figures from official PCC reports.

15. Berniece Kennel info; GH, Mar. 18, 1969, 259.

16. GH, Dec. 30, 1969, 1120; Kennel list; PCC Reports, 1969, 1976; MY, 1972, 11; Paul Burkholder info; Kennel info; in the late 1970s the congregation purchased a chapel at Adair Village, some ten miles north of Corvallis, and adopted the name Prince of Peace Mennonite Church.

17. Congregational records; PCC Reports reflect the year it recognized the ordinations.

18. Appeals and statements from concern groups; minutes of Feb. 17, 1964, PCC exec. comm. meeting; PCC Report, 1965, 3; MsEv, Sum. 1965, 6.

19. Nelson Kauffman letter to Shetler and Yoder, June 16, 1966, with copies to PCC and MC leaders, in PCC sec. files; Nelson Kauffman letter to HL, Mar. 5, 1976.

20. Meeting times from Barbara Garber diaries; PCC sec. files; copy of appeal to 1966 conference.

21. Statement in BMF folder; MsEv: Sum. 1966, 11; Win. 1965, 8-9; Theron Schlabach, *Gospel Versus Gospel* (GVG) (Scottdale, 1980), 112-117.

22. MsEv, Win. 1967, 8-9; PCC Report, 1967, 6.

23. David Mann letter to Howard Zehr, Dec. 12, 1967, in PCC sec. files; Barbara Garber diary notes.

24. PCC Report, 1968 5; minutes of Jan. 27, 1968, meeting, in PCC sec. files.

25. David Mann letter to PCC exec. comm., Apr. 20, 1968, in PCC sec. files; Barbara Garber diary note for May 11, 1968, about an all-day meeting at Sheridan.

26. PCC Reports: 1968, 3; 1969, 1-4; MsEv, Win. 1969, 4-5; Marcus Lind letter to HL, Mar. 18, 1986.

27. Survey of PCC membership records.

28. Copy of letter in author's possession.

29. MsEv: 1964-1966; Osborne continued as editor through Fall 1969; Marcus Lind, op. cit.

30. Copy of letter in PCC sec. file, 1967-1968.

31. David Mann letter to Marcus Lind, July 21, 1967, PCC sec. files, 1967; Millard Osborne letter to Clifford Lind, Nov. 14, 1968, in author's possession.

32. Program of the First Annual Meeting of the Bible Mennonite Fellowship, held at Sheridan on Nov. 8-10, 1968; Clifford Lind notes of Saturday speeches.

33. Letter in author's possession; writer wishes to be anonymous.

34. Survey of PCC Reports.

35. In 1981, at the request of the few remaining members of the Maranatha congregation at Ballston, Marcus Lind assumed bishop leadership there. Maranatha

had never joined the PCC, but it associated with the Tangent-Harrisburg-Porter group for some years and later had more contacts with the BMF. Upon accepting this responsibility, Lind placed his membership there, which then removed him from membership in a PCC congregation. MY, 1977, 56; survey of PCC Reports, 1955-1976; MsEv, Win. 1974, 7; Lind correspondence in Maranatha folder; Marcus Lind letter, op. cit.; survey of BMF programs.

36. Marcus Lind letter, op. cit.
37. PCC Reports, sec. notes, MsEv.
38. Ibid.; PCC Report, 1975, 1.
39. Survey of PCC Reports.
40. PCC Report, 1976; MY, 1977, 56.

Chapter 6

1. Waldo Hills/Emmanuel withdrew from the PDC in 1984; in 1987 the EMB denomination adopted Fellowship of Evangelical Bible Churches as its name.
2. HW, Apr. 1878, 65; HT: June 1878, 102; Dec. 1879, 230; Lehman, op. cit., Chaps. 2-3; J. C. Wenger, notes on ms. draft; Gratz, *Bernese Anabaptists* (Goshen, 1953) 12; Gratz also wrote that several of those named moved to Oregon in 1876, but this date, remembered in 1949 by elderly people in Oregon, does not coincide with Wenger's contemporary account; GH, Nov. 22, 1928, 719; Eunice Deter, *Descendants of Ulrich Steiner . . .* (Morrison, Illinois, 1947), 36; *History of Oregon, Vol. III* (Chicago and Portland, Pioneer Historical Publishing Company, 1922), 577; leaflet, "Seventy-fifth Anniversary of the Emmanuel Mennonite Church," Apr. 22, 1965; Waldo Hills (Emmanuel Mennonite Church) Register, 13, 58ff., 39-40, 34-38, 73b; Bertha Kenagy and Rose Roth, op. cit.; LD research notes; info from Ira Miller, Wauseon, Ohio, and Edwin Riegsecker, Feb. 1987; various congregational records; some of the names had more than one spelling.
3. Daniel J. Steiner speech at the 50th anniversary of Emmanuel Mennonite Church, copy of script in author's possession; Waldo Hills Register, 47; Lewis A. McArthur, *Oregon Geographic Names,* 4th edition (Portland, 1974), 600.
4. Steiner, ibid.
5. HT, May 1878, 86; *Nachrichten aus der Heidenwelt,* May 1879, 35.
6. Perry A. Klopfenstein, *Marching to Zion; A History of the Apostolic Christian Church, 1847-1982* (Fort Scott, 1984), 18, 26-27, 118-119, 247; James O. Lehman, *Crosswinds: From Switzerland to Crown Hill* (Rittman, 1975), 27-30; Harry F. Weber, *Centennial History of the Mennonites in Illinois, 1829-1929* (Goshen, 1931), 36ff., 101ff.; Gratz, op. cit., 114-115.
7. HL interviews, Aug. 18, 1976, at Silverton, with Steve Kauffman and Grover Lichty; congregational records reported by Ernest Werner; Marion County Deed Records, Books 30: 581; 46: 357; 137: 250; Weber, op. cit., 101; author's survey of ACC cemetery.
8. HT: Aug. 1880, 146; Dec. 1880, 217; Sep. 1, 1884, 264; Sep. 15, 1884, 281; Mar. 15, 1892, 88; GH, Nov. 22, 1928, 719; Waldo Hills Register, 54, 68; Bertha Kenagy and Rose Roth, op. cit.; Clayton Steiner, *From Switzerland to Sonnenberg* (Goshen, 1976), 11, 14, 18.
9. Steiner, op. cit.; "Pioneering," a short, undated paper.
10. Kenagy and Roth, op. cit.
11. HT, Oct. 1, 1899, 299; Melvin Gingerich, "The Christian B. Steiner Mennonite Church," MHB, July 1963, 7; John Lais info.
12. Gingerich, op. cit.; John Heyerly, op. cit.; Mabel Geiger Conrad, Jan. 1977 reply to HL letter.
13. Pannabecker, *Open Doors,* Chaps. 3-5, discusses the South German, Swiss, and Russian origins.
14. Emmanuel church register, 201-202, 214; Seventy-fifth anniversary booklet; Dan J. Steiner, fiftieth anniversary speech; ME, I, 229; Pannabecker, op. cit., 81-81.

15. John D. Steiner info; program of dedication service, 1970; church register, minutes of Dec. 26, 1910, annual meeting.

16. Dan J. Steiner, op. cit.; TM: July 22, 1926, 3; May 18, 1943, 16; June 19, 1945, 11-12; John M. Franz statistical info; LD ms.; 1970 dedication program; survey of PDC membership records, 1925, 1944-1976; PDC Reports: 1958, 17; 1972, 17; Wilbert A. Regier reply to HL letter, Mar. 11, 1987; MWR: S. S. Baumgartner, Oct. 9, 1940; Nov. 18, 1976; Mar. 17, 1977, 11.

17. Survey of membership records; LD info from John D. Steiner.

18. LD, thesis, 23-29; LD draft of Chap. 2, 29; ME, IV, 876; HT: June 1, 1882, 170; Jan. 1, 1883, 9; June 1, 1887, 169; Mildred Schrock, *For His Sake* (Gordonville, Pa., 1972), first printing, 126, 128; Reuben Goertz letter to LD, Oct. 31, 1971, in author's possession; Polk County Deed Records, 1882-1892; Edwin P. Graber, *Memoirs of Rev. John Schrag and family* (n.p., 1952), 5-9, 15-16.

19. Story told by Ray Mishler, found in Dick, op. cit., 86-87; also told with variations in Schrock, op. cit., 139-147.

20. Graber, op. cit.; all the early records of J. R. Schrag were destroyed by fire after he moved to Schrag, Washington, according to an Aug. 7, 1970, letter to LD from Schrag's daughter, Leona Gering; Toews, op. cit., 53, 72-75, 139, 366-367.

21. Lane and Polk County Deed Records; HT, June 15, 1891, 85; Dick, op. cit., 37-39; Schrock, op. cit., 153-156; Mike O'Brien, "Alvadore moving into its new church . . ." *Eugene Register-Guard,* Oct. 18, 1969, 2A; PDC minutes, 1896, from LD draft, "The Pacific District Conference. . . ."

22. Schrock, op. cit., 153, 158-159; Lane County Land Records; LD, thesis, 40; historical writings about the Menno congregation, Lind, Washington, comp. by Joe Jantz, 9-21-75; P. C. Jantz, "History of the Menno Mennonite Church," a short unpublished article, nd.

23. O'Brien, op. cit.

24. Polk County Deed Records.

25. Polk County Deed Records; Zion Church register; spelling is variant of Redekop; John Dyck, "The Oregon Trail of Manitoba Mennonites," *Mennonite Historian,* Sep. 1988, 1-2.

26. *Dallas Itemizer,* June 14, 1893, 2.

27. Zion Register; ChrLead, July 1, 1947, 1, 8; Polk County Deed Records.

28. Gustav Schunke, "God's Trailblazer in the West," *1955 Annual* (Baptist), 19ff.; LD draft, 32.

29. LD draft, 33, Schunke, op. cit.

30. PDC Report, 1949, 3, 5.

31. Pannabecker, op. cit., 203; Emmanuel Church register; minutes of 1896 conference, as noted and written by LD; LD ms. of PDC; PDC Report, 1959, 3.

32. PDC Report, 3, 5; TM, Nov. 15, 1960, 736.

33. LD notes from church records; other LD info; family records through 1911, translated from the Zion Church Journal; the church constitution which appears in the journal with the membership record was apparently first written in 1913, according to Jan. 16, 1913, business meeting entry; ME, I, 684; GC statistics, 1914.

34. LD notes from church records and other LD info; Diamond Jublilee History account, probably prepared by Gay Rempel.

35. Neufelt Memoirs; LD info.

36. ME, II, 560; LD info; LD, thesis, 74; Diamond Jubilee History.

37. LD notes from church records; other LD info.

38. Ibid.

39. LD notes from church records; other LD info; LD, thesis, 75; MWR, Nov. 18, 1971.

40. LD info; LD notes from church records; MY (GC), 1939, 41; WE, Mar. 1939, 3; ME II, 560; PDC Reports, 1935-39.

41. LD info; survey of WE, 1934-1939; TM, Mar. 29, 1960, 206; program of dedication services, Sep. 15, 1968.

42. LD info; survey of TM: 1939-1948; June 29, 1948, 2, obituary quotes; PDC Reports: 1940, 206; 1948, 14, for membership statistic (Leisy obituary gives membership as 280); Widmer report in 1939 MY (GC), 41; WE, Oct. 1942, unp.

43. LD info; Jan. 15, 1966, letter to Grace Mennonite from Flickinger, copy in Grace folder; PDC reports, membership survey.

44. PDC Reports; LD info.

45. LD notes of PDC minutes, 1900; 1949 PDC Report, 3; LD notes from PDC minutes name Mishler the first three years; Chris. Widmer, [from Albany], is named as an 1899 PDC delegate; HT: Feb. 15, 1897, 55; June 1, 1897, 169; Jan. 1, 1898, 9; Jan. 15, 1899, 25; Dec. 15, 1899, 378; June 15, 1902, 178.

46. LD notes of PDC minutes, 1896-1901; PDC Report, 1949, 7.

47. LD notes of PDC Reports, unpub. ms. of the PDC history; congregational records.

48. PDC Report, 1949, 3-4; Pannabecker, op. cit., 382-383.

49. LD: notes of PDC Reports, ms. of PDC history, 20, and other info; PDC minutes: 1924, 1938; TM: Jan. 17, 1929, 7; Aug. 13, 1931, 8; Aug. 1, 1939, 13; Alberta directory 1966; MY (GC), 1927; ME, IV, 1057; Mary Lou Cummings, ed., *Full Circle* (Newton, 1978), Lois Barrett chapter about Catherine Niswander, 179; Lois Barrett, *The Vision and the Reality* (Newton, 1983), 137.

50. TM: Aug. 13, 1931, 8; Oct. 1, 1931, 15; July 20, 1933, 2-3; Aug. 6, 1935, 23; Nov. 10, 1936, 22; Feb. 27, 1940, 7; WE, Nov. 1937, 3; 1966 Alberta directory, lists only ten names; MY (GC), 1932, 8-9; LD notes; Cummings, op. cit., 178-180; Barrett, op. cit., 136-137.

51. Survey of membership from PDC Reports; survey of WE, 1945-1959; LD info.

52. PDM, July 1965, unp.; TM: May 27, 1975, A-2; Jan. 27, 1976, A-1, 2; survey of PDC Reports, 1969-1976; LD draft of congregational history.

53. See Chap. 3 for additional background; LD: ms. of Grace, also interview with Mr. and Mrs. Elmer Widmer, Apr. 16, 1975, at Albany; membership book; discrepancies give the charter membership as 17, in TM: Oct. 1, 1931, 15; and 24, in Oct. 29, 1931, 5-6; the latter figure probably included persons added after June 29, before the congregation became incorporated; survey of correspondence and news in TM and WE; survey of PDC Reports for membership.

54. LD: notes of minutes and church board minute book and other info; survey of PDC Reports for membership; survey of WE; E. H. Widmer letters to Albert Epp, Feb. 28, 1968, and Oct. 22, 1968, copies in Grace file; recommendations to Special Church Business Meeting, Oct. 16, 1968; Floyd Whitaker, op. cit.

55. See Chap. 5 for background details; LD notes, apparently from official church record book; ME, I, 495; TM, Feb. 13, 1945, 16; charter list returned with questionnaire, informant not identified; the spelling of Stuwe is uncertain from the handwriting—Margaret Shetler says it could also be Stuve; WE survey; MWR, May 11, 1972.

56. Survey of WE; LD: notes from record book and other info; info from Mendenhall; survey of PDC Reports for membership; pastor's reports, 1968, in Calvary file.

57. PDC Reports: 1948, 7; 1949, 15-16; 1951, 9; 1953, 11; 1954, 20; LD info; TM, May 10, 1949, 9; Ivan Emmert info.

58. PDC Reports: 1949, 15-16, quote; 1951, 6, 21; Ivan Emmert's list of charter members.

59. Survey of PDC Reports/workbooks, 1957-1977; WE, unp.: July 1963, Oct. 1963; LD info; *The New Era*, Sweet Home, Jan. 20, 1972, 7.

60. Survey of PDC records and reports, including WE and PDM; MY, 1977, 60, for Evangel membership; WE, May 1939, 3; LD info in PDC ms.

61. LD analysis, 1975, in her PDC ms., 48-49, in author's possession.

62. Toews, op. cit., 148-149, 202, 450 n. 49; John H. Lorenz, *The Mennonite Brethren Church* (Hillsboro, 1950), 168-170.

63. *Der Sendbote,* May 4, 1904, 286, Helzer obit, says he lived in Portland 18 years; Esther Jost, ed., with Kevin Enns-Rempel, Loyal Martin, Paul Toews, *75 Years of Fellowship; Pacific District Conference of the Mennonite Brethren Churches, 1912-1987* (Fresno, 1987), 10, 34; Lorenz, op. cit., 170; Kevin Enns-Rempel letter to HL, Apr. 22, 1988; Art. of Inc., Nos. 2013, 8461, in Oregon State Archives; HL interview with J. B. Toews, May 22, 1982, at Eugene; J. A. Toews, op. cit., 160; E. Kimbark MacColl, *The Shaping of a City; Business and Politics in Portland, Oregon, 1885-1915* (Portland, 1976), 47, 112, 126, 133, 136-137; Reisbich is also spelled in related sources as Reisbig, Reisdich and Reiswick; membership survey from PDC Yearbooks; Erma Neufeld info with photo—says Sixth Street was a location. In 1988 it is Sixth Avenue.

64. Dyck, op. cit., 106-107; ChrLead, June 11, 1963, 14, obit. of P. C. Hiebert; Enns letter; survey of PDC Yearbooks, translations by Elizabeth Horsch Bender.

65. Survey of PDC Yearbooks to 1940; J. B. Toews, op. cit.

66. Polk County Deed Records; (n.a.), "History of the Mennonite Brethren Church at Dallas, Oregon," ChrLead, July 1, 1947, 1, 8; Toews, op. cit., 139-148; spellings of the same name differ in various sources; *The Chronicle of the Abraham M. Buhler Family* (no biblio. data on author's photocopied pages), 74ff.; Dyck, op. cit., 31; LD draft, 33; Art. of Inc., No. 2034, in state index; Albert W. Warden, Jr., *A History of North American Baptists in Oregon* (Portland, 1956), 23; Bergan also spelled Bergen.

67. Buhler chronicle, 74-75; Otto Bier, *Salt Creek/Dallas Mennonite Brethren Church* (no place named, 1983); PDC Yearbook, 1940, 170-171; Art. of Inc., No. 10650, in State Archives; Voth letter to G.H. Jantzen, July 20, 1947, copy in North Dallas file; survey of membership in PDC Yearbooks. as provided by Rachel Hiebert of MB Archives at Fresno; Esther Voth Enns letter to LD, Jan. 29, 1978, with copy of July 20, 1947, letter from Henirich S. and Susie Voth, in North Dallas file; ME, III, 917; C. J. Dyck, ed., *Something Meaningful for God,* op. cit., 106-107, 120.

68. Erma Neufeld letter to HL, Apr. 6, 1987; P. H. Berg letter to the Dallas MB Church, July 27, 1947, in Dallas MB file; ME, III, 917; PDC Yearbooks: 1919; 1940, 171; ChrLead, July 1, 1947, 1, 8; LD ms., first draft; LD interview with Mary Hildebrand Bier, Apr. 30, 1975, at Dallas.

69. Neufeld letter, op. cit., and other info; ME, II, 4; PDC Yearbook: 1926, 10; 1940, 29, 171; LD interview with Otto and Mary Bier, op. cit.; Berg, op. cit.; ChrLead: Nov. 1, 1946, 6; Nov. 15, 1955, 18; Otto Bier, 1983, 9; LD draft read by Erma Neufeld; LD notes of minutes, Nov. 24, 1942, and Aug. 12, 1942, and other info.

70. LD info; Bier, 1983, 9; Neufeld info; ME, II, 4; membership survey from PDC Yearbooks; ChrLead: survey 1955-1976.

71. Ibid.; 1947 Voth letter; Jost, et al., 11, 18-19, 116.

72. LD notes from official minutes; info from Evelyn Boese; program for 25th anniversary and dedication service; survey of ChrLead, 1944-1973.

73. LD notes from business meetings and on questionnaire; survey of membership from PDC Yearbooks; Boese info and notes on 1982 draft; survey of ChrLead, incl. Sep. 20, 1960, 22; Nov. 23, 1963; July 15, 1969, 20; Oct. 14, 1975, 20.

74. Info from Rufuz Franz; ChrLead, May 14, 1963, 22-23.

75. Franz info; survey of ChrLead, 1964-1976, incl. Aug. 3, 1965, 21; membership survey in PDC Yearbooks.

76. PDC Yearbook, 1976, membership summary; J. A. Toews, op. cit., 372.
77. ME, II, 4; HL interview with Sol H. Warkentin, Apr. 8, 1982, at Salem; P. H. Quiring, "The E.M.B. Church at Dallas, Oregon," in G. S. Rempel's *A Historical Sketch of the Churches of the Evangelical Mennonite Brethren* (n.p., n.d. [about 1939 or 1940]); program of Fiftieth Anniversary; spelling of OakVilla according to Rufus Franz; Alfred Quiring letter to LD, May 6, 1975, from LD notes in EMB file; LD interview with Mr. and Mrs. David Thiessen, May 6, 1975, at Dallas; Rufus Franz info.
78. Quiring, Thiessen, and Warkentin, op. cit.; LD interview with Anna Ediger, May 7, 1975, at Dallas; LD info; Franz info; ME, IV, 404.
79. Gertrude Regier response with questionnaire; Quiring history; LD info.
80. LD and Sol Warkentin info; ME, IV, 404; LD telephone conversation with D. P. Schultz, Apr. 12, 1975; HL interviews: with Rufus Franz, Mar. 9, 1982; Sol Warkentin, Apr. 2, 1982; Sol Warkentin letter to HL, Apr. 9, 1982.
81. Sol Warkentin info.
82. HT, May 1878, 86; David Luthy, op. cit., 393-395; Luthy, FL, Aug./Sep. 1978, 18; S. G. Shetler, CH, 9, 12; Luthy letter to HL, Feb. 21, 1977; names gathered from DJH, JBH, HH, HT, Shetler, Weber, Anna Weirich, Eli Plank, David Luthy, and other misc sources; info from Lynn D. Kuenzi, Salem, from a Kuenzi family book.
83. Luthy letter to HL, Jan. 29, 1980; *The Twelfth Census of the United States, 1890 . . . Vol. 50, Part 7*, pp. 490-491; it also reports 16 members in Washington County, but there are no other known records or traditions to verify the existence of an Amish group in that Oregon county at any time. An 1881 letter from the U.S. Census Office, in the MCA, Goshen, to Samuel Guengerich of Amish, Johnson County, Iowa, requesting info about the small body of Amish in Oregon, suggests that Guengerich may have provided the info. There is no copy of his reply. Probably the U.S. Census taker confused Washington County, Iowa, and Washington County, Oregon. Melvin Gingerich, *Mennonites in Iowa*, op. cit., 26, indicated that Amish had settled in Washington County, Iowa, about four decades earlier. No documentation was available for Shetler, CH, 9, that seven ministers were among the Amish at one time. ME, IV, 1103, except Linn County info should be for Marion County; Eli Plank tape recording of May 24, 1976; Noah Roth interview with Ken Goe, Feb. 5, 1976, copy in Zion library; J&G, 475-476; MY survey of membership records; Vinnie Yoder info; FL, May 1976, 21; Schrock, *For His Sake*, op. cit., 130.
84. Hostetler, op. cit., 50, 306-311; Orva Helmuth letter to HL, May 23, 1976; survey of HT correspondence; info from Anna Weirich.
85. Luthy, op. cit., 396-397; membership survey in MY; Margaret Shetler's inventory of the Zion cemetery.
86. David Luthy letter to HL, June 11, 1981; FL, Aug. 1978, 19-21; ME, III, 433; info from Anna Weirich.
87. FL: Aug. 1978, 20-21; May 1974, 17-18; MY, 1908, 57; Philip H. Parrish, op. cit., 224.
88. FL: May 1974, 17-20; Aug. 1978, 21; Anna Weirich's story of Dan Miller's request.
89. Survey of Luthy articles.
90. Anna Weirich info; Eli J. Bontreger, *My Life Story* (self-published, 1953-1960), 25, 42, copy in MHL; this is not the Eli E. Bontrager of earlier in the century.
91. Weirich info; Barclay, op. cit., 145-146.
92. FL, July 1979, 20; Bontreger, op. cit., 42; Weirich info; survey of membership in MY.
93. Weirich info; Herman and Mae Smucker interview with Swartzentruber, from their Jan. 4, 1977, letter to HL; Lloyd Lind info from Alvin Weirich, Mar. 30, 1981, to HL.

94. Weirich info.
95. Info from Franklin Jantz, Scio, Oregon; Hiebert, op. cit., 243; [n.a.], *Histories of the Congregations of the Church of God in Christ, Mennonite* (n.p., 1963), 155f.
96. Jantz info; ME I, 630; Hiebert, op. cit., 304-305.
97. Amanda Toews letter to LD, May 23, 1975, in Evergreen file; Barclay, op. cit., 144; Jo Sommer, "'The Holdeman People' Stirring Controversy," Salem *Statesman*, Apr. 27, 1975, I-7; Jantz info; Hiebert, op. cit., 497, 499, 502.
98. Wittlinger, op. cit., 153, 451-452.
99. Joyce Books Chamberlain letter to HL, Apr. 10, 1984; Books quote in EV, Dec. 4, 1944; Wittlinger, op. cit., 452.
100. Survey of EV correspondence, incl. June 6, 1949, 203; Chamberlain, op. cit.
101. Ibid.
102. EV, Feb. 25, 1973, 8-9; survey of EV, 1973-1976.
103. GH: July 29, 1937, 393; July 7, 1938, 321; Nov. 30, 1945, 664; MsEv: Jan. 1952, 10-11; Apr. 1948, 8; Oct. 1948, 7; Jan. 1955, 8-9; Apr. 1955, 1, 15-16; Ethel Snyder info; Margaret Shetler letter to HL, Mar. 8, 1987, in Chap. 14 file; PCC sec. files, reports and letters.
104. MsEv: Jan. 1949, 6; Oct. 1950, 11; Jan. 1952, 9-10; July 1952, 1, 16; Jan. 1957, 10; Milo and Martha Schultz, op. cit.; GH, May 2, 1950, 427.
105. Minutes of May 3, 1964, meeting; Schultz info; MsEv: Oct. 1960, 14; Apr. 1963, 12; Chester Kauffman comments to HL, Oct. 12, 1985, at Rickreall, Oregon.
106. Survey of correspondence in MsEv, 1947-1961, and in GH, 1936 and later; Ruth Krehbiel info.
107. Krehbiel info; Anna Weirich letter to HL, Jan. 21, 1975; HL and LD interview with Anna Weirich, May 12, 1975; Barclay, op. cit., 147; membership survey from MY.
108. Hopewell records from Sterling Roth; HL telephone interview with Ralph Shank, Jan. 23, 1981; MsEv, Fall 1968, Bethel correspondence, 13; letters to HL from: Omar G. Miller, May 10, 1975, in Bethel folder; Ina Yoder, May 5, 1980; Jonathan Zook, Nov. 25, 1980, and Dec. 29, 1980; Wilbert Kropf, Jan. 30, 1981; Olive Miller, May 5, 1980; info from Ralph Shank and Lloyd Lind; HL telephone interview with Lloyd Kropf, Jan. 12, 1981.
109. First BMF constitution; Enos Schrock letter to HL, Oct. 18, 1985.
110. Letters: David W. Mann, PCC sec., to Howard J. Zehr, Dec. 12, 1967; Nelson E. Kauffman to the BMF, May 26, 1972, both in PCC sec. files; Enos Schrock to HL, Oct. 18, 1985; Kauffman conversation with HL on Aug. 2, 1975, in Missouri.

Chapter 7

1. HT: Apr. 15, 1885, 120; Aug. 15, 1889, 249; Dec. 1, 1889, 362; May 1, 1891, 138-139; GH, Oct. 2, 1924, 528; MFH, Apr. 1985, 71; LD draft, using MY (GC), 1944, 34.
2. ME, IV, 61; H. D. Burkholder, *The Story of Our Conference and Churches* (Pacific District Conference, 1951), 23-24; MY (GC), 1944, 34; PDC Reports: 1953, 16; 1954, 15; 1963, 14; Lee Price Campbell, *Seventy-five years . . . A History of the Pacific District Conference*, Master of Divinity thesis at Western Evangelical Seminary, 1973, 35-36.
3. P. C. Jantz history, at dedication of building, July 17, 1950; Burkholder, op. cit., 26-28; ME, III, 576; TM, Mar. 9, 1943, 1-3; survey of PDC Reports; Minnie Franz info.
4. Jantz, op. cit.; ME, IV, 1118; TM: Oct. 22, 1931, 5; Mar. 9, 1943, 1; Minnie Franz info in Menno file; survey of PDC Reports.

5. Burkholder, op. cit., 29-30, 33-34; ME, III, 741; Campbell, op. cit., 32-33, 60-62; survey of PDC Reports.
6. Burkholder, op. cit., 31-32; ME, IV, 602; survey of PDC Reports.
7. ME, IV, 1075; WE, Nov. 1937, 3; Campbell, op. cit., 31; PDC Report, 1944, 11.
8. Survey of PDC Reports; Burkholder, op. cit., 35-36; TM, Jan. 9, 1945, 7; Campbell, op. cit., 64-65.
9. Campbell, op. cit., 69-70; survey of PDC Reports.
10. Patricia Reesor info; GH: Oct. 3, 1961, 875; survey of MsEv correspondence and reports; MWR, Apr. 5, 1979, 13; MY 1977, 61.
11. Survey of PDC Reports; Campbell, op. cit., 70-73.
12. C. J. Dyck, "In the California Gold Rush," ML, Jan. 1956, 25-28; HT, Sep. 1878, 161; ME, I, 491; Lucile Boshart-Carr, et al., *Christian E. Boshart and Catherine Buerge Family History and Genealogy* (Newport, 1978), 18-19; Wilma Brentz, *Christian Schertz Genealogy and History, 1815-1971* ([Farmington, IL, 1971]), 1, 3.
13. PCC Report, 1948, 6.
14. Phyllis Bergman history for 75th anniversary.
15. Ibid.; Burkholder, op. cit., 38-43; Campbell, op. cit., 29-31, 81-85; survey of PDC Reports.
16. ME, IV, 788; CE, Jan. 31, 1928, 46; TM: Jan. 11, 1938, 16; May 1, 1951, 291; survey of PDC Reports; Burkholder, op. cit., 44-45; Campbell, op. cit., 86-91.
17. "The First Mennonite Church, 1906-1956, Reedley, California; Fiftieth Anniversary Program and a Brief History of the Church"; TM, Oct. 22, 1931, 6-7; *Reedley First Mennonite Church, The First Seventy-five Years, 1906-1981* (Newton, n.d.), 50, 66-67; LD notes about Russian refugees; Campbell, op. cit., 95-96; survey of PDC Reports.
18. Barrett, op. cit., 81-85; Burkholder, op. cit., 49-52; ME, III, 13; Campbell, op. cit., 96-100; survey of PDC Reports.
19. ME: I, 494; III, 401; HT: Mar. 1, 1902, 74; Mar. 1, 1906, 66; GH, Mar. 23, 1916, 841, and subsequent correspondence; Shetler, CH, 48-51; survey of PCC Reports; GVG, 150-151, footnotes of [S.C.] Yoder correspondence with C. Snyder and H. Shoup; reports and correspondence in PCC sec. files.
20. HT: Feb. 2, 1905, 34; Nov. 16, 1905, 364; GH: Dec. 20, 1934, 814.
21. Shetler, CH, 45-46; HT: Mar. 23, 1905, 92; Feb. 15, 1906, 52; Sharer autobiography, op. cit.; GH: Apr. 22, 1909, 59; Mar. 30, 1916, 859; PCC Report, 1911.
22. Shetler, CH, 46; GH, Mar. 30, 1916, 859.
23. ME, II, 249.
24. ME, IV, 977; LD notes, source not given.
25. GH: May 27, 1909, 138; Mar. 3, 1910, 777; Oct. 3, 1918, 479; Jan. 22, 1920, 804; Feb. 16, 1928, 1002; Feb. 13, 1930, 953; Aug. 13, 1942, 421; Shetler, CH, 47, 90; HL interview with Claud Hostetler, May 15, 1984.
26. ME, IV, 509; LD notes from MY (GC), 1938, 41; PDC Reports: 1964, 20; 1965, 19; WE, Dec. 1934-Jan. 1935, 3, gives date as 1934, other later sources say 1935.
27. ME, IV, 1077; TM, Aug. 13, 1931, 7; LD notes from Home Missions report, 1933-35, source not given; WE, Jan. 1934, 2; Campbell, op. cit., 28.
28. LD notes, source not included; MWR, Oct. 21, 1924; TM, Mar. 6, 1945, 16; PDC Reports: 1945, 9; 1946, 10-11, 1956, 19; 1957, 11.
29. ME, IV, 964; history ms. of the MC and GC congregations.
30. Shetler, CH, 47-48; Mary (Mrs. Luke) Weaver, op. cit.; minutes of Feb. 12, 1929, meeting of PCC Mission Board and conference exec. comm., and other reports of Winton in PCC sec. files; GH: Apr. 10, 1930, 41; Sep. 25, 1930, 552; Mar. 5, 1931, 1032; Apr. 4, 1931, 40; Apr. 6, 1933, Field Notes; survey of membership records in PCC sec. files; MsEv: July 1948, 6-7; Hiebert, op. cit., 268-275; 292.

31. ME, I, 313; Burkholder, op. cit., 55-57; Hiebert, op. cit.; TM: Feb. 6, 1940, 14-15; Mar. 12, 1940, 11; July 23, 1940, 13; Nov. 19, 1940, 11; Nov. 18, 1941, 17; Feb. 27, 1951, 147; Apr. 3, 1951, 227; Dec. 4, 1951, 771; WE, Dec. 1950, 3; PDC Reports: 1951, 5; 1952, 9; 1953, 11; 1956, 15; 1960, 9.

32. Mary Weaver, op. cit.; survey of PDC Reports; MY, 1977, 64, gives membership from 1975 report as 85; MYs indicate that it was never affiliated with SWC but was listed with UM congregations. Apparently Sharon continued for a time: MY 1969 lists both Sharon, of the SWC, with a membership of 48, and United, with UM congregations, with a membership of 54, pp. 75, 81; MY 1966-1968 and 1970-1971, not available; Sharon not listed in 1972.

33. GW, May 29, 1907, 137; petitions, reports, and letters in PCC sec. files; PCC Report, 1941, 4; GH: Feb. 26, 1942, 1025; HL interview with Claud Hostetler, May 15, 1984.

34. ME, IV, 507-508; GH: Feb. 4, 1943, 953; Jan. 27, 1944, 921; Hostetler, op. cit.; 1948 membership report in PCC sec. files.

35. MsEv: April 1957, 1, 5, 15-16; HL interview with Lloyd, Merle, and Joe Kropf, Nov. 10, 1981, at Harrisburg.

36. ME, III, 619; survey of PDC Reports; WE, Jan. 1955, unp.; TM, Nov. 27, 1973, A-2.

37. PDC Report, 1957, 7-8, gives 1957 date; survey of PDC Reports; ME, IV, 1065; Campbell, op. cit., 103-104.

38. Survey of PDC Reports, incl. 1973, 25, for organization date.

39. Barney Fix, op. cit.; HT, Dec. 1, 1889, 362.

40. HT: Apr. 15, 1899, 121; Jan. 1, 1900, 10; Feb. 15, 1900, 57; Feb. 26, 1904, 68; GH: Dec. 20, 1934, 814; July 2, 1936, 296; Feb. 4, 1937, 957, 1005, 1008; Shetler, CH, 23; Shetler, MY, 1916, 29, 31; Anne Garber info; HL, Nampa ms.; MY, 1977, 56.

41. ME: I, 7; II, 203, says Emmanuel disbanded in 1930; F. L. and Anna Wenger, "The Mennonites of Aberdeen, Idaho," ML, July 1957, 120ff., says Emmanuel disbanded in 1929; "History and Constitution of the First Mennonite Church . . . of Aberdeen, Idaho," 1973, 3.

42. Wengers, op. cit.; Otto Becker and Aaron Epp info; survey of PDC Reports.

43. Wilbur Lantz letter to HL, March 1, 1980; Pannabeacker, *Faith in Ferment*, op. cit., 178, 204; ME, IV, 1127; HL interview with E. S. Garber, Jan. 15, 1981; Mary Weaver info.

44. Shetler, CH, 35; history prepared by Allie Kauffman for 50th anniversary meeting on May 3, 1964; ME, II, 329; survey of membership in MY.

45. "The Dutch Flats of Dubois," by Aaron J. Epp, Aberdeen, 1972, mimeographed booklet of 32 pages; whether the "Klane Gemeente" group was part of the Kleine Gemeinde, organized in Russia in 1814, is not clear; Epp interpreted the phrase as "the small congregation," 17, 19.

46. Amos Shenk ms. and list of charter members; survey of membership in MY; PCC report workbook, 1979, 12; HL interview with Wes Hooley, July 1, 1979, at Nampa; survey of MsEv correspondence.

47. ME, I, 490; TM, Dec. 5, 1950, 797, gives charter membership as 15, in contrast to ME, 24; both articles written by Menno J. Kliewer; PDC Report, 1947, 14, also says 15; LD notes of Lyman Springer letter to PD Unruh, May 21, 1956; Walter H. Dyck report, Apr. 11, 1958, copy in Caldwell folder; PDC Report, 1963, 15, 20; Campbell, op. cit., 19-20.

48. Info from Florence (Mrs. Dan) Shank; Campbell, op. cit., 18; PDC Reports: 1958, 21; 1968, 48.

49. Info from: Kenneth Snyder, Jerry Gingerich; Ida Horst letter to HL, Feb. 1, 1981; PCC Report, 1961, 2; "Record of Membership" dated Nov. 24, 1963; legal correspondence in Highland file.

50. HL, E. S. Garber biography, 43; GH, June 24, 1943, 252; survey of MsEv correspondence; Anne Garber info; survey of MY membership records; interview with Robert Garber, June 29, 1979, at Nampa.

51. Shetler, CH, 26-29, 89-90; Glenn L. Roth info; ME, III, 762-763; PCC Reports: 1916, 11; 1919, 4; N. A. Lind Collection, III, 13-1 in MCA.

52. Minutes of Feb. 5, 1946, meeting, MHB, July 1982, 3; ME, IV, 663; PCC sec. files; MsEv, Oct. 1946, 4.

53. PDC Reports: 1964, 20, and survey; Campbell, op. cit., 78-81.

54. Files of reports and letters of the Joint Administrative Committee for Tucson and Orange County; PDC report workbook, 1976, has no membership listed for Evangel for 1975; 1977 MY, 60; MY, 1978, reported 32 members for 1977, and by 1978, reflected in 1979 MY, Evangel was no longer listed with SWC.

55. PDC report workbook, 1976, 12; MY: 1976, 62; 1977, 60.

56. TM, June 11, 1985, 228-229; PDC workbook, 1976; survey of MY, 1977-1979.

Chapter 8

1. LD notes of PDC minutes, 1896, 1937, in LD ms., 3, 26; MY (GC), 1939, 26-28; LD info.

2. MWR, Jan. 6, 1983, 11; John Lais info.

3. Western info from Hilda Reist; LD ms. of Dallas, 4; HL notes from Hopewell's 75th anniversary program, Aug. 12, 1978; GH, Aug. 22, 1918, 369; Kropf ms., 3; MY: 1933, 62; 1934, 62.

4. LD notes of PDC minutes, from LD ms., 3; HT, Oct. 27, 1904, 346; Shetler, CH, 52; copies of printed programs, 1905-1907; survey of PCC and PDC programs, minutes, and reports of later years.

5. Theron F. Schlabach, "Mennonites and revivalism," *Goshen College Bulletin,* July 1983, 3; Schlabach, GVG, Chap. 1, especially pp. 31-47; Norman Kraus, "Toward a Theology for the Disciple Community," KCC, 111-112; PCC Report, 1951, 5.

6. Bier, op. cit., 5; GH, Feb. 26, 1920, 905; Ray Mishler at Hopewell's 75th anniversary program, op. cit.; Stoltzfus, op. cit., 233; Schlabach, GVG, quoting SEA, 174, 270-271.

7. ME, I, 328-329; LD notes of 1896 PDC minutes, from LD ms. of PDC, 3; PDC Report, 193; Chap. 12 tells more about WMS and Salem Academy.

8. Urie E. Kenagy notes, in PCC archives.

9. HL interview with Lloyd Lind, Dec. 9, 1977; Gerig, op. cit.; Vinson Synan, *The Holiness-Pentecostal Movement in the United States* (Grand Rapids, 1971), 197-198; see Robert Steele, *Storming Heaven . . .* (New York, 1970) and *The Vanishing Evangelist* (New York, 1959) for comprehensive biographical writings about McPherson; Clifton E. Olmstead, *History of Religion in the United States* (Englewood Cliffs, N.J, 1960), 550; "Lighthouse Temple to Mark 60th Anniversary," *Eugene Register-Guard,* Feb. 8, 1986; Bier, op. cit., 9; WE, March 1941, unp.

10. MsEv: July 1953, 1, 15-16; July 1954, 1, 16; July 1956, 4; Oct. 1956, 4-5; GH, Feb. 26, 1957, 205.

11. Marsden, op. cit., is a basic source for the study of Fundamentalism.

12. Marsden, op. cit., 11-21; Edwin Scott Gaustad, *A Religious History of America* (New York, 1966), 258-260; Olmstead, op. cit., 465-467; Kathryn Yoder, "A History of Education Among Mennonites on the West Coast," unpub. ms., 1949, in MHL, 4-6; PCC Report, 1921, 4; PDC (MB) Yearbook, 1945, 36.

13. ME, II, 418-419; Marsden, op. cit., 118-123; Gaustad, op. cit.; Olmstead, op. cit., 467-470.

14. Kraus, op. cit., 103-117; ME: I, 329-332; II, 418-419; GVG, 112-117.

15. Alice Gingerich, *The Life and Times of Daniel Kauffman* (Scottdale, 1954), 22, 26; Melvin Gingerich, *Mennonite Attire Through Four Centuries,* op. cit.,

150; Daniel Kauffman, *Manual of Bible Doctrines* (Elkhart, 1898), 13-14; MCD, 57, article on Christian ordinances; Daniel Hertzler, ed., *Not By Might* (Scottdale, 1983), 15; "In Honor of Elizabeth Bender on Her Ninetieth Birthday," MHB, Jan. 1985, 5-7.

16. Kauffman, op. cit., 11-14, 186, 196-204; John F. Funk and John S. Coffman, *Confession of Faith and Minister's Manual* (Elkhart, 1906, 4th ed.), 19; *Mennonite Confession of Faith* (Scottdale, 1968), 3; delegates at the 1921 session of MGC at Garden City, Missouri, did adopt an addendum to the Dordrecht Confession, entitled "Christian Fundamentals," which a later section will discuss.

17. Gingerich, op. cit., is a primary source on the subject of attire; see also ME: II, 99-104; IV, 183-84.

18. Gingerich, op. cit., 34-35, 81ff., 96-106; Wenger, *Faithfully, Geo. R.,* op. cit., 59-60; "Conversations with Elizabeth Bender, III," MHB, Apr. 1986, 6.

19. Wenger, op. cit., 53, Brunk quote; HT, June 15, 1902, 178; notes from Hopewell record of Brunk's and Garber's visit; PCC Report, 1917, 5; although the resolution is included in the official report, it does not specifically say that this particular resolution was adopted, only that it was written; author's conversations with Oregon people, and their estimates of the prevalence of the necktie.

20. Gingerich, op. cit., 148ff.; "Rules and Discipline," 1906, 7; PCC Constitution and Discipline: 1915, 10; 1924, in Shetler, CH, 73ff.; 1942, 8; 1953, 12-13; author's conversations with Oregon people.

21. Kraus, op. cit., 109-110.

22. Many persons fifty years or older, of Mennonite (MC) heritage, remember the "all things" emphasis and the concept of "staying saved" by obedience to church regulations; GVG, 51-52; Miller, "West Coast Echoes," July 1950, 1.

23. Chaps. 3-5 discuss these changes in the PCC in more detail.

24. Survey of PCC constitutions; S&T and John Horsch, *The Mennonite Church and Modernism* (Scottdale, 1924), and other books by Horsch include detailed arguments against Modernism; Schlabach, GVG, 111-117; S. F. Coffman, ed., *Mennonite Confession of Faith*, MPH, 1931 printing, 58ff.; in this document the spelling is Dortrecht, not Dordrecht; Wenger, op. cit., 70; Wilbert R. Shenk letter to HL, Apr. 28, 1987; comments about capital "F" in author's memory.

25. King, "Lessons from the Churches . . . " S&T, July 1931, 9; George R. Brunk, "Faulty Fundamentalists," S&T, 1931 article reprinted in Feb. 1946, 486; "Trumpet Echoes on Sources of Error," S&T, July 1939, 93-95; Schlabach, op. cit.

26. ME, II, 253-254; LD info.

27. Church constitution of the Zion Church near Dallas, in a congregational "journal," undated, but obviously before the Dec. 19, 1896, meeting which made a change in it; Pannebecker, *Open Doors,* op. cit., 175-176; 406-409; LD info; PDC Report, 1968, 20-21; GH, Feb. 21, 1984, 134.

28. *Confession of Faith of the General Conference of Mennonite Brethren Churches* (Hillsboro, 1976), quote from 9, also 5-7; confession of faith on back of card titled "The Mennonite Brethren Church Covenant," from Rufus Franz; *Evangelical Mennonite Brethren Missionary Manual,* 1955, 11.

29. HL interview with William Neufeld, May 3, 1985, at Eugene; Hiebert, op. cit., 275-277, 498; Whittlinger, op, cit., 88-89, 95-96; PDC Report, 1968, 21; David Luthy, op. cit.; ME II, 99-104.

30. Marsden, op. cit., 31, 37, 46-47, 51-59, 64-65; "A Dispensational Chart by C. E. Putnam," Bible Institute Colportage Association, Chicago, 1918; Erb, *The Alpha and the Omega* (Scottdale, 1955), 16, 24-26; quotes 25, 26; see also 16, 24; *The Scofield Reference Bible. . . .* (New York, 1917).

31. Erb, op. cit., 22-26, 37; Erb, *South Central Frontiers,* op. cit., 82; HT, Aug. 17, 1897, 249; ME: I, 557-558 Coffman quote; IV, 917; John Zook letter to Missouri relatives, July 24, 1897, copy in HL files; Mary Miller, *A Pillar of Cloud* (North Newton, 1959), 240; Sanford G. Shetler, *Preacher of the People,* op. cit., 80-81, 100-101; HL telephone conversation with Ben Kenagy, Dec. 18, 1989.

32. ME, I, 558; PCC sec. records; Miller comments at Hopewell Church, Aug. 12, 1978; survey of S&T files; author knows of various persons who have subscribed in recent years to S&T; Program for the Fall Bible Conference of 1954, noting the previous year's conference; GH: Dec. 20, 1934, 812, quote about Thut; other issues, Oct. to Dec. 1934, also refer to Thut's work in the West; May 26, 1938, 164; Sep. 31, 1939, 532; Amos Conrad speaking at Albany's 75th anniversary celebration, Jan. 26, 1975; for additional info about Derstine, see Urie A. Bender, *Four Earthen Vessels*, op. cit., chapter on Derstine, esp. 235-236; and Smith, op. cit., 310-313; handbill announcing meetings.

33. David Peterson, *Children of Freedom or Children of Menno? The Oregon Mennonite Church in the Two World Wars*, master's thesis at University of Oregon, 1981, 13; G. Richard Culp, "Comments on a Review of Biblical Prophecy" (pamphlet, n.p., n.d.), 4; HL conversation with Ben Kenagy, Feb. 17, 1985, at Eugene; Orrie D. Yoder, "Can We Trust the Word of God?" S&T, July 1944, 225-227; MsEv: Apr. 1959, 4.

34. G. Richard Culp, *Studies in Prophecy* (privately published, 1971, 112), 287-288, 295; the author has a Scofield Bible formerly owned by Wilbert Lind, earlier of Oregon; HL telephone conversation with Harold Hochstetler, Mar. 5, 1986; GH: Apr. 23, 1942, 85, 89; MsEv: July 1960, 13, quote by unidentified Blaine correspondent; Win. 1972, 15.

35. PCC Report, 1963, 1, 3; Letter from David Mann to Marcus Lind, July 21, 1967, in PCC sec. files.

36. Culp, op. cit., 147, 149, 286-287, 291-292; Wilbur D. Kropf info; author's personal knowledge of a reference to Culp's "misuse" of the Scriptures.

37. ME: I, 558-559; II, 247-248; HL interview with Rufus Franz, Nov. 21, 1986, in Eugene; survey of PDC reports, 1944-1976; HL conversations with La Vernae Dick Hohnbaum, Mar. 6-7, 1986, and Randy Friesen, Mar. 9, 1986, at Eugene.

38. TM: Feb. 22, 1938, 7, quote from Albany; Nov. 19, 1940, 8, Thiessen quote; WE: Nov. 1943, unp., reporter not identified; Sep. 1950, 7; Apr. 1954, unp.

39. ME: I, 559; II, 248; Toews, op. cit., 377-379; Bier, op. cit., 14-15; Wittlinger, op. cit., 60, 417; Hiebert, op. cit., 384; Culp, op. cit., 286.

40. Scofield, op. cit., 1000; Toews, op. cit., 376; Guy Hershberger, *War, Peace and Nonresistance* (Scottdale, 1955), 49ff.

41. Marsden, op. cit., 72-79, 96; Melvin E. Dieter, *The Holiness Revival of the Nineteenth Century* (Metuchen, NJ, 1980), esp. 4, 27, 159; J. C. Wenger, *Introduction to Theology* (Scottdale, 1954), 290; Wilbert R. Shenk, *Henry Venn—Missionary Statesman* (Maryknoll, NY, 1983), 112, especially to the missionary movement in England; Synan, op. cit., discusses the movement in relation to American religious and cultural history, 17-19; Putnam's dispensational chart, op. cit.; Joseph S. Miller, *Beyond the Mystic Border* (Hillsboro/Hesston, 1985), 43.

42. Synan, op. cit., 52, 77, 207-211, 220, 223; Wilbert R. Shenk letter to HL, Apr. 28, 1987.

43. Kauffman, op. cit., 262ff.; Marsden, op. cit., 78-79, 93-95; ME, IV, 414-415; Record, op. cit., 20, 29.

44. KN Record, op. cit., 97, 104-105; Erb, *The Alpha and the Omega*, op. cit., 243; Miller, op. cit., 41-74; GH, July 24, 1984, 523; Erb, *South Central Frontiers*, op. cit., 242ff.; Wenger, *Faithfully, George R.*, op. cit., 142-143, 167.

45. Stoltzfus, op. cit., quote from HT, Nov. 15, 1900, on 232; also, 232-233, 304-305; 364; ME, I, 313; CM, Nov. 1931, 336-337.

46. Stoltzfus, op. cit., 304-305; MsEv, July 1959, 1, 11-12; HT, Dec. 19, 1907, 473; GH: Mar. 19, 1963, 246; Jan. 1, 1931, 841; July 16, 1931, 361; Aug. 11, 1944, 383-384, quote about Shenk; GVG, 99; Augsburgers in Roy S. and Martha Koch, ed., *My Personal Pentecost* (MPP) (Scottdale, 1977), 172, 175; MsEv: July 1962, 2; GH: Jan. 16, 1930, 863, Leah H. Kauffman obituary; Bethel membership list.

47. PCC Report, 1906.

48. PCC Reports: 1907, 1908, 1910, 1911 in PCC sec. notebook.

49. PCC Report, 1913.

50. PCC Report, 1922, 5-6; Shetler, CH, 89; GH: Aug. 11, 1944, 383; Apr. 20, 1948, 383; MsEv, July 1962, 2.

51. PCC Report, 1924, 5, emphasis added.

52. Shetler, CH, 11, 25; PCC Reports 1926, 1932, 1946, 1955; programs of ministers' meetings, 1936, 1939, 1944.

53. GH: Feb. 18, 1937, 1001; June 17, 1937, 249; Jan. 20, 1944, 904; Jan. 27, 1944, 921; MsEv, Jan. 1950, 4; Wilbert R. Shenk letter to HL, Apr. 28, 1987; Mildred Schrock, unpub. ms., unpaged.

54. Shetler, CH, 25; GH: Mar. 19, 1914, 784; Mar. 26, 1914, 800, 805; Apr. 14, 1953, 355; survey of Indian Cove correspondence in church periodicals, incl.: MsEv, July 1946, 7-8; Jan. 1949, 12; Apr. 1961, 13; Jan. 1963, 12,; Sum. 1973, 15; Amos Shenk, unpub. ms.

55. MsEv: Oct. 1948, 2; July 1954, 8-9.

56. PCC Report 1952, 4; MsEv, July 1953, 1, 15; Kraus in KCC, 110.

57. Faye Byers in MPP, 146-150; PCC conference program, 1954; MsEv, Jan. 1958, 14-15.

58. Letter to "Dear Brother" from "The Committee" with program, Jan. 10, 1960, in PCC sec. files; 1965 program of minsters' meeting.

59. Byron Shenk in MPP, 188-189; Wilbert R. Shenk letters to HL, Apr. 28, 1987, and May 19, 1987, and other info from Shenk; MsEv: Jan. 1954, 9; Sep. 1958, 10; July 1963, 15; survey of correspondence in periodicals from Logsden and McMinnville.

60. "Rejoice Committee Statement and Fact Sheet; MWR, Jan. 29, 1976, 1; PCC Conference sec.'s report to delegates, 1975, unp.; 1976 "Rejoice" program.

61. ME, II, 790; Whittlinger, op. cit., 321-338, quote on 330; Hiebert, op. cit., 415, quote on 433; John Hostetler, *Amish Life*, op. cit., 26, quotes on 29.

62. Marsden, op. cit., quote on 79, 128-129.

63. TM: May 28, 1931, 15; Jan. 1, 1931, 3-7; LD notes of Regier letter, in Chap. 10 files; PDC Reports: 1949, 21; 1967, 11-12; LD info from her Calvary ms., 6.

64. LD interview with David F. Thiessen, May 6, 1975; Marsden, op. cit., 75, 79; Bier, op. cit., 13; William Neufeld, op. cit.

65. Marsden, op. cit., 117, quote on 224.

Chapter 9

1. Barrett, op. cit., Chap. 1, esp. 4; GVG, 35-40.

2. PDC minutes: 1896, 1904, 1907, 1908, according to LD unpub. ms. of PDC; 1903 minutes, handwritten translation in PDC file; 1959, 6, 9, 20.

3. KN Record, op. cit., 131-32; quoted from Shetler, CH, 65.

4. Ethel Snyder info; Milo Schultz, op. cit.; C. J. Dyck, ed., *Something Meaningful for God,* op. cit., 106-107; Esther Voth Enns letter to LD, Jan. 29, 1978.

5. LD notes of Zion minutes: Apr. 9, 1905; May 20, 1906; Jan. 1, 1907; Jan. 1, 1908; HT: Apr. 1, 1897, 105; July 15, 1898, 218; "Account Book of the Mennonite Church," 102, 106.

6. Survey of programs of quarterly mission meetings; Shetler, CH, 68-69.

7. GH: Jan. 3, 1935, p. 854-855; Aug. 6, 1936, 429; Sep. 3, 1936, 490; Aug. 26, 1937, p. 475-476.

8. LD info in Dallas MB ms., 12-13; TM, Oct. 12, 1948, 12; WE: May 1932, 3; Mar. 1934, 4; LD info in Liberty Gardens, unp., unpub. ms.

9. Report in PCC sec. notebook, apparently sometime in 1928; TM, Aug. 14, 1930, 4-5; WE, Oct. 1943, unp.; LD info from John C. Jantz in her ms. about the PDC, 23-24; MsEv: July 1944, 1; Yoder quote, Apr. 1946, 2.

10. Kathryn Yoder Miller, op. cit.; Zion file; Dallas EMB file.

11. WE, Feb. 1942, Grace/Dallas corr., unp.; MsEv, Win. 1975, 16; ChrLead, Mar. 29, 1966, 23; PCC Report, 1912; GH, Sep. 9, 1986, 610; GVG, 227.

12. ME, IV, 654; GH: Aug. 15, 1929, 425; June 4, 1963, 487; quote from MsEv, Jan. 1951, 3; Iva Shrock Snyder conversation with HL, June 16, 1984.

13. Dallas EMB history; Rufus Franz info; GH, Nov. 18, 1947, 729; Ralph Shank talk on Aug. 12, 1978, at Hopewell; survey of MsEv, 1949-1962.

14. GH, Feb. 13, 1941, 985; MsEv, Oct. 1950, 12-13; Harrisburg history.

15. GH: Mar. 23, 1922, 1000; Nov. 4, 1926, 681; July 23, 1931, p. 394; Mar. 4, 1937, p. 1043; July 22, 1937, p. 378; MsEv, Jan. 1947, 2-3.

16. MsEv: Oct. 1951, 14; Apr. 1952, 14; survey, 1970 through Win. 1973; 1974 Miss. Bd. report.

17. LD notes of Emmanuel; poem written by Mrs. John Frey, copy in Dallas EMB file; survey of reports of women's activities in various periodicals; Zion Sewing Circle records; *WMSC Pulse,* Apr. 1975, 14.

18. LD info from interview with Mary Hildebrand Bier, Apr. 30, 1975; author remembers boys in the Western group in the early 1960s.

19. Ethel Snyder, "Love Builds by Serving," mimeo booklet, 1964, 2-10; survey of reports of women's activities.

20. ME, I, 581; PDC Report, ca. 1927, from sec. notebook; Emmanuel info; CE Report, 1920, as noted in Dick PDC ms., 21; TM, Aug. 14, 1930, 4-6; WE, Oct. 1947, unp.

21. Faye Hooley, "The Youth Projects of Oregon," unpub. ms. for a class at Hesston taught by Paul Yoder [1949], in PCA; Albany info; Shirley Gerig, "Literaries in Oregon," unpub. ms., 1949, in PCA.

22. PDC Reports 1948-1976; WE: Sep. 1948, 4; Mar. 1953, unp., Alberta correspondence; info from Emmanuel, Calvary, Liberty Gardens, Albany, Lebanon, Logsden, Sweet Home, Salem, Eugene.

23. GH: Apr. 7, 1953, 324; copies of messages for Aug. 1955, in author's files; MsEv: Oct. 1953, 12; Oct. 1954, p. 12; July 1955, 9.

24. Articles of Incorporation, op. cit.; HL interview with J. B. Toews, May 22, 1982, at Eugene; PDC (MB) Yearbooks: 1915, 105-106; 1930, 9; Jost, et al., op. cit., in several places gives 1937 as date of disbanding; see Chap. 6 for further details about the Portland MB congregation and Alberta/Peace.

25. HT: June 15, 1888, 184; Oct. 1, 1891, 299; Nov. 1, 1891, 331-332; Mar. 22, 1906, 94; Feb. 14, 1907; Oct. 31, 1907, (first page of issue); Dec. 19, 1907, 473; Orie Conrad info; GW: Mar. 21, 1906, 486; Report, 1906, 1907, 1908, 1910; PCC Report, 1911; Shetler, CH, 39-40, 69; some histories mistakenly give 1906 or 1908 as the beginning date of Bressler work; Robert Lee, "History of the Portland Mennonite Church . . ." Goshen College paper, 1953, 2f., quoting Myrtle Miller, and 5, 7; Claud Hostetler in "Portland Glimpses," June 1973, 3; GH: Apr. 22, 1915, 60; Apr. 29, 1915, 72.

26. PCC Report, 1922, 12; Lee, op. cit., 9-10; GH: Nov. 9, 1922, 628.

27. Paul E. Yoder in "Mennonite Gospel Mission Newsletter," Feb. 1946, 1; Muriel E. Snyder history of Portland mission in MsEv, Jan. 1957, 1, 2, 16; FA, 1925, 6-10; Lee, op. cit., 12; Heatwole quote in GH, Mar. 5, 1925, 970.

28. Lee, op. cit.; quotes from Snyder history, op. cit.

29. Lee, op. cit., 11-12, 22-23; Snyder history; GH: Sep. 20, 1923, 514; Dec. 20, 1923, 770; Aug. 14, 1924, 404-405; Sep. 4, 1924, 471; Aug. 15, 1929, 421.

30. Lee, op. cit., 24-28; YCC, Sep. 25, 1927, 722; Jess Kauffman, *A Vision and a Legacy* (Newton, 1984), 13-16.

31. Lee, op. cit., 18-20, 28, 31; GH: quotes from Mar. 5, 1925, 970-971; May 7, 1925, 100; Aug. 13, 1925, 408-409; Aug. 4, 1927, 428; Aug. 11, 1927, 440; Dec. 22, 1927, 826-827; Jan. 12, 1928, 884; Mar. 1, 1928, 1051-1052; Mar. 20, 1930, 1048; HL interview with Claud Hostetler, Nov. 10, 1981, at Albany.

32. GH, Jan. 7, 1932, 890-891; Lee, op. cit., 28.
33. Lee, op. cit., 33-34, 41-42; Shetler, op. cit., 95; GH, Oct. 7, 1937, 581; MsEv, July 1947, 1-3; Ethel Snyder info.
34. GH: Nov. 5, 1936, 698; Apr. 7, 1938, 28, quote; Feb. 17, 1938, 1008; May 26, 1938, 164; Mar. 16, 1939, 1073; Sep. 21, 1939, 532.
35. Lee, op. cit., 36; MsEv: Apr. 1945, 3; July 1945, 2; Oct. 1946, 4; Jan. 1950, 4, 5, 14; Apr. 1951, 6-7; Apr. 1955, 3, 15; "Portland Glimpses," June 1973, 8.
36. Lee, op. cit., 20, 26-27, 41-42.
37. Lee, op. cit., 35-39; MsEv: Jan. 1955, 6; Jan. 1956, 9; July 1956, 14-15; July 1962, 14; Apr. 1963, 13-14; July 1963, 14; PCC Report, 1956, 8; Hostetler notes with HL draft of Portland history; "Portland Glimpses," op. cit.
38. Survey of correspondence and articles related to Portland, incl. GH: Oct. 7, 1937; May 26, 1938, 164; Lee, op. cit., 25; MsEv: Apr. 1946, 4; Oct. 1954, 6-7; July 1955, p. 6; July 1956, 14-15; Oct. 1964, 5; Jan. 1965, 9; Fall 1965, 5; Spr. 1966, 4-5; Sum. 1966, 5, 15; Spr. 1968, 2; Sum. 1968, 4; Sum. 1971, 16; correspondence and reports in the Walnut Park folder.
39. MsEv: Apr. 1950, 3; Jan. 1954, 2, 5; July 1954, 8-9; Jan. 1955, 3; Jan. 1964, 14; Win. 1969, 11-12; Spr. 1969, 14; Fall 1970, 2-3; Fall 1973, 15; Spr. 1974, 10-11; PMACC (Portland Mennonite Advisory-Coordination Council) and N.W. Portland Board files; MY, 1974, 69; GH, Oct. 30, 1973, 825-28; survey of reports and correspondence.
40. GH: June 26, 1951, 614; Oct. 30, 1973, 825-828; MY and PCC reports of membership; MsEv, Spr. 1974, 10-11.
41. ME, IV, 1097-8; GH: Apr. 25, 1935, 85, first quote; Aug. 6, 1936, 410; Dec. 30, 1943, 836; Nov. 13, 1951, 1100; Dec. 29, 1953, 948; PCC Reports: 1934, 13; 1935, 12; 1936, 13; 1941, 12; 1943, 11-12, last quote; 1944, 14; MsEv: Jan. 1950, 8-9; July 1952, 3; Oct. 1955, 1; July 1962, 2, second quotes.
42. PCC Reports: 1953, 13; 1960, 7; 1961, 7; 1968, 3; MsEv, Win. 1968, 6; survey of reports in GH and MsEv.
43. LD info from Wilbert Regier report, 1946; TM, Feb. 25, 1947, 13.
44. ME, IV, 1117; GH: Sep. 7, 1948, 837; Sep. 28, 1948, 910; Nov. 23, 1948, 1121; Oct. 6, 1953, 964; survey of reports in MsEv, Jan. 1948, and following.
45. Survey of reports in MsEv; Sheridan and Berean files; Mission Board files on Rescue Mission; MsEv, Win. 1968, 6, annual meeting minutes; PCC Report, 1966, 8; L. L. Lind postcard to HL, Jan. 10, 1981, in Rescue Mission folder; *Eugene Register Guard,* Jan. 21, 1981, 9D.
46. Survey of MsEv reports; Apr. 1956, 1, 15-16, gives history of the mission; Lloyd Kropf info; Wilbert R. Shenk letter to HL, May 19, 1987; GH: Mar. 8, 1955, 228; Mar. 25, 1958, 279.
47. MsEv: Jan. 1947, 4; Jan. 1948, 2; Apr. 1953, 15; Jan. 1957, 4; May 1958, 3.
48. "Information Sheet" from Board in 1950 PCC sec. files; survey of MsEv reports, 1950-64; Mabel L. Kropf, "Mennonite Ministry Among Oregon Migrants," 1960, unpub. ms. in WMS library.
49. Shetler and Mission Board correspondence in PCC sec. files; quote from Eldon Shetler letter to Ivan Headings, PCC sec., Feb. 14, 1956; MsEv correspondence and reports, July 1951 through July 1959.
50. C and HL visited Shenk home in August 1959; survey of MsEv correspondence and reports, 1962-1968; ME: II, 266; III, 196-199; IV, 576-578; GH, Jan. 23, 1962, 90; Harvey Voth reply to HL, Dec. 10, 1981, letter; Sheridan history about Mishler; PCC Report, 1962, 8; HL conversation with Merle Kropf, Nov. 1981; WR Nafziger letter to the Vanderhoof congregation, July 7, 1965, in PCC sec. files.
51. CM, Sep. 1912, 651; Jan. 1938, 15, quote; Mar. 1939, 78-79; GH, July 6, 1933, 293-294; July 21, 1938, 348; Apr. 20, 1948, 383; Omar G. Miller letter to HL, May 10, 1975; PCC Report, 1944, 14-15.

52. PCC Reports, 1927-1943; MsEv: Apr. 1957, 6; July 1957, 5; Oct. 1957, 4.

53. Survey of records and correspondence from congregations; Chap. 12 discusses the urbanization of Oregon Mennonites in more detail.

54. GH: Jan. 2, 1951, 14-15; Sep. 9, 1986, 610-611; J. D. Graber, *The Church Apostolic* (Scottdale, 1960), 25ff., Graber quote; PCC Report, 1968, 3-4, last quote; Sam Hernandez file with Mission Board files; MsEv: Sum. 1972, 7; Sum. 1973, 2-3; 1976 Report to PCC delegates, Showalter and Kauffman reports, unp.

55. Boise: MsEv: various issues Sum. 1970 to Spr. 1977; Ranch Chapel: MsEv: Sum. 1973, 5-6; Sum. 1974, 4; Fall 1975, 18-19; Win. 1977, 19.

56. PDC (GC) Reports: 1959, 15-17; 1975, 14-15; PDC (MB) Yearbooks: 1964, 7-10; 1970, 23.

57. Files of congregations; Margaret Shetler info; GH: Feb. 27, 1936; 75th anniversary booklet of Zion, 4-5.

58. Dallas MB info; ME, I, 690; Pannabecker, *Open Doors*, op. cit., 281-282, 334-337; Pannabecker, *Faith in Ferment*, op. cit., 162-164, 285ff., 352-354; Jeanne Zook info.

59. MsEv, July 1950, 10-11; Wilbert R. Shenk letter to HL, May 19, 1987.

60. MsEv: Oct. 1949, 13-15, minutes of Oct. 15, 1949, Board meeting, quotes from 14; July 1950, 11; Jan. 1950, 3, 14-15; Apr. 1949, 6; Apr. 1952, 3, 8; GH: Dec. 12, 1950, 1227; Feb. 6, 1951, 139; Jan. 15, 1952, 69; Feb. 26, 1952, 205, mistakenly indicates steps being taken for cooperation of the PCC Mission Board with EMBMC.

61. MsEv: Apr. 1952, 3; Oct. 1952, 15; Jan. 1954, 2-3, quotes.

62. MsEv: July 1954, 5; Apr. 1955, 3; July 1955, 1, 3, 15-16, quote from 15; Oct. 1955, 2; Jan. 1956, 2-3; Oct. 1956, 3; July 1957; Oct. 1957, 3; MPP, 146.

63. Survey of MsEv regarding LAF, incl. Oct. 1956, 4, first quote; July 1957, 2, second quote; PCC Report, 1960, 7, last quote; Wilbert R. Shenk letter to HL, May 19, 1987; 1976 PCC Report to delegates from Showalter and Kauffman, unp.

64. Survey of MsEv, 1958-1976; James and Noreen Roth letter "To whom it may concern," Apr. 13, 1959, in 1959-60 Mexico folder with Mission Board records; PCC Report, 1966, 5; 1969 Report to Delegates by Mission Board.

65. MsEv: Fall 1968, 2; Spr. 1969, 4; Sum. 1974, 2; Fall 1975, 2; Sum. 1976, 2; Fall 1976, 2-3; PCC Reports: 1971, 8; 1972, 8-9; 1976, 4.

66. The *Telephone Register*, McMinnville, Jan. 12, 1950, 1-3; MsEv: Jan. 1946, 5; Oct. 1949, 12, says 28 heifers; WE, May 1951, 4; Jan. 1959, 6-7; ChrLead: May 10, 1966, 14; June 19, 1966, 23; Katie Funk Wiebe, *Day of Disaster* (Scottdale, 1976), 94ff.; PCC Report, 1957, 12; GH, Aug. 27, 1957, 752.

Chapter 10

1. Emma Goldman, *Living My Life, Volume 1* (New York, 1970), 224-226, 290-296, 309-313; Todd & Curti, op. cit., 507; Dulles, op. cit., 84, 179; Paul Avrich, *The Russian Anarchists* (Princeton, 1967), 163-164, 198; Richard and Anna Maria Drinnon, eds., *Nowhere at Home: Letters from Exile of Emma Goldman and Alexander Berkman* (New York, 1975), xxv-xxviii; Steven K. Smith study of the Isaaks, incl. letter to HL, July 4, 1988.

2. Almanac donated to the PCC Archives; Ralph Lais, op. cit.

3. Paul Toews, "Dissolving the boundaries and strengthening the centers," GH, Jan. 25, 1983, 49-52.

4. Connie Petty, "Patriarch embodies pure, simple living," *Albany Democrat-Herald*, June 20, 1975, 13; accounts of various early families and communities; Kathryn Yoder Miller, op. cit.

5. Orie Conrad letter to HL, Feb. 10, 1975; HT, Oct. 1, 1896, 291; "Account Book of the Mennonite Church" (Hopewell), pp. 7-8; Ralph Lais, op. cit.

6. Omar G. Miller, "A Story of Isaac S. Miller," n.d., unpub. ms.; Omar G. Miller letter to HL, Apr. 12, 1977; Edward Kenagy, "The Brick and Tile Industry,"

Mennonite Community, Feb. 1949, 24-27; Margeret Shetler letter to HL, July 11, 1986.

7. LD mss.: MB, 1; EMB, unp.; Zion and Grace, notes crediting Yearbook, 1929, 45.

8. Peace Section Census of 1940 in MCA; HL conversations: with E. S. Garber, July 19, 1981, at Albany; with L. L. Lind, July 13, 1986, at Eugene; Emma Sommers, "The Zion Community at Hubbard Oregon [sic]," *Mennonite Community,* Feb. 1949, 20-22; Peace Section Census, op. cit.

9. Ethel Reeser, "Where Should Young Women Find Work?" *Mennonite Community,* Feb. 1950, 18-19, 29.

10. Information on congregational questionnaires and from related sources; incomplete responses suggest that from ten to twenty congregations had no farmers in 1976.

11. Ibid.; incomplete returns suggest that at least some women in most congregations worked outside the home.

12. ME: II, 221-222; III, 290-292; IV, 141-142, 186-188; Theodore O. Wedel, "Reminiscences & Reflections," ML, Oct. 1948, 40; Cummings, op. cit., 179.

13. Anna Weirich info, op. cit.; LD mss., records and notes: of Dallas MB minutes; of Zion church records; of PDC (GC) records, 1907; historical sketch in the Grace Diamond Jubilee Service, no author credited; Cummings, op. cit., 179; WE, Feb. 1940, 4.

14. ME, II, 221-222; John Zook letter, May 4, 1896, quote; Shetler, CH, 17; HT, July 1, 1894, 907; Kathryn Yoder Miller, op. cit.; Henry and Bertha Gerig, op. cit.; Ken Goe, op. cit.; Berneice Kennel letter to HL, Mar. 29, 1977; penciled notes in Zion folder, undated, no author named; Floyd Emmert at Hopewell anniversary meeting, Aug. 12, 1978; Shetler, MY 1916, 26, 28; Funk's "Second Count of Mennonites," 1895-1900; Jerry Brenneman, "Mennonites in Oregon . . ." op. cit.; Amos Schmucker ms. of Fairview, 12; Wilbur Kropf ms. of Harrisburg.

15. ME, IV, 493-494; Constitution of the Zion Church; LD info, ms. of Zion and notes of meetings, Feb. 6, 1898, and Mar. 12, 1899; PDC Report, 1968, 21-22; Shetler, MY, 1916, 28; "Account Book of the Mennonite Church [Hopewell]," pp. 56-57, 68, 83; *Mennonite Confession of Faith,* op. cit., 23.

16. *Evangelical Mennonite Brethren Missionary Manual* (Omaha, 1955), 20; *Confession of Faith of the General Conference of Mennonite Brethren Churches,* 1976, 20; Barclay, op. cit., 156-158.

17. ME: III, 43; 343-344; 796 801.

18. Policy of Insurance and Certificate of Membership for Zion, 1917 and 1922; ME, III, 343-44, 796-801; "Account Book of the Mennonite Church" [Hopewell], 79.

19. PCC Report, 1943, 5; author remembers stories of persons who struggled with the question of auto liability insurance.

20. ME, III, 343-344; Kauffman, op. cit., 533ff., quotes from 533 and 543; PCC Constitutions: 1906, 1915, 1924, 1942, 1953; Barclay, op. cit., 156-157.

21. Info from Anna Weirich, Dan Widmer, and Wilbur Kropf.

22. ME, IV, 245; info from Dan Widmer; GH, May 7, 1931, 123; PCC Report, 1938, 4; "Faith Practice and Government of the Tangent Mennonite Church," 1965, 14; Hiebert, op. cit., 448, 462; Barclay, op. cit., 148, 156.

23. PCC Constitution and Discipline, 1953, 13; Report of Committee in PCC sec. files; PCC Report, 1959, 3; ChrLead: Dec. 1, 1956, Harry Neufeld article, p. 5; ChrLead, Apr. 13, 1961, 4-5, 17; Feb. 6, 1962, 5.

24. PCC Constitutions: 1915 and following; 1942, 9, quote; PCC Report, 1908, quote; Toews, op. cit., 344-345, quoting an 1888 conference resolution; Pannabecker, *Open Doors,* op. cit., 383-384; WE, Nov. 1940, 2; news clippings from *Register-Guard,* Eugene, June 23, 1976, through Sep. 2, 1976; John A. Lapp letter to HL, Aug. 19, 1988; John Atkins, "Kenagys crusade to protect farmland," *Corvallis Gazette-Times,* Mar. 20, 1978.

25. Survey of constitutions; PCC Reports: 1921, 5; 1922, 6; 1934, 6; 1935, 5; 1945, 4; 1948, 5; 1949, 9; 1950, 4-5; MWR, Dec. 4, 1986, 3.

26. Information in Tangent files.

27. LD copy of Zion constitution; LD notes of PDC Report; WE: Nov. 1943, unp.; Mar. 1945, unp.; LD copy of Regier letter to Evangelization Committee members King and Harder, 4/6/47; PDC (GC) Report, 1968, 21; Toews, op. cit., 371; ChrLead, Apr. 15, 1955, p. 15; EMB Missionary Manual, op. cit., 22.

28. PCC 1906, "Rules and Discipline," 6-7; PCC Constitution and Discipline: 1915, 10; 1942, 8-9; 1953, 12-13; S&T, July 1930, 15; Kathryn Yoder Miller info.

29. ME, III, 266-267; Guy F. Hershberger, op. cit., 208-213, 270-272, 324, 327; John C. Wenger, *Separated unto God* (Scottdale, 1952), 266-270; Dulles, op. cit., 75-88, 384-396, 471-474, 509-511; Arnold Regier letter to LD, Mar. 28, 1975; George B. Dodds, *Oregon; A Bicentennial History* (New York, 1976), 217-218.

30. *Words of Cheer*, Aug. 4, 1935, 3; PCC Report, 1936, 3-5; GH, June 17, 1937, 249; "Industrial Relations; A Statement of Position . . . 1941," Hershberger, op. cit., 324-327; ME, III, 266; Report of the Labor Union Committee to PCC, Nov. 12-13, 1958, in PCC sec. files.

31. Survey of PCC Reports; 1970 Annual Report to the PCC.

32. "Mennonite Confession of Faith," 1931, containing the 1632 Dordrecht confession, 42-44; ME: II, 74-75; III, 510.

33. GH, Oct. 12, 1939, 596; ME, II, 74-75; PDC (MB) Yearbook, 1976, 26-27; PDC (GC) Report, 1968, 21; LD notes about Grace; PCC Reports to delegates, 1970, 4b; 1972, Report of PCC Ex. Comm. Actions for July 9, 1971, unp.; Chr. Ed. Cabinet report, 1975, 1976, unp.

34. Survey of PDC (GC) Reports; PDC (MB) Yearbook: 1970, 2, 6; 1973, 39-50.

35. GH, June 4, 1925, 200; MWR, Apr. 1972; PCC Report, 1975, 5-6, Brunner quote.

Chapter 11

1. Matthew 5:39, KJV; Wenger in GH, Nov. 11, 1986, 775, corrects erroneous tradition that Constantine made Christianity legal in 325; Wenger, *Introduction to Theology*, op. cit., 314; T. Walter Wallbank and Alastair M. Taylor, *Civilization Past and Present*, Volume 1 (Chicago, Scott, 1949), 226, mention only Theodosius and give year as 395; Dyck, *An Introduction to Mennonite History*, op. cit., 10-21; John Horsch, *Mennonites in Europe* (Scottdale, 1942), 1; John S. C. Abbott, *The History of Christianity . . . .* (Portland, Maine: George Stinson & Co., 1885), 303-324; Wenger, *Separated unto God* (Scottdale, 1952), 253; Bender, "The Anabaptist Vision," in Wenger, *The Mennonite Church in America* (Scottdale, 1966), 315-331; Pannabecker, *Open Doors*, op. cit., 394-395; Guy F. Hershberger, *War, Peace and Nonresistance* (WPN), op. cit., 77, 89; ME, III, 898-901; James C. Juhnke, "Mennonites in Militarist America . . ." in KCC, 171.

2. WPN, 58ff.; Marlin E. Miller, "The Gospel of Peace," 9ff., and John H. Yoder, "The Evangelical Revival and the Peace Churches," 96-103; Robert L. Ramseyer, ed., *Mission and the Peace Witness* (Scottdale, 1979); C. Norman Kraus, "Toward a Theology for the Disciple Community," KCC, 110-112; GVG, 47-53; Horsch, op. cit., 68; Horsch, "War and the Christian Conscience," pamphlet (Scottdale, 1940 reprint [noted on p. 15]), 16.

3. Zion record book, Vol. II, and Vol. I, Dec. 19, 1896, congregational meeting; HT, May 15, 1899, 154.

4. Denlinger, op. cit., section on "Pacifism," notes items in HT, GW, and GH, gives examples of writings against war in Mennonite publications; Peterson, op. cit., 21-24, notes frequent discussions in publications against war.

5. Wallbank and Taylor, op. cit., vol. 2, 384; WPN, 115; Ray H. Abrams, *Preachers Present Arms* (Scottdale, 1969), in this documentary on World War I, discusses the social forces and the war psychology that caused most American

clergymen to support the war effort from their pulpits and otherwise and to vigorously denounce conscientious and other objectors to the war; Smith, op. cit., 540-541; MHB, July 1972, 4; WPN, 110f.; J. S. Hartzler, *Mennonites in the World War* (Scottdale, 1921), 50-51.

6. Allan Teichroew, "Military Surveillance of Mennonites in World War I," MQR, Apr. 1979, 95ff.; WPN, 11; Guy F. Hershberger quote in ME, I, 696; Smith, op. cit., 543; James Juhnke, *A People of Two Kingdoms* (Newton, 1970, 100; Theron Schlabach letter to HL, July 15, 1988.

7. PCC Reports: 1914, 6, 8-9; 1917, 3; MHB, July 1972, 4; HL conversation with Sarah Wall of Dallas, at Albany, Oct. 11, 1986; quotes from Peterson, op. cit., 27-28, 33; Abrams, op. cit., 95ff., discusses the atrocity mongers.

8. E. Z. Yoder letter to Sanford C. Yoder, June 26, 1918, MCA; Wilbur Kropf history of Harrisburg congregation, unpub. ms., 7, copy in author's file, says that Frank Kropf held that the Harrisburg banker's claim that Albany area Mennonites were buying war bonds proved to be false, upon investigation; but Peterson's research indicates that at least several did purchase bonds; Peterson, op. cit., 31-33, quotes on 31, 33 from *Albany Daily Democrat;* Kathryn Yoder Miller, op. cit.; Shetler, CH, 29-30.

9. Peterson, p. 33, for *Harrisburg Bulletin* quote; Wilbur Kropf, op. cit., 6-7; interviews with Frank Kropf and Joe Kropf, as reported in Dick, 61, and Peterson, 46; Wilbur Kropf does not want to be the source of documentation for the Frank Kropf stories; Daniel Kropf's home still showed evidence of gunshot many years later; Orie Kropf, who was present when the Daniel Kropf deliverance occurred, told the story at a Mennonite history workshop at Canby, Oreg., June 23, 1986; some stories include the deacon [perhaps Joseph C. Hostetler, who was ordained in 1922] and Frank Kropf along with Daniel Kropf as being visited by the men from town.

10. Peterson, op. cit., 22-22a; C. Henry Smith, op. cit., 541ff., recounts experiences of conscientious objectors on a national level.

11. Lois Kenagy taped interview with Orie Conrad, Dec. 3, 1979, at Albany, copy of tape in author's possession; Peterson, op. cit., 43.

12. Letters: from E. Z. Yoder to S. C. Yoder: Jan. 28, 1918; Apr. 7, 1918; June 26, 1918; July 18, 1918; Sep. 10, 1918; Oct. 27, 1918; Dec. 29, 1918; from S. C. Yoder to E. Z. Yoder, Mar. 8, 1918; E.Z. Yoder to D. D. Miller, Jan. 28, 1918; all letters in MCA; Peterson, op. cit., 21, 26, 39; Kathryn Yoder Miller, op. cit.

13. Smith, op. cit., 284; Pannebecker, op. cit., 91, 115-116; Toews, op. cit., 130; WPN, 97; Haury, op. cit., 20, note refers to J. B. Toews' study on why Mennonites left Russia in 1874; Bier, op. cit., 11-12; HL conversation with Sarah Wall, Oct. 11, 1986, at Salem; LD ms. of PDC (GC) does not note nonresistance as a subject of discussion before or during WWI; Jost, op. cit., 75; LD records; letters to HL: Erma Neufeld, Oct. 24, 1986; Sol H. Warkentin, Nov. 19, 1986.

14. Letters in MCA: E. Z. Yoder to S. C. Yoder, July 18, 1986; S. C. Yoder to Aaron Loucks, Apr. 26, 1918; S. C. Yoder to D. H. Bender, Apr. 26, 1918; Haury, op. cit., 199; Kathryn Yoder Miller, op. cit.

15. Melvin Gingerich, *Service for Peace* (SFP) (Akron, 1949), 16, 18, 21-28, 33-38, 50-52, 84; chaps. 2-5 detail Mennonite efforts to promote a positive peace testimony and to procure an acceptable plan for an alternative to military and noncombatant service; C. J. Dyck, *From the Files of MCC* (Scottdale, 1980), 9; James C. Juhnke, "Mennonites in Militarist America: Some Consequences of World War I," KCC, 172-174; Juhnke, op. cit., 113-116.

16. Info from Sarah Wall and Sol Warkentin; directory of CPS; MCC Draft Census, in MCA.

17. LD draft of Dallas ms., 9-10; MCC Draft Census records show a wide discrepancy for the I-A-O and I-A classifications; CPS Directory; Toews, op. cit., 350-351; LD notes from minutes of West Salem business meetings, Sep. 14, 1942, to Apr. 12, 1944; Evelyn Boese notes.

18. TM, Aug. 14, 1930, 4-6; May 19, 1942, 15; Nov. 20, 1945, 14; PDC Reports: 1940, 206; 1941, 207, 211; 1942, 214; 1943 in TM, Sep. 14, 1943, 7; WE: Dec. 1941, unp.; Feb. 1942, unp.; March 1942, unp.; May 1942, unp.

19. J. Winfield Fretz, "The Draft Status of General Conference Men in World War II," TM, July 24, 1945, 1-2; MCC Draft Census, ca. 1948; another census of Oregon congregations, apparently earlier, shows a lower percentage classified as IV-E and a higher percentage as I-A; CPS Directory; info from Calvary; HL conversation with Randy Friesen, Nov. 21, 1986, at Eugene; WE: Dec. 1940, unp.; May 1943, unp.; TM: Feb. 3, 1942, 16; Mar. 3, 1942, 15; May 12, 1942, 14; May 19, 1942, 15, quote; Sep. 1, 1942, 13-14; Jan. 22, 1946, 15.

20. LD draft of Dallas ms.; WE: May 1944, unp., for Albany quote; Dec. 1944-Jan. 1945, unp.; TM: Nov. 17, 1942, 3-4; June 6, 1944, 6; June 2, 1945, 14-15; Apr. 9, 1946, 16; TM, Apr. 9, 1946, 16, Dallas quote; Arnold Regier letter to LD, Mar. 28, 1975, in Alberta file; Arnold Regier, in MWR, June 14, 1984, 4; LD interview with Elmer Widmer, Apr. 16, 1975, p. 6, LD ms.

21. SFP, 168-66 l9, 380f.; Regier, op. cit.

22. Program file of Armistice Day meetings, which continued at least through 1957; GH: Nov. 23, 1939, 738; Nov. 9, 1945, 624; PCC Reports: 1933, 4; 1938, 6; 1940, 4-5; ME, III, 889-890; Peterson, op. cit., 68, 75, 85.

23. Guy F. Hershberger, *The Mennonite Church in the Second World War* (MCISWW) (Scottdale, 1951), 30; Peterson, op. cit., 80; *Harrisburg Bulletin* quotes in Peterson: Dec. 11, 1941, on 78; Aug. 10, 1944, on 81; Wilbur Kropf ms., 7.

24. Peterson, op. cit., 82; Miller, Oct. 1946; essence of story from anonymous source.

25. SFP, 52, 74; MCISWW, 37, 40; MsEv, July 1944, Fairview cor., unp.; MCC Draft Census, MCA; Peterson, op. cit., 86, puts CPS at 73 percent.

26. SFP, 52ff., 84; MsEv, Oct. 1944, names and addresses of men in CPS, unp.; PCC Reports: 1941, 5; 1943, 4; 1944, 6-7; MCISWW, 91.

27. Peterson, op. cit., 79, 84, 98; SFP, 84; 348-349, 378, Chap. 23, 395 ff.; MsEv, July 1945, unp.

28. MsEv, July 1945, unp.; SFP, 403-7; Peterson, 100-102.

29. SFP, 168, 203, 274; HL interview with Rufus Franz, Nov. 21, 1986, at Eugene; ME: I, 607-609; IV, 358; Eva Emmert info; N. A. Lind Memoirs, II, 40; MCISWW, 71; Peterson, op. cit., 101; GH, May 7, 1946, 120; TM, Apr. 9, 1946, 11.

30. Emmanuel history notes; TM: Feb. 3, 1942, 16; Feb. 10, 1942, 2; Wendell E. Harmon, "Glimpses of Our Civilian Public Service Camps," Mar. 10, 1942, 9-12; Arnold Regier letter to LD, op. cit.; Peterson, op. cit., 94-97; SFP, 128, 168, 388-389.

31. PCC Reports: 1941, 2, 4; 1943, 4; MCISWW, Lind quote, 104; MsEv, Jan. 1945, probably an annual report, not one for the total war, unp.

32. Peterson, op. cit., 86ff.; Draft Census records in MCA; J. Winfield Fretz, "The Draft Status of General Conference Mennonite Men in World War II," TM, July 24, 1945, 102; MCISWW, 43-44.

33. Peterson, op. cit., 85n; MsEv, Jan. 1945, Zion cor., unp.; Zion boys may not all have been members; Ethel Snyder at Mennonite history workshop, June 23, 1986, at Canby.

34. Statement in PCC sec. files; Peterson, op. cit., 102; PCC Report, 1947, 5; MCISWW, 266.

35. MsEv: July 1947, 4, 7; Jan. 1949, 12; WE, Mar. 1952, unp.

36. Pannabecker, op. cit., 260ff.; Urie Bender, *Soldiers of Compassion* (Scottdale, 1969), 266ff.; 282ff.; MsEv: Oct. 1964, 9; Win. 1966, 15.

37. MsEv: July 1953, 8; Win. 1966, 2-3, 8; Spr. 1966, 16; occasional listings in subsequent issues; personnel lists in Civilian Peace Service [C.P.S.] Coordinator manuals, 1966-1969, 1969-1972, in PCA; letters in PCC sec. files: Marcus Lind to Exec. of PCC, Mar. 22, 1968; Marcus Smucker to CPS Sponsorship Committee and

others, Oct. 14, 1969; David Mann to Marcus Smucker, Nov. 5, 1969; Jost, op. cit., 77.

38. PDC (GC) Reports: 1953, 9; 1954, 9; 1956, 20-21; other committee reports through 1976; WE: Sep. 1948, unp.; June 1951, unp.; Jan. 1952, unp.; May 1953 unp.; TM, June 12, 1951, 376; Toews, op. cit., 351-52, quotes from 375-376.

39. TM, June 12, 1951, 376; Pannebecker, op. cit, 265; John D. Steiner in Emmanuel questionnaire; WE: 1951-57; file notes of Emmanuel, Grace (Dallas), Grace (Albany) and Calvary; info not available for Alberta/Peace and Sweet Home; Toews, op. cit., 351-352,; "U.S. Mennonite Brethren Churches Survey of Students, Christian Service [,] MCC, IW [Sic], Military," 1969-1970, 1970-1971, 1971-1972, 1972-1973, 1973-1974, CMBS; ChrLead: Dec. 19, 1967, 22; June 4, 1968, 23.

40. Abrams, op. cit., 277ff.; Haury, op. cit., 219ff.; Albert N. Keim, "Service or Resistance? The Mennonite Response to Conscription in World War II," MQR, Apr. 1978, 141ff; PDC (MB) Yearbook, 1969, 4-6, 31.

41. GH: Sep. 16, 1969, 802-803; Oct. 7, 1969, 865, 869; MsEv, Sum. 1969, 16; Marcus Lind letter to HL, Mar. 18, 1986.

42. PCC Report, 1970, 4-5; informal surveys and the author's general awareness suggest that in Oregon, only three young men from Zion, students at Goshen College, were draft resisters.

43. HL interviews: Sarah Wall, Oct. 11, 1986, at Albany; Sol Warkentin, Apr. 2, 1983, at Salem; EMB Report on Church Membership and Church Organizations: annual reports, 1965-1975, CMBS.

44. Hostetler, op. cit., 49; MY reports of membership; MCC Draft Census in MCA; *The Telephone Register,* McMinnville, Jan. 12, 1950, 1-3.

45. Oregon BIC persons have not responded to HL queries; MsEv: Fall 1973, 10; Spr. 1974, 18; Spr. 1975, 11; Wittlinger, op. cit., 531; Hiebert, op. cit., 469; Amanda Toews letter to LD, May 23, 1975, letter in author's file.

46. John Driver, *Community and Commitment* (Scottdale, 1976), 70.

Chapter 12

1. Kathryn Yoder, "A History of Education Among the Mennonites on the West Coast," op. cit., 4-6; PCC Reports: 1911; 1917, 8, 5; 1919, 6-7; 1920, 2-4; 1921, 4; GH: Aug. 26, 1920, 432; Nov. 11, 1920, 652.

2. GH: Jan. 27, 1921, 867-868; Feb. 17, 1921, 928; Shetler, CH, 71; "Pacific Coast Bible School"—a printed one-page report, almost identical to a typed paper found in Ina (Hostetler) Wolfer's papers after her death.

3. GH: Feb. 24, 1921, 944; Oct. 20, 1921, 576; Nov. 3, 1921, 600; Oct. 29, 1925, 640; Dec. 17, 1925, 777; Feb. 4, 1926, 923; Feb. 24, 1927, 1017; Dec. 29, 1927, 840; Jan. 25, 1928, 937; Jan. 10, 1929, 852; Shetler, *Preacher of the People,* op. cit., 186, 208-209; minutes of Bishops' meeting, Nov. 17, 1921, MCA, Collection 111-13-1; programs of Bible schools at Sheridan in 1937 and 1938; PCC Reports: 1922, 8; 1924, 4, quote; 1926, 4; 1927, 6-7; 1928, 4-5; 1929, 5-6, 8; Shetler, CH, 70-72; "Bulletin for the Short Term Bible Schools . . . 1928"; the School Committee later became known as the School Board.

4. PCC Report, 1930, 5-6; Yoder, op. cit., 10-11.

5. PCC Reports: 1930, 5-6; 1935, 5; announcement leaflets of Sheridan and Zion schools; GH, Jan. 30, 1941, 940.

6. ME, IV, 1009; PCC Reports: 1934, 4-5; 1935, 5; 1938, 6; 1943, 4-5; 1946, 5, 9; programs of young people's institutes [1935]-1940; Yoder, op. cit., 13; reports from the Young People's Institute Committee: 1944-1945, in author's files; quote from 1946, Report D in Yoder, op. cit.; also Yoder, 13; handwritten program of Fairview institute.

7. PDC minutes: 1925, 1927, 1928, from LD ms., 23; "Second Annual Report of the Pacific District Conference Retreat Committee" by L. J. Horsch, Sec., in TM [1927]; TM: July 22, 1926, 3; June 3, 1941, 15; CE, July 17, 1928, 237; PDC

Report, 1946, 8; succeeding reports, beginning with 1947, 9-10, 25-26, tell of a Young People's Union which did not include Bible training in its purpose; WE: Oct. 1933, 4; Nov. 1943, unp.; Dec. 1940, unp.; July 1952, unp.; Oct. 1952, unp.; Nov. 1952, unp.; Dec. 1956, unp.; TM: Apr. 16, 1935, 7; Aug. 6, 1935, 8-9; Feb. 6, 1940, 8; PDC (MB) Yearbooks: 1931, 17; 1932, 10; 1940, 51-52; Toews, op. cit., 259; Warkentin and Gingerich, *Who's Who Among the Mennonites* (WWM), op. cit., 24-25.

    8. ME: I, 332; IV, 403; PDC (MB) Yearbooks: 1939, 41-42; 1940, 51-52; Otto Bier, op. cit., 12-13; Erma Neufeld info in Dallas MB file; LD info in Dallas EMB file; WWM, 334-335; WE: Dec. 1940, unp.; May 1941, unp.; Nov. 1941, unp.; Apr. 1942, unp.; May 1945, unp.

    9. PDC (MB) Yearbooks, 1945 through 1956; ME, IV, 403.

    10. Ibid.; quote from GH Jantzen, 1946 report, 41; articles about Aganetha Toews in *Eugene Register Guard*, June 11, 1984, 1-2C; Bier, op. cit., 12-13.

    11. GH, Jan. 4, 1946, 764; PCC Report, 1945, 5; Kathryn Yoder, op. cit., 14-16 and appendix; PCC Report, 1945, 5; Miller, "West Coast Echoes," July-Sep. 1951, unp.

    12. Marcus Lind letter to HL, July 28, 1986; Yoder, op. cit., 19; Diana C. Blackstone, "The History of Western Mennonite School," unpub. ms. at WMS, 1983, 3; ME: I, 308; II, 122-124.

    13. PCC Report, 1951, 4; HL conversation with Clifford Lind, July 15, 1986; misc SBT announcements 1948 through 1953; HL telephone interview with Bernard Showalter, Dec. 1, 1988.

    14. MsEv, July 1956, 8,; panel discussion at Board Appreciation Night, Feb. 23, 1987, at Salem; MY: 1969, 19; 1974, 65; 1975, 92; 1976, 94; misc reports and conversations about WMS.

    15. ME, II, 151; "Report of the Committee to Study the Need and Possibility of Church Controlled Schools," in PCC sec. files, 1945; Yoder, op. cit., 19-20; MsEv: July 1948, 7; July 1950, 13; May 1958, 11; GH, Mar. 29, 1949, 309; letters to Hope Lind: Sterling Roth; Omar Miller, May 10, 1975; Maynard Headings, Aug. 16, 1978; Shirley Yoder talk at Zion, Feb. 19, 1976; Margaret Shetler info.

    16. Letters to HL: Wilbert Kropf, May 9, 1975; Wilbur Kropf, Dec. 3, 1981; MY: 1976, 94; 1986, 144; HL telephone interview with Beverly Knox, Nov. 30, 1977; Mildred Schrock info.

    17. ME: I, 302-303; II, 817; PCC Report, 1946, 5; Barrett, op. cit., 169-171; GVG, 109; Aaron J. Epp, "Bethany Lives On," small booklet giving history of Bethany hospital; PDC minutes as recorded in LD ms., 16-17.

    18. ME, IV, 403; Warkentin and Gingerich, op. cit., 321, 365; L. L. Lind, July 19, 1986, at Eugene, said that N. A. Lind served on the board for a time; Epp, op. cit., 1-3; Rufus Franz comments at Oregon Advisory Committee meeting, June 7, 1986, at Salem; Arno Wiebe, "Nurses Began Salem Mennonite Witness," MWR, June 25, 1987, 11, gives December 1916 as opening date; Arno Wiebe letter to HL, May 21, 1988.

    19. WE: Nov. 1934, 3; Apr. 1941, unp.; Apr. 1945, unp.; CE: Apr. 25, 1924, 144; July 4, 1924, 224; PDC (MB) Yearbook, 1945, 19; Jerry Easterling, "He feels like a father to Salem Memorial," *Oregon Territory*, Jan. 16, 1977, 3.

    20. Peg Hatfield, "History of the Lebanon Community Hospital," unpub. ms. [1975], unp., copy in author's possession.

    21. Ibid.; PCC Reports: 1946, 5, gives year of initial contact—Hatfield date of 1947 is in error; MsEv: Apr. 1946, 3; Jan. 1948, 2-3; CL, May 1962, 26-28, 33; Allen Erb, *Privileged to Serve* (Elkhart, 1975), 161ff.; GH, Jan. 17, 1951, 60-61.

    22. Erb, op. cit. 163-64, 180-81; GH: Jan. 17, 1951, 60-61; July 1, 1962, 663; Aug. 19, 1952, 828; Hatfield, op. cit.; PCC Report, 1950, 5, 13; Miller, "West Coast Echoes," July 1950 Suppl, unp.

    23. GH, Jan. 17, 1951, 60-61; 1986 Kanagy response to draft of ms.; MY, 1977, 97; Hatfield, op. cit.

24. PCC Reports: 1914, 7; 1915, 10; 1916, 8-9; 1921, 5; 1922, 4; 1923, 8; 1925, 5; 1929, 8; GH, May 1, 1924, 89, quote; Lee, op. cit., 26-28; ME, III, 811; MsEv: July 1944, 4; Apr. 1946, 2; Oct. 1946, 7; survey of 1947-49 issues; Oct. 1949, 13; Jan. 1950, 14; Apr. 1950, 11.

25. GH, Dec. 14, 1939, 793; PDC (MB) Yearbook, 1947, 56; dedication program for the Mennonite Home for the Aged at Albany.

26. "A brief statement in the matter of obtaining an Old People's Home . . ." no author, in 1945 PCC sec. file; GH, Aug. 3, 1945, 330; PCC Reports: 1939, 5; 1941, 5-6, quote; 1944, 5; 1945, 6.

27. GH: Aug. 3, 1945, 530; May 13, 1947, 163-164; Aug. 26, 1947, 475; MsEv: July 1945, 2; Jan. 1946, 1; Apr. 1946, 2, 4-5; Jan. 1947, quote from 1, 4; leaflet: "Drawing of the Proposed Mennonite Old Peoples [sic] Home . . ."; PCC Report, 1946, 13.

28. PCC Report: 1947, 8; MsEv: July 1947, 7; survey of MsEv, 1950s; GH, Nov. 23, 1954, 1116; Luke Birky info.

29. PDC (MB) Yearbooks: 1947, 56-57; survey of reports in yearbooks through 1966, the last year of a report for the Dallas Home; Bier, op. cit., 15; Erma Neufeld info.

30. MsEv: Apr. 1956, 4, quotes; Oct. 1956, 3; Jan. 1957, 3, 9; July 1957, 9.

31. MsEv: Jan. 1959, 11; Apr. 1960, 3; July 1960, 7; July 1961, 6; July 1963, 6; Fall 1966, 4; Fall 1972, 17; Mission Board Report to Conference, 1973, in report to delegates, unp.; MWR, Dec. 2, 1976, 11; Ralph Holderman info.

32. MsEv: Apr. 1946, 4; July 1956, 15; Margaret Shetler letter to HL, Dec. 3, 1986.

33. GH: Feb. 11, 1947, 996; July 6, 1948, 636; survey of PCC Reports; printed program of the 1947 camp; Margaret Shetler letter to HL, Mar. 3, 1987; "Willamette Youth Fellowship," a short history, no author named, written 1957; Rebecca Horst, "History of Oregon Mennonite Youth Camps," unpub. ms., 1960, at WMS; Berneice Kennel letter to Becky Horst, Apr. 4, 1960, in Kennel's files; copy of 1948 program in author's files.

34. Programs or announcements of 1949, 1950, 1951, 1953 camps; survey of PCC Reports; the anon. ms., op. cit., and the Horst ms., op. cit., are not consistent in regard to camping and retreats between 1948 and 1957; Jess Kauffman, op. cit., 59; MsEv: July 1951, 3; July 1963, 8; Sum. 1965, 8; Win. 1972, 8; Fall 1975, 14; Sum. 1976, 9; Margaret Shetler letters to HL, Dec. 3, 1986, and Mar. 3, 1987.

35. MsEv: July 1951, 3, 20; July 1953, 2; July 1955, 3, 16; July 1959, 3; July 1962, 6-7; Apr. 1964, 7; July 1964, 1, 10; Apr. 1965, 7; Spr. 1975, 12.

36. MsEv: July 1956, 15, Martha Hostetler quote; Kauffman, op. cit.

37. MsEv: Oct. 1960, 5; Apr. 1961, 4; Jan. 1963, 8; Jan. 1964, 8; "Drift Creek Currents," Apr. 28, 1985; HL telephone conversation with Ben Kenagy, May 30, 1987.

38. Survey of reports in MsEv, 1964 through Win. 1977, Sum. 1979.

39. MY, 1977, 89-90; misc info about BMF; TM, Aug. 28, 1945, 10-11; Vivian Schellenberg letter to HL, Sep. 3, 1986; PDC (GC) Reports, 1969-1974, report of organization; PDM, May 29, 1973, A-3; survey of PDC (MB) Yearbooks; LD ms. of Dallas EMB, 7; GH, Feb. 1, 1949, 119, lists Amanda Anderson as a daughter of Henry J. Yoder.

Chapter 13

1. Emmanuel withdrew from the PDC (GC) early in 1984; Sweet Home Community Chapel withdrew about then or soon after.

2. GH, Jan. 31, 1984, 69; HL conversation with Ray Zehr, Apr. 22, 1984, at Eugene.

3. ME, III, 622; PCC Report, 1932, 6.

4. PCC Reports: 1970, 4; 1971, 4; 1972, 4; MsEv: Sum. 1974, quote on 16, 14; Fall 1975, 8-9.

5. Daniel Hertzler, ed., *Not by Might,* op. cit., 161, quotes from 162; MsEv: Win. 1974, 15; Fall 1975, 9; Win. 1976, 1, 2, 20.

6. Barclay, op. cit., 147-148; MWR: Aug. 17, 1972; July 17, 1975, 6, and article in same issue, "Nationwide Bible Meeting Planned"; July 22, 1976, 7.

7. Pannabecker, op. cit., 382ff.; 346-347; LD, "Mennonites at the End of the Oregon Trail," ca. 1977, unpub. ms., copy in author's possession; Wilbert Regier statements from LD notes.

8. Dick, op. cit., 8-9; PDC Report, 1964, 18.

9. Otto Bier, op. cit., quote on 12, 16; LD notes of Kingwood minutes; Rufus Franz info; LD ms. of Dallas MB, 16; WWM, 23, 109; ChrLead: Oct. 1940, 25; Jan. 1, 1948, 11; MWR, May 20, 1982, 12; list of pastors at Dallas; J. A. Toews, op. cit., 269-270, 273.

10. ME, II, 264; MY, 1977, 122; HL conversation Frank and Sarah Wall at Salem, Nov. 10, 1986; Dallas EMB questionnaire; EV: Mar. 10, 1976, 15; May 10, 1976; July 10, 1976, 15; Sep. 25, 1976, 15; MY, 1977, 122; Hiebert, op. cit., 304-305; Nov. 9, 1981, draft in Evergreen folder.

11. Oregon's Amish community had essentially disbanded by the time the Amish publishing venture at Alymer, Ontario, developed; ME, II, 264; Hiebert, op. cit., 325-327, 587-589; Wittlinger, op. cit., 258-269, 415-418.

12. PCC Reports: 1907; 1923, 7; 1933, 5; 1934, 6; 1938, 4; 1958, 4; 1961, 2; 1964, 3-4; ME, III, 634; MsEv: Apr. 1959, 4; Sum. 1971, 11-13; Spr. 1972, 12-14; Fall 1975, 10; anecdote told by J. C. Wenger to HL, Oct. 11, 1984, at Goshen; data from MPH in PCC sec. files.

13. TM: Mar. 31, 1942, 16; June 2, 1942, 1; Sep. 14, 1943, 13; Jan. 15, 1947, 7; PDC Yearbook, 1940, 53; ChrLead, Oct. 1940, 22; survey of ChrLead files.

14. Comments of Mary Zehr Lind, in author's hearing; MY&D, 1930, 23; PCC Reports: 1931, 5; 1944, 5; 1955, 5; David Peterson, "The Culture of Oregon Mennonitism Between the Two World Wars," 1982, unpub. ms., copy in author's possession, 18-19, 30; no studies have been done of Oregon youth attending Mennonite schools in post-World War II years; HL relationship with Oregon Mennonites since the early 1950s and residence in the state since 1960 leads to the observation; incomplete responses on questionnaire; ME, II, 547; MY, 1977, 92, indicates Rosedale Bible School began in 1951, the Institute in 1966.

15. WE: Apr. 1935, 4; Nov. 1937, 4; Dallas corr. in July 1952, and Dec. 1956; ME, II, 559-560; Haury, op. cit., 232ff., 250; PDC Report, 1951, 8; LD notes for 1948, including an unidentified writer about Bethel College, from PDC records; LD ms. of Emmanuel, 4; survey of correspondence from Oregon congregations in WE and TM, incl. WE: Jan. 1955, unp.; Mar. 1955, unp.

16. Bier, op. cit., 13-14; ChrLead: Oct. 1944, 12; Jan. 1, 1955, 11; LD info; Toews, op. cit., 229, 274-6; GH, Jan. 25, 1983, 51; Kingwood and North Park questionnaires.

17. MY, 1977, 122; Dallas EMB questionnaire.

18. ME, III, 44-48; survey of HT corr. 1876 and later; GW, Dec. 19, 1906, 601; GH: July 10, 1913, 232-233; Oct. 19, 1916, 541 quote; Dec. 16, 1926, 816; WE: Apr. 1935, 3; May 1944; Apr. 1, 1947, 13-14; Rufus Franz info.

19. Pannabecker, 47, quote; survey of PCC reports through 1959; SSHs addressed to Berniece Kropf, with expiration date on label about eighteen months later, several copies in author's files; Margaret Shetler info; MsEv, Win. 1975, 14; at least one of Orie Kropf's daughters, Albany congregation, attended Upland College; Wittlinger, op. cit., 306.

20. WE, Nov. 1943, unp.; TM, Apr. 22, 1947, 15; Bertha Harder letter to LD, March 22, 1975, in Inter-Mennonite folder; survey of congregational records and correspondence from several publications.

21. PCC Report, 1947, 5; WE, May 1959, unp.; PDM, July 1959, unp.; Jan. 29, 1974, A-1; ChrLead, May 9, 1967, 23; MsEv: Fall 1971, 2; Spr. 1975, 11; "A

Festival of Praise," program; PDC Report, 1973, 12, Brunner quote; LD, ms. of PDC history, 47.

22. Earlier chapters illustrate GC, MB, and EMB cooperation with other denominations; PCC Reports: 1916, 14-15; 1920, 3; survey of reports and info from congregations and periodicals.

23. Jeanne Zook info.

Chapter 14

1. ME, I, 656.

2. Floyd Emmert in MsEv, Apr. 1947, 5; CE, June 19, 1928, 194.

3. PCC Report, 1975, unp.; Wilbert Shenk letters to HL, Apr. 28, 1987, and May 19, 1987.

4. Joan Didion, "The Coast," *Esquire,* Feb. 1976, 10, 14; Naisbitt, *Megatrends* (New York, 1982), 210-211.

5. Stanley Hauerwas, *The Peaceable Kingdom* (Notre Dame, 1983), 70; Henry Steele Commager, *The Nature and Study of History* (Columbus, 1965), 92-93.

6. PCC Report, 1986, 7; author's observations during June 20, 1986, delegate session.

7. HL consultation with Harold Hochstetler, Jan. 16, 1986, at Eugene.

8. Katie Funk Wiebe, "The power of a promise," GH, Nov. 18, 1986, 786.

9. Harold Hochstetler, op. cit.

10. Paul Toews, "Mennonite myths and realities," CL, Oct. 1986, 21-26, quotes from 23 and 24.

Appendix
Leaders in Oregon Mennonite Congregations Through 1976

Men who served as ordained ministers influenced their congregations, some significantly but all to some degree. (Before 1976 no women served any Oregon congregation in such a designated capacity, though a number served as strong congregational leaders.) They preached and taught the Bible and encouraged their members to live as faithful followers of Christ. Bishops or elders were ministers with additional responsibilities, such as organizing congregations, administering baptism and communion, and performing ordinations and marriages. Occasionally in later years a minister was licensed rather than ordained—at his or the congregation's discretion—for a time of testing which often led to later ordination. For older congregations it is not always possible to determine who was the leading minister or designated pastor. This list includes many assisting and perhaps some retired ministers.

Deacons administered alms funds or assisted financially needy members in other ways. Many also assisted in congregational discipline. Some, especially in Amish Mennonite congregations, took a turn at preaching. Mennonite Brethren informants did not list their many deacons, whose status did not carry the level of authority common in AM and MC congregations. Several other groups also did not list deacons.

Mennonites believed in the priesthood of all believers, that individual Christians did not need an intermediary between them and God. But they still accorded respect and authority to their chosen leaders. This list recognizes those leaders, their influence on Oregon congregations and conferences, and the sacrifices many of them made to serve God and his people in this way.

Key

bp followed by dates: years as resident bishop. This designation was most common among groups with Swiss Mennonite heritage.

d followed by dates: years as deacon.

e followed by dates: years as elder. Known records do not identify all who were elders. This designation was most common among groups with Dutch/Russian Mennonite heritage.

l followed by dates: years as licensed minister.

Dates with no other designation: years as minister.

Asterisk (°) indicates years as nonresident bishop, in addition to serving as resident leader.

ca: circa (about).

[year]–(dash) with no date following: continuing through 1976. If 1976 is part of date, person terminated during 1976.

Other Explanation

Full information is not available for every ordained person.

Sources include *Mennonite Yearbook* (MC), *Mennonite Yearbook* (GC), *Yearbook of the Pacific District Conference* (MB), conference reports, information from congregational historians, obituaries and notes from various church periodicals, and other published Amish or Mennonite histories.

Congregations are listed in order of organization, with the conference affiliation or lack of it shown in parentheses. The list of abbreviations located near the front of the book details those used to identify each congregation in 1976. Dates following the congregation's name indicate organization date and, if applicable, the date of disbanding. Earlier congregational names or affiliations may also be included.

■ ■ ■

NEEDY AMISH (OOA), ca
1879-ca 1918, at Needy
Joseph Meyer, ca 1879-ca early
1880s
Peter Christner, ? -ca 1883 or
1887
Jonas J. Kauffman, bp 1880-1907
Jacob F. Swartzendruber, ca
1881-ca 1882
John A. Miller, several years in
early 1880s; 1890-1893
David C. Schrock, 1895-ca 1897
Noah Schrock, ca 1907- ?

C. B. STEINER SWISS MENNO-
NITE (UM), ca 1880-1928,
first at Pratum, later at homes
in Clackamas County
Christian Geiger, ca 1880-1884;
bp 1884-1913
John Beer, 1884-1928
Peter Neuschwander,
d 1884-1898
C. B. Steiner, bp 1885-1903

PORTLAND (MB), ca 1886-ca
1938, in Portland
Heinrich Helzer, 1886-1893;
e 1893-1904
P. C. Hiebert, 1907-1908 (lived
and served also at Dallas)
H. S. Voth, 1909-1915 (lived and
served also at Dallas)
Heinrich Reisbich, 1916-1924
Peter Heinrich, (l ?) 1916-1924,
1926-1929
K. Wittenberg, 1918-1919
N. L. Popp, d 1921-1929
F. F. Friesen, 1923-1924,
1936-ca 1938
Heinr. Pauli, 1925-1926
C. Urbach, 1930-ca 1933

LANE COUNTY (AM), ca 1887-ca
1898, west of Eugene
Peter Christner, bp ca 1887-ca
1898 (but largely inactive after
1889)
Peter D. Mishler, 1892-1893;
bp 1893-1894

Jacob D. Mishler, 1893-1895;
bp 1895-1898
Levi J. Yoder, d 1893-1895;
1895-1898

EMMANUEL (GC), 1890, east of
Salem, earlier known as Waldo
Hills Mennonite Church
John Rich, e 1890-1894
Peter J. Gerig, 1894-1909
S. S. Baumgartner, 1910-1925
John M. Franz, 1925-1940
Daniel J. Unruh, 1940-1943
John R. Turnbull, 1943-1944
Wilbert A. Regier, 1944-1952
Frank Harder, 1953-1957
Allan R. Tschiegg, 1958-1972
Wilbert A. Regier, 1972-1973
Barry Horner, 1973-1974
Glen Makin, 1974-1975
Frank Schutzwohl, 1975-

PERRYDALE (CGC), ca 1890-ca
1902
Samuel Boese, 1893-1902

ZION (MC) (1893), near Hubbard,
earlier AM
Amos P. Troyer, d 1893-1895;
1895; bp 1895-1935
Daniel J. Kropf, 1893-1911
Daniel Roth, d 1900-1923
Edward Z. Yoder, 1911-1954
Daniel B. Kauffman, 1919-1928
Levi J. Yoder, 1922-1930 (but
largely inactive)
Clarence I. Kropf, d 1923-1935;
bp 1935-ca 1960
Paul N. Roth, 1936-1944
Christian G. Yoder, d 1936-1946
Chester Kauffman, 1945-1950
John E. Gingerich, d 1947-
Edward (Kelly) Kenagy, 1949-ca
1953
John M. Lederach, 1957-1960;
bp 1960-1966
John E. Garber, d 1961-
Linford Hackman, 1964-1965
Paul Brunner, 1966-1975
John P. Oyer, 1975-

FAIRVIEW (UM), 1894, east of Albany, earlier AM and MC
Jacob Roth, 1894; bp 1895–1903
Daniel Erb, d 1897–1898;
  1898–1937
Peter Neuschwander,
  d 1898–1911
C. R. Gerig, 1904–1908;
  bp 1908–1942
Joseph Schrock, 1909–1923
Joseph E. Whitaker, 1912–1919
C. C. Steckley, d 1912–1944
Frank E. Roth, 1919–ca 1932
Melvin Schrock, 1934–ca 1949
Henry Gerig, 1934–1963
N. M. Birky, bp 1938–1960
Verl Nofziger, d 1948–1954;
  1954–1960; bp 1960–
Merrill Boshart, d 1956–
Neil Birky, l 1957–1958;
  1958–1963
Percy Gerig, l 1965–1966
Clarence Gerig, l 1965–1970;
  1970–
Roy Hostetler, 1970–

GRACE (GC), 1896, at Dallas, earlier a separate rural congregation named Zion
H. A. Bachman, 1899–ca 1901
Isaac Dyck, l 1903–1904;
  1904–1908
John P. Neufelt, 1909–1919
Bernhard H. Janzen, ca
  1920–1922
John M. Franz, 1923–1925
S. S. Baumgartner, 1926–1929
  (lived and served also at Portland)
Gerhard Baergen, 1929–1933
Herbert E. Widmer, 1933–1939
Homer Leisy, 1939–1948
John R. Warkentin, 1948–ca 1949
J. J. Regier, 1949–ca 1952
Earl Peterson, 1952–1953
John M. Franz, 1953–1955
Harold D. Burkholder,
  1955–1960
Waldo J. Flickinger, 1960–1965

J. R. Duerkson, 1965–1966
J. J. Esau, 1965–1966
Olin Krehbiel, 1966–1970
Ted Fast, 1970–

MCMINNVILLE AMISH (OOA),
  1897–1904, 1906–1930,
  1935–1961, near McMinnville
David C. Schrock, 1897–1902
Tobias T. Yoder, 1898–1899;
  bp 1899–1902
David Y. Miller, ca 1908–1912;
  bp 1912–1913, 1919–1922
David D. Schlabach, bp
  1909–1912
Daniel E. Miller, ca 1910–1912;
  1916–1917; bp 1917–1921,
  1948–1952
Daniel Coblentz, d 1911–1913
Alvin M. Beachy, 1915–1922
Moses W. Yoder, ca 1935–1939;
  bp 1939–ca 1947
Menno Swartzentruber, ca
  1938–1951; bp 1951–1961
Samuel Weaver, 1945–1961
Ben Slabaugh/Schlabach,
  1945–1960
William D. Miller, ca 1947–ca
  1952

HOPEWELL (UM), 1899, near
  Hubbard, earlier MC
J. D. Mishler, bp 1899–1923
Levi Welty, d 1899–1902
Noah L. Hershberger, 1904–1956
Alex I. Miller, d 1904–1914
John F. Bressler, ca 1906–1909
William Bond, 1911–1941
S. G. Shetler, 1913–1915;
  bp 1915–1916, 1920–1921
Daniel F. Shenk, d 1915–1922
John K. Lehman, 1915–1917
Lloy A. Kniss, 1920–1921
Hugh Wolfer, d 1920–1929
Henry Wolfer, 1923–1927;
  bp 1927–1943
Oliver W. King, d 1933–1964
Leroy Cowan, 1939–1946
Allan Good, 1939–ca 1940

James Bucher, 1946-1968
LeRoy Hooley, 1948-1952
Jacob S. Roth, 1949-1966
Maynard Headings, 1957-1960;
1972-
James Roth, 1959, 1976-
Glen Roth, l 1960-1961
Levi Strubhar, l 1963-1965;
d 1965-
Sterling Roth, l 1968-1969;
1969-1976

ALBANY (MC) (1899), at Albany,
earlier known as Twelfth
Street Mennonite Church
Levi J. Yoder, 1899-ca 1908
David Hilty, 1901-1902; °
1904-1907
John P. Bontrager, 1905-1911;
bp 1911-1919; ° 1919-1921,
1940-1949
Moses E. Brenneman,
d 1911-1915; 1915-1957
John Steckley, 1913-1929
Ephraim Martin, 1916-1962
Joseph E. Whitaker, 1919-1929
Norman A. Lind, 1919-1921;
bp 1921-1940
John H. Whitaker, d 1930-1966
George Kauffman, 1938-1957
Paul E. Yoder, 1949-1955
Allen H. Erb, bp 1953-1957; °
1957-1960
David Mann, 1955-1960;
bp 1960-1970
Nelson E. Kauffman,
bp 1970-1972
James M. Lapp, 1972-

NORTH DALLAS (MB),
1905-1923, north of Dallas
Jacob Toews, e 1905-ca 1906
Peter P. Buhler, d 1905-1923
P. C. Hiebert, 1907-1908
H. S. Voth, 1909-1915
P. H. Berg
John Enns, ? -ca 1920
Dietrich D. Bartel, ? -1923
Abraham Buhler, 1917-1923
H. F. Klassen

HARRISBURG (UM), 1911, near
Harrisburg, formerly Conserva-
tive Amish Mennonite
Daniel J. Kropf, 1911-1914;
bp 1914-1927
Peter Neuschwander,
d 1911-1916
Enos Hostetler, 1912-1913
Jacob Roth, 1921-1926
Joseph C. Hostetler,
d 1922-1927; bp 1927-1931
Joseph Schrock, 1923-1943
Levi Kropf, 1927-
John P. Yoder, d 1930-1932;
bp 1932-
Orrie Yoder, 1934
Ira Headings, d 1942-1946
Jacob S. Roth, 1942-1944
Noah Miller, 1945-1948
Wilbur D. Kropf, 1949-
Herman Kropf, d 1949-
Wilbert D. Kropf, 1955-1957;
bp 1957-
Willard L. Stutzman, 1959-1966
Joe Birky, d 1959- (without offi-
cial charge)

DALLAS (EMB), 1912, at Dallas,
earlier called Bruderthaler
Solomon Ediger, 1912-1920
H. H. Dick, 1920-1928
Jacob H. Quiring, 1920-1935;
e 1935-1941
John J. Friesen, d 1920-ca 1960
Abr. F. Friesen, ca 1922- ?
John J. Schmidt, 1928-1929
John P. Neufelt, ca 1934- ?
J. N. Wall, 1930s
A. C. Wall, 1930s, perhaps 1940s,
1947-1948
Peter Fast, 1930s
H. S. Unruh, ca 1941- ?
D. P. Schultz, 1941-1947
A. P. Toews, 1947-1952
Arno Wiebe, 1953-1961
Allen Wiebe, 1961-1968
Peter Unrau, 1969-
John Ratzlaff, 1971-1974
Allen Tschiegg, 1975-1976
Randy Benson, 1976-

FIRDALE (MC), 1915–1924, near
 Airlie and Suver
 E. C. Weaver, d 1914–1922
 G. D. Shenk, 1916–1921;
  bp 1921–1924
 M. B. Weaver, d 1920–1923
 Luke E. Weaver, 1921–1924
  (stayed through 1928)

BETHEL (UM), 1919–1969, near
 Canby, earlier AM and MC
 Fred J. Gingerich, 1919–1921;
  bp 1921–1955
 Chris Snyder, d 1920–1948
 Orrie D. Yoder, 1930–ca 1933;
  1934–ca 1937
 Sam Shrock, 1935–1973
 Omar G. Miller, 1935–1969 (in-
  cluding Molalla for a time
  before it disbanded)
 Ernest Bontrager, 1943–1955
 Jonathan C. Zook, d 1948–1951;
  bp 1951–1969
 J. A. Birky, d 1953–1958
 Harold Reeder, d 1960–1969
 Joe H. Yoder, 1962–1968

DALLAS (MB), 1919, in Dallas
 D. A. Peters, 1919–1920
 P. H. Berg, 1919–1921
 John M. Enns, 1919–1921,
  1935–1936
 P. E. Penner, 1921– ?
 George/Gerhard G. Wiens,
  1921–ca 1930
 D. D. Bartel, ca 1920–ca 1925
 F. F. Wall, 1923–1938, 1946
 John J. Kliewer, 1924
 H. D. Wiebe, 1925–ca 1936,
  1940–1942, 1943–1944,
  1954–1958, 1965–1967
 F. F. Friesen, 1926–1936
 Abraham Buhler, 1928–1929
 N. N. Hiebert, 1935–1939
 D. J. Dick, 1936–ca 1948
 J. J. Toews, 1940–1943
 Henry Hooge, 1942–1946,
  1954–63
 G. N. Jantzen, 1945–1951

David P. Schultz, 1950–1951,
  1954–
 Walter Penner, 1952–1955
 Lando Hiebert, summer 1955
 D. J. Wiens, 1955–1959
 Lando Hiebert, summer 1959
 Arthur Flaming, 1959–1964
 P. B. Pauls, 1962–1963
 Herman Neufeld, 1963–1973
 Orlando Wiebe, summer 1964
 Louis Goertz, 1964–1969
 John Neufeld, 1 1966–
 Eugene Gerbrandt, 1969–1972
 Ted Fast, 1969–1970
 Stanley Lyman, 1972–
 Glenn Makin, 1974–

SHERIDAN (UM), 1923, at
 Sheridan, earlier MC
 J. D. Mishler, bp 1923–1928
 Daniel F. Shenk, 1923–1962
 G. D. Shenk, bp 1924–1961
 William Beachy, d 1924–ca 1938
 Hugh Wolfer, d 1929–1947
 Amos Kilmer, 1931–1945
 James Bucher, 1942–1946
 Henry Wolfer, 1943–1945,
  1947–1955
 Max Yoder, 1945–1955
 Leroy Cowan, 1946–1965
 Raymond Mishler, 1947–1956;
  bp 1956–
 Oscar Wideman, ordained 1950
  (served in Portland)
 Eldon Hamilton, 1952–1962
  (served in Honduras)
 Enos Schrock, d 1961–
 David Hostetler, 1962–
 Lee Mast, 1963–1965
 James Eigsti, 1972–

PORTLAND (MC), 1924, in Port-
 land
 Allan Good, 1924–1932
 Paul N. Roth, 1924–1936
 Henry J. Yoder, d 1927–1942
 Glenn W. Whitaker, 1936–1939
 Marcus Lind, 1940–1945
 Chester D. Hartzler,
  d 1942–1957

Claud M. Hostetler, 1948-1961
Luke E. Weaver, 1957-1972
Amsa Kauffman, 1962-1963
Glen Roth, short time in 1963
Marcus Smucker, 1963–
Cleo Mann, 1969-1971
Lee J. Miller, 1970-1972

PEACE (GC), 1931, in Portland,
  formerly known as Alberta at
  an earlier location
Albert Claassen, 1933-1935
Edmund J. Miller, 1937-1940
Arnold Regier, 1940-1943
Herman Wiebe, 1943-1945
Clyde Dirks, 1945-1951
James Braga, 1951-1952
Harry Albrecht, 1952-1959
Samuel Ediger, 1959-1961
Nobel Sack, 1961–ca 1969,
  1970-1971
Melvin C. Williams, 1969-1970
Elmer Friesen, 1971–

GRACE (GC), 1931-1968, in Al-
  bany
W. Harley King, 1931-1934
William Augsburger, 1935-1940
J. M. Franz, 1940-1941
P. A. Kliewer, 1941-1949
William Templin, 1943– ? (ap-
  parently a short time)
Henry Dalke, 1949-1953
E. J. Peters, 1953-1954
Herbert King, 1955-1959
P. D. Loewen, ca 1960-1962
Enoch Zimmerman, briefly in
  1962
Clyde Dirks, 1962-1968

SALEM (EMB), 1933-1941, in
  Salem
Henry C. Unruh
John J. Schmidt
Abe Voth
H. H. Dick
David P. Schultz, 1940-1941

MOLALLA (MC), 1934-1951, at
  Molalla

Joe H. Yoder, 1935-1945
George Miller, 1937-1938
Archie Kauffman, 1937-1941
Henry J. Yoder, d 1942-1946
Jacob S. Roth, 1945-1949
Omar G. Miller, 1949-1951 (as-
  sisting from Bethel)

SWEET HOME (MC), 1940, at
  Sweet Home
N. A. Lind, bp 1940-1956
Archie Kauffman, 1941-1959
Willard L. Stutzman, d
  1942-1948; 1948-1959
Glen Birky, d 1950–
Merle Kropf, 1959-1960
Orie Roth, l 1960-1961;
  1961-1963; bp 1963-1969
Eugene Garber, 1969–

KINGWOOD (MB), 1940, at Salem,
  earlier known as the Menno-
  nite Brethren Church of West
  Salem
Abe A. Loewen, 1940-1949
Albert Fadenrecht, 1946-1949
John E. Friesen
Alex Sauerwein, 1950-1953
Henry Hooge, 1953-1954
Frank Wiens, 1954-1959
Peter Becker, 1955-1957
A. C. Fuller, 1959-1960
Leonard J. Vogt, 1960-1974
Rudolph Toews, 1961-1965,
  1972-1974
John Larrabee, 1969-1971
Rick Allen, 1971-1972
Larry Nickel, 1973-1975
Allen Tschiegg, 1975
Ralfe E. Kaiser, 1975–
Donald R. Heinrichs, 1976–

CALVARY (GC), 1944, near Aurora,
  earlier at Barlow
Paul N. Roth, 1944-1956,
  1973-1974
Nobel V. Sack, 1956-1957,
  1959-1960
Henry Penner, 1957-1959
Harry W. Howard, 1960-1973

Richard Gydesen, 1967– ?
Gerald Mendenhall, 1974–
Chester Kauffman, 1976–

REDWOOD COUNTRY (BIC),
 1945, near Grants Pass
Benjamin M. Books, 1945–1949
Hess Brubaker, e 1949–?
Glenn Diller, 1952–1955 or
 longer
William F. Lewis, before and
 after 1964
Amos Buckwalter, 1969–?
Sam Hollingsworth, 1976–

CLOVERDALE (CGC), 1945–1957
Jacob G. Loewen, 1945–1957
 (perhaps unordained)

ROSEBURG CONSERVATIVE
 AMISH MENNONITE (UM),
 1947–1951, near Sutherlin, ca
 1951 moved to South Carolina
Ira J. Headings, d 1947–[1951
 and longer]
Menno J. Schrock, 1949–[1951
 and longer]

WESTERN (MC), 1948, about ten
 miles north of Salem
Marcus Lind, 1948–1955;
 bp 1955–1976
Joe A. Birky, d 1948–1952
Menno S. Snyder, d 1955–1965
Paul Yoder, 1955–1957
David Hostetler, 1959–1962
Henry Becker, 1959–1961
Eldon Hamilton, 1964–1976
Richard Wenger, 1975–

PLEASANT VALLEY AMISH MEN-
 NONITE (UM), 1949–ca 1963,
 near Yoncalla, later in Santa
 Clara area north of Eugene
 before moving to Wisconsin ca
 1963
Roy Headings, 1949–1950;
 bp 1950–[continuing in 1976
 in Wisconsin]

Elmer Hostetler, ca 1953, later
 silenced

LABISH VILLAGE (BIC), ca 1949,
 near Salem
Benjamin M. Books, ca 1949–ca
 1960
Arthur Cooper, ca 1963–

TANGENT (UM), 1950, in Tangent,
 earlier MC
Melvin Schrock, 1950–
Henry Wolfer, ° 1950–1955,
 bp 1955–1960
Merle Stutzman, 1952–1973
Harold Reeder, d 1955–1960
Victor Kropf, 1962–1963;
 bp 1963–
Jason Schrock, d 1974–

SWEET HOME COMMUNITY
 CHAPEL (GC), 1951, in Sweet
 Home
Alfred Schwartz, 1951–1956 (and
 from 1949 until it organized)
Peter Peters, 1957–1963
Able C. Siebert, 1963–1966
Don Emmert, 1966
Richard Geysden, 1966–1967
Larry Sloan, 1967–

CHAPEL IN THE HILLS (UM), ca
 1953, ten miles southeast of
 Silverton, became a community
 church by 1960
Edward (Kelly) Kenagy, 1953–
 (and from his ordination in
 1949)

WINSTON (UM), 1955, in Winston,
 earlier MC
Roy Hostetler, 1955–1970
Eldon Shetler, 1970–1971
Harold Reeder, d 1971–
Timothy Zook, l 1974–

PORTER (UM), 1955, seven miles
 east of Estacada, earlier MC
Ernest J. Bontrager, 1955–ca

1969 (and from his ordination
in 1943); bp ca 1969–
Joe Birky, d 1956, 1962, short
periods
Rhine Benner, 1963 short period
Isaac Baer, 1967 short period
Leander N. Mast, 1967–1969
Clifford W. Yoder, 1970–1973
John Yoder, 1976–
James Bucher, 1976–

LOGSDEN (MC), 1956, about
seven miles east of Siletz
Eugene Lemons, l 1956–1959
Roy D. Roth, 1959–1970
James E. Horsch, l 1963–1964
Lynford Hershey, 1970 winter
Larry L. Bardell, l 1970–1973
George M. Kauffman, 1970 sum-
mer, 1974
Alfred W. Burkey, l 1974–1976;
1976–

BLAINE (MC), 1956, seven miles
east of Beaver
Jacob D. Kauffman, 1956– (and
from his ordination in 1947)

EAST FAIRVIEW (UM), 1957,
between Lebanon and Sweet
Home, earlier MC
Ivan Headings, 1957–1963 (and
from 1953 until it organized)
Ivan Bare, d 1959–1968
Clifford Lind, l 1961–1963
Gary Knuths, l 1963–1964; 1964–

LEBANON (MC), 1957, in Lebanon
Allen Erb, bp 1957–1959
George M. Kauffman, 1957–1959
Millard E. Osborne, l 1959–1960;
1960–1970
Dan Longenecker, 1970–1973
Richard Headings, 1974–

GRANTS PASS (MC), 1957, in
Grants Pass
Max Yoder, 1957–1958;
bp 1958–1971

Al Nikkel, 1971 summer
Lowell Stutzman, l 1971–1972
Ralph E. Myers, Jr., l 1972;
1972–1976

FIRST MENNONITE (MC), 1957,
in McMinnville
Paul E. Yoder, 1957–1960;
bp 1960–1966
Oscar Wideman, 1962–1974
Henry Becker, 1968–1972
Lynn Miller, l 1973–1974; 1974–

EVERGREEEN (CGC), 1957, near
Scio
Edward Jantz, 1959–
Henry Baize, d 1961–1970
Monroe Toews, d 1961–1975
Ben Ulrich, d 1971–

LIBERTY GARDENS (EMB), 1958,
in Salem
Frank C. Wiens, 1958–1963
Henry Nickel, 1963–1966
Wayne Bass, 1967–1968
Samuel Ediger, 1969–1970
Wayne Deason, 1970–1976

MEADOWBROOK (UM), 1958, five
miles northwest of Molalla, be-
came a community church
Chester Kauffman, 1958–1964
(and from 1949 until it orga-
nized)
Frank Horst, 1961–1963
John Chilcott
Howard Hornby
Harold Maycumber, 1976–

BROWNSVILLE (UM), 1960, in
Brownsville, earlier MC
Henry Wolfer, bp 1960–1963
Lloyd Kropf, 1960–
E. S. Garber, bp 1963–

CHURCH IN THE WILDWOOD
(MC), 1961, about twenty
miles west of Sheridan

Joe Kropf, 1961– (and from his ordination in 1958)
Hugo Krehbiel, 1970–

SALEM (MC), 1961, in the Keizer area
Wilbert Nafziger, 1961–1967
Henry Becker, 1962–1966
John Heyerly, 1967–1972
John Willems, 1973–

BEACHY AMISH, ca 1961, near Amity, remnant of OOA group
Ben Slabaugh/Schlabach, bp ca 1962–

CASCADIA (MC), 1963, about thirteen miles east of Sweet Home
Melvin Paulus, 1963– (l 1961–1964)

NORTH PARK COMMUNITY (MB), 1964, in Eugene
Harold Schroeder, 1964–1967
Walter Friesen, 1967–1970
Loyal Funk, 1970–1972
Paul N. Roth, 1972 interim
Don MacNeill, 1972–

EUGENE (MC), 1965, in Eugene
Cleo Mann, 1966–1968
Harold Hochstetler, bp 1968–

MARANATHA (UM), 1965, at Ballston, a few miles southeast of Sheridan
LeRoy Cowan, 1965–
Jacob S. Roth, 1966–ca 1971
John R. Yoder, 1967–1975
Merle Stutzman, 1976–

BETHANY (MC), 1966, near Albany
David Groh, 1966–1975
Cloy Troyer, 1975–

BEREAN (UM), ca 1968–1976, in Portland
Joe H. Yoder, 1968–1976
James Bucher, 1968–1976

CORVALLIS (MC), 1969, near Corvallis; changed location and name after 1976
Elmer S. Yoder, l 1969–1970
Paul G. Burkholder, 1970–1971
Walter C. Hines, 1971–1974
George Kauffman, 1974–1975, 1976–
Lester Yoder, 1974–1975 (lay leader)
Robert H. Yoder, 1975–1976

Bibliographical Note

Because a formal bibliography would expand the size of this book beyond that which its editors recommend, readers are reminded that the footnotes give a great number of sources.

Earliest research focused on congregational responses to questionnaires and to related information provided by representatives from congregations, whether or not they returned the questionnaires. The requested information concerned first settlers and dates they moved to the area; dates of first meeting, organization, incorporation, and meetinghouse use; location and description of meetinghouses and cemeteries; membership survey, sources of and reasons for growth or decline of membership; names and other information about ordained leaders; dates, early leaders, size, languages and facilities used, and significance of the Sunday school; dates, first leaders, scope of activities and significance of women's, men's, and youth groups; descriptions of morning, evening, and midweek worship services; mission interests, projects, and participants; financial practices including system of giving, pastoral support, and how offerings were used; congregational patterns of authority, leadership, and discipline; relationship of the congregation to a larger body; occupations of members; numbers of men serving in alternative or military service during times of conscription; women employed outside the home; number of children in the average family; leisure activities; young people in college; outstanding events in the congregation's history; and whether they could suggest other sources of information.

Additional later interviews, letters, and conversations with designated or ad hoc congregational historians and various other persons provided insight and understanding. At least one individual and often several from most Oregon congregations read the subsequent detailed drafts of their congregation's history and clarified and corrected parts of that draft. Articles in *Mennonite*

Encyclopedia helped, though further research occasionally uncovered errors in those earlier articles.

Not all congregational respondents had access to official minutes and other records. Denominational periodicals often provided missing information through contemporary letters from congregational or regional correspondents. In addition, such periodicals offered glimpses into the life and thought of the larger churches they represented and helped place Oregon Mennonites in their larger context. Particularly helpful were *Herald of Truth, Gospel Herald, The Mennonite, Christian Leader,* and *Evangelical Visitor.*

Official conference minutes provided additional insights into the thoughts and actions of Oregon Mennonites. Elizabeth Horsch Bender translated pertinent sections of the Pacific District Conference (MB) German reports, and Leonard Gross, archivist at the Mennonite Church Archives at Goshen, Indiana, made them available for this research. Conference publications, particularly *Missionary Evangel,* "Workers' Exchange," and the Pacific District (GC) *Messenger,* gave much information about congregational and conference life. *Missionary Evangel* was particularly helpful in researching the stories of schools, homes, camps, and the Lebanon hospital—institutions related to the Pacific Coast Conference.

Oregon's historical libraries have few materials relating to the state's Mennonites, but staffs of a number of Mennonite and related libraries and archives provided cheerful assistance. Especially helpful were persons at: the Center for Mennonite Brethren Studies at Fresno, Calif.; Archives of the Mennonite Church and the Mennonite Historical Library at Goshen, Ind.; Mennonite Library and Archives at North Newton, Kans.; Mennonite Historical Library at Bluffton, Ohio; Archives of the Brethren in Christ Church, Grantham, Pa.; Menno Simons Historical Library, Harrisonburg, Va.; and Western Mennonite High School at Salem, Oreg. Portions of the N. A. Lind, S. C. Yoder, and D. H. Bender manuscript collections at the Mennonite Church Archives offered unique insights. The Yoder and Bender papers became available through the courtesy of David Peterson.

A number of term papers from Western Mennonite School provided youthful but occasionally insightful glimpses of particular Oregon Mennonite congregations or activities. Research papers by students at Hesston College and Goshen College also helped. Through previous research for an earlier work, excerpts from the

Barbara (Wenger) Garber (1896-1988) diaries were available. Berniece Kennel provided copies of letters by John L. and Fannie (Yoder) Zook, written from Oregon in the 1890s. Dorothy King gave copies of several letters written about that time by Fannie's father, Abraham Yoder.

Earlier histories of Oregon Mennonites, whether in published or thesis form, provided helpful information for this volume but also include details that it could not. In the order of their appearance, they are: S. G. Shetler, *Church History of the Pacific Coast Mennonite Conference District* (Scottdale, [1932]); H. D. Burkholder, *The Story of Our Conference and Churches* (North Newton, 1951); La Vernae J. Dick, *Early Mennonites in Oregon* (Oregon College of Education, 1972); Lee Price Campbell, *Seventy-five Years on the Shore of the Peaceful Sea, A History of the Pacific District Conference of the General Conference Mennonite Church of North America* (Western Evangelical Seminary, 1973); and David Chris Peterson, *Children of Freedom or Children of Menno? The Oregon Mennonite Church in the Two World Wars* (University of Oregon, 1981). David Luthy's early articles in *Family Life* magazine and the chapters about Oregon in his subsequent book, *The Amish in America: Settlements That Failed, 1840-1960* (Aylmer, Ontario and Lagrange, Indiana, 1986) provide additional information about Oregon's Old Order Amish.

Many published works supplemented and enhanced the research for this volume, as the footnotes indicate. A number of volumes published as Studies in Anabaptist and Mennonite History in the book series sponsored by the Mennonite Historical Society were particularly useful. Additional volumes which deserve mention are: John Richard Burkholder and Calvin Redekop, eds., *Kingdom, Cross, and Community: Essays on Mennonite Themes in Honor of Guy F. Hershberger* (Scottdale, 1976); and George M. Marsden, *Fundamentalism and American Culture: The Shaping of Twentieth-Century Evangelicalism, 1870-1925* (Oxford, 1980). In addition to the noted sources about Anabaptist and Mennonite history and thought, searchers may find many additional materials at Mennonite archives and historical libraries which are listed in the biennial *Mennonite Yearbook* (Scottdale, Pennsylvania). Some of the periodicals included in the key to abbreviations located at the beginning of this book give a continuing picture of the groups they represent.

Index

A

Abrams, 163
Adlon, 100
Aeschliman, 118
Aeschliman, Dan, 260
Aeschliman, Eva, 260
Aeschliman, Merlin, 117
Aeschliman, Paul R., 148,
    153, 185, 205, 222,
    236, 326, 334
agriculture, 31, 36, 48, 59,
    63, 103, 110, 136,
    143, 146, 171ff.,
    185-6, 189ff., 197,
    229, 267ff., 294,
    297
  declining, 274, 277
  economic depression,
    172
  innovations, 30, 267
  land speculators, 258
  modern methods, 75
  prosperous, 67
  role of irrigation, 187,
    193, 196, 197, 198,
    261
  transition from, 269
  unproductive, 37, 59,
    74, 75, 119, 143,
    198, 267
  see also ruralism
Airlie, 74
Albany Mennonite Church,
    53, 54, 63ff., 87, 93,
    94, 95, 102, 122,
    153, 156, 209, 225,
    244, 245, 275, 276,
    296, 321, 329
Albany Mennonite Home,
    318
Alberta Community
    Mennonite Church,
    154ff., 244, 245,
    279, 290, 291, 332
Alberta-Saskatchewan
    Conference
  see Northwest
    Conference
alcohol, 31, 60, 95, 173,
    207, 209, 276, 277,
    278, 280, 295
Allgyer, S. E., 78, 207, 226
Alliman, 101
all things, 76, 215, 237
Alpine Mennonite Church
  see Seventh Street
    Mennonite Church
alternative service, 289ff.,
    299ff., 331
  after World War II, 298
  influences pro, con, 297
  in Portland, 251
  I-W, 101, 106, 299, 303
  promoting leadership,
    304
  Vietnam War, 300
  see also Civilian Public
    Service
American Sunday School
    Union, 239, 258
amillennialism, 219ff.
  see also Premillennialism
Amish, 78
  on Holy Spirit, 232
  origins and groups, 33
  see also Old Order
    Amish
Amish Mennonites, 33,
    41ff., 185
  joining Apostolic
    Christian Church,
    137
  merging with (old)
    Mennonites, 33, 63
Amstutz, 136, 140
amusements, 67, 95, 125,
    278
alternatives, 168
Anabaptism, 32, 33, 336
anarchism and
    Mennonites, 266
Anderson, Amanda
    (Yoder), 323
Antioch Mennonite
    Church, 74
  see also First Mennonite
    Church (Nampa,
    ID)
Apostolic Christian
    Church, 137ff., 170,
    341
Arizona, 201
Armistice Day programs,
    292
attire, 53-4, 57, 61, 66-7,
    79, 95, 112, 177,
    179, 209, 213-4,
    338
  and congregational
    dissention, 87, 156
  and mission, 247, 261-2
  at church colleges, 332
  essential of
    nonconformity, 213
  Evangelical Menn.
    Breth. emphasis,
    278
  fruit of faith, 215
  GC non-emphasis, 218
  hair styles, 112, 125
  hooks and eyes
    controversy, 46, 53
  Old Order Amish, 218
  plain coat, 77, 81, 124,
    214, 251, 256, 261,
    265

AM opposition, 214
see also humility;
    nonconformity;
    prayer veiling
Augsburger, Carolyn
    (King), 226
Augsburger, Fred, 226
Augsburger, Myron, 210
authority
    challenged, 88
    diversity, 75
    locus of, 97, 114, 124,
        214ff.
    of church community,
        28
    of conferences, 62, 75,
        81, 96, 115, 215
    of ordained leaders, 28
    shifting, 95, 123, 133,
        215-6
    see also Bible, authority;
        conference
        discipline;
        leadership
automobile, 175

B

Bachman, 148
Bachman, H. A., 148, 192
Baergen, Gerhard, 150
Baer, J. B. (John B.), 137,
    140, 146-7
Bailey, 101
Baker, 101, 116
Baker, Earl, 56
Baker, Earl, Jr., 116
Balzer, 151, 165
Banker, 157
baptism, 147, 153, 164,
    213
    and church membership,
        207
    of adults, 140
    of the Holy Spirit, 224ff.
        at Dallas Evang.
        Menn. Breth., 233
    Pacific Coast Conf. on,
        207
    see also entire
        sanctification;
        holiness; Pente-
        costalism; second
        work; glossolalia

Barber, 107
Bare, 106
Bare, Ivan, 106
Bartel, 154
Bartel, Mr. and Mrs. Loyal,
    260
Bauman, 91
Baumgartner, Samuel S.,
    141, 154, 289
Beachy, 78, 110
Beachy, Alvin M., 174
Beachy Amish, 33, 175,
    272
Beachy, Daniel, 173
Beachy, Will, 231
Beacon Bible School, 310
Becker, 118, 144-5, 148,
    176
Becker, Henry, 318
Beckler, 120
Beer, 136
Beer, John, 138, 140
Beier, 163, 165
Beiler, 171
Bekker, 148
Bekker, Abraham, 146
Bekker families, 146
Benson, Randy, 169
Berean church, 181
Berg, 164
Berg, P. H., 163-4
Bergan, Elias, 163
Bergen, 145
Bergey, 122
Berkey, 57, 74, 108, 110,
    157
Berkey, Jacob, 59
Berkey, Kenneth, 268
Berkey, Mervin, 231
Berkey, Peter, 268
Bestvater, Wm. J., 223,
    309
Bethany Mennonite
    Church, 53, 120,
    121
Bethel College, 330, 333
Bethel Community
    Mennonite Church,
    195
Bethel Mennonite Church
    (Canby), 49, 51, 62,
    67, 83ff., 94, 99,
    126, 181, 220, 227,
    236, 240, 252, 257,
    285, 313

Bethel Mennonite Church
    (Dubois, ID), 198
Bethel Mennonite Church
    (West Liberty, OH),
    225-6
Bethel Mennonite Church
    (Winton, CA), 194
Beugli, 136
Beutler, 136, 140
Beutler, Lillian, 253
Beutler, Mrs. Sam, 136
Bible, authority, 25, 82,
    97, 112ff., 215, 281,
    307, 337
    and evolution, 211
    Dallas GC statement,
        217
    differing concepts, 123,
        128, 131
    dispensationalism, 223
    foundational, 216, 217
    Fundamentalist
        influence, 125, 211,
        218
    upheld, 123
    verbal inspiration, 125,
        211, 216
    see also
        Fundamentalism;
        inspiration;
        interpretation
Bible conferences, 148,
    207-8, 219, 308
    and revival meetings,
        207
    on Holy Spirit, 230
    (or schools, institutes,
        normals), 207
Bible Institute of Los
    Angeles, 217, 221,
    223, 233, 250, 333
Bible Mennonite
    Fellowship, 115ff.,
    126, 129-30, 178,
    181-2, 222, 257,
    319, 329, 336
    camping, 323
    mission work, 255
Bible schools, 87, 100,
    308-9
    at Dallas, 309
    Pacific Coast Bible
        School, 307
    "Special Bible Term",
        312

see also Young people's
  institutes
Bier, Otto, 207, 223, 233,
  311, 330
Biery, 136
Bilyeu, 103
Birky, 74, 107, 119
Birky, Jack, 119
Birky, Joe, 92, 114
Birky, Loretta (Phillips),
  119
Birky, Luke, 298
Birky, Nick (N. M.), 33,
  90, 121
Birky, Verna, 298
bishops
  authority, 86, 87, 92, 96,
    111, 122, 215, 320
  irregular administration,
    98
  replaced by overseer,
    126
  role, 47, 173
Blacks, 178
Blaine Mennonite Church,
  103, 104, 221, 341
Bledsoe, 74
Blosser, 136
Blosser, John, 227
Blosser, Kate, 74
Boehr, Mrs. Richard, 281
Boese, 176
Boese, Samuel, 176
Bond, 81
Bond, Ordena, 313
Bond, William, 69
Bontrager, 100, 122
Bontrager, Ernest J., 89,
  94-5, 99, 100, 230,
  257
Bontrager, Ida (Boyer), 94,
  99, 100, 257
Bontrager, John P., 71,
  73-4, 191, 193,
  225-6, 289, 334
Bookrack Evangelism, 241
Books, Benjamin M., 177-8
Books, Priscilla, 177-8
Borkholder, 171
borrowing, lending, 61, 65,
  274
Boyer, 74
Braun, 148, 165
Braun, Gerhard, 145
Brenneman, Moses E., 71,
  72, 73, 83

Brenneman, Orpha
  (Mishler), 72
Bressler, John F., 246
Brethren in Christ, 34,
  117-8, 135, 177-8,
  303, 334, 341
  endorsing
    Premillennialism,
    223
  Grants Pass, 177
Brewer, 159
brotherhood, 168
Brown, 91, 181
Brownsville Mennonite
  Church, 57, 115-6,
  270
Brubaker, 78, 81, 110
Brubaker, J. K., 60
Brunk, George R., I, 53,
  64ff., 153, 213ff.,
  220, 225, 273ff.
  on progressive holiness,
    225
  on uniform plainness,
    214
Brunk, George R., II, 210,
  220, 230
Brunk, Lawrence
  and Holy Spirit baptism,
    230
Brunner, Paul, 122, 132,
  281, 335, 339
  on Holy Spirit, 231
Bucher, 181
Bucher, Elsie, 313
Bucher, James, 82, 180-1,
  194, 253
Buck, 122
Buckles, Fred, 195
Buerge, Claude, 322
Buhler, 163, 165
Buhler, Jacob, 163
Burck, 57, 157
Burck, Frank, 41
Burck, Harley, 41
Burck, Lovina (Miller), 41
Burk, 106
Burkey, 107, 111, 119-20
Burkey, Alfred, 132
Burkholder, 51, 57, 159
Burkholder, Ezra, 70
Burkholder, Harold D.,
  152, 217, 333
Burkholder, Paul G., 122

business, 36, 84, 268, 270
  and church planting,
    103, 108
  failed saw mill in Lane
    County, 61
  see also economics
Byers, 104, 108, 110, 118
Byers, Cecil, 262-3
Byers, Faye, 262
Byers, Willard, 109
Byers, Willis, 92

C

California, 188ff.
Calvary Mennonite
  Church, 88, 157,
  191, 217, 233, 264,
  291, 300, 335
Camp Fremont, 286, 287
Camp Lewis, 287ff.
  conscientious objectors
    at, 288
camping, 251
  EMB, 323
  for children
    mission emph., 321
  GC, 323
  MB, 323
  Portland mission, 320
  youth, 320
    opposition, 320
  see also Drift Creek
    Camp
Carpenter, 103
Cascadia Mennonite
  Church, 118-9, 341
C. B. Steiner Church, 59,
  138ff.
Cemetery Church
  see C. B. Steiner Church
Central America, 260-1
Central Conference of
  Mennonites, 198
Chapel in the Hills, 93,
  178-9, 239
charismatic movement,
  188, 196, 199, 211,
  224ff., 343
child evangelism, 166,
  243, 322
  see also camping;
    mission, summer;
    mission, Sunday

children's activities, 243
children's homes, 317
children's meetings, 69,
    148, 207, 236, 237
Chinese workers, 171
Christian Endeavor, 243
Christian Leader, 332
Christian Workers'
    Conference, 206
Christner, 51, 53, 66, 70,
    171
Christner, Barbra (Haas),
    57, 59
Christner, Chris, 59
Christner, Peter, 43, 57,
    58, 60, 140
church, concept of, 38, 61,
    97, 112ff., 124, 131,
    134, 159, 167,
    174-5, 180, 201-2,
    215ff., 259
  membership, barriers,
    235
  separation from state,
    28, 32, 125
  see also authority;
    discipline; laity
Church in the Wildwood,
    116-7, 231, 332,
    341
Church of God in Christ,
    Mennonite
    (Holdeman), 33,
    135, 168, 176-7,
    303, 331
  early Polk County, 176
  on Holy Spirit, 232
  second, third groups in
    Oregon, 176
church-state separation
  see church, concept of
City Acres Mennonite
    Church, 200
Civilian Public Service,
    289ff., 303
  men's diversity, 295, 296
  Oregon camps, 295, 296
  types of work, 294
  valued contributions,
    295, 296
  values v. negative
    elements, 295
  see also conscientious
Claassen, Albert, 154
Claassen, J. E., 189

Clackamas County, 34, 41,
    49, 84, 139
Clay, 116
climate, 31, 34, 59, 63,
    146
  influencing migration,
    37
Cloverdale congregation,
    176
Coblentz, 108, 117
colleges, Mennonite,
    332-3, 339
  see also Bethel; Eastern
    Menn.; Goshen;
    Hesston; Rosedale;
    schools; Tabor
colonization evangelism,
    258, 262
Columbia Basin Mennonite
    Church, 188
community
  competition from the
    state, 282, 304
  contemporary
    challenges, 342
  diminished by
    revivalism, 207
  of faith, 25ff., 204
  religious concept, 337,
    343
  sense of, 37, 61
  tension with
    individualism, 28,
    134, 168, 182, 205,
    281
  transferring to another,
    48, 175, 265-6
  vs. a private faith, 216
  weakness and strength,
    342
  see also individualism
community churches, 117,
    158, 178ff., 188,
    193, 199, 331
  unsupportive of
    nonresistance, 303
  vs. Mennonite standards,
    256, 303
"Concern Group", 116,
    124ff.
conference discipline, 62,
    74-5
  and Mennonite
    Confession of Faith
    (1963), 126

authority of, 95, 96, 123
  diminishing, 99, 112,
    113
  controversies about, 77,
    191
  governing Western
    Mennonite School,
    311
  re state aid, 277
  see also authority;
    congregationalism;
    discipline; ministry
conference organization
  see Pacific Coast Conf.,
    Pacific Dist. Conf.
conferences
  see ministers' meetings;
    mission conf.
confessions of faith, 126
conflict resolution
  accommodation, 77, 96,
    197
  between IN and MO
    AMs, 44
  conciliation, 43, 59, 64,
    65-6, 87-8, 120-1,
    130, 149-50, 175,
    256
    in Mexico mission
    work, 264
  division, 61, 139,
    147-50, 175, 180,
    199
  excommunication, 152
  migration, 34, 38, 48,
    55, 88, 110, 118,
    172ff., 226, 229
  reconciliation, 78, 131,
    174
  restitution, 65
  withdrawal, 49, 53ff., 61,
    87-8, 91-2, 98-9,
    106, 110, 115-6,
    120-1, 126-7, 133,
    152, 156ff., 164,
    168, 180, 187, 191,
    194ff., 229, 233,
    256
Congo Inland Mission, 260
congregationalism, 75,
    115, 131, 135, 160,
    218
congregations
  see extinct; house
    fellowship; names of
    particular congregs.

AM practice, 55
GC, 329
vs. conference
discipline, 62
see also conference
dicipline
congregational outreach
see mission
Conrad, 111, 157
Conrad, Amos, 37, 38, 268
Conrad, Barbara, 51
Conrad, Joe, 37
Conrad, Orie, 206, 287,
322
Conrad, Paul, 260
conscientious objection,
objectors, 198,
284ff.
see also Camp Lewis;
Civilian Public
Service; draft;
military; names of
wars; noncombatant;
noncooperation;
nonresistance;
peace witness; war
bonds
Conservative Amish
Mennonite, 33
constitutions, 77, 96
Bible Mennonite
Fellowship, 126,
181
Waldo Hills, 141
see also Pacific Coast
Conference
Cook, 106, 161
Cooper Arthur, 178
Corliss, 119
Corning, CA, 192
Corvallis Mennonite
Church, 121-122,
231
Counts, 179
Cowan, 118, 180
Cowan, Cheryl, 312
Cowan, LeRoy, 180
Creswell, 176
Culp, G. Richard, 222

D

Dalke, Henry, 157
Dalke, Robert R., 194

Dallas Bible School, 310
see Beacon Bible School
Dallas Evangelical
Mennonite
Brethren, 168-9,
223, 233, 238ff.,
245, 260, 268, 289,
303, 330
music in evangelism,
239
Dallas Home for the Aged,
or Dallas Rest
Home, 318
Dallas Mennonite
Brethren, 164-5,
206, 207, 209, 223,
233, 237, 240, 243,
260, 268, 290, 300,
318, 330ff.
Dapp, 136
Davies, 117
Davis, 74
deaconesses, 314
deafness, 56
Deason, Wayne, 170
Deetz, 171
Denlinger, Don, 165
Derstine, Clayton. F., 82,
220
Detweiler, 110
Detweiler, Lizzie, 69
deVries, 140
Dick, 151, 168, 169
Dick, George, 194
Dick, H. H., 310
Dick, J. S., 310
Dick, La Vernae, 160, 238
Dickason, Betty, 103
Diehm, 148
Diehm, Anna (Rempel), 37
Diehm, Johann George, 37
Dill, 161
Diller, Donavin, 201
Dillon, 107
Dimick, 118
Dinuba, California, 191
Dirks, Clyde, 155, 160
discipleship, 28, 98, 204,
207, 215
and nonconformity, 97
see also attire
fruits of faith, 172, 203
newly defined, 114
varying practices, 66
see also obedience

discipline
agreement between
congregations, 78
Amish, 33
at Fairview, 98
Bruderthaler emph., 34
congregational, 83, 139
disagreement about, 47
Garber and Brunk, 66
Holdeman, 34
Pacific District
Conference (GC),
153
patterns, 218
Strasbourg Discipline,
213
see also authority;
conference
discipline;
obedience
dispensationalism, 219ff.
among GCs, 222, 223
among MBs, 223
and Holy Spirit, 224
see also
premillennialism;
Scofield
diversity among
Mennonites, 25, 38,
43-4, 57, 75, 95,
108, 158, 160-1,
189, 231, 291, 328,
329, 343
approved, 123
in Eugene MB congreg.,
167
on nonresistance, 304
re attire and language,
45
urban, 120
divine healing, 209, 228ff.
George Hostetler on, 45
divorce, 175
and mission, 280
opposed, 95, 279
with remarriage, 131,
194, 280
see also marriage
doctrines—as beliefs,
practices, 82
Doerksen, 167, 169
Doerksen, David R., 169
Dordrecht Confession, 213
Dorsing, 91
Dos Palos, California, 193

Douglas County, 61
Dow, 181
draft resistance, 127,
    301-2
  see also conscientious;
    noncooperation
Drift Creek Camp, 251,
    321, 322, 323
  impetus for, 322
  offenders ministry, 323
Duerksen, 151, 165, 168
Dutch Flats, 136
Dyck, 145, 148
Dyck, Isaac, 148
Dyck, Johannes Dietrich,
    188

E

Easch, Jacob, 44
Eash, 57, 110
Eash, Amos, 109
Eastern Mennonite
    College, 332
East Fairview Mennonite
    Church, 104ff.
Ebersole, 181
economics
  see agriculture; finances;
    labor unions;
    logging,
    manufacturing;
    Needy Brick Co.;
    occupations; Panic
    of; railroads;
    sawmills; war bonds;
    war taxes; wealth;
    World War II
ecumenism
  see interdenominational
Ediger, 168, 170
Ediger, John W., 310
Ediger, Peter J., 195
Ediger, Solomon, 168, 233
education, 306ff.
  agent of change, 311
  opposition in Pacific
    Coast Conference,
    311
  through publications, 76
  see also schools
Egli, 157
Eicher, 53, 120
Eicher, S. E., 295, 296,
    316

Eigsti, Jim, 329
Elliot, 159
Ellis, John, 146
Emanuel Mennonite
    Church (Aberdeen,
    ID), 197
  see also Waldo Hills
Emmanuel Mennonite
    Church (Pratum),
    135, 140ff., 218,
    223, 232, 237, 242,
    243, 244, 253, 260,
    289, 290-1, 300,
    334, 341
Emmaus Mennonite
    Church, 141, 144ff.
Emmert, 66, 78, 84, 89,
    91, 159, 179, 269
Emmert, Anna (Schrag),
    90, 145
Emmert, Ben, 57, 90, 91,
    145
Emmert, Floyd, 69
Emmert, Mark, 262
Emmert, Twila, 262
end-time preaching
  see eschatology
Enns, Abram, 146
entire sanctification
  see holiness; Holy Spirit;
    second work of
    grace
Erb, 46, 66, 107, 156
Erb, Allen, 97-8, 106, 108,
    111, 245, 316
Erb brothers, 320
Erb, Daniel (of Albany),
    54
Erb, Daniel (of Hubbard),
    44
Erb, Katherina (Roth), 52
Erb, Paul, 128, 320, 329
Erb, Stella (Cooprider), 98
Ernst, 111
Esau, 145, 165, 176
eschatology, 207, 219, 221,
    233
  differing views, 221
  see also amillennialism;
    dispensationalism;
    premillennialism
Escondido, CA, 192
essentials and
    non-essentials idea,
    87, 160, 283, 291,
    304, 329, 343

and "staying saved", 215
eternal security, 215, 217
  see also salvation
ethnicity, 27, 161, 189,
    235, 334, 337, 344
  in Russia and U.S., 34
Eugene Mennonite
    Brethren
    congregation, 166-7
  see also North Park
Eugene Mennonite
    Church, 119, 120
Evangelical Mennonite
    Brethren, 34, 135,
    149, 164, 168ff.
  language usage, 272
Evangelical Visitor, 331
evangelism
  John P. Bontrager
    emph., 72
  literature, 80, 235,
    240-1, 244, 248,
    253, 257, 262
  personal, 80
  promoted above
    nonresistance, 283,
    290-1
  see also mission
Evangel Mennonite
    Church, 201
Evans, Edith, 253
Eveleth, 110
Evergreen congregation
    (CGC), 176, 303,
    331
Evers, 57, 74, 180
Evers, Lois Catherine, 279
Evers, Moses, 58, 61
Evers, Nancy (Culp), 61
Ewert, Frank, 186
excommunication, 33, 88,
    99, 112, 168, 194,
    297
extinct congregations, 41,
    51, 61, 74, 84, 157,
    162, 170, 181,
    186ff.

F

Fadenrecht, 165
Fahndrich, Richard, 231
Fairmeade, California, 193

Fairview Mennonite
    Church, 52ff., 62,
    70, 76-7, 88, 98,
    104, 120, 127, 139,
    209, 236, 241, 245,
    270, 272, 275, 285,
    294, 314, 321
Faith Mennonite Church,
    199
Family Almanac, 76
farming
    see agriculture
Fast, 151, 161
Fast, George A., 160
Fast, H. A., 330
Fast, H. P., 223
Fast, Ted, 152
Filer Mennonite Church,
    198
finances, 99, 200, 310
    contributing to
        disbanding, 157,
        162, 170, 200
    for Pacific Coast Bible
        School, 306ff.
    prosperity in World War
        II, 294
Firdale Mennonite
    Church, 74, 75
First Mennonite Church
    (Aberdeen, ID), 197
First Mennonite Church
    (Caldwell, ID), 199
First Mennonite Church
    (Colfax, WA)
    see Onecho Mennonite
    Church
First Mennonite Church
    (Deer Park, WA),
    187
First Mennonite Church
    (McMinnville),
    109-10, 176, 231
First Mennonite Church
    (Monroe, WA), 186
First Mennonite Church
    (Nampa, ID), 196,
    200, 225-6
First Mennonite Church
    (Paso Robles, CA),
    189
First Mennonite Church
    (Phoenix, AZ), 201
First Mennonite Church
    (Reedley, CA), 190

First Mennonite Church
    (Upland, CA), 190
Fleischman, 163
Flickinger, Waldo J., 152
foot washing, 139, 209,
    213
Fort Rock, 258, 259
Franz, 151, 167
Franz, Ella, 269
Franz, John B., 264
Franz, John M., 84, 142,
    143, 149, 186, 222,
    290, 292
Franz, Oscar, 268
Franz, Rufus, 222, 292,
    295
Fretz, J. Winfield, 270,
    300, 337
Fretz, John L., 238
Frey, 168
Frey, Marcella, 263
Frey, Ray, 152
Frey, Vincent, 263
Friesen, 148, 161ff., 168-9
Friesen, Elmer, 155-6, 330
Friesen, Frank F., family,
    162
Friesen, Loren, 188
Friesen, Nels, 238
frontier spirit, 37, 39, 340
Fry, 117
Fuller, 74, 117
Fundamentalism, 82, 211ff.
    influences
        in education, 314
        of and on Mennonites,
        116, 124, 125, 143,
        216, 219, 329, 336
        vs. nonresistance,
        303-4, 282ff., 300ff.
    (old) Mennonite
        adaptations, 82,
        212ff.
    see also Bible, authority;
        dispensationalism;
        Grace Bible; Holy
        Spirit emph.;
        premillennialism;
        Scofield
Funk, 156, 168, 169

G

Gahler, John, 242

Galle, M. J., 186-7, 232,
    309
Garber, David, 64ff., 73,
    191, 196, 274
Garber, E. S., 81, 116, 197
Garber, Eugene, 123, 241
Garber, Robert E., 200
Gardner, 122
Geiger, 136
Geiger, Christian, 138, 140
Geiser, 136
General Conference
    Mennonites, 34, 64,
    135, 140ff.
    early, at Dallas, 143,
    146ff., 163
    identifying emphases, 33
    see also Bethel College;
        Central Conf.;
        congregationalism;
        Pacific District
geographical influences,
    28, 33, 38-9, 62, 73,
    102-3, 109, 132,
    136, 153, 160,
    188-9, 202, 328ff.,
    339
Gerber, 136, 140, 145
Gerber, Lowell, 197
Gerig, 53, 120, 136, 140,
    148
Gerig, Christian R. (C. R.),
    54, 81, 208, 209,
    272
Gerig, Clarence, 182
Gerig, Daniel, 193
Gerig, Henry, 81, 90
Gerig, Peter, Jr., 141
Gering, 143
German Baptists, 140, 146,
    163
Giesbrecht, 176
Gingerich, 51
Gingerich, Dan L., 181
Gingerich, Fred J., 51, 81,
    220, 307
Gingerich, John, 93
girls' sewing circles, 243
Glendale Mennonite
    Church, 187
Glick, 74
Glick, Joseph E., 74
glossolalia, 224, 229ff.
    see also Holy Spirit;
        Pentecostalism

Goertz, 163
Goerz, 167
gold prospecting, 136, 188
Good, 74, 81
Good, Allan, 81, 246ff.,
    320
    and mission, 248ff.
Good, Fannie (Miller), 81,
    246, 247
Goossen, 149
Goshen College, 332
Gospel Herald, 67, 75, 83,
    212, 228, 240, 249,
    331
Gospel Tidings, 331
Gospel Tract Mission, 240
Graber, 143, 148
Graber, J. D., 239, 258
Graber, Jake, 144
Grace Bible Institute, 152,
    217, 223, 333
    Evang. Menn. Breth.
    support, 333
    vs. Bethel College, 333
    see also Fundamentalism
Grace Mennonite Church
    (Albany), 70, 72, 84,
    156ff., 222, 243,
    291
Grace Mennonite Church
    (Dallas), 150ff., 209,
    217, 222, 290-1,
    300
Grants Pass Mennonite
    Church, 108-9, 231
Great Depression, 85, 249,
    269, 332
    and World War II, 293
Grenfell, 103
Grieser, 120
Groff, 91
Groh, David, 120-1, 328
Grubb, E. F., 190
Guenther, 165
Guidelines for Today, 124
Gunn, 154

H

Haima, 120
hair styles
    see attire
Hamilton, 57, 74, 78, 84,
    103, 179

Hamilton, Eldon, 261
Hamilton, Jessie, 261
Hamilton, Mary, 66
Hamm, 168-9
Hammer Tent Revival, 210
Hanger, 103
Harder, Frank S., 333
Harder, Leland, 259
Harder, Milton, 188
Harms, 165
Harms, Harold, 260
Harms, Joyce, 260
Harrisburg Mennonite
    Church, 48, 53ff.,
    61, 114, 206, 220,
    222, 240, 255, 264,
    267ff., 275, 313
    in World War I, 285-6
Hartzler, 157
Hatfield, Mark, 276
Haury, S. S., 137
Headings, 106
Headings, Helen
    (Kaltenbach), 180,
    263
Headings, Ira J., 61
Headings, Ivan, 101, 106,
    245
Headings, Maynard, 180,
    263, 329
Headings, Richard, 132
Hege, Jacob, 189, 197
Heinrich, 161
Heinrich, Peter, 161
Helzer, 161
Helzer, Heinrich, 161
Herald of Truth, 27, 60,
    67, 75, 334
Hernandez, Sam, 259
Herold der Wahrheit, 27
Herr, 136, 140
Hershberger, 57, 66, 99,
    119
Hershberger, Levi, 60
Hershberger, Noah, 66, 69
Hershey, Jeanie, 323
Hershey, Lynford (Lyn),
    132, 259, 323
Hershey, T. K., 279
Hess, 100
Hess, D. B., 194
Hesston College, 220, 308,
    332
    Oregon attendance, 211
Heyerly, 53, 111, 157

Heyerly, John E., 118
Heyerly, John, Jr., 53, 139
Heyerly, John, Sr., 136,
    139
Heyerly, Keith, 268
Hicks, 154
Hiebert, 165, 167
Hiebert, Cornelius, 145
Hiebert, Lando, 330
Hiebert, N. N., 165, 310,
    330
Hiebert, Peter C., 161,
    163, 236
Highland Mennonite
    Chapel, 199
Hildebrand, 164
Hilty, David, 66, 71, 73,
    225ff.
Hines, Walter, 122
Hispanics, 133, 178, 200,
    341
    Woodburn Hispanic
    congregation, 259
Hochstetler, 118
Hochstetler, Harold, 119,
    122, 130, 132
Hofstetter, 136
Hofstetter, Lyman, 195
Holdeman, John, 176
Holdemans
    see Church of God in
    Christ, Mennonite
Holderman, 118
Holderman, Ralph, 319
Holderread, 122
holiness movement, 98,
    224ff.
    influence on George R.
    Brunk I, 213
    Oregon Mennonite
    origins, 225ff.
    progressive holiness,
    224ff., 232-3
    Quaker influence, 225
    see also second work
Hollingsworth, Sam, 178
Holy Spirit emph., 88, 113,
    131, 199, 210, 226,
    227ff.
    among Brethren in
    Christ, 232
    among smaller
    Mennonite groups,
    232
    promoting evangelism,
    232

and mission, 224, 229ff.,
262
divisiveness, 230
Indian Cove, 229
in Pacific District
Conference (GC),
232
problems in Pacific
Coast Conference,
228
Sheridan, 228
see also baptism, Holy
Spirit; trance
homes, 314ff.
homes for the aged, 317ff.
Honderich, Samuel, 198,
227
Hondrick, 157
Hooley, 46, 167
Hopewell Mennonite
Church, 44, 64ff.,
73-4, 81, 84, 88,
126, 153, 206, 236,
240, 246, 268, 273,
285, 313
Horn, 100
Horsch, John, 216
Horsch, L. J., 309, 333
Horsch, Michael M., 190
Horst, 118
Horst, Clarence A., 199
Horst, Frank, 187, 199
hospitals, 314ff.
Hostetler, 46, 56, 78, 91,
101, 104, 110, 118,
157
Hostetler, Christian J., 55,
61
Hostetler, Claud, 72, 94,
96, 229, 250, 251
Hostetler, David (of
Missouri), 49
Hostetler, David (of
Oregon), 101, 102,
255
Hostetler, Enos, 56
Hostetler, George, 43ff.,
196, 281
Hostetler, Guy, 253, 255
Hostetler, John, 37, 172
Hostetler, Joseph C., 267
Hostetler, Lester, 339
Hostetler, Levi (father),
49, 55-6, 61
Hostetler, Levi (son), 56

Hostetler, M. H., 73, 307
Hostetler, Mary, 253
Hostetler, Nora, 250
Hostetler, Paulina (Easch),
45
Hostetler, Roy, 101, 182
Hostetler, Simon, 44
Hostetter, Gladys, 311
house fellowship, 196,
201-2
Howard, Harry, 158
Howes, 118
Hubler, 118
humility
Amish emph., 172
and nonconformity, 97
basis for plain clothing,
213
John M. Brenneman on,
26
lost, 212
see also attire;
nonconformity
Huwa, 161
Hyde Park (in Boise), 259

I

Idaho, 196ff.
identity as Mennonites, 27,
39, 183, 235, 325ff.,
340ff.
AM reluctance, 77
and Fundamentalism,
121
and isolation, 109
and mission, 341-2
diminished, 143, 157,
166-7, 179, 180,
330
strengthening of, 267,
340
vs. community church,
104, 158, 167
identity, personal, 132
Immanuel Mennonite
Church, 190, 195
immersion, 137, 166
Indian Cove Mennonite
Church, 198, 227ff.,
252
Indians, 30, 102
individualism, 28, 85, 153,
205

and nonresistance, 291
challenging community,
40, 86, 134, 143,
172, 337
in community churches,
182, 265
in Fundamentalism, 211,
233
vs. humility, 340, 344
see also community
influence of Oregon
Mennonites, 328
inspiration of the Bible,
216ff, 337
see also Bible, authority;
Fundamentalism
institutes, 323
see also retreats
insurance, 273ff.
life, *see* life insurance
see also mutual aid
interdenominational
relations, 44, 51, 60,
83, 108, 117, 138,
141, 143, 150, 154,
159, 185, 194,
206-7, 310, 334ff.
opposed, 125
proselytizing
Mennonites, 196,
199
Salem Academy, 310
inter-Mennonite relations,
139, 147, 153-4,
168, 187, 193,
197-8, 256, 295,
298, 310-1, 314,
318, 323ff.
Pacific Coast
Conference
with Harrisburg
Mennonite Church,
334
with Brethren in
Christ, 334
shifting, 329
interpretation of Scripture,
27, 33, 97, 113, 134,
338
and social concerns, 121
changing methods, 215
diversity, 97, 128-9, 267,
337
millennialism, 219ff.

re Holy Spirit
variations, 230
see also inspiration
Isaak, Abe, 266
Isaak, Mary (Dyck), 266
itinerant preaching, 39,
51, 60, 103, 135,
137, 140, 146, 154,
198, 205
and General Conference
Mennonites, 147
and nonconformity, 82,
89
and withdrawals, 115,
124, 129
minister-at-large, 148
Oregon as mission field,
235, 236, 245
promoting Mennonite
doctrines, 212
strengthening
denominational
relations, 327
see also Baer, J. B.

J

Jantz, Edward, 176
Jantzen, G. H., 310
Jantzi, 103, 111
Jantzi, John, 103
Janz, 167
Janzen, 151
Janzen, Archie, 259
Janzen, Herman, 192
Jewish evangelism, 181,
237, 252-3
and dispensationalism,
221-2
Johnson, 46, 66, 84, 91
Johnstone, 101
Jones, 122, 157

K

Kaiser, Ralfe, 166
Kaltenbach, 180
Kanagy, 107
Kanagy, Gene, 317
Kansas-Nebraska
Conference, 64ff.,
73, 153, 225, 227
Kassabaum, Nick, 185

Kauffman, 46, 51, 104,
107, 118, 136, 143,
157, 171, 179
Kauffman, Chester, 93,
158, 179, 180
Kauffman, Christian, 144
Kauffman, Daniel
(Scottdale, PA),
212ff., 224, 275,
279
Kauffman, Daniel B., 93,
227
Kauffman, Daniel D., 200
Kauffman, David H.,
226-7, 252
Kauffman, Elvon, 321
Kauffman, Florence, 239
Kauffman, George, 93,
108, 111, 122, 123
Kauffman, Jacob (of
Almota, WA), 185
Kauffman, Jacob (of
Blaine), 104, 221
Kauffman, John D., 45,
48-9, 55, 61
Kauffman, Jonas J., 171ff.
Kauffman, Magdalena, 185
Kauffman, Merle, 187
Kauffman, Nelson E., 132
Kauffman, Rachel, 171,
173
Keck, Jane, 170
Kenagy, 46, 99, 156
Kenagy, Ben, 124, 322
Kenagy, Clif, 265, 276
Kenagy, Edna (Gingerich),
93
Kenagy, Edward (Kelly),
93, 179, 245
Kenagy, Emmanuel, 44,
47, 221
Kenagy, George, 83, 156
Kenagy, Jacob C., 219
Kenagy, Lois, 276
Kenagy, Urie, 208
Kennedy, 180
Kennel, 103, 122
Kennel, Christian R., 52-3
Kennel, Earl, 75, 322
Kennel, Magdalina
(Swartzendruber),
52
Kentta, 103
Kentta, Rosalie, 102
Kester, 84, 110

Kilmer, 57, 74, 78
Kilmer, C. I., 59
King, 46, 57, 66, 81, 118,
122, 157
King, Ben B., 217, 225-6
King, Donald, 317
King, Leo, 117
King, Sadie, 250-1
King, W. Harley, 157, 199
Kingwood Bible Church,
165-6, 300, 330
Sunday school as
mission, 239
see also West Salem
Menn. Breth.
"Kirchliche" Mennonites,
163
Kliewer, 148, 151
Kliewer, Franz, 145ff.
Kliewer, J. J., 186
Kliewer, Menno, 199
Kliewer, P. A., 157
Kniss, Lloy A., 307
Knuths, 111
Knuths, Gary, 110
Knuths, Mildred, 110
Koch, 161
Koehn Church, 194
Koehn F. D., 187
Koehn, Joel T., 194
Koinonia Fellowship, 202
Kramer, 171
Krehbiel, 117, 122, 180
Krehbiel, Christian, 185
Krehbiel, H. J., 190
Krehbiel, Harry, 309
Krehbiel, Jacob, 145
Krehbiel, Olin, 152
Kreider, 171
Kreider, John, 196
Kreider, Urias, 188
Kreider, Verlene, 196
Kroeker, 164, 167
Kroeker, Mr. and Mrs. A.
F., 260
Kropf, 46, 56, 111, 116ff.
Kropf, Adah, 117, 261
Kropf, Anna (Hostetler),
48
Kropf, Charity, 317
Kropf, Daniel J., 46ff., 56,
267, 286
Kropf, Frank, 267, 285,
318
Kropf, Herman, 56

Kropf, Ivan, 269
Kropf, John (1888
    immigrant), 43
Kropf, Joseph (Joe), 117,
    255, 261-2
Kropf, Leroy, 312
Kropf, Lester, 265
Kropf, Levi, 56
Kropf, Lloyd, 116, 181,
    182, 255, 329
Kropf, Merle, 195, 255,
    257
Kropf, Wilbert D., 56
Kropf, Wilbur D., 56-7
Krug, 154
Kuhns, 120
Kulp, Isaac L., 69
Kurtz, Sarah, 73

L

Labish Village BIC, 178
labor unions, 278-9
    and nonresistance, 279
Lackey, 157
Lais, 46, 120
Lais, Amos, 268
Lais, John (1879
    immigrant), 45, 47
Lais, John (grandson of
    immigrant), 293
Lais, Katie (Troyer), 268
Lais, Susannah (Plank), 45
laity
    and mission Sunday
        schools, 239
    designated leadership,
        56, 71, 74
    participation, 59, 132,
        134, 216
        increased after
            alternative service,
            304
    see also church, concept
Lancaster, CA, 193
Landis, 107, 111
Landis, Amos, 63
Landis, Louis, 111
Landis, Mark, 229
Landis, Sabina (Ebersole),
    63
land speculator, 144
Lane County, 34, 43, 50,
    53, 57, 61, 64-5, 69,
    143ff., 176, 185

Lane County AMs, 57ff.,
    67, 71, 145
    division, 64
language usage, 48, 53, 60,
    96, 140, 144, 154,
    162, 174, 176, 197,
    272, 335
    change to English, 272
    German vs. English, 53,
        55, 191, 271-2
    in World War I, 149,
        272, 289
    Spanish as barrier, 240
Lanier, 100
Lantz, 118
Lantz, Gideon, 170
Lantz, Lee, 197
Lantz, Robert, 117
Lapp, James M., 132, 329
Larrew, 78, 104
Larrew, Frank, 78, 103-4
Larrew, James, 103
Larrew, Loyd, 103
Larrew, May (Detweiler),
    103-4
Larrew, Orval, 312
Larson, 51
Latin American
    Fellowship, 262
Lauber, 110
lawsuits, 149, 276
leadership
    see conference
        authority; laity;
        ministry; seminary;
        teacher
Lebanon Community
    Hospital, 97, 106,
    108, 315ff.
Lebanon Mennonite
    Church, 106ff.
Lederach, John, 111,
    121-2
Lee, Nancy, 252
Lee, Robert, 249, 252, 260
Lehman, 84, 120, 180
Lehman, Henry C., 84
Lehman, J. S., 60
Leichty, 120
Leisy, 154
Leisy, Bertha (Roth), 151
Leisy, Homer, 151-2, 222,
    290-1, 310
Lemons, 103
Lemons, Eugene, 103

Leppert, George, 186
Liberty Gardens Bible
    Church, 170, 237,
    244, 303, 331
Lichti, Cathy, 202
Lichti, Don, 202
Lichty, 136
Lichty, Alexander, 138
Lichty, Elizabeth, 27, 135,
    137
Lichty, John, 27, 135, 137
life insurance, 82, 83, 156,
    274, 277
Lind, 91, 119
Lind, Cliff, 119, 323
Lind, Gilbert, 317
Lind, Hope (Kauffman),
    119, 323
Lind, Iola, 317
Lind, Janet, 119
Lind, Leah (Kauffman),
    116
Lind, Lloyd, 92
Lind, Marcus, 92-3, 116,
    130ff., 220-1, 311,
    329, 331
Lind, Millard, 328, 331
Lind, N. A., 72-3, 81, 83,
    87, 90ff., 209, 294,
    296
Lind, Robert, 264
Lind, Sarah (Flohr), 91
Lindsay, Hal, 221
Linn County, 34, 43, 48,
    51ff., 62, 69, 139
Linscheid, 149
literary societies, 244
literature evangelism
    see evangelism, lit.
lodges
    see secret orders
Loewen, 145, 165, 176
Loewen, Abe A., 165
Loewen, Agnes, 165
Loewen, Jacob G., 176
logging, 84, 89, 103, 118,
    176, 269, 270, 315
Logsden Mennonite
    Church, 101ff., 221,
    231, 240, 245
Los Angeles, 72, 191
Loucks, 100
Loucks, Mildred, 100
Lyman, Charles, 185
Lyman, Stan, 165

M

MacNeill, Don, 167
Major, Herbert, 186
Makin, Glenn, 165
Mann, Cleo, 119
Mann, David, 94, 111,
119ff., 132, 221,
322
manufacturing, 36, 59, 268
Maranatha Mennonite
Church, 180
Marion County, 34, 41ff.
Marner, 108, 180
marriage, 209, 213, 279
only with members, 95
with non-members, 87,
157
see also divorce
Martens, 161
Martens, Mary, 161
Martin, 66, 81, 118, 167
Martin, C. Z., 228, 261
Martin, J. Z., 268
Martins, 136
Maurer, Barbara (Gerig),
51, 54
Maurer, Joseph, 43, 51
Maust, Sherman, 195
Maycumber, Harold, 180
McClintock, Donald, 190
McDowell, 91
McNabb, J. L., 186
McPherson, Aimee
(Semple), 209
McTimmonds, 108
McTimmonds, Berle, 108
McTimmonds, Clysta
(Nice), 108
McTimmonds, Elmer, 89,
108, 286-7
Meadowbrook Mennonite
Church, 85, 93,
179-80, 239
Mendenhall, Gerald, 158
Mengershausen, 179
Menno Mennonite Church,
145, 185
Mennonite, The, 160, 211,
332
Mennonite Aid Plan, 274,
335
see also Menn. Mutual;
mutual aid
Mennonite Biblical
Seminary, 167

Mennonite Brethren, 34,
135, 146ff., 160ff.
and Fundamentalism,
218
at Donald, Woodburn,
165
early, at Dallas, 146-7,
163
in Russia, 163
language usage, 272
Oregon congregations,
167
relations with Baptists,
146-7, 163ff., 209
Mennonite Central
Committee, 264,
289, 295ff., 335
Pacific Coast
Conference
disapproval of, 298
peace education, 289
programs, 299
Mennonite Church (MC)
or (old)
see esp. chs. 3-5
Mennonite Church of
Estrella, 189
Mennonite Community
Church, 195
Mennonite Confession of
Faith (1963), 125
Mennonite Country
Church, 186
Mennonite Covenant
Fellowship at
Clackamas, 341
Mennonite Disaster
Service, 264-5
Mennonite Mutual Aid,
275, 277
see also Mennonite Aid
Mennonite Publishing
House, 99, 331
Mennonite Youth
Fellowship, 94, 244
*Mennonitische Rundschau,
Die*, 37
men's organizations, 94,
235, 244
Messenger, The, 160
Mexico, 260ff.
Meyer, 140
Meyer, Joseph, 170-1
Meyers, 136

migration
conflict resolution, 172
disillusion, 38, 143ff.
for employment, 118
from Canada, 54, 164
from China, 187, 190
from Europe, 32, 43, 54,
136
from other states, 164
from Russia, 186
motives, 52-3, 85, 168,
185, 188, 229
nonresistance, 282,
288
Old Order Amish, 171
patterns, 39, 136
to Oregon, 43, 56, 67,
168
disillusion, 37, 46
motives, 34, 36, 169
westward, 185
within Oregon, 48
within U.S., 33, 43-4, 54,
164, 186
motives, 151
see also extinct;
missions, swarming;
settlement
military service, 282ff.
accepted by some
Mennonites, 301
and church membership,
297
see also conscientious;
nonresistance;
peace; names of
wars
Miller, 56-7, 70, 78, 100,
106-7, 120, 157,
159, 171
Miller, Abraham, 41, 100
Miller, Alex, 58, 66
Miller, Almira, 41
Miller, Benedict, 41, 43,
57
Miller, Christine, 155, 160
Miller, Daniel D., 170, 172
Miller, Daniel E., 174
Miller, David Y., 174
Miller, Doris, 263, 264
Miller, Edmund J., 155,
185
Miller, Eli, 202
Miller, Isaac S., 36, 268
Miller, Jacob K., 171, 174

Miller, John, 263, 264
Miller, L. J., 209
Miller, Leo L., 190
Miller, Mattie (Christner), 57
Miller, Milo, 41
Miller, Mose, 140
Miller, Myrtle, 251
Miller, Obed and sons, 269
Miller, Olive (Bucher), 100
Miller, Omar G., 67, 75, 83, 86, 88, 100, 206, 215, 220, 293, 311, 316
  and Modernism, 83
Miller, Paul W., 88, 229ff.
  on Holy Spirit, 229
Miller, Rachel (Mast), 41
Miller, Roy, 231
Miller, S. J., 221
Miller, Sam, 250, 320
Miller, Solomon L., 57
Miller, Twila, 100
ministers' meetings, 69, 88, 153, 228, 230
ministry and ministers
  authority, 106
  characteristics, 205
  conflicting expectations, 122
  influence in conference, 92, 111, 123
  need for, 27, 38, 43, 64, 137, 146, 174, 246, 251
  patterns of transfer, 72
  see also ordination; seminary
Mishler, 66, 70, 78, 84
Mishler, Carrie (Schrag), 145
Mishler, Elsie (Nice), 78, 257
Mishler, Emily, 262
Mishler, J. B., 84, 246
Mishler, Jacob D., 57ff., 64ff., 73, 78-9, 153
Mishler, Jim (J. M.), 78, 145
Mishler, Melvin, 102, 262
Mishler, Nellie, 262
Mishler, Peter D., 41ff., 57ff., 72
Mishler, Rachel (Miller), 41, 72

Mishler, Raymond (Ray), 78, 94, 124, 181, 221, 230, 257
Mishler, Robert, 262
mission and missions, 89, 95, 158, 204, 235ff., 306, 320, 324, 338
  among migrants, 240
  and American Indians, 201, 240
  and divorce and remarriage, 280
  and nonresistance, 283, 290
  as a regional focus, 328
  Breth. in Christ, 177-8
  by congregations, 238ff.
  changing theories, 258, 259
  congregational, 166, 167
  deaconess, 314
  denominational focus, 167
  financial support, 236, 245
  focus on children
    Sunday schools, 248
  foreign, 155, 181, 260ff.
  homes, hospitals, 314, 319
  identified by Pacific Coast Conference promotion, 236
  lay initiative, 84
  literature, 240
  MB, 161
  medical, 244
  Mexico, 133, 200
  music in, 238, 245
  Portland, 81, 161, 245ff.
  radio, 245
  role of laity, 236, 238, 247, 255
  rural, 99, 102, 110, 257, 258
    declining emph., 258
  summer Bible schools, 101, 102, 106, 239, 240
  Sunday schools, 53, 79, 84, 91, 93, 100, 102, 104, 178-9, 200, 239-40, 251, 257
    popularity, 257
    "swarming", 122

  to children
    see child evangelism
  urban, 190, 191, 196, 246
  Vanderhoof, B.C., 256
  vs. church planting, 97
  women's groups, 241
  see also evangelism; Good, Allan; Jewish; mission boards, etc.; Portland; rescue
Missionary Evangel, 108, 120, 128, 229, 238, 328
mission boards, committees, 76, 153, 159ff., 177, 191, 196, 235ff., 329, 338
  for Central America, 261
  lack of trust, 260
  non-Mennonite, 260
  re Portland AM/MC work, 246
mission conferences and meetings, 62, 148, 237, 335, 338
Mitchell, 108, 120
Modernism, 82-3
Molalla Mennonite Church, 67, 84, 179, 277
Monroe Community Chapel, 186
Montana, 200
Moody Bible Institute, 142, 168, 217, 219, 220
Moody, D. L., 219
Moore, 117
Morgan, 74
Morris, 157
Morrow County, 37
Moser, 136
Mountain View Mennonite Church, 200
movies, 206, 277
Mueller, 136
Mueller, C. F., 237, 243
Muller, 140
Multnomah School of the Bible, 223, 333
music, 235
  and mission, 179, 238
  and revival meetings, 207

instruments, 57, 95, 151,
156, 168, 209
singing, 139, 151
singing schools, 69
opposition, 139
"special", 237
mutual aid, 89, 270ff.,
335ff.
organized, 274
see also Mennonite Aid
Myers, 116
Myers, Gottlieb, 136
Myers, Ralph, Sr., 116

N

Nachtigal, 161, 163
Nafziger, 118
Nafziger, Dave, 323
Nafziger, Florence, 260
Nafziger, Marjorie, 323
Nafziger, Wilbert R., 117
Nampa Mennonite Church
see First Mennonite
Church (Nampa,
ID)
nationalism
United States, 29
Neal, 180
Neavoll, George, 105
Needy Brick and Tile Co.,
36, 268
Neo-Pentecostalism
see charismatic;
Pentecostal
Neuenschwander, 136
see also Neuschwander
Neufeld, Ernest, 201
Neufelt, 148-9, 168
Neufelt, John P., 149
Neufelt, Nick, 149
Neuschwander, 53, 56, 120
see also
Neuenschwander
Neuschwander, Emma
(Biery), 36, 55
Neuschwander, Peter, 36,
55, 138, 139
Nevada, 201
Nice, 78, 108, 120
Nice, Howard, 108
Nickel, 169
Nickel, Phil, 110
Nightengale, 161

Nightengale, David, 161
Nisly, 117, 180
Nisly, Alvin, 116
Nisly, Wilma (Shenk), 116,
117, 231
Niswander, 154
Niswander, Catherine,
154, 309
Niswander, Menno, 197
Nofziger, 51, 53, 57, 107,
120
Nofziger, C. G., family,
272
Nofziger, Dan, 316
Nofziger, Verl, 122, 188
noncombatant service,
284ff.
see also conscientious
nonconformity, 89, 95, 97,
209
and attire, 77, 81
as Menn. fundamental,
212-3
changes after World
War II, 298
"drift" from, 89, 112,
115
fruit of salvation, 97
Paul W. Miller, on, 88
promoting
nonresistance, 293
see also attire;
nonresistance;
separation from
world
noncooperation with
Selective Service,
301ff.
see also draft
nonjuring
see oath-taking
nonmillennialism
see amillennialism
nonresistance, 32, 44, 89,
95, 125, 153, 190,
204, 209, 213, 270,
276, 282ff.
and attire, 54, 77, 97
and mission, 283, 290
and war bonds, 283
as Menn. fundamental,
212
enlarged concept, 304
influences pro, con, 297
lack of teaching, 283,
284, 288, 290-1

noncooperation with
Selective Service
see noncooperation
non-essential to faith,
87, 122
promoted, 292
shifting Pacific Coast
Conf. position, 302
societal endorsement,
301
teaching, 290, 292, 300
vs. dispensationalism,
223
see also conscientious;
peace witness; war
bonds; war taxes
North Dallas Mennonite
Brethren, 163ff.,
236, 333
North Park Community
Church (Menn.
Breth.), 167, 260,
264, 300, 330
North Pomona Mennonite
Church, 194
Northwest Conference,
201
Northwest Fellowship of
Unaffiliated
Conservative
Mennonites, 180,
329
nurture, 89, 204-5, 208,
211, 233, 306, 324
and mission, 265
see also Bible conf.;
Bible schools;
Sunday schools
Nusbaum, 57

O

oath-taking, 153
obedience
and progressive holiness,
225
to biblical teachings, 97
see also discipleship;
discipline
Obelander, 179
occupations, 59, 267ff.
of women, 269-70
Oglesby, Debbie, 201
Oglesby, Nathan, 201, 202

(old) Mennonites
  see esp. chs. 3-5
Old Order Amish, 33, 135,
  170ff., 272, 331,
  338
  California settlement,
  174
  early Yamhill County,
  173
  Hubbard, Needy, 170
  McMinnville, 173, 264,
  303
  second, third
  settlements, 173ff.
  membership, 172ff.
  see also Amish
Olsen, 84
Olson, 170
Onecho Mennonite
  Church, 148, 185
Orange Mennonite
  Fellowship, 196
ordination
  by lot, 47
  dissatisfaction with,
  47, 88, 93, 194
  by vote
  dissatisfaction with,
  73, 93
  irregularities, 49, 88
  of deacons to preach, 78
  status rejected, 59
  see also ministry
Oregon history, 29ff.
Osborne, Millard, 107-8,
  111, 128, 132, 317
Ösch (Oesch), 66
Oswald, 107
Oyer, John P., 132

P

Pacific Coast Bible School,
  68-9, 306ff.
  and mission, 307
Pacific Coast Conference,
  62-3, 74, 131, 153,
  183, 215; *and esp.*
  chs. 3-5
  and Bookrack
  Evangelism, 241
  and denom. standards,
  87
  conference minister as
  overseer, 131

constitution, 95-6, 112,
  124ff., 131
  membership, 74-5, 85,
  89, 111, 127, 133
  merging with AMs, 76
  on Holy Spirit, 226ff.
  on Sunday schools, 239
  organization, 63, 74
  withdrawals, 114, 123,
  126ff.
Pacific College, 333
Pacific District
  Conference (GC),
  148, 152ff., 160,
  183
  and eschatology, 222
  and missions, 235-6
  membership, 160
  on Holy Spirit, 233
  organization, 147, 147
Pacific District
  Conference (MB),
  160, 167
  membership, 167
  on Holy Spirit, 233
pacifism
  see nonresistance
Panic of 1893, 59, 172,
  176, 268
Pankratz, 165
Pankratz, Peter, 318
Parker, 111, 159
Paschall, 167
pastoral support, 94, 150,
  155, 167
patriotism, 277, 291
Paul, 165
Pauli, 161
Paulus, 116, 118
Paulus, Melvin, 118, 124,
  181, 329
Pax service, 299
Peace Mennonite Church,
  155, 341
  see also Alberta
  Community Menn.
  Church
peace witness, 280ff.,
  299ff., 324, 330,
  336
  education, 289
  interdenominational,
  336
  see also nonresistance
Peck, 154

Penner, 145
Pentecostal emph., 57, 209
  at Indian Cove, 229
  influences, 200, 224,
  228ff.
  on smaller groups, 232
  in Mexico mission work,
  262-3
  in Pacific District
  Conference (GC),
  232
  reaction to, 228
  vs. traditional practice,
  228
  see also charismatic
Pentecostalism, 209
Peters, 145, 148, 163, 164,
  168
Peters, D. A., 164
Peters, E. J., 157
Peters, Isbrand, 147, 163
Peterson, 181
Peterson, Kenneth J., 190
Phernetton, 100
Phoenix, 110
Pietsch, W. E., 164, 209,
  223
plain coat, clothing
  see attire
Plainview Mennonite
  Church, 110-1
Plank, David J., 174
Pleasant Valley Amish
  Mennonite congreg.,
  62
Pletcher, 74
political involvement, 276
  and peace witness, 304
  disapproved, 125, 185,
  276
  Menn. Breth., 276
  increasing, 276
  voting, 112, 276
  see also nonresistance;
  church-state; state
  aid
Polk County, 34, 74,
  143ff., 163, 176
Polk Station, 145ff.
Popp, 161
Porter Mennonite Church,
  99-100, 112, 114,
  221, 313, 336
Portland
  early OM mission work,
  246

GC Menn. mission, 245
Menn. Breth. mission,
    245
mission beginnings, 247
Portland Mennonite
    Brethren congreg.,
    161-2, 236
Portland Mennonite
    Church, 80, 181,
    220, 229, 239, 246,
    251-2, 300
camping, 251
children's activities, 250
diversity, 251, 252
end of mission status,
    250, 251
focus on children, 249
in Great Depression,
    249-50
mission origin, 246ff.
Pratt, 179
Pratum, 136
prayer meetings, 69, 98,
    217
charismatic, 231
prayer veiling, 95, 124-5,
    139, 213-4
see also attire
premillennialism, 211,
    219ff.
among smaller
    Mennonite groups,
    222-3
see also amillennialism;
    dispensationalism;
    Fundamentalism
Prince of Peace
    Mennonite Church
see Corvallis Menn. Ch.
progressive holiness
see holiness movement
prophecy
see eschatology
publications
aid to identity, 331
airing controversies, 64
exposing error, 217
influences *re*
    Fundamentalism, 217
    migration, 37, 60, 67
    missions, 237ff., 249
    unity, 75
    withdrawals, 124
promotion of, 331-2
teaching doctrines, 212

uneven acceptance, 331

Q

quarterly mission
    meetings, 108,
    236-7
see also mission
    meetings
Quenzer, Floyd, 195
Quiring, 145, 148, 168
Quiring, Jacob H., 168

R

railroads and
    development, 186-7, 196
    migrations, 30, 185
    wood industries, 90
Ramseyer, 136
Ranch Chapel, 132, 259,
    341
Randall, 100
Rariden, 103
Ratzlaff, 110, 163, 176
Ratzlaff (Ratzloff), John,
    109, 110, 319
Ratzloff, 118, 179
Ratzloff, Elvina, 319
recreation, 319ff.
Reddekopp or Redekop,
    148
Redekop, Peter, 145
Rediger, 46
Redwood Country Church,
    177
Reeder, 99, 106
Reeder, Harold, 254, 318
Reeder, Myrtle, 318
Rees, Henry, 188, 190
Reeser, Ethel, 270
Regehr, 164
Regier, Arnold, 291-2, 332
Regier, J. J., 223
Regier, Wilbert A., 142,
    232, 277, 310
regulation coat
see attire, plain
Reimer, 148, 164, 170
Reisbich, 161
Reist, 78
Reist, Hilda, 206
Reist, Reuben, 92

Rejoice conference, 231
relationships of
    Mennonites
to government, 276
to larger society, 30
with Fundamentalist
    institutes, 310
with larger society, 30,
    266, 289, 323, ch.
    10
with their conferences,
    183
with their denomination,
    125, 128, 142, 152,
    160, 183, 202, 298,
    325, 327, 339, 343
see also ecumenism;
    economic;
    inter-Mennonite;
    political
relief and service, 204,
    298, 303, 336, 338
and societal acceptance,
    289
material aid, 264, 298
personnel, 264, 298
see also voluntary serv.
Rempel, 145, 148, 168
Rempel, Gerhard J., 37
Reno, Nevada, 202
rescue missions
farm, 254, 319
Harrisburg members,
    initiators, 57
Portland, 117, 181,
    253-4
Sacramento, 116-7, 195,
    255
retreats, 309, 323
revivalism, 60, 78, 206ff.,
    211, 220
and individualism, 28
and missions, 237, 261
characteristics, 207
desire for, 46
Holy Spirit emph., 224ff.
influence of other
    denominations, 209
influence on
    nonresistance, 282
Mennonite style, 207
methodology, 228
Pentecostal, 53
revival meetings, 62, 69,
    85, 152, 163-4, 168,
    335

at Pacific Coast Bible
  School, 308
see also tent revivals
Reznicsek, 157
Rich, 136, 140
Rich, John, 140, 147
Riegsecker, Chris, 136
Riegsecker, Jacob, 136
Riegsecker, Joseph, 136
Rieser, 156
Riesser, 197
Rinks, Riley, 186
Robertson, 159
Robla Mennonite Church,
  195, 255
Rock of Ages Mennonite
  Home, 109, 319
Rogie, Alice, 240
Rogie, Alvin, 83
Ropp, 53, 120
Rose, 148
Roseburg Conservative
  Amish Mennonite
  congregation, 61
Rosedale Bible Institute,
  333
Ross, 161, 181
Ross, Kenneth, 192
Roth, 46, 81, 91, 99, 106,
  118, 120, 136, 157
Roth, Catherina, 52
Roth, Catherine, 51
Roth, Christian, 51
Roth, Daniel (of Albany),
  52
Roth, Earl, 157, 260
Roth, Glen A., 313
Roth, Jacob, 44, 52, 200
Roth, Jacob S., 194
Roth, Jake, 104, 105, 106
Roth, James, 263
Roth, Jeanne (Robitaille),
  104ff.
Roth, John, 52
Roth, Ken, 323
Roth, Lois, 313
Roth, Marlene, 119
Roth, Martin, 52
Roth, Mary (Eicher), 52
Roth, Myrna, 323
Roth, Noreen, 263
Roth, Orie, 122
Roth, Paul N., 81, 87-8,
  157, 158, 217, 250,
  276

Roth, Roy D., 103, 111,
  132
Roth, Ruth (Jantzen), 157,
  260
Roth, S. E., 240
Roth, Velma (Burck), 158,
  250
Roupp, 149
Ruckert, 111
ruralism, 149, 164
  declining, 270
see also agriculture;
  urbanization
Russian Mennonites
  (so-called), 60, 135,
  140, 143, 145, 190,
  272, 288
in Russia, 34
inter-Mennonite
  relations, 334
Ruth, Emma, 237, 290,
  292

S

Sack, Nobel, 155, 217
Salem Academy, 208, 211,
  310-1
Salem Deaconess Home
  and Hospital, 314
Salem Evang. Menn. Breth.
  (1930s), 169
Salem General Hospital
  see Salem Deaconess
Salem Memorial Hospital
  see Salem Deaconess
Salem Mennonite Church,
  117ff.
Salem Mennonite Church
  (Aberdeen, ID)
  see First Mennonite
  Church at Aberdeen
Salem Mennonite Church
  (Ruff, WA), 186
Salt Creek, 146
salvation
  and church membership,
  159, 179, 200, 207,
  209
  and discipleship, 113,
  283
  and holy living, 232
  and Holy Spirit, 225,
  227, 230, 232

and peace, 282, 291
Apostolic Christian
  Church emph., 137
Breth. in Christ emph.,
  34
eternal security, 217
evidence of, 215
Salzman, Earl, 190
San Marcos Menn. Church,
  189
see also Second
  Mennonite Church
  of Paso Robles
Sather, 167
Sauer, 161
sawmills, 36, 59, 61, 104,
  108, 158, 268ff.,
  279, 293, 315
Schantz, 119
Schimmelfeming, 176
Schlabach, 57, 118
Schlabach, Isaac, 57
Schlegel, 53
Schlegel, Joseph, 46-7, 59,
  62
Schmidt, 165
Schmidt, A. G., 192
Schmidt, Gladwyn, 298
Schmidt, J. J., 233
Schmidt, Wilbur, 187
Schmucker, 66, 120
Schmucker, Amos, 53, 241
Schmucker, Oliver, 318
Schneider, 167
Schnell, 161
schools
  church, 211
  elementary, 144, 313
  German, 148, 172, 272,
  313
  influenced by war spirit,
  297
see also Bible schools;
  colleges; Salem
  Acad.; seminary;
  Western Menn.
  School
Schrag, 149
Schrag, Barbara (Graber),
  143, 145
Schrag, Jacob R., 60, 144,
  185
Schrag, Joseph, 143-4
Schrag, Lizzie, 143
Schrag, Mary, 143

Schrag Mennonites, 143ff., 172, 185
Schrag, Nellie, 144
Schrock, 53, 99, 104, 107, 111, 148, 171
Schrock, David C., 173
Schrock, Fannie, 107, 298
Schrock, Joseph, 81
Schrock, Kathryn, 313
Schrock, Melvin, 81, 90, 98-9
Schrock, Mildred, 80
Schrock, Paul, 99
Schrock, Perry, 110
Schrock, V. L., 192
Schroeder, 167-8
Schroeder, Harold, 167
Schuler, Martha, 315
Schuler, Mary, 315
Schultz, 46, 51, 57, 84, 170, 179
Schultz, D. P., 169-70
Schumacher, 157
Schunke, Gustav, 146-47, 163
Schwartz, 159
Schwartz, Alfred, 159
Schweitzer, 100
Schweitzer, Royden, 198
Schwindt, 161
Scofield Reference Bible, 217ff., 232
see also dispensa-
    tionalism
Seattle Mennonite Church
    see South Seattle
        Mennonite Church
second coming of Christ, 219
see also eschatology
Second Mennonite Church
    of Paso Robles, 190
see also First Mennonite
    Church (Paso
    Robles, CA)
second work of grace, 224ff., 230, 233
Breth. in Christ emph., 34, 232
see also baptism;
    charismatic,
    holiness; Holy
    Spirit; Pentecostal
secret orders, 95, 153, 209, 213, 273

opposed, 273
seminary training, 95, 111, 118, 123, 132, 142, 205
see also Menn. Bibl. S.
separation from the world, 97, 125, 215, 275, 281
in language used, 271
see also nonconformity
separation, church-state
    see church, concept of
Sermon on the Mount, 282
Mennonites vs.
    dispensationalists, 223
settlement, 34
eastern Oregon, 37
Lane County, 43, 57
Linn County, 43, 48, 51
Polk County, 37, 74, 143, 163
Salem, Silverton, 27, 36, 136
Sheridan, 78
Woodburn, Hubbard, 36, 41, 43
see also extinct;
    migration
Seventh Street Mennonite
    Church, 195
Shafter, California, 192
Shank, 91, 111
Shank, Beulah, 313
Shank, Ralph, 181, 182
Sharer, 74, 110
Sharer, Delilah, 192
Sharer, Elmer, 109
Sharon Mennonite Church, 194
Shenk, 74, 78, 104, 117-8, 122
Shenk, Amos (son of A. M. Shenk), 198, 229
Shenk, Amos M., 198, 226, 229
Shenk, Barb, 256
Shenk, Daniel F., 78ff., 84, 102-3, 227, 275
Shenk, Fannie (Schrag), 79
Shenk, Gabriel D., 74, 80, 116-7, 220
Shenk, Juanita
    (Brenneman), 119
Shenk, Luella (Sharer), 80

Shenk, Ron, 256
Shenk, Wilbert R., 119, 262, 328
Sheridan Mennonite
    Church, 67, 75, 78ff., 101ff., 110, 126, 180, 220, 228ff., 254, 256, 261, 264, 275, 279, 308, 311, 314, 336
Shetler, Eldon, 256
Shetler, Lois, 256
Shetler, Maggie, 307
Shetler, Ralph, 251, 320, 322
Shetler, S. G., 64ff., 73, 220, 229, 307
Shoemaker, 159
Showalter, 118
Showalter, Bernard, 117
Shrock, Sam, 240
Siemens, 145, 148
Sills, 116
Silverton Hills, 93
Sims, 117
Singer, 161
Singh, Ajmer, 99
Singh, Verna (Hersh-
    berger), 99
Sittner, 161
Slabach, 70
Slabaugh, 78
Slabaugh, Ben M., 175
Slatter, 317
"sleeping preachers"
    see trance preaching
Sloan, Larry, 159
Smith, 110, 117
Smith, J. B., 82, 220, 222
Smucker, 56, 101, 111, 120
Smucker, Dottie, 251
Smucker, Jonathan P., 41, 43, 185
Smucker, Marcus, 122, 251-2
Snyder, 81
Snyder, Anna, 239, 251, 257, 298-9
Snyder, Chris (Christian), 51, 200, 246, 257, 261
Snyder, Delbert, 119
Snyder, Jon, 299
Snyder, Kenneth, 313

Snyder, Lee (Kropf), 119, 312
Snyder, Muriel (Ethel), 247
social change, 131, 155, 162, 175, 280, 298, 325, 332, 338
  among Amish, 175
  and interpretation of Scripture, 338
  and wars, 214, 304
social concerns, 131-2, 188, 212, 252, 259, 276, 280, 304
  see also alcohol, amusements, tobacco
Sommer, 140
Sommers, 110, 136
South Nampa Mennonite Church, 197, 199
South Pacific Conference, 89, 189, 194, 201
South Seattle Mennonite Church, 188
Southwest Conference, 189
  see also South Pacific Conference
speaking in tongues
  see glossolalia
Spirit preaching
  see trance preaching
Spring Valley Mennonite Church, 186
Stahley, Emanuel, 192, 226
Stanley, 157
state aid, 277, 338
Stauffer, 81, 106, 140, 156
Stauffer, Anna, 309
Steckly, 74
Steffen, 136, 140, 144
Steffen, Peter, 136
Steiner, 122, 136, 140, 144
Steiner, C. B., 137ff.
Steiner, Catherine, 138
Steiner, D. J., 148
Stockton, 180
Stoltzfus, Amos, 323
Stoltzfus, Maxine, 323
Strong, 84
Strong, Nada, 84, 277
Strubhar, 57
Strubhar, Anne (Tolmshoff), 178

Strubhar, Clifford, 244
Strubhar, Dwight, 313, 329
Strubhar, Naomi, 179
Strubhar, Tim, 124, 179
Stump, 148
Stutsman, 122
Stutzman, 56, 99, 106, 108, 111, 120, 157
Stutzman, Dave, Sr., 92
Stutzman, J. P., 57
Stutzman, Merle, 99
Stutzman, Verle, 188
Stutzman, Willard L., 114
Stuwe, 157
summer Bible schools, 179, 180, 235, 248, 258, 335
  opposition, 61
Sunday schools, 78, 154, 191, 192, 205, 235, 258, 335
  agents of nurture, 206
  Amish, 174ff.
  avoiding union Sunday schools, 71
  conferences and convention, 62, 67, 69, 76, 148
  German, 172, 175
  mission, 72
  opposition, 53, 61, 139, 140, 172
  Pacific District Conference (GC), 206
  see also child evangelism; union
Sunday School Times, The, 224-5
Sunnyslope Mennonite Church, 201
Sutter, 53, 136
Suver, 74
Swartzendruber, 171
Swartzentruber, Menno, 174-5
Sweet Home Community Chapel, 91, 158-9
Sweet Home Mennonite Church, 73, 89-90, 118, 241
Swiss Mennonites, 37, 55, 135ff., 335
  join Apostolic Christian Church, 137

Switzerland, Oregon, 136
Sword and Trumpet, The, 124, 217, 220-1
  see also Brunk, George R., I and II
Sycamore Grove congregation (Missouri), 43ff., 209, 219

T

Tabor College, 330, 333
Tadeo, Raul, 263-4
Tadeo, Vanita, 263-4
Tangent Mennonite Church, 53, 88, 98-9, 112, 114, 116, 230, 270, 277, 313
teacher training classes, 206
telephones, 275
tent revivals, 116, 177, 210, 220, 240
  and Holy Spirit emph., 230
  see also revivalism, revival meetings
Terra Bella, California, 192
theology, 113
  accusations of unorthodoxy, 129
  and Holy Spirit emph., 224
  Calvinism opposed, 217
  distinctively Mennonite, 28, 209
  distrusted, 82
  divisive, 190
  Fundamentalist vs. Mennonite, 28, 115, 211
  influences on Oregon Mennonites, 205
  membership defined, 76
  Mennonite doctrines, 212
  Pacific District Conference (GC), 153
  re Christ, 54, 211
  re end times, 222
  re life insurance, 275

salvation within
  community, 27
Thiessen, 151, 168-9
Thiessen, Alfred, 168
Thiessen, David, 168
Thiessen, Helen, 222, 323
Thiessen, Mrs., 318
tobacco, 67, 209, 277, 295
Toevs, John, 197
Toews, 151, 163, 176
Toews, Jacob, 163
Toews, Jacob J., 164
Toews, John A., 218, 300
trance preaching, 45, 48,
  55, 61
  in Missouri and Oregon,
  49
Troyer, 46, 110, 157
Troyer, Amos P., 36, 46ff.,
  59, 81, 93, 220,
  267-8
Troyer, Bertha, 251
Troyer, Delilah [Lyle]
  (Yoder), 36, 48, 268
Troyer, Edna, 41
Troyer, Jim, 41
Troyer, Mattie (Miller), 41
Tschiegg, Allan R., 142
Tucson Mennonite
  Fellowship, 202
Turnbull, J. H., 223
Twelfth Street Mennonite
  Church
  see Albany Mennonite
  Church
two-trackism, 282-3
Tyson, 74

U

Ulrich, 197
Unaffiliated Mennonite
  Groups, 178ff.
unequal yoke, 125, 273,
  298
Unger, 66, 144-5
Unger, David, 145
Union County, 63
union Sunday schools, 44,
  51, 70, 103, 192,
  273, 335
United Mennonite Church,
  194
Unrau, 111

Unrau, Pete, 169, 331
Unruh, 168-9, 176
Unruh, Daniel J., 291
Unruh, Merle, 194
Urbach, 161
urbanization, 106, 117ff.,
  149, 162, 164, 251,
  252, 258, 268ff.,
  281
  and missions, 255
  rural, decline, 258
  influence on
  families, 280
  migration, 176
  of youth, 247

V

Victorville, CA, 191
Vietnam War, 300ff.
Village Missions, 180, 258
Vimont, Ben, 256
Virgin, Bill, 199
Vogt, Leona (Kleiver), 166
Vogt, Leonard, 166
Vogt, Wilhelm, 145
Volga Germans, 161
voluntary service, 155,
  178, 188, 251-2,
  299
  among migrants, 256
  at Yale, WA, 256
  camping, 256
  summer Bible schools,
  256
  see also Pax; Menn.
  Disaster Serv.
Voth, 163
Voth, H. D., 192
Voth, Heinrich (church
  elder), 161, 163
Voth, Heinrich (H. S.),
  161ff., 223, 236
Voth, Henry, 163
voting
  see political partic.

W

Waldo Hills congregation,
  139-40, 147-8
  see also Emmanuel
  Mennonite Church
  (Pratum)

Walker, 108
Wall, 169
Wallace, Elster, family,
  201
Waltner, 144
Waltner, John, 186
war bonds, 285
  see also nonresistance
Warden Mennonite
  Church, 187
Warkentin, 145, 148, 170
war taxes, 131
Way, The, 241
wealth, 37, 44, 131, 281
Weaver, 74, 179
Weaver, E. C., 191
Weaver (Becker), Gladys,
  260
Weaver, Luke E., 75, 192
Weaver, Mary (Glick), 75
Weaver, Samuel A., 175
Weber, 84
wedding ring, 95, 112,
  124, 338
Wedel, Franz (F. B.), 314
Wedel, Irwin, 315
Wedel, Peter, 163
Weirich, 171
Weirich, Anna, 176
Weirich, William, 176
Welty, 66, 136, 144
Wenger, 136
Wenger, A. D., 63-4, 219
Wenger, Christian C., 27,
  36, 37, 135ff.
Wenger, J. C., 128, 222,
  329
Wenger, Magdalena, 27,
  135
Wenger, Viola, 250-1, 317
"West Coast Echoes", 75,
  86, 215, 293, 311,
  316
Western District AM
  Conference, 45, 62
  from congreg. to conf.
  authority, 62
Western Evangelical
  Seminary, 155, 180,
  217
Western Mennonite
  Church, 91, 92, 112,
  118, 243
Western Mennonite
  School, 91, 208,
  222, 230, 311, 313

West, Harry, 74
West, Harry, family, 285
West Salem Mennonite
    Brethren, 165, 290
    see also Kingwood Bible
        Church
Wheeler, 157
Whitaker, 122
Whitaker, Ferne, 237, 250
Whitaker, Glenn, 250
Whitaker, J. E., 73
White, 108
Wideman, 78, 110
Wideman, Louise, 253
Wideman, Oscar, 110, 253
Widmer, 53, 56, 70, 118,
    120, 156
Widmer, C. R., 69, 72, 246
Widmer, Daniel, 117
Widmer, Herbert E., 150
Wiebe, A. J., 189
Wiebe, Allan, 260
Wiebe, Elisabeth, 318
Wiebe, Herman D., 310,
    318
Wiebe, Orlando, 330
Wiebe, Selma, 260
Wiens, 151, 159, 164, 168,
    170
Wiens, Frank C., 170
Wiens, Jacob, 145
Wiens, Sarah (Lohrentz),
    206, 243, 315
Willems, 108, 165
Willems, John, 118
Willow Creek Mennonite
    Church
    see Second Mennonite
        Church of Paso
        Robles
Winston Mennonite
    Church, 101, 109,
    127, 314
Winton Mennonite
    Church, 193
Wisseman, 120
Wittenberg, 161
Wittrig, 108
Wolfer, 91, 103, 106, 116,
    118
Wolfer, Dewey, 101, 102
Wolfer, Florence
    (Mishler), 102
Wolfer, Henry A., 88,
    115ff., 191, 246,
    253

Wolfer, Hugh, 253
Wolfer, Ina, 253
Wolfer, Mary, 88, 246
women, participation of,
    72ff., 102, 116, 131,
    179, 243, 307
deaconesses, 314
designated leadership,
    154, 161
    in summer Bible
        schools, 239
empowered to organize
    Sunday schools, 239
hospital work, 314, 315
in administration, 313,
    317ff., 323
in Bible institute, 309
informal roles, 49, 178
in larger society, 268
in livelihood, 267, 270,
    295
in missions, 155, 157,
    241, 247, 250, 253,
    260, 262
    quoted, 247, 250
in public meetings, 206,
    237
ministers' wives, 74
missionary projects, 244
peace work, 290, 292
    quoted, 66, 80, 103, 117,
    206, 222, 231
    re Civilian Public
        Service, 296
teaching, 69, 105, 206,
    308ff.
women's groups, 72, 76,
    151, 182, 235,
    241-2, 290
    promoting spiritual
        growth, 243
    re Civilian Public
        Service, 296
Wood, 106
Woodlake, California, 192
Workers' Exchange, 151,
    160, 238
World War I, 198, 283ff.,
    288, 303
army camps, 286-7
display of flag, 285
hostility toward
    Mennonites, 283ff.
varying Mennonite
    responses, 284

war bonds, 285-6
World War II, 290ff.
economic advantages,
    294
hostility *re* Mennonites,
    56, 293-4
influence, Portland
    Mennonite Church,
    250
war bonds, 293
Wyatt, 179

Y

Yale, WA, 256
Yamhill County, 173-4
Yoder, 46, 51, 57, 66, 70,
    74, 78, 81, 84, 101,
    108, 110, 117, 122,
    157, 171, 181
Yoder, A., 283
Yoder, Alice (Troyer),
    49-50, 93
Yoder, Allen, 231
Yoder, Daniel J., 41, 45
Yoder, Edward Z., 49-50,
    87, 93-4, 227, 287,
    289
    in World War I, 287,
    289
Yoder, Fannie (Weaver),
    206
Yoder, Henry, 250
Yoder, Hiram, 261
Yoder, Ina (Hamilton), 84,
    255
Yoder, Joe (not Joe H.),
    231
Yoder, Joe H., 84-5, 181,
    201, 255
Yoder, John, 317
Yoder, Lester, 231
Yoder, Levi J., 43, 57ff.,
    64ff., 153, 170, 226
Yoder, Louisa (Miller), 41
Yoder, Lydia, 250
Yoder, Max G., 94, 108-9,
    113, 130, 132, 196,
    230, 232, 261
    and Holy Spirit emph.,
    231
Yoder, Mose (Amish
    bishop), 174-5
Yoder, Moses (from MO),
    43

Yoder, Orrie D., 195,
    220-1, 227, 237,
    241, 252, 331
Yoder, Paul E., 94, 109,
    122, 238, 321
Yoder, Rhea, 251
Yoder, Sanford C., 287,
    289
Yoder, Tobias T., 173
young people's institutes,
    309
    see also nurture
youth activities, 69, 151,
    168, 235, 243-4,
    320
    mission organizations,
    243
    see also Menn. Youth
    Fell.; young

Yutzi, 53
Yutzy, 110
Yutzy, Sol, 109

Z

Zehr, 101, 119
Zimmerman, 106
Zimmerman, Don, 264
Zimmerman, Elvina, 264
Zimmerman, Peter, 44, 49
Zion Mennonite Church
    (AM/MC), 44ff., 54,
    62, 69, 85ff., 93ff.,
    140, 157, 173, 178,
    206, 217, 220, 236,
    239, 242ff., 267,
    283, 285, 296-7,
    309, 321, 334-5

language usage, 272
quilting reputation, 243
sewing circle, 242
Zion Mennonite Church
    (GC), 148ff., 217,
    236, 268, 272ff.
    on nonresistance, 283
    see also Grace
    Mennonite Church
    (Dallas)
Zook, 66, 118, 154, 180
Zook, Jeanne, 155, 260,
    336
Zook, John, 155, 244, 260
Zook, Jonathan, 181
Zook, Samuel, 177
Zuercher, E. E., 83

The Author

Hope Kauffman Lind was born in Mountain Lake, Minnesota. She lived in Wood River, Nebraska, from middle childhood until her marriage to Clifford Lind. She has lived in Oregon since 1960.

She went to church conferences with her family from early years onward (even getting lost at the first one she remembers). She shared in her parents' frequent hospitality to evangelists, missionaries, representatives from church colleges, and other Mennonite visitors. Such activities introduced her to the larger Mennonite community beyond her small home congregations.

Hope graduated from Hesston College, Kansas (1955) and Eastern Mennonite College, Virginia (1957). She has served on both Mennonite Church and Pacific Coast Conference (MC) committees.

After teaching school for several years, Hope began freelance writing and has been published in numerous Mennonite and other religious periodicals. Many of her children's stories featured historical subjects, as did her biography of E. S. Garber, a Mennonite leader. She wrote four articles for *Mennonite Encyclopedia V.*

Since 1974, she has served the Pacific Coast Conference as Conference Historian. In 1988 she initiated the Oregon Mennonite Historical and Genealogical Society and became its first chair.

Hope and her husband, Clifford, have lived in Eugene, Oregon, since 1964. They attend the Eugene Mennonite Church. They are the parents of Janet Lind (married to Calvin Esh), Myron Lind, Julia Lind, and Carl Lind.